The Afghan Conundrum: intervention, statebuilding and resistance

This book covers the period spanning the international invasion of Afghanistan in 2001 to the foreign military withdrawal in 2014. It explores and dissects the conflictual encounter between international troops, statebuilders and donors on the one hand, and Afghan elites and the wider population on the other. It brings together a group of leading experts and analysts on Afghanistan who examine the varied reasons behind the mixed and often perverse effects of exogenous statebuilding and reflects upon their implications for wider theory and practice. The starting point of the various contributions is a serious engagement with empirical realities, drawing upon extended experience and field research. Their exploration of the unfolding dynamics and effects of external intervention raise fundamental questions about the core premises underlying the statebuilding project.

This book was published as a special issue of *Central Asian Survey*.

Jonathan Goodhand is a Professor of Conflict and Development Studies at the University of SOAS. He has more than twenty five years of experience working in and on Afghanistan and has published widely on the political economy of conflict and peacebuilding.

Mark Sedra is an Adjunct Assistant Professor of Political Science at the University of Waterloo and Balsillie School of International Affairs. He is also the Executive Director of the Centre for Security Governance, a non-profit think tank dedicated to the study of security transitions in fragile, failed and conflict-affected states.

Thirdworlds

Edited by Shahid Qadir, *University of London*

THIRDWORLDS will focus on the political economy, development and cultures of those parts of the world that have experienced the most political, social, and economic upheaval, and which have faced the greatest challenges of the postcolonial world under globalization: poverty, displacement and diaspora, environmental degradation, human and civil rights abuses, war, hunger, and disease.

THIRDWORLDS serves as a signifier of oppositional emerging economies and cultures ranging from Africa, Asia, Latin America, Middle East, and even those 'Souths' within a larger perceived North, such as the U.S. South and Mediterranean Europe. The study of these otherwise disparate and discontinuous areas, known collectively as the Global South, demonstrates that as globalization pervades the planet, the south, as a synonym for subalterity, also transcends geographical and ideological frontiers.

The Afghan Conundrum: intervention, statebuilding and resistance

Edited by
Jonathan Goodhand and Mark Sedra

Routledge
Taylor & Francis Group

LONDON AND NEW YORK

First published 2015
by Routledge
2 Park Square, Milton Park, Abingdon, Oxfordshire OX14 4RN

and by Routledge
711 Third Avenue, New York, NY 10017, USA

First issued in paperback 2016

Routledge is an imprint of the Taylor & Francis Group, an informa business

British Library Cataloguing in Publication Data
A catalogue record for this book is available from the British Library

ISBN 13: 978-1-138-20969-5 (pbk)
ISBN 13: 978-1-138-83048-6 (hbk)

Typeset in Times New Roman
by RefineCatch Limited, Bungay, Suffolk

Publisher's Note
The publisher accepts responsibility for any inconsistencies that may have arisen during the conversion of this book from journal articles to book chapters, namely the possible inclusion of journal terminology.

Disclaimer
Every effort has been made to contact copyright holders for their permission to reprint material in this book. The publishers would be grateful to hear from any copyright holder who is not here acknowledged and will undertake to rectify any errors or omissions in future editions of this book.

Contents

Citation Information

The chapters in this book were originally published in *Central Asian Survey*, volume 32, issue 3 (September 2013). When citing this material, please use the original page numbering for each article, as follows:

Chapter 1
Rethinking liberal peacebuilding, statebuilding and transition in Afghanistan: an introduction
Jonathan Goodhand and Mark Sedra
Central Asian Survey, volume 32, issue 3 (September 2013) pp. 239–254

Chapter 2
Statebuilding in Afghanistan: challenges and pathologies
William Maley
Central Asian Survey, volume 32, issue 3 (September 2013) pp. 255–270

Chapter 3
Statebuilding in Afghanistan: a contradictory engagement
Astri Suhrke
Central Asian Survey, volume 32, issue 3 (September 2013) pp. 271–286

Chapter 4
Contested boundaries: NGOs and civil–military relations in Afghanistan
Jonathan Goodhand
Central Asian Survey, volume 32, issue 3 (September 2013) pp. 287–305

Chapter 5
A tale of two retreats: Afghan transition in historical perspective
Jonathan Steele
Central Asian Survey, volume 32, issue 3 (September 2013) pp. 306–317

Chapter 6
March towards democracy? The development of political movements in Afghanistan
Antonio Giustozzi
Central Asian Survey, volume 32, issue 3 (September 2013) pp. 318–335

Please direct any queries you may have about the citations to
clsuk.permissions@cengage.com

Rethinking liberal peacebuilding, statebuilding and transition in Afghanistan: an introduction

Jonathan Goodhand and Mark Sedra

This special issue coincides with a period of large-scale international troop withdrawals from Afghanistan, with a scheduled transition to 'Afghan ownership' in 2014. This latest 'transition' in Afghanistan's protracted conflict represents an interesting juncture at which to analyse and assess the record of statebuilding efforts in the country and their wider implications. In many respects, the changing narratives around intervention and statebuilding in Afghanistan resonate with and reflect wider shifts in thinking and policies related to security, peacebuilding, and statebuilding.

The US-led intervention was initially shaped by a minimalist doctrine related to narrow objectives of the war on terror, but it subsequently expanded to encompass a maximalist agenda related to statebuilding and democratization. However, interveners fell victim to their own hubris and to many of the familiar pathologies of colonialism, including dependency, domination, and defiance (Gregory 2012). This led to a more limited, pragmatic, and illiberal engagement, aimed at expediting a hasty exit.

The legacies of this latest international intervention will, like the earlier Anglo-Afghan wars and Soviet intervention, continue to shape and inflect processes of statebuilding within the country and the wider region for decades to come. It will also inform wider international debates and policies on the efficacy and legitimacy of exogenous statebuilding. To what extent will Afghanistan be seen as the high point and the subsequent *dénouement* of liberal peacebuilding? Will it be the last of the 'new protectorates' (Mayall and de Oliveira 2011)? Could it trigger a retreat from donor-supported transformational statebuilding? Liberal peacebuilding (which we discuss below), with its vast social-engineering ambitions, has become more difficult to sustain and defend.

This special issue examines the varied reasons behind the mixed and often perverse effects of exogenous statebuilding and reflects upon their implications for wider theory and practice. The starting point of the various contributions is a serious engagement with empirical realities, drawing upon extended experience and field research. Their explorations of the unfolding dynamics and effects of external intervention raise fundamental questions about the core premises underlying the statebuilding project. In this introductory article, before looking at the contributions, we briefly reflect upon how the Afghan experience informs wider debates on liberal peacebuilding and statebuilding.

Rethinking liberal peacebuilding: legacies and lessons

Liberal peacebuilding is understood here as the simultaneous pursuit of conflict resolution, market sovereignty, and liberal democracy (Pugh, Cooper, and Goodhand 2004). A great deal has been written about the post–Cold War emergence and evolution of liberal peacebuilding as the dominant paradigm and policy response to insecurity, seen to be rooted in failing or fragile states. The doctrine has deep roots, but in its post–Cold War guise, there has been a peculiar blending of anxiety and optimism – on the one hand, complacency about the victory of the West, and on the other, unanchored anxiety about new kinds of security threats (Roxborough 2012, 182). Unruly borderlands are seen to be a source of these threats, even though, as Afghanistan shows, they were in part created by the West during the late–Cold War period (Coll 2004; Mamdani 2005; Rubin 2002).

Statebuilding, from this perspective, is viewed as the antidote to internal conflict, and over time there has been a convergence between peacebuilding and statebuilding, to the extent that they are seen as being mutually reinforcing and indeed inseparable from one another. This transformative agenda is operationalized through a range of interconnected initiatives, including security sector reform, constitution writing, good governance and rule of law initiatives, macro-economic reforms, reconstruction, rural development, and so forth. It is exported through the 'strategic complexes' of the liberal peace, composed of state and non-state, for-profit and non-profit organizations involved in complex sub-contracting arrangements (Duffield 2001).

To what extent is liberal peacebuilding, as sketched above, a useful framing device and starting point for analysing intervention in Afghanistan? Can the intervention be understood as the endpoint of a process that began with the fall of the Berlin Wall and was marked by the emergence of a more radical, militarized, and unbounded approach to building peace? Critical theorists point to the genealogy of liberal peacebuilding, linking colonial policies of indirect rule, to modernization theory, to its latest incarnation in contemporary peace and stability operations, so as to expose the underlying ambitions to colonize and occupy (Beate 2007; Gregory 2004; Jabri 2007). Liberal peacebuilders themselves may not recognize their role in exercising power; according to Chandler (2006), the liberal peace can be understood as an 'empire in denial'.

The proponents of international peace operations attempt to draw a clear line between self-interested neocolonialism and altruistic peacebuilding, arguing that Afghanistan and Iraq should be seen as outliers. For example, Roland Paris, in his 2010 article 'Saving Liberal Peacebuilding', distinguishes between post-conquest and post-settlement peacebuilding, the former being coercive and the latter consensual. Yet, both supporters and critics of liberal peacebuilding tend to take the liberal goals of its sponsors at face value. If these goals are not achieved, it is assumed that this is due to peacebuilders diverging from the liberal path by not being liberal enough or by deploying illiberal means to achieve ostensibly liberal ends. In Afghanistan, there has been a constant divergence between proclaimed commitments to liberal principles and actual practices on the ground. This started with the Bonn agreement of December 2001, which, far from being a transmission mechanism for the liberal peace template, was the result of messy compromises between internal and external players and contained distinctly illiberal and non-democratic dimensions. Therefore, liberal peace, as a doctrine for policy makers, is sufficiently expansive and systematically evasive to accommodate coercive-realist elements and emancipatory elements (Mac Ginty 2010, 401). The Afghan intervention vacillated over time along a spectrum of consent and coercion, manifesting itself in a constant tension between transformational aspirations linked to statebuilding, democratization, and human rights on the one hand, and pragmatic, illiberal practices aimed at building a coercive apparatus of control on the other. This tension became more acute as the insurgency grew, a reaction in part to the heavier international footprint (see Suhrke, this volume). This led to a search for more 'local', 'hybrid', and 'Afghan-led' approaches to stabilization and a retreat from the grand ambitions of statebuilding.

Analytically, a liberal framing of intervention fails to explain these underlying tensions and misses the abiding influence of imperialism, geopolitics, and non-liberal political strategies and ideologies. To explain failed war-to-peace transitions solely in terms of shortcomings in post-conflict peacebuilding or the liberal peace paradigm is reductionist in the extreme (Selby 2013, 80). As with Iraq, the Afghan intervention was dominated by the United States in military, diplomatic, and financial terms, and its strategic goals were initially limited to the pursuit of the war on terror. This followed 9/11 and the US identification of Taliban-controlled Afghanistan as its primary security threat. The US was in the beginning a reluctant statebuilder, but this position changed over time as statebuilding came to be seen as the vehicle for stabilization, re-election for President Bush in 2004, and the achievement of an exit strategy. Whilst long-term occupation was never the goal of the United States, this does not mean that more distinctly imperial ambitions were irrelevant. Afghanistan has long constituted a troublesome borderland on an imperial frontier, and this latest intervention can be understood as an attempt by the US to extend its zone of security outwards, deploying an invisible empire or 'security supply chain' (Gregory 2012) through the use of the CIA, drones, detention centres, and rendition. The contracting-out of warfare and neoliberal forms of capital accumulation are interlinked – as Naomi Klein (2008) argues, landscapes of post-war reconstruction can be understood as frontiers of capital. But the business of supplying war produces volatile and violent spaces in which the 'geopolitical and geoeconomic are locked in a deadly embrace' (Gregory 2012). Notions of war and peace become unstable and contested. Building peace is a violent business, and night raids, aerial bombardment, drones, militia formation, and detention centres co-exist alongside (and are in many ways inseparable from) road building, aid for war widows, constitution making, support for elections, and so forth; the latter may have the effect of masking or legitimizing the destructiveness of the former.[1]

The post–Cold War experiments in liberal peacebuilding may be a less useful reference point for Afghanistan than the late-colonial wars of the Cold War period (Feichtinger, Malinoski, and Chase 2012). Indeed, it is the historical lessons of Malaysia, Algeria, and Vietnam that foreign militaries and counterinsurgency experts in Afghanistan have turned to as a guide for action, rather than more recent interventions in Cambodia, East Timor, or the Balkans. As the international drawdown goes through its final phases, the pre-eminent concern of international actors is not with liberalization but with legitimizing international exit.

Much of the critical writing on the liberal peace emphasizes its hegemonic power and its coherence – the liberal peace is framed in Foucauldian terms, as a technology of governance, a disciplinary regime, which bends polities and societies to its will through forms of hard and soft compliance. According to Mac Ginty, it acts like a monopoly, squeezing out alternative ways of doing things and alternative sources of power. In practice, it's the only game in town (Mac Ginty 2007). The language of coherence, integrated missions, and 'whole of government approaches' is frequently taken at face value; the global is seen as the site of elite consensus, whilst the local is a terrain of conflict, resistance, messy compromises, and backsliding (Selby 2013, 62).

Yet, the Afghan mission differs markedly from this representation. The mission is far from hegemonic, in that liberal peacebuilding competes with (and is undermined and colonized by) alternative power centres, institutions, and sources of authority and legitimacy. And it is far from internally coherent, with the exporters of liberal peacebuilding being as fragmented, conflictual, and dysfunctional as the importers (and resisters) of the liberal peace. Over time, the ambitions of the mission expanded, in the belief that 'all good things come together' – that the war on terror, statebuilding, development, democratization, counter-narcotics, and reinventing the NATO alliance were commonly held and mutually reinforcing goals. But this could not mask the fundamental contradiction of pursuing a war whilst trying to build peace (see Suhrke, this volume). In the end, the former was prioritized over, and distorted, the efforts of the latter. The statebuilding project faltered because it was undermined as much by its sponsors as by its recipients.

Liberal peacebuilders and their critics both tend to have an inflated view of the significance and power of the liberal peace. Whilst, relative to the countries in which they intervene, peacebuilders have enormous material and coercive power, their effects are less than impressive. There may be initial 'shock', but after a while there is not a great deal of 'awe'. The transformational hubris of the liberal peace doctrine disappeared on the battlefields of Helmand and Kandahar, as well as on the streets of Kabul, as the international community retreated into their diplomatic enclaves and high-security compounds. Over time, the peacebuilders lost any semblance of moral authority as they were seen by many Afghans to have engaged in highly coercive, illiberal, or corrupt practices. Public-opinion polls showed declining support over time for the international presence, reflecting a growing Afghan scepticism towards both the liberal remedies offering salvation and the violent pacification that promised security.

Rethinking statebuilding

As noted earlier, in the orthodox perspective, peacebuilding and statebuilding were viewed as being mutually supportive and interdependent. The trope of failed or fragile states was used to justify intervention, necessitating radical political and societal restructuring. 'A failed state is implicated in the production of "ungoverned spaces" and peoples, hence its transformation requires the institutional design requisite of government' (Jabri 2013, 11).

The liberal peace is therefore a project of institution-building geared towards the transformation of the state itself. This version of statebuilding is based on the idea that state legitimacy is bound up with its role as the provider or facilitator of public services and the notion of a Lockean social contract. States which diverge from the neoliberal model are somehow deficient and need to have their capacities built in order to conform to the basic principles of 'good governance'. This prescriptive and functionalist approach is based upon a depoliticized and reified understanding of the state. It suffers from historical amnesia (Cramer 2006), because it is blind to the processes of historical change which shaped European state formation.

As Ottoway (2003) notes, international actors set out to create particular sets of organizations, in spite of the fact that raw power, rather than organizational design, was a more important determinant of the trajectory of war-to-peace transitions. The liberal approach has been characterized as 'peacebuilding without politics' (Chandler 2010). Statebuilding is presented as technical exercise, even though it is fundamentally about the distribution, production, and transformation of political power, which inevitably will be contested, often violently so.

There is a significant gap between the assumptions underlying top-down neo-liberal statebuilding and the insights generated by the classical literature on European state formation (Mann 1984; Migdal 2001; Taylor and Botea 2008; Tilly 1992). This literature shows that: state formation was a lengthy process; it was violently contested; there were different historic paths and trajectories, which in the main were led by endogenous elites; and the outcomes were seldom envisaged or the result of conscious planning and design (Roxborough 2012). This work moves us beyond the 'idea of the state' and instead engages with its empirical reality (Abrams 1988).

Drawing on Migdal (2001), the state can be viewed in dual terms as a 'field of power': first, as a powerful image of a clearly bounded, unified organization that can be spoken of in singular terms; and second, as the practices of a heap of loosely connected parts or fragments, often with ill-defined boundaries between them (Migdal 2001, 22–23). In analysing the Afghan state in transition, we should therefore not restrict ourselves to studying the formal apparatus of government. The state can also be viewed as an amorphous ensemble of forces, institutional forms, relations, actors, and practices, in which the boundaries between public and private, state and non-state, legal and illegal are fuzzy and contested. In many respects, the Afghan state can be characterized as a rhizome state (Bayart 1993), in which underground or parallel power structures symbiotically coexist with the visible and formal offices of the state.

This takes us beyond a singular focus on formal institutions and towards looking at underlying configurations of power and interest, which were transformed through various phases of war. To an extent, there was a pluralization of regulatory authority as a result of the diffusion of the means of violence and the crisis in the legitimacy and capacity of the state. Arguably, the Taliban, when in power, were proto-statebuilders intent on achieving a monopoly in the means of violence. Paradoxically, external intervention overthrew a relatively stable political order (under the Taliban) and replaced it with an inherently unstable and violent order, based upon an exclusive and, for many, illegitimate political settlement. Intervention thus interrupted a brutal process of state formation, and the occupation stimulated a new round of war and state failure – very different from the official narrative of a war-to-peace transition.

Statebuilding, like peacebuilding, is sufficiently expansive and vague to accommodate different ideologies and viewpoints. The liberal version of 'virtuous statebuilding' (Giustozzi 2011) may have been ascendant between 2002 and 2006, when there remained a degree of optimism and some convergence of interests between exogenous and endogenous statebuilders. But, over time, the statebuilding narrative changed. In 2002 it was the absence of a strong, centralized state that was seen to be the source of the problem of terrorism and insecurity. By 2008, an overly centralized, corrupt, and illegitimate state was seen as the problem that was helping catalyze the insurgency (Barfield 2012). Statebuilding based on good-governance principles was clearly not working. It was seen to be too top-down, too bureaucratic and slow, and perversely leading to the creation of a corrupt, rentier state. The Taliban increasingly appeared to be 'outgoverning' the Afghan government and NATO forces in much of the country (Kilcullen 2011). The interests of the hosts and guests appeared to be rapidly diverging.

This led to a search for more local, bottom-up solutions to the perceived problems of governance and insecurity. The valorization of local traditions and the recognition of more hybrid and pluralized forms of authority appeared in some ways to be a welcome departure from liberal fantasies of the Weberian state. Yet, celebratory accounts of embedded governance and hybrid orders were also extremely naive or disingenuous and did not necessarily reflect Afghan popular expectations of the state. As Hakimi's account (this volume) shows, the experience of war has changed perceptions of the state as a provider of public goods, and many Afghans want more state, not less. Local forms of authority are not necessarily more legitimate or embedded, and decentralization may be a recipe for a return to warlord rule. Furthermore, international actors were ill equipped to play the game of local politics, having only a very limited understanding of the Afghan political economy. Aid workers, provincial reconstruction team advisers and special forces units were easily co-opted or manipulated by local intermediaries. Finally, localization can be seen as a vehicle for passing on responsibility to local actors, evading accountability, masking underlying power relations, and ultimately justifying withdrawal.

Therefore, our analysis points to the complexity, messiness, and incoherence of intervention. Attempts to build a liberal peace meet friction and resistance and are mediated through competing interests and hybrid institutional arrangements; it is hardly surprising that peacebuilding looks very different when it hits the ground. As Barnett and Zurcher (2009) note, in the complex negotiating relationships between international actors, national elites, and peripheral elites, the default position is a 'co-opted peace' in which local actors pay lip service to the conditionalities of external actors but in practice continue to pursue their own sets of interests, which are at odds with ostensibly liberal goals.

Exogenous statebuilding is shot through with conflicting objectives and paradoxical effects. It aims to build ownership, but undermines the authority of state actors by retaining control over key decisions and imposing conditionalities; it promotes the idea of a Lockean social contract, whilst providing unmonitored resources that create a corrupt rentier state; it centralizes and bureaucratizes the means of coercion, whilst supporting the formation of local militias; it aims to strengthen the service-delivery role of the state whilst supporting a plethora of parallel projects channelled through NGOs and foreign militaries; and it promotes the rule of law and human security whilst building up a paramilitary police force.

The drawdown of foreign troops and the decline in external finance will have profound impacts on the Afghan political economy. As noted by Steele (this volume), Najibullah was able to maintain an apparatus of control so long as external resources flowed from the Soviets. And Najibullah, unlike Karzai, did not have to contend with 'good governance' conditionalities, even though Karzai's funders have rarely held themselves accountable to such standards. Rather than good governance or security sector reform being taken at face value, they should instead be treated as ideologies of North–South relations – they reveal more about the way Western powers try to present themselves than they do about how these actors operate on the ground (Giustozzi 2011, 4). Western peacebuilders' notions of 'virtuous state building' (Giustozzi 2011) can therefore be best understood largely as an ideology or legitimizing narrative rather than a template for exogenously supported statebuilding.

Rethinking transition

The literature on peacebuilding is replete with 'lessons learned', and history is frequently invoked in order to draw contemporary lessons. In the hands of liberal peacebuilders or counter-insurgency (COIN) experts, history is a resource: it is invoked either to safeguard interventions from criticism or to conduct them better than they are conducted at present. This utilitarian outlook transforms past colonial experience into a modern-day classroom for international bureaucrats, peacekeepers, or soldiers (Bain 2011). Afghanistan is a site of learning, a laboratory for field-testing ways of fighting and ways of governing which are copied, refined, and developed elsewhere.

One of the most striking features of the international intervention has been the growth of the information-and-research marketplace and the role that knowledge brokers and experts have played within this marketplace, all dedicated to making Afghan society more legible and therefore more governable. These include dedicated research-and-analysis NGOs, COIN experts, security advisers, 'human terrain teams', and intelligence experts. Wimplemann (this volume), for example, shows how these networks advanced the informal rule of law agenda based on claims about its authenticity and legitimacy. Attempts to draw upon local knowledge and comprehend the granular details of Afghan society are redolent of colonial administrators, whose invocation of local knowledge was blind to the fact that such knowledge is always the ideology or world-view of a particular stratum of powerful intermediaries (Roxborough 2012, 198).

One of the most important dimensions of this information economy is the way that intervention is represented and packaged to Western audiences. Population-centric warfare is as much about maintaining the support of Western electorates as it is about winning the hearts and minds of the Afghan population. It is self-evident that the dynamics of intervention are inseparable from the electoral cycles and the battles for legitimacy and representation in Western polities – and there is no straightforward connection between this and progress along predetermined timelines and benchmarks in Afghanistan.

Peacebuilding and statebuilding are therefore not apolitical, technical activities; they are *nolens volens*, ideological. They involve convincing enough people that a set of activities, forms of behaviour, social relations, and institutions are acceptable, as well as presenting effective obstacles and sanctions in the way of those who do not. At the heart of this is the challenge of legitimation, as almost all forms of peace put limits on the range of behaviour and this has to be agreed to by the wielders of violence and society at large.

Ideologies involve not just sets of ideas but powerful, legitimating obfuscations (or even inversions) of reality (Paige 1998). For example, the notion of 'transition' places boundaries around action and obfuscates reality. Intervention in Afghanistan was framed as helping facilitate a war-to-peace transition; particularly for NATO troop-contributing countries like Germany and Holland, who wished to differentiate between Afghanistan and Iraq, there were strong political imperatives to present the former as a 'post-war', 'stabilization and reconstruction' context. The notion of transition is bound up with the liberal *telos* of progress, improvement, a state of becoming – progress that can be ticked off with the achievement of key benchmarks, including the signing of the Bonn Agreement, the formation of a transitional authority, the writing of the constitution, the holding of presidential and parliamentary elections, and the implementation of disarmament, demobilization and reintegration programmes. These highly symbolic events were meant to signal a process of transformation, introducing irreversible changes that denote a transition from war to peace.

However, the Bonn Agreement, in hindsight, is best conceptualized less as the marker of a war-to-peace transition than as another turning-point in a protracted conflict that has undergone several phases and has mutated over time. Afghanistan's 'transition' has been less about transformation than about the reproduction of wartime dynamics and structures. Of course there have been major changes, including rapid urbanization, increased education, and the growth of the middle class; but there have also been strong underlying continuities between 'war' and 'peace', and the underlying rules of the game have not fundamentally changed. This is illustrated in several of the contributions to this volume, which show that the wartime political economy persists into and shapes the 'peacetime'. In many respects, a durable disorder became systemic, with different sets of interests being tied up in the continuation of a war system, which generated rents for those involved. Therefore, notions of transition have less to do with fundamental shifts in the Afghan political economy than with external conceptualizations of the context which are used to justify changes in strategy. For instance, over time, one can detect a shift from linear, ends-based or goal-oriented interventions to one which involved understanding the limits to change in the non-linear or hybrid politics of social or everyday practices and interactions (Chandler 2013, 20). The failures of statebuilding and the growth of the insurgency led to growing focus on the societal sphere. Chandler eloquently points to the dangers of such a change:

> Peacebuilding interventions working on the ontological basis of hybridity would merely institutionalise lower expectations and horizons, allocating responsibility for this to local agency. Failure would be represented as success, both in recognising local agency and in rejecting the 'hubris' of the liberal past. (Chandler 2013, 32)

This latest transition has involved a radical redefinition of success – the desired end state is now a regime that is sufficiently robust not to collapse and with the coercive capacity to prevent the Taliban from retaking Kabul and al-Qaeda from regaining a foothold in the region. Evidently, the international footprint will not disappear, and it will continue in different forms, including the presence of special forces, aid advisers, drones, and continued financial support. One can also expect, with a reduced Western presence, an increased assertion of regional power interests, including China. Some may read this retreat from liberal peacebuilding as a return to the imperial strategies of the Cold War period – away from the liberal interlude, with its transformational aspirations, which involved telling the recipients of intervention, 'You do it our way', back to a more modest and pragmatic interaction with client states of 'You do it your way' (Amsden 2009). However, it may not be as straightforward as this – for example, the furore in the

British press over the February 2009 passing of the Shia Family Law is illustrative of the fact that Western electorates and taxpayers may not always be so tolerant of allowing aid recipients to do things 'their way'.[2] Furthermore, as Hakimi and Wimplemann show in their contributions, there may be no internal consensus about what constitutes 'our way'.

Introducing the contributions

This collection of essays does not claim to provide comprehensive coverage of the gamut of issues that have shaped exogenous statebuilding in Afghanistan. Rather, the various articles, which are based on extensive empirical research grounded in different disciplinary approaches, critically examine the various dimensions of the donor-sponsored transition and reflect upon its impacts and legacies. While there are some commonalities in the arguments presented, the authors offer different diagnoses and prognoses. The following section does not attempt to summarize these contributions but rather provides an overview that identifies common critical threads that run through them.

The collection depicts a deeply flawed and ever-shifting intervention that failed to meet its stated transformative goals and instead generated a range of perverse effects. The two overview articles, by Maley and Suhrke, provide critical if somewhat divergent analyses of the Afghan statebuilding experience. Maley argues that the process was hardly doomed from the start but rather 'was undermined by a series of strategic misjudgements and miscalculations'. He highlights errors in design, decision-making, timing and leadership, which led to a series of breakdowns and crises that stymied the process. He touches on three broad and interrelated themes that run throughout the collection and help to explain the gradual breakdown of donor-assisted statebuilding: the interveners' flawed understanding of Afghanistan (its history, politics, and culture); the gradual embrace of hybridity[3] in the security and governance spheres, exemplified by the turn to informal militias and judicial structures; and the many internal contradictions of the statebuilding model itself.

In contrast, Suhrke argues that the intensive and intrusive nature of the Western-supported process of state transformation set it on the road to failure from the outset. She highlights three specific tensions within the liberal statebuilding agenda that eroded the project and demonstrated its futility: the tension created by massive aid flows, fostering aid dependency and the creation of rentier state structures; the tension between the goal of local ownership and the intrinsic desire of donors to retain control; and the competing imperatives of waging war and building peace. In light of these tensions, the attempts to paper over the cracks and setbacks in the statebuilding project through the provision of more aid, the deployment of more foreign troops, and the contracting of more technical assistance – coalescing into a 'second civil service' – were bound to fail, and demonstrated the normative rigidity of the process itself. Although Maley argues that changes in donor approaches could have produced better results in Afghanistan, he does concede the inherent rigidity of the statebuilding strategy, noting that the Western-driven, Westphalian model of international society that framed donors' actions limited their capacity to engage and adapt to local realities.

Exogenous statebuilding was certainly not unilinear, instead following a shifting trajectory that veered from the 'light footprint' approach inaugurated at the 2001 Bonn Conference, to a much heavier footprint by the middle of the last decade in response to deteriorating security and political conditions, and finally to a mixed or 'hybrid footprint', a corollary of NATO's embrace of COIN doctrine. This trajectory was marked by what Maley describes as a debilitating 'slide away from institutionalization in the direction of neopatrimonialism', something he sees as a 'dysfunctional form of hybridity'. Sedra also describes a 'slide towards expediency' in his analysis of the security sector reform (SSR) process, in which the liberal normative core of SSR was gradually hollowed out, leaving only a conventional train-and-equip strategy focused more on immediate NATO military objectives than on Afghan human security needs. The liberal aspirations of the statebuilding process were gradually stripped away as the transition evolved and the futility of exogenous statebuilding strategies and approaches became apparent.

Maley describes how Western actions such as the blocking of the International Security Assistance Force (ISAF) expansion, which emboldened regional strongmen to consolidate their powerbases or mini-fiefdoms, encouraged neopatrimonialism and the move of President Karzai to embrace the type of 'Peshawar politics' that prevailed during the era of the anti-Soviet *jihad*. Sharan's essay expands on this analysis, laying out how the Afghan state is held together through 'a system of patronage and opportunism' that was entrenched by the interveners' strategy of striking bargains with former *mujahideen* commanders to reconstitute the state. The efforts of the interveners to distribute patronage and employ proxies to advance military and stabilization objectives were at odds with the purported goals of institutionalization and democratization. It fostered what Sharan refers to as a 'network form of a state', built upon the self-interested competition of various elite political networks, all fuelled by the donor-aid regime.

In his article on the development of political movements in Afghanistan, Giustozzi notes how candidates for elected office have been principally motivated by the desire to access the spoils of the transition at the political centre and have tended to rely on their patronage networks to rally votes rather than to build an electoral infrastructure. This marked a significant departure from the political developments in the 1960s and 1970s that saw the rise of new political technologies of mass mobilization. Post-2001 political developments veered away from this 'democratic opening', with contemporary political parties structured more as patronage machines built on wartime networks rather than grass-roots party organization. In fact, few of the new political groupings that contested Afghanistan's parliamentary and presidential elections have 'understood the demands of Western-style competitive elections in terms of institution building and voters' rights'. Instead, they have viewed their participation in these elections both as a means to signal their support for the post-2001 political order and as a mechanism to access patronage. As Wilde and Mielke note, the massive resource flows channelled by donors through Afghanistan have provided a powerful incentive for elites and political networks to capture parts of the state and, in turn, the Western-supported statebuilding agenda.

Suhrke explains how donors have facilitated the creation of vast networks of patronage that have become the 'principal safety net for the governing elites on both the national and the subnational levels'. This is not surprising considering the enormous size of the intervention, with the flow of money overwhelming the state's capacity to absorb and spend it in a transparent, socially responsible, and legally acceptable manner. Drawing on Suhrke's work, Goodhand aptly points out that 'too much aid spent too quickly with little oversight can be delegitimizing and destabilizing'. There is such a thing as bad aid, and in complex environments like Afghanistan, less can be more. Aid was treated as a force multiplier in Afghanistan, meant to support military operations. The problem with this logic, as Goodhand points out, is that the empirical relation between underdevelopment, poverty, and insurgency is questionable and unproven. One thing that aid definitively did do in Afghanistan was to foster a rentier state, with unprecedented levels of aid dependence and, relatedly, high levels of corruption. Suhrke and many other contributors to this volume detail how widespread corruption, both grand and petty, has distorted and undermined the statebuilding project, consolidating the rentier state and its deleterious features. Corruption is so pervasive that it has become, in the words of Sharan, a 'normalized' feature of society, contributing to malfunctioning institutions and a crisis of state legitimacy.

Several of the contributions to this volume explore how knowledge production has been used and misused to support donor activities and reinforce Western strategic objectives, often overriding local norms, ideas, and opinions. The dominant role played by external 'experts' and 'technical assistance' providers points to a neocolonial use of ideas and knowledge to perpetuate the exercise of power. Part of the problem with the statebuilding process, according to Sharan, was that the interveners overlooked local knowledge in devising their strategies, particularly around the role of the elite-based patronage politics that came to define and underpin the state and the statebuilding process. This often wilful failure of external actors to understand Afghanistan, instead treating it as a *tabula rasa,* is a consistent theme throughout the volume. As the statebuilding process evolved, different statebuilders adopted different lenses through which to interpret Afghanistan and justify their activities, whether it was Afghanistan as a blank slate or Afghanistan as a pre-modern, tribal, and stateless society. These lenses were based on particular readings of Afghan history that several authors cite as deeply problematic. Jonathan Steele explains in detail how the West failed to learn the implicit lessons of the Soviet experience and may be repeating some of its mistakes. Giustozzi shows how the different stages of Afghanistan's decades-long civil war fundamentally altered the country's social and political landscape, a reality that Wilde and Mielke, as well as Hakimi, recognize and draw upon.

A common criticism of the post-Bonn era and statebuilding strategy revolves around the limited engagement of secular, liberal political groups, as evidenced by their absence at the Bonn Conference itself in December 2001. Giustozzi recognizes the marginalization of these groups, which featured prominently in the era prior to the 1979 Soviet intervention, but cautions that the historical changes which took place during the subsequent civil war meant that 'the post-Bonn phase of Afghan history could not simply have been the resumption of a pattern of development abandoned in the early 1970s'. In other words, the 'democratic opening' that occurred in the 1970s could not have been merely resumed in a seamless fashion. In a similar vein, forms of tribal politics and governance prevalent across many parts of Afghanistan during the nineteenth and early twentieth centuries cannot be easily reconstituted, as many donors have endeavoured to do through their hybrid transition strategies, with external aid and support.

Wilde and Mielke contest dominant Western perceptions of order and governance in the Afghan context, arguing that the knowledge upon which Western strategies are based is unsound and formed using the wrong analytical lens. Drawing on their research in Afghanistan's north-east and on longer-term historical trends studied through archival material, they explain how the basic instruments of social order – reciprocity, patronage, eldership, and mediation – endure despite the changes in power and authority structures brought about by the civil war. Even though 'conventional elders' have been displaced in many areas by a new stratum of wartime elites – entrepreneurs of violence, or 'warlords' as they are often called – traditional practices of social order have remained intact, often overlooked or concealed by the constantly shifting elite networks, regime changes, and external interventions. Wilde and Mielke argue that the central pillars of social order – patronage, mediation, and brokering – are not adequately grasped by statebuilders in Afghanistan, contributing to the problems of the exogenous statebuilding project. A growing tension emerged in donor programming between the desire for transformation and radical normative change which characterized the early phases of the statebuilding process and the renewed enthusiasm for historical continuity and reproduction that dominated the latter phases. The turn to forms of hybrid political order defined this move towards reification, recapturing authentic forms of governance and security from Afghanistan's past. This was often based on superficial and frequently romanticized perceptions.

As already noted, governance in Afghanistan and elsewhere consists of complex mixes of the formal and informal. The attempt by liberal peacebuilders to engage with traditional or customary forms of governance was partly a reflection of the inherent hybridity of politics and governance in Afghanistan, and partly a pragmatic response in the face of resistance from local populations to the imposition of Western-oriented state structures.

In his article detailing the evolution of the Afghan Local Police (ALP), particularly the pilot phase in Wardak, Hakimi explains how donors anchored their strategies of promoting informal governance and security to nineteenth-century historical, anthropological, and ethnographic accounts of Afghanistan conducted by agents of the colonial powers to solidify their control of Afghanistan. The ALP in particular was based on 'an idealized and reified vision of the past' that proved outdated under present conditions. It was part of a broader trend towards embracing informal security, driven to a great extent by the growth of the Taliban-led insurgency. Wimpelmann similarly details how the emergence and burgeoning growth of interest in the informal and traditional in the rule of law sphere was driven by major breakdowns and setbacks in Western stabilization efforts. Couched as a bottom-up approach, hybrid statebuilding programmes were intended, Wimpelmann argues, to 'restore Afghanistan to its allegedly harmonious traditions of the past'. However, as Wimpelmann and Hakimi convincingly show, the ALP and informal-justice structures have been opposed by many Afghans at the local level and have actually had little to do with providing actual protection or access to justice for civilians. Although described as 'authentic' bottom-up processes, they tended to be implemented in a top-down fashion rooted in external perceptions and interests, thereby contradicting claims of local ownership. Traditional security and justice structures, as conceived by donors, were instrumentalized to advance counter-insurgency and counter-terrorism ends.

Programmes such as the ALP illustrate another general dilemma or tension in donor statebuilding assistance in Afghanistan, mentioned by Goodhand: often it appears more geared to winning the hearts and minds of those living in the West, 'who need to be convinced of the validity of the struggle', than to improving the lives of Afghans. In other words, it is debatable which interests are being advanced by the external intervention: the interests of the interveners or the interests of the objects of the intervention.

Although often described as 'Afghan-led' and 'authentic', the efforts to develop a national policy on informal justice were, as Wimpelmann details, externally driven. Donors sought to circumvent Afghan governmental and civil-society opposition to such plans, centred on concerns over the status of women and human rights norms, by employing 'expert knowledge steeped in orientalist frames'. Despite donor exhortations about the importance of local ownership as an indispensible element of statebuilding practice, donors regularly overrode Afghan institutions, particularly once the military came on board with this idea and hitched it to their COIN strategy. There is wide agreement in the volume that local-level ownership was often sacrificed in advancing the broader objectives of the interveners. Maley goes as far as stating that local-level leaders were effectively 'disenfranchised' on many key issues.

The employment of hybrid statebuilding strategies clearly had mixed results, partly due to the lack of nuance in the interveners' understanding of the Afghan political milieu and partly due to the tendency of those same interveners to selectively instrumentalize aspects of Afghan history and culture to advance their strategic interests. The 'valorization' of informal non-state structures was no more attuned to local realities than the attempts to transplant a modern, centralized Weberian state. According to Maley, the Afghan experience has shown that hybridity is an approach that should be neither universally condemned nor universally lauded; its viability and impact will be dictated by the conditions present in each context.

Shifts in intervention strategies in Afghanistan reflected a number of internal contradictions in the statebuilding exercise. As stated earlier, Suhrke identifies one of the fundamental paradoxes at the centre of Afghanistan's statebuilding agenda: the employment of heavy-handed and intrusive external assistance to produce a self-sufficient, Afghan-owned, and liberal political order. The failure of this intrusive presence to deliver on its promises of more security, development, and good governance delegitimized the process itself and drove statebuilders into 'a modified retreat' in the form of hybridity and finally the transition to Afghan rule and 'good enough' governance. By 2013, statebuilders had ostensibly abandoned ambitious plans for a liberal democratic order in Afghanistan, talking instead about compromised or mediated forms of democratic governance that were liberal in a minimalist sense and geared to reflect local power realities and institutional pathologies like corruption and clientelism. While some would argue that the liberal character of the intervention was always a veneer that donors used to conceal and legitimize their use of illiberal means to achieve external strategic ends, even this pretence of liberalism was abandoned as the transition evolved. The embrace of 'good enough' served to justify Western disengagement, laying blame for the failure of the liberal democratic project on Afghans while seeking to establish outcomes that supposedly better reflected local realities and limitations.

Another internal contradiction of the statebuilding project is the statebuilding agenda's over-arching focus on formal central state authority despite the de facto decentralization of power in the country. Maley details how the lion's share of donor attention has been dedicated to the strengthening of central state institutions and agencies, which is problematic considering that the majority of Afghans have no interaction with these levels of governance. Long-standing urban–rural tensions have been exacerbated by the fact that rural Afghans have not received a 'peace dividend' on a par with those in major urban centres, undermining the legitimacy of the state in the rural periphery and giving a boost to anti-government elements. There is also a disparity between the aid and assistance provided to areas affected by the insurgency and to those that are not, with the former receiving the bulk of support. As Goodhand notes, this creates a perverse incentive whereby relatively stable communities must demonstrate instability to receive a greater share of aid.

In contrast to Maley's criticism of the over-centralization of the statebuilding project, Hakimi takes issue with the gradual localization of donor efforts as the transition evolved and NATO embraced COIN strategy. Hakimi notes how Afghanistan's protracted conflict has had profound effects on state–society relations. Contrary to the dominant perceptions of Afghan hostility to the state, he explains how many local elders have begun to demand national solutions to persistent problems like insecurity and have resisted attempts to confine them to outdated patterns of 'indigeneity' through the promotion of traditional structures, norms, and actors. Local elites might actually want more state rather than less, contradicting some dominant Western perceptions which, as Goodhand says, 'tend to reify the local, celebrating "the community" as a place of virtue, solidarity, and resilience'. The tendency of donors to view Afghan politics as static (based on dated perceptions and colonial images) rather than dynamic and fluid has complicated and even undercut their statebuilding efforts.

The temporal aspects of statebuilding present a further contradiction. Although framed as a long-term evolutionary process, exogenous statebuilding in Afghanistan has been implemented with a short-term outlook, characteristically prioritizing the immediate military and security needs of the interveners, with little consideration of the longer-term transformative goals of the intervention. Maley laments the failure of the US and NATO to develop a coherent strategic vision for Afghanistan, noting how 'all too often, international actors have scrambled to produce short-term palliatives rather than address problems synoptically'. Statebuilders have tended to view their intervention in Afghanistan as a new turning-point in Afghanistan's modern history, starting from a 'blank slate', rather than as another phase in a longer-term process of state formation. Given that the engagement in Afghanistan was partially driven by external, Western security concerns – the 'war on terrorism' – the long-term rhythms and patterns of political development and state formation have tended to be overlooked.

Looking at the statebuilding concept and its future after Afghanistan, Goodhand's exploration of NGO roles in the context of civil–military relations is revealing, showing the process to be 'fractured and contested from within and based upon flawed premises and strategies'. Many of the core assumptions and practices upon which statebuilding orthodoxy is based are unproven and questionable. Viewing SSR as a microcosm of statebuilding, Sedra questions the very viability of the liberal statebuilding model in conflict-affected countries like Afghanistan, showing it to be woefully ill-equipped to achieve its ambitious transformative aims. Indeed, as Maley explains, the Afghan statebuilding experience has left a deeply ambiguous legacy. Afghanistan may have marked the zenith of the liberal statebuilding model, which is now the subject of vigorous criticism in academic and policy circles from all parts of the political spectrum. Partly as a result of the Afghan experience, in the near future the world is more likely to see limited statebuilding interventions, on the lines of recent Western engagements in Libya and Mali, rather than the grand transformative projects of Afghanistan and Iraq.

What does this all mean for Afghanistan after 2014? The authors are generally pessimistic on the prospects for the country beyond NATO's drawdown. According to Steele, 'Afghanistan will end up hopelessly fractured.' After all, in many ways the Soviets left Afghanistan in a more stable position than NATO is likely to in 2014. For instance, the security forces, seen as a key to transition today, were more effective and better equipped under Najibullah at the time of the Soviet withdrawal. Hakimi shares Steele's pessimism, describing an Afghanistan that has changed a great deal from the Taliban period but is perhaps more insecure, with power fractured among a range of predatory militia groups held in check only by fragile mini-bargains with the state and interveners. Any achievements of the statebuilding process, and particularly its informal-justice initiatives, are little more than a 'veneer', in the words of Wimpelmann, concealing deep instability and continuing violence. Giustozzi expresses concern about the fragility of the incipient electoral system, which the Afghans are unlikely to be able to sustain without massive external subsidies, raising questions about the sustainability of the entire democratic process. Speaking about the potential for Afghanistan's fledgling political parties, he expresses some optimism in that they 'will have to reconnect to their society, find solid constituencies, or perish', but adds the caveat that 'this cannot happen without a major crisis happening first'.

Suhrke is somewhat more optimistic regarding Afghanistan's future. Given her contention that it was the intrusive international aid presence that fostered crisis in Afghanistan, she argues that the reduction of that overarching foreign presence will create space for Afghans to address the prevailing weaknesses of the state, 'based on long-term bargains between elites and subjects as well as compromises among contesting ethnic and sectarian groups'. In fact, the withdrawal of foreign troops could be considered an essential precondition for re-establishing the internal legitimacy of the Afghan state and advancing a more sustainable, locally owned statebuilding process. In the absence of the intrusive international presence and its distorting effects, Afghans will revert to the fundamental instruments of social order that Wilde and Mielke describe. Here again, the Soviet experience is worth recalling. As Steele notes, the Soviet withdrawal was total, allowing 'Najib's government to present itself as fully sovereign'. NATO, on the other hand, intends to maintain thousands of troops in the country, which could serve to 'maintain the image, and reality, of an occupation' and possibly restrict the sovereign space needed for state consolidation and the striking of new bargains for peace.

Conclusions

There are dangers in reading (or indeed predicting) too much from this one episode, and there is a need to recognize the variable geography of the liberal peace; interventions have varied markedly from case to case and over time. As the contributions to this volume show, Afghanistan needs to be studied seriously in its own right, rather than used simply as a case study to illustrate wider trends and policy debates. The authors, as noted already, do not have a common position, and nor have most attempted to spell out what should have been done or what could have been done differently. However, within these contributions, and the writing more broadly on Afghanistan, three different positions can be identified.

First, there is the window-of-opportunity narrative. This states that although there were early successes, the statebuilding agenda got side-tracked by the war against the Taliban, poor integration, bad coordination, and the lack of funding and fire-power early on. According to this position, a heavier, better coordinated and more strategic footprint, particularly in the initial stages, could have made a positive difference. Conversely, a sudden reduction in foreign troops and aid will have deleterious effects and could lead to another outbreak of civil war. The broader lesson drawn from this position is that 'bargain basement' statebuilding (Ottoway 2003) does not work and a more sustained and heavier international footprint is required to help states recover from and rebuild after war.

A second argument is that the project was doomed to failure from the outset. Statebuilding was built upon shaky foundations, including an illegitimate political settlement, the absence of a convincing political track to reconcile or incorporate the Taliban, and the large inflow of resources and military fire-power which produced massive contradictions and perverse effects. According to this thesis, exogenous statebuilding could never have worked, as it was always part of the problem. However, this conclusion leads to a more optimistic prognosis on the transition, since, as Suhrke argues (this volume), it may open up new spaces for Afghans and regional actors to negotiate a more inclusive political settlement. The wider implications of this view are that liberal peacebuilding is unlikely to work in circumstances where the political settlement is exclusive, the national elite are fragmented, and external intervention is mixed in with a range of geostrategic and geo-economic interests. This does not mean that external support cannot play a supportive role on the margins, but it must be strategic and well timed, and respond to local realities.

Finally, there is the imperial argument: that intervention had nothing to do with the liberal peace in the first place. It was all about national security and geopolitical interests. Intervention could never have 'worked' according to the liberal template, as that was never the goal. The implication of this position is that external powers should stop meddling in the internal affairs of poor, unstable countries because their actions will always be tainted by self-interest.

Which position or combination of positions will stand the test of time, it is too early to tell. However, it is clear that liberal peacebuilders have come out of the Afghan experience more chastened, cautious, and perhaps more cynical than they were before the intervention. As already noted, Afghanistan may well mark the end of the 'new protectorates', signifying a return to more limited external engagement in civil wars. The global financial crisis, the calamitous effects of intervention in Afghanistan and Iraq, and the growing political and economic clout of Brazil, Russia, India, China and South Africa (who are all more sceptical of liberal interventionism) may see a return to something like the old Westphalian order. If this is correct, then liberal peacebuilding will probably be seen, in retrospect, as a brief interlude. Its significance lies less in its practical effects than in what it tells us about a particular moment of Western hegemony. As Mayall and de Oliveira (2011, 29) note, the new protectorates are noteworthy because of 'their heuristic value for an understanding of an age during which they rose to prominence, rather than their meagre practical impact'. Yet, notwithstanding their limited intended impacts, exogenous statebuilding may have profound and unforeseen negative effects, as the contributions to this volume show. The consequences and legacies of (il)liberal peacebuilding will continue to reverberate in Afghan society long after the last foreign troops have withdrawn and the peacebuilders have gone home.

Acknowledgements

We would like to thank Deniz Kandiyoti and Astri Suhrke for useful comments on an earlier draft of this article.

Notes

1. Eyal Weizman (2011), for example, writes about 'humanitarian violence', the result of what he calls humanitarianism as the 'practice of lesser evils', a philosophy that links the interventions of Medicins Sans Frontieres in humanitarian crises and Israel's projection of power in Gaza. Humanitarian action and military interventions are both 'crucial means by which the economy of violence is calculated and managed' (4). Both are based upon a notion of proportionality which is not about clear lines of prohibition 'but rather about calculating and determining balances and degrees' (11).
2. The Shia Family Law, part of which pertained to sexual relations between husband and wife, made international headlines. Article 132 specifies that Shia women are required to sexually submit to their husband's demands. Karzai's approval of the law was interpreted by many as an attempt to secure the support of Shia power brokers.
3. Hybridity refers to the coexistence of liberal and illiberal norms, institutions, and actors (Belloni, 2012, 24). Oliver Richmond refers to hybridity and the effort to 'engage more closely with local context' as a 'post-liberal peace' (2009, 328, 331).

References

Abrams, P. 1988. "Notes on the Difficulty of Studying the State." *Journal of Historical Sociology* 1 (1): 58–89.

Amsden, A. 2009. *Escape from Empire: The Developing World's Journey through Heaven and Hell.* Cambridge, MA: MIT Press.

Bain, W. 2011. "Protectorates New and Old: A Conceptual Critique." In *The New Protectorates. International Tutelage and the Making of Liberal States*, edited by J. Mayall and R. de Oliveira, 31–48. London: Hurst.

Barfield, T. 2012. "Afghans Look at 2014." *Current History* 111 (744): April, 123–128.

Barnett, M., and C. Zurcher. 2009. "The Peacebuilder's Contract: How External Statebuilding Reinforces Weak Statehood." In *The Dilemmas of Statebuilding. Confronting the Contradictions of Post War Peace Operations*, edited by R. Paris and T. Sisk, 23–52. London: Routledge.

Bayart, J. 1993. *The State in Africa: The Politics of the Belly.* London: Longman.

Beate, J. 2007. "The Tragedy of Liberal Diplomacy: Democracy, Intervention, Statebuilding' (parts 1 and 2)." *Journal of Intervention and Statebuilding* Part I, 1 (1): 87–106; Part II, 1 (2): 211–29.

Belloni, R. 2012. "Hybrid Peace Governance: Its Emergence and Significance." *Global Governance* 18: 21–38.

Chandler, D. 2006. *Empire in Denial. The Politics of Statebuilding.* London: Pluto Press.

Chandler, D. 2010. *International Statebuilding. The Rise of Post Liberal Governance.* London: Routledge.

Chandler, David. 2013. "Peacebuilding and the Politics of Non-linearity: Rethinking 'Hidden' Agencies and 'Resistance'." *Peacebuilding* 1 (1): 17–32.

Coll, S. 2004. *Ghost Wars. The secret history of the CIA, Afghanistan and Bin Laden, from the Soviet Invasion to September 10, 2001.* London, UK: Penguin.

Cramer, C. 2006. *Civil War is not a Stupid Thing. Accounting for Violence in Developing Countries.* London, UK: Hurst.

Duffield, M. 2001. *Global Governance and the New Wars. The Merging of Development and Security.* London, US: Zed Books.

Feichtinger, M., Stephan Malinoski, and Richard Chase. 2012. "Transformative Invasions; Western Post-9/11 Counterinsurgency and the Lessons of Colonialism." *Humanity* Spring, 3 (1): 35–63.

Giustozzi, A. 2011. *The Art of Coercion. The Primitive Accumulation and Management of Coercive Power.* London: Hurst.

Gregory, D. 2004. *The Colonial Present: Afghanistan, Palestine, Iraq.* London, UK: Wiley-Blackwell.

Gregory, D. 2012. "Supplying War in Afghanistan. The Frictions of Distance." *Open Democracy*, 11 June, 2012. http://www.opendemocracy.net/author/derek-gregory

Jabri, V. 2007. *War and the Transformation of Global Politics.* London: Palgrave.

Jabri, V. 2013. "Peacebuilding, the Local and the International: A Colonial or Post Colonial Rationality?" *Peacebuilding* 1 (1): 3–16.

Kilcullen, D. 2011. "Deiokes and the Taliban: Local Governance, Bottom –up State Formation and the Rule of Law in Counter-insurgency." In *The Rule of Law in Afghanistan: Missing in Inaction*, edited by W. Mason, 35–50. Cambridge University Press.

Klcin, N. 2008. *The Shock Doctrine. The Rise of Disaster Capitalism.* London, UK: Penguin.

MacGinty, R. 2007. "Reconstructing Post-war Lebanon: A Challenge to the Liberal Peace?" *Conflict, Security, Development* 7 (3): 457–482.

Mac Ginty, R. 2010. "Hybrid Peace: The Interaction Between Top-Down and Bottom-Up Peace." *Security Dialogue* 41 (4): 391–412.

Mamdani, M. 2005. *Good Muslim, Bad Muslim. America the Cold War and the Roots of Terror*. Publishing, US: Three Leaves.

Mann, M. 1984. "The Autonomous Power of the State. Its Origins, Mechanisms and Results." *European Journal of Sociology* 25 (2): 185–213.

MayallJ., and R. S. de Oliveira, eds. 2011. *The New Protectorates. International Tutelage and the Making of Liberal States*, 1–30. London: Hurst. Introduction.

Migdal, J. 2001. *State in Society. Studying How States and Societies Transform and Constitute One Another*. Cambridge, UK: Cambridge University Press.

Ottoway, Marina. 2003. "Rebuilding State Institutions in Collapsed States." In *State Failure, Collapse and Reconstruction*, edited by Jennifer Milliken, 245–266. Oxford: Blackwell.

Paige, J. 1998. *Coffee and Power: Revolution and the Rise of Democracy in Central America*. Cambridge, MA: Harvard University Press.

Paris, R. 2010. "Saving Liberal Peacebuilding." *Review of International Studies* 36: 337–365.

Pugh, M., and N. Cooper with J. Goodhand. 2004. *War Economies in a Regional Context: Challenges for Transformation*. London, UK: International Peace Academy, Lynne Rienner.

Richmond, O. 2009. "Becoming Liberal, Unbecoming Liberalism: Liberal- Local Hybridity via the Everyday as a Response to the Paradoxes of Liberal Peacebuilding." *Journal of Intervention and Statebuilding* 3 (3): 324–344.

Roxborough, I. 2012. "Building Other Peoples' States: The Sociology of Statebuilding." *Comparative Sociology* 11: 179–201.

Rubin, Barnett. 2002. *The Fragmentation of Afghanistan. State formation and Collapse in the International System*. New Haven, CT: Yale University Press.

Selby, Jan. 2013. "The Myth of Liberal Peacebuilding." *Conflict, Security and Development* 13 (1): 57–56.

Taylor, Brian, and Roxana Botea. 2008. "Tilly Tally: War-Making and State-Making in the Contemporary Third World." *International Studies Review* 10: 27–56.

Tilly, C. 1992. *Coercion, Capital, and European States, AD990-1992*.

Weizman, E. 2011. *The Least of All Possible Evils. Humanitarian Violence from Arendt to Gaza*. London, UK: Hurst.

Statebuilding in Afghanistan: challenges and pathologies

William Maley

Asia-Pacific College of Diplomacy, The Australian National University, Canberra, Australia

The process of statebuilding in Afghanistan since 2001 has been complicated by a diverse set of problems, including the unintended consequences of early political decisions, the choice of institutional forms that have fostered dysfunctional policy-making, and the slide towards a neopatrimonial system combining bureaucracy with patronage. These problems have had a corrosive effect on the statebuilding enterprise, leaving an ambiguous legacy as Afghanistan proceeds towards one of the most challenging phases of its modern history.

Introduction

The overthrow of the Taliban regime in late 2001 inaugurated a complex phase of statebuilding in Afghanistan with multifarious consequences, not all of which are yet fully obvious. Nonetheless, while Afghanistan has witnessed a range of positive developments in the decade or so since then (Ignatius 2013), few would hold up the Afghan statebuilding enterprise as a model for emulation by other countries. In key respects, the experience has fallen far short of the expectations held both by ordinary people in Afghanistan and by donors who initially committed themselves not to abandon the people of Afghanistan but to provide them with opportunities that they had notably failed to receive following the collapse of the communist regime in Kabul in April 1992. While there is always a risk that military forces will outstay their welcome (Edelstein 2008), the Afghanistan enterprise was not doomed from the outset; rather, it was undermined by a series of strategic misjudgements and miscalculations that combined to produce a dispiriting, rather than inspiring, outcome.

My aim in this article is to highlight some of these problems, but also to set them in a wider context. Decisions are often constrained by a range of factors beyond the immediate control of any single actor, and, as is so often the case when major disasters occur, it is the complex interaction of multiple contributing factors, rather than one big mistake (for which a single actor can be held to account), that explains why some complex undertaking ran into difficulties. This has certainly been true in the Afghan case. The various sections of this article elaborate these points. The first section examines how contentious and complex the discussion of statebuilding has become, and how a Westphalian model of international society constrained what could be attempted in Afghanistan. The second identifies some specific design flaws in the statebuilding enterprise, and some further problems with the post-2001 constitutional and political systems. The third shows how systemic weaknesses facilitated a fatal slide away from institutionalization in the direction of neopatrimonialism, setting the scene for the massive electoral fraud that marred the 2009 presidential election. It notes the problems of distrust and elite fragmentation that resulted, highlights the prevalence and corrosive effects of corruption, and discusses the problem of abuse of power and the weakness of the rule of law. The fourth traces the effects of an overly centralized state and addresses the failure of the state to secure the lives of ordinary people. The fifth offers some brief conclusions.

Conundrums of statebuilding

Much ink has been spilt with the objective of defining the state, not least because of the polysemic character of the term itself (see Gill 2003; Poggi 1978; van Creveld 1999). On the one hand, the word 'state' can be used to define a territorial unit of a particular kind; in this use it is virtually synonymous with the word 'country'. In that sense of the term, Afghanistan has long been a state, historically meeting the criteria set out in the 1933 Montevideo Convention on the Rights and Duties of States (165 League of Nations *Treaty Series* 19), recognized as such in the wider international system, and confirmed in its identity by decades of membership in the United Nations. The other main sense of the term refers to the key political and administrative structures within such territorial units, seeking to monopolize, in Max Weber's famous terminology, the legitimate means of violence, and using distinctive forms of revenue raising, notably taxation, to fund its activities. 'Statebuilding' typically refers to attempts to create such structures, or to re-create them when they have either broken down or been severely disrupted. Nonetheless, the idea of 'statebuilding' is a complex one. On a narrow reading it might seem to imply a conscious process of planning followed by construction, but that would exclude what Adam Ferguson in the eighteenth century described as 'establishments, which are indeed the result of human action, but not the execution of any human design' (Ferguson 1995, 119) – which is why the term 'state for-mation' might in some ways be more illuminating. Nevertheless, it does not follow from this that either conscious design choices, or for that matter decisions taken *without* attention to their poss-ible ramifications, have not played a significant role in shaping Afghanistan's experience. On the contrary, I argue that key choices made at crucial moments about particular issues go a long way towards explaining Afghanistan's predicament.

It is also the case that in recent times, conscious attempts to build new state structures have often been undertaken in the context of peace operations directed at restoring order in severely disrupted territories, resulting in a proliferation of analyses of 'nationbuilding' and 'peacebuild-ing', which often give a central place to the reconstitution of state structures as well (see Call and Wyeth 2008; Fukuyama 2006; Jenkins and Plowden 2006; Meienberg 2012; Richmond and Franks 2009). These discussions are increasingly nested within a complex literature that criti-cally appraises the feasibility of statebuilding as part of a liberal political agenda (Tadjbakhsh and Richmond 2011). This literature notes that statebuilding programmes often focus on build-ing up the central instrumentalities of the state, even though it may be in the 'periphery' that the bulk of the population is located and key political contests are played out (see Schetter 2013); it warns against efforts that are over-ambitious and under-resourced (Ottaway 2002); and it high-lights the peril of assuming that a single model will fit all cases. In its more radical versions, it critiques liberal intervention itself (Chandler 2011); and a number of authors take up the issue of hybridity, the 'synthesis of the formal and informal, the old and the new, the local and the global' (Roberts 2013, 95; see also Edwards 2010).

Some see hybridity as a positive goal, although this is in some respects an old idea in new clothes. Some argue, as did Eckstein long ago, that 'a government will tend to be stable if its authority pattern is congruent with the other authority patterns of the society of which it is a part' (Eckstein 1992, 188). But, that said, while the reality of such syntheses on the ground is something that the case of Afghanistan clearly illustrates (Giustozzi and Ibrahimi 2013, 256–259), it does not follow that respect for the informal, the old, or the local is intrinsically desirable. On occasion it may be a good idea to attempt a break from 'traditional' ways of doing things that privilege the power of some aspirants over others by entrenching norms of partiality (Ullmann-Margalit 1977).

The success of statebuilding endeavours is conditioned by local history, culture, and life experiences (see Barry 2011), and also by the complex set of principles, norms, and standard operating procedures to which any statebuilding project must conform, at least to some degree, if it is to be internationally accepted. The Taliban's refusal to accept the validity of such principles and norms contributed significantly to their pariah status, even before the September 2001 attacks (Maley 2000).

These principles and norms come in a number of different forms. At a deep level, scholars have sought to identify constitutional principles of international society (Reus-Smit 1999, 30). These are not necessarily the product of explicit or conscious negotiation between actors within the system; on the contrary, they may evolve progressively as different parties interact with each other and come to accept particular patterns of behaviour as necessary and appropriate for the regulation of such interactions. At the deepest level of all, such principles may define what is considered to be a relevant actor in the first place. The so-called 'Westphalian' order, dating from the Peace of Westphalia of 1648, came to assign a central role to actors defined as 'sovereign states', and although the complex 'principles' of sovereignty have been much violated when powerful actors found it in their interests to do so (Krasner 1999; Pemberton 2009), the *ideal* of the 'sovereign state' has strongly influenced statebuilding endeavours – an influence amplified by the deeply negative connotations of an obvious alternative model, that of colonialism.

Two other bodies of norms also served to constrain what the architects of Afghanistan's statebuilding enterprise could attempt. On the one hand, Afghanistan remains subject to a range of international obligations arising from its past ratification of binding international treaties, or accession to them. These cover a range of different areas, including most importantly human rights and the laws of armed conflict. Such obligations do not evaporate simply because a state has run into severe difficulties. Indeed, some would argue that in such circumstances, norms of this kind are more important than ever in seeking to constrain the power of those who might be minded to act either recklessly or ruthlessly. On the other hand, Afghanistan is potentially subject to another norm, arguably still embryonic in form and certainly more recent in provenance, that has nonetheless received much attention in the era of complex peace operations: the 'norm of democratic governance' (Maley 2009a). This norm mandates that at some point, ordinary people must be given the opportunity to choose whom they wish to have as their rulers; and underpinning it are important procedural requirements to ensure that acts of choice are free and fair (Elklit and Svensson 1997). Whether these norms are useful or not in the Afghan context is beside the point. The key point is that they cannot simply be wished away. They formed a critical part of the background to the November–December 2001 Bonn Conference that inaugurated Afghanistan's twenty-first-century statebuilding experiment.

Design flaws

The Bonn Conference, hosted by the German government and organized by the United Nations, brought together a number of key non-Taliban Afghan political actors to lay out a pathway for political transition in the country. On the whole, it has had bad press, not entirely deserved. In contrast to transitions such as that in South Africa between the release of Nelson Mandela in 1989 and the holding of multiracial elections in 1994, the UN in the case of Afghanistan was faced with acute time pressures. From mid-November 2001, the Afghan capital had been in the hands of the anti-Taliban forces that also held Afghanistan's seat in the UN General

Assembly, and there was a widespread belief that any alternative dispensation would have to be put in place swiftly. It has also been suggested that it was a mistake on the UN's part not to include the Taliban in the Bonn Conference, but this criticism fails to take note of the atmosphere at the time. The occupants of Kabul were still outraged at the assassination on 9 September 2001 of their long-time leader Ahmad Shah Massoud, and it is inconceivable that they would have agreed to negotiate with the Taliban – if, indeed, anyone could have been found who could have credibly presented himself as the Taliban's delegate (Maley 2011a).

There are three key dimensions to any statebuilding enterprise. The first is institutional *design*, and the second is the development of institutional capacity, to both of which I will turn shortly. A third, however, of fundamental importance, is the securing of *generalized normative support* (that is, legitimacy) for the institutions and arrangements that a statebuilding enterprise has put in place. Developing institutional capacity lay beyond what was possible at Bonn, and some key issues of institutional design were explicitly left for a later constitutional *Loya Jirga* (Great Assembly) to resolve. However, the Bonn conference did as much as could reasonably have been expected to identify ways of securing legitimacy for the structures and institutions that the Bonn process was intended to produce. The particular legitimation strategies which it employed wove together a number of distinct approaches in the hope that their confluence would provide a robust foundation for new state structures. The Bonn Agreement (United Nations 2001), struck at the end of the conference on 5 December 2001, drew on *traditional* factors by employing the language of *Loya Jirga* and by seeking to exploit goodwill towards the former monarchy by granting the last king of Afghanistan, Zahir Shah, the title of Father of the Nation. It sought to make use of *legal-rational* factors by anticipating the holding of free and fair elections to fill key offices of the state. And it sought to harness the *perceived charisma* of Hamid Karzai by naming him the head of an Interim Administration that was subsequently inaugurated on 22 December 2001 (Maley 2009b, 224–229).

That said, legitimacy is also related to performance (Maley 2008), and the great failure of the Bonn Agreement was that it put in place some arrangements that would blight the performance of the new administration from the outset. The most serious failure at Bonn was the complete neglect of questions relating to the appropriate scope and strength of the future state. 'Scope' refers to the range of activities that the state pursues; 'strength' relates to the powers which it can exercise to pursue those activities. Together, the two do a great deal to determine the character of the state (Fukuyama 2004). At Bonn, there was virtually no meaningful discussion of either of these dimensions of state power. Instead, the Bonn Agreement blithely provided for up to 29 departments of government. In part, this reflected an unthinking return to the model of the Afghan state that had taken shape in the 1950s and 1960s under the influence of the statist ideologies that prevailed at that time (see Rubin 2002). But the main reason for the decision to opt for a grandiose state structure was painfully clear: departments were to be distributed as rewards to the various factions that took part in the conference, and there had to be enough rewards to go around.

This proved to be disastrous on two levels, both related to the dynamics of political competition. While a number of Afghans doubtless supported the idea of a 'strong' state, on the basis of a Hobbesian need for a common power to hold all other actors in awe, the ambition to develop such a state inevitably sharpened political competition by holding out the prospect that a strong state could be a significant political asset to control. Yet, paradoxically, the aspiration to develop a strong state was undermined by the bureaucratic structure of the state. With different factions in control of departments, with considerable ostensible overlap in the responsibilities of different agencies, and with incoming donor money as a stake over which to struggle, the scene was set for a state that would be weakened by administrative complexity and by bitter rivalry between different ministers, ministries, and officials (Maley 2006). There have been successes as well as failures in the policy process, and some young Afghan officials are outstandingly impressive. Nonetheless, too many agencies have become political fiefdoms, and a recent study has concluded that 'the fortunes and the strength of ministries remain fragile and weakly institutionalized, and are rather embedded in the personalities of their leadership' (Parkinson 2010, 2).

Whilst the administrative character of the new Afghan system was determined at Bonn, the new constitutional framework was the product of the December 2003–January 2004 meeting of the 'Constitutional *Loya Jirga*' for which the Bonn Agreement provided. In the appraisal of institutions, Robert Goodin has suggested that four features are desirable as attributes: revisability, robustness, sensitivity to motivational complexity, and variability (Goodin 1996, 39–43). The 2004 Afghan Constitution presented some significant problems where some of these features were concerned. While its human rights guarantees struck a positive note, its wider structure set the scene for major problems as time went on.

The most serious single weakness in the Afghan constitution was that it put in place a strongly presidential system of government. Presidential systems are not simply political systems that provide for the office of president, since this office can be found in essentially parliamentary systems such as that used in the Federal Republic of Germany. The key feature of a presidential system is that the president functions as the chief executive within the political system more broadly, and has a mandate which is not dependent on the continuing confidence of a legislative body, as is the case in Westminster systems. The perils of presidentialism have long been recognized by scholars (Linz 1990). Such systems often depend on near-superhuman capabilities on the part of an incumbent president, and can easily run into difficulties if the occupant of that office falls short of expectations. Furthermore, presidential systems are notoriously difficult to revise, since the initiative to move away from a presidential system must come from the very individual who occupies the presidential office, and who is least likely to be willing to concede that the system is dysfunctional.

In the Afghan case, the presidential system has proved dysfunctional in a number of respects. First, President Karzai has had to function simultaneously as both symbolic Head of State and executive Head of Government. Each could be a full-time position; handed to one person, they represent a recipe for overload and exhaustion. Second, given the bureaucratic tensions noted earlier, the president has also had to function as a one-man mechanism of interagency coordination. Third, and most seriously, in presidential systems, subordinate actors almost inevitably look to the president to provide leadership in both policy development and implementation; and indeed, one of the reasons that the United States supported a presidential system for Afghanistan was that key US leaders believed that a strong chief executive was required both to drive policy and to provide a simple point of contact for Afghanistan's key external supporters (Suhrke 2011, 169). Yet President Karzai, like most of the Afghans who might have been considered as serious candidates for presidential office, had grown up politically in an essentially state-free environment, in Karzai's case, working in the 1980s for the leader of a minor Afghan resistance party based in the Pakistani city of Peshawar. He had no particular claim to expertise in policy development or implementation, and this became excruciatingly apparent as expectations of what he should do shifted over time from symbolic leadership to a more hands-on approach. It was no wonder that in 2010, US Ambassador Karl Eikenberry was to complain of Karzai's 'inability to grasp the most rudimentary principles of state-building' (quoted in Sanger 2012, 45).

This did not lead to humility on the part of the executive branch. If anything, the executive has been notable for its hubris. The main victim has been the bicameral parliament, and in particular its lower house, the Wolesi Jirga. An elected parliament can provide a check on unhealthy concentrations of power, and can facilitate the articulation of diverse political interests. While the tempestuous antics of some of its members deserve little respect, the Wolesi Jirga has to a certain degree played these roles. But only to a certain degree. The 'single non-transferable vote' electoral system used to choose its members makes it very difficult for political parties to thrive, and instead has thrown up what has been largely a clutch of independents, coalescing into loose blocs – not in the open, but in secretive ways (Reynolds and Carey 2012). The legislature has been most effective when providing a platform for public concerns to be aired; it has been much less effective in providing solutions, although this is in large measure because it is the executive rather than the legislature that has the formal power to do so. Furthermore, it is at risk of being manipulated by outsiders with patronage networks at their disposal, a problem that hit the headlines when conservative Shiite religious figure Asef Mohseni succeeded in promoting a Shiite Personal Status Law that proved highly controversial both internationally and amongst many Shia (Oates 2009). Legislators have also been manipulated by the Palace.

Pathologies of the state

By far the worst consequence of the adoption of a presidential system was that it facilitated a slide into neopatrimonialism, which represents a particularly dysfunctional form of hybridity. While various definitions of neopatrimonialism have been deployed since S.N. Eisenstadt (1973) first coined the term, the characterization offered by Bratton and Van de Walle (1994, 458) remains extremely useful:

> In neopatrimonial regimes, the chief executive retains authority through personal patronage, rather than through ideology or law. As with classic patrimonialism, the right to rule is ascribed to a person rather than an office. In contemporary neopatrimonialism, relationships of loyalty and dependence pervade a formal political and administrative system and leaders occupy bureaucratic office less to perform public service than to acquire personal wealth and status. The distinction between private and public interests is purposely blurred. The essence of neopatrimonialism is the award by public officials of personal favors, both within the state (notably public sector jobs) and in society (for instance, licenses, contracts, and projects). In return for material rewards, clients mobilize political support and refer all decisions upward as a mark of deference to patrons.

Beyond this, there are further distinctions that can usefully be made, notably that drawn by Bach (2011, 277) between 'regulated' and 'predatory' forms of neopatrimonialism: in the former, 'patrimonial practices tend to be regulated and capped', whereas in the latter they can reach monstrous extremes.

Karzai's neopatrimonialism is not remotely to be compared with the predatory forms witnessed under leaders such as Mobutu in Zaire or Bokassa in the Central African Empire, who were self-indulgent and sultanistic. Rather, it represents a continuation of the Peshawar politics in which Karzai was schooled in the 1980s – a state-free environment in which one's very conception of politics was based on alliances, networking, and patron–client relationships. Nor was the neopatrimonial path taken without input from Karzai's backers. The US decision in early 2002 to block expansion beyond Kabul of the International Security Assistance Force (ISAF) left Karzai with little option but to use patronage to bolster his position in rural areas; and former US Defense Secretary Donald H. Rumsfeld claimed in his memoirs that he had counselled Karzai to emulate the patronage politics of the notorious Mayor Richard J. Daley of Chicago (Rumsfeld 2011).

Neopatrimonialism has had a corrosive effect on the statebuilding enterprise in Afghanistan for three reasons. First, over time it has made Karzai a target for flattery and cajoling of a kind that few actors would be able to resist, which has led to his becoming more and more remote from the concerns of ordinary Afghans, and inclined to trust his own judgment and the advice of a small group of relatives and cronies rather than relying on a wide circle of advisers (Rubin 2009). By many accounts it has also led to a kind of hypervigilance – after all, many neopatrimonial leaders have met with sticky ends, since they tend to accumulate enemies as well as friends – and high levels of suspicion, dramatically on display in some of his criticisms of his US allies, and possibly also in his decision to remove two of his most accomplished ministers – the finance minister, Dr Ashraf Ghani, in 2004, and the foreign minister, Dr Abdullah, in 2006. Second, it set the scene for gargantuan electoral fraud when Karzai came up for re-election in 2009. There is no evidence that Karzai was directly involved, but in neopatrimonial systems, a ruler's associates have very strong incentives to do the dirty work for him. A detailed study of the fraud has concluded that 'the overwhelming part of the election fraud seems to have been committed in favour of the incumbent, which may be explained by the close relationships between election officers and government officials' (Weidmann and Callen 2013, 74). Free and fair elections are a direct threat to neopatrimonial networks and relationships, and the 2009 fraud was utterly predictable. Third, it tends to perpetuate elite fragmentation and distrust, just at the moment when civic trust and a consensually unified elite are most important as a basis for political stability (see Higley and Burton 1989; Maley 1997, 2003).

While Karzai has certainly leaned on supporters from his Popalzai tribe, notably his brother Ahmed Wali Karzai (murdered in Kandahar on 12 July 2011) and Jan Mohammad Khan of Uruzgan (murdered six days later in Kabul), neopatrimonialism should not be confused with the personalistic politics of Afghan tribes, especially given the near-legendary feuding that can occur within tribes and families, including the Karzais (see Chayes 2006; Risen 2009, 2012). The crucial difference is that in the neopatrimonial system that has taken shape since 2001, the complex personalistic ties of the ruler are intertwined with the power and resources of the state. Nor should neopatrimonialism be seen as the unavoidable destiny of a 'traditional society'. With an estimated 70% of the Afghan population below the age of 25, and globalization affecting Afghanistan in manifold ways, simplistic notions of 'tradition' do little more than de-authenticate the aspirations of a large section of the population (see for example Hakimi, this volume). Neopatrimonialism is a distinctively modern form of political organization, with its own pathologies, and while it may not have led – yet – to a full-blown crisis of legitimacy, it has set the scene for rampant corruption and the failure of the rule of law to take root.

Corruption is widely regarded as one of Afghanistan's most serious problems. A 2012 survey carried out for the Asia Foundation (2012, 107) found that over half of respondents (52%) saw corruption as a major problem in their neighbourhood, 56% in their daily life, 60% in their local authorities, 70% in their provincial government, and 79% in Afghanistan as a whole.

Further aspects of the 2012 data are particularly alarming. First, the 'perception that corruption is a major problem in Afghanistan as a whole is at its highest point in 2012 (79%) since the first survey in 2006' (108). Second, the belief that corruption is a major problem in respondents' daily lives has climbed steadily, from 42% in 2006 to 56% in 2012 (109). These findings are broadly consistent with other studies that highlight corruption as a major concern. In a 2009 survey, Integrity Watch found that one Afghan in seven experienced direct bribery, and that the average value of bribes was USD 156 – in a country where average annual income was only USD 502 (Integrity Watch Afghanistan 2010, 10). This represents corruption on a scale that dwarfs any previous Afghan experience. Writing of Afghanistan's historical experience of corruption, Jonathan Goodhand has noted that 'not all forms of corruption are equally harmful or equally wrong in the eyes of most Afghans.... It seems probable the people will tolerate corruption if the state can deliver some tangible benefits to them and their families' (Goodhand 2008, 416). But with perceptions of corruption as widespread as they presently are, Afghans' patience may end up being stretched to the breaking point.

The main form that corruption has taken in Afghanistan is not direct embezzlement from the state budget (of which there is little evidence) but the abusive seizure of private assets, the solicitation of bribes in exchange for contracts and positional goods, and the favouring of relatives in contracting and appointments. The donor community bears a heavy responsibility for some of these problems, having flooded the country with money when absorptive capacity was low and bureaucratic complexity high, exactly the environment in which bribery could be expected to flourish. Even the Taliban managed to benefit from this largesse (Wissing 2012). Charged with monitoring the over USD 89.5 billion provided for Afghanistan since 2001, the US Special Inspector General for Afghanistan Reconstruction (SIGAR) in January 2013 offered an unflinching assessment of reconstruction efforts, finding that reconstruction efforts suffered from inadequate planning, insufficient coordination, poor execution, and a lack of meaningful metrics for progress. This had led to 'lost opportunities and incalculable waste' (SIGAR 2013, iv). He also warned that 'carrying defective practices and weak oversight into the Afghan "Decade of Transformation," even at lower levels of funding and effort, would carry great risk of massive new waste, fraud, and abuse' (SIGAR 2013, 11). But, that said, the Karzai Administration has been extremely lax in addressing the problem of corruption in any meaningful fashion, with Karzai himself intervening to protect associates suspected of misconduct (Chandrasekaran 2010; Felbab-Brown 2013, 100). Furthermore, as the 2009 election showed, Karzai has not been squeamish about benefiting from corruption (although he continues to maintain, in the face of all the evidence, that he was the *victim* rather than the beneficiary of fraud).

The episode that brought corruption in Afghanistan to a worldwide audience was doubtless the collapse of the Kabul Bank. Though touted as an example of Afghanistan's entering the twenty-first century, the Kabul Bank was run by its chairman and its chief executive officer as a Ponzi scheme, with new deposits funding unsecured loans to the high and mighty. In Felbab-Brown's words (2013, 104), it became a 'personal piggy bank for many of Afghanistan's most influential power brokers and highest government officials including President Karzai's brother Mahmoud Karzai'. In November 2012, an 'Independent Joint Anti-Corruption Monitoring and Evaluation Committee' published a damning report on the bank's collapse. The committee did a remarkable job, but a single passage in the report highlights how difficult it is to confront corruption in a neopatrimonial system: 'Unfortunately, a small number of organizations declined to participate in the inquiry, the most central being the Afghan High Office of Oversight. Despite the lack of participation, the Committee was able to secure enough information to fill in any gaps. It is our hope that those organizations that did not participate take the results of our inquiry more seriously than they did the process' (Independent Joint Anti-Corruption Monitoring and Evaluation Committee 2012, 3). The chair of the High Office of Oversight and Anti-corruption is a longtime Karzai associate who was chair of the Independent Election Commission at the time of the fraud-ridden 2009 election.

The development of a neopatrimonial system also helps explain why the rule of law remains so weak in Afghanistan (Maley 2011b). There is, of course, a vicious circle here. The rule of law is above all else a principle to constrain the arbitrary exercise of power, but neopatrimonialism generates behaviour of precisely this kind, and asymmetries of power and wealth, combined with weakness in the rule of law, underpin corruption (Uslaner 2008). When meaningful justice proves impossible for ordinary people to obtain, the moral foundations of a political order begin to decay, and with time the legitimacy of that order may be severely compromised.

Among the key elements of the rule of law identified by legal theorist Joseph Raz (1979, 214–218), it is the independence of the judiciary that is the most important, and also by far the most difficult to achieve. A judiciary which is simply a craven echo of the executive is hardly worth the money it costs to run it. Yet developing an independent judiciary is by no means easy; and according to a sophisticated recent analysis, it has a vital ideational dimension. 'Sincere judicial attitudes are not inert background characteristics, awaiting the right strategic conditions to be released or activated; rather, they are themselves crucial to explaining judges' proclivity to assert their authority against powerful actors' (Hilbink 2012, 589). To sustain an independent judiciary is even more difficult: it requires a 'self-enforcing equilibrium', since if no one expects anyone else to follow the law, there is little likelihood that law will play much of a role in shaping behaviour (Weingast 1997). Arguably, this is exactly the problem in Afghanistan. The neopatrimonial system was entrenched while attempts to build the rule of law were still getting off the ground, and consequently, judges were co-opted as part of the wider system from the outset. As Fukuyama has argued, 'We should admit to ourselves that we have very little historical experience in successfully constructing a rule of law in societies where . . . a strong state precedes law' (2010, 43).

The performance of the state-based courts has been so disappointing (Tondini 2010) that serious scholars have investigated a range of alternatives. Ali Wardak (2004; see also United Nations Development Program 2007) has argued for a hybrid model that draws on the legitimacy of community-based dispute-resolution mechanisms while promoting respect for key human rights norms. Such a model does not involve a retreat from 'modernity' in favour of 'tradition': on the contrary, it embodies ideas about restorative justice that are at the cutting edge of modern criminology and are particularly appropriate where punitive measures risk triggering cycles of revenge (see Braithwaite and Wardak 2013; Wardak and Braithwaite 2013). It should also be noted that there has been growing criticism of the use of informal justice as an adjunct to counterinsurgency operations (see Wimpelmann, this volume). Unfortunately, while the Afghan judiciary may be weak at delivering justice, it has a well-developed sense of self-preservation, and according to Suhrke, the chief justice responded to the United Nations Development Program report cited above by banning it, 'claiming quoting or citing it was illegal' (2011, 214). As Migdal has put it, 'State leaders, especially, have had a very strong interest in presenting their idea of law as if no other meanings of it existed or mattered' (2001, 151).

State, society and security

Much discussion of statebuilding in Afghanistan has focused simply on the top leadership of the state and its central agencies. But most Afghans have few if any direct encounters at these levels; they are much more likely to come into contact with what Migdal has called the *trenches*, consisting of 'the officials who must execute state directives directly in the face of possibly strong societal resistance', and the *dispersed field offices*, the 'regional and local bodies that rework and organize state policies and directives for local consumption, or even formulate and implement wholly local policies' (1994, 16). There is little evidence that engagements at these levels have been a source of much joy. The strongly centralized nature of the state has seen to that.

Rural Afghanistan presents an exceptionally complex political landscape, in which the agencies of the Afghan state provide but one set of participants in a ceaseless renegotiation of power relations involving civil society, the state, and transnational actors, all using diverse strategies to realize their objectives (Monsutti 2012). Yet it is also a venue of central importance for political legitimation. While Afghanistan is becoming increasingly urbanized, it is through popular opposition in rural areas that Afghan regimes have often been destabilized in the past. The *mujahideen* of the 1980s flourished in the countryside. Much has changed in rural areas: radio and even television have spread at high speed, and according to the 2012 Asia Foundation survey, 83% of rural respondents had access in their household to a radio, 63% to a mobile phone, and 40% to a television (171). While this is more the product of private entrepreneurial activity than direct state assistance, citizens who are networked to this extent cannot be ignored, and 'delivering the goods' in rural Afghanistan therefore matters.

Afghanistan also has a long history of local community governance (Shahrani 1998). This is not synonymous with tribal power relations, since significant components of the Afghan population are not tribally structured. The key word here is 'governance', which connotes structures that are legitimate and do not depend for their authority on a relationship with some other power holder. In the post-2001 era, community governance has been largely bypassed, and community leaders at this level disenfranchised in a number of ways. On the one hand, they have lacked the technical expertise to play much of a role in interacting with key donors; such roles were quickly assumed by urban 'technocrats', many of them émigrés who returned after the Taliban was overthrown. On the other hand, the centralized neopatrimonial state has left many of them marginalized, even in their own localities. Furthermore, the de facto and de jure states do not align; much real power is exercised by armed commanders or others with powerful patrons in Kabul; and a 'circle of corruption and power' results (Gardizi, Hussmann and Torabi 2010, 17). A 2011 study concluded that 'rent-taking occurs at every available opportunity, and the influence of powerholders and patronage networks remains pervasive' (Saltmarshe and Mehdi 2011, 2).

As Goodhand and Mansfield (2013) have noted, positions within the state are highly prized at local levels. They provide access to resources, and are perceived to bring with them a degree of legitimacy. Some 'leaders' in rural areas, such as Matiullah Khan in Uruzgan, have built careers for themselves by exploiting the desire of foreign forces to find local partners (see Filkins 2010; Schmeidl 2010). And when a Matiullah Khan becomes provincial chief of police, as happened in Uruzgan, it lifts him from the ambiguous status of 'warlord' into a more elevated realm. But what it does not do is to automatically make him a policeman for 'all Afghans', as opposed to favoured members of his Durrani tribe. Indeed, under the prevailing Afghan system, all key appointments come from Kabul (many from the president personally), and resources for distribution are locally allocated portions of the resource base of the *central* state. Loyalty to the centre, rather than efficiency in the eyes of locals, is the pre-eminent criterion for determining an official's worth. As a result, a large number of unappetizing figures have made lucrative careers for themselves within the structures of the state, blighting its wider reputation (see MacGinty 2010).

This is not to say that all officials of the state in rural Afghanistan are venal and inefficient. On the contrary, some young officials of real quality have caught the attention of acute observers, for example Faridullah, the *woleswal* (administrator) of Alisheng district in Laghman province (Foschini 2012). Unfortunately, it is at this level that officials are also at grave risk of assassination – this was the fate of Faridullah in August 2012 – although more senior figures are vulnerable, too (Ahmed 2012; Maley 2012a).

If a state proves incapable of providing basic security for its people, its standing is likely to be increasingly questioned. While much of Afghanistan remains relatively quiet, there are few guarantees that a sudden upsurge in violence will not occur. At the very least, this is a source of pervasive stress; and for those who have suffered severely in the past, it provides an incentive to seek a means of exit. Here, the overarching problem for both the Afghan government and its backers is the persistence of insurgency, which the blocking of ISAF expansion and the drift of US attention from Afghanistan to Iraq in 2002–2003 greatly facilitated. The resumption of insurgent activity in Afghanistan – involving Taliban groups, the so-called 'Haqqani network', and the extremist group Hezb-e Islami (led by Gulbuddin Hekmaytar) – came in 2003–2004 when Asia Foundation (2004) data suggested a high level of *optimism* about the direction in which the country was moving; one should therefore be wary of simply pinning the blame for insurgency on poor performance by the Afghan government and its international supporters.

This is not to say that the security performance of the Afghan state has been up to scratch. The Afghan National Army (ANA), funded by the United States, has won respect as a national institution, but it is far too costly to be sustainably funded from internal revenue sources, and it is unclear how cohesive it will prove to be once foreign forces (currently providing air cover and medical evacuation capabilities) have left, or how effectively its management structures will perform the bureaucratic tasks required to support front-line troops (see Sedra, this volume). The 2012 scandal surrounding malnutrition amongst patients at the Dawood National Military Hospital in Kabul certainly gives cause for concern (Abi-Habib 2011; Wendle 2012). The Afghan National Police (ANP) have been widely and credibly criticized as corrupt and preda-tory; they have also suffered huge casualties at the hands of insurgents (see Giustozzi and Ishaq-zadeh 2013; Murray 2011; Wilder 2007).

Another concern, with respect to the standing of the Afghan state, is the sensitive issue of civilian casualties, on which President Karzai has focused a great deal of his rhetoric. On the one hand, civilian casualties, even in small numbers, are tragic for the victims and their families; the symbolic effects of civilian casualties can be significant; and ghastly events (such as the deaths of civilians in a German air strike near Kunduz in September 2009) can undermine inter-national support for a deployment (Mettelsiefen and Reuter 2010). But on the other hand, the vast bulk of civilian casualties in Afghanistan since 2001 have been at the hands of the Taliban and their associates (of whom Karzai has been notably less critical than of his Western partners), and the scale of mortality has been only a small fraction of what it was in the 1980s – or even of the annual road toll in Afghanistan (Maley 2012b; United Nations 2013).

President Karzai's concerns here are far from illegitimate, and this is one reason why the United States has toyed with counterinsurgency ideas that highlight respect for the civilian popu-lation (see Kaplan 2013). However, the United States has not approached the Afghanistan situ-ation with a consistent *strategic* vision; nor, for that matter, have its NATO allies (Rynning 2012, 183). All too often, international actors have scrambled to produce short-term palliatives rather than addressing problems synoptically. Thus the much-fêted Provincial Reconstruction Teams too often became substitutes for the Afghan state, creating perverse incentives for local political actors. At the same time, however, they proved unequal to the (near-impossible) task of stabilizing Afghanistan on a province-by-province basis (see Hynek and Marton 2012; Stapleton 2012).

The main reason that this was a hopeless task is that sanctuaries in Pakistan provided a crucial foundation for insurgent activity. This was recognized on both sides of the conflict. In August 2007, during a visit to Kabul, Pakistani president Pervez Musharraf candidly remarked, 'There is no doubt Afghan militants are supported from Pakistani soil. The problem that you have in your region is because support is provided from our side' (Shah and Gall 2007). US Ambassador Eikenberry made a similar point from Kabul: 'Pakistan will remain the single great-est source of Afghan instability so long as the border sanctuaries remain. Until this sanctuary problem is fully addressed, the gains from sending additional forces may be fleeting' (quoted in Sanger 2012, 33). There is strong evidence that this has resulted from a deliberate 'double game' in which Pakistan's Inter-Services Intelligence directorate has sought to sustain the Taliban as a tool for future influence in Afghanistan (Maley 2011c; Waldman 2010), something which is completely consistent with its use of surrogates elsewhere for asymmetric warfare. The response of the United States to this duplicity proved completely ineffectual. On the one hand, it pressed Karzai to hold his tongue, arguing – in the face of mounting evidence to the contrary – that Washington knew how to handle Islamabad. On the other hand, when pressure should have been applied, it dithered, and it consistently underestimated its capacity to bring pressure to bear on Pakistani actors. With the death of Osama Bin Laden in May 2011, the US moved to extract itself from Afghanistan, leaving the problem of Pakistan's meddling unresolved, and Afghans gazing into an abyss not of their making.

Conclusion

As the long-running drama of Afghan statebuilding limps towards what may be its concluding episodes, it is useful to take stock of what has happened since the process was initiated. The experience of the last decade in Afghanistan has left an ambiguous legacy with respect to the idea of statebuilding. Afghanistan, now exposed to the forces of globalization as never before, is a very different country from what it was in 2001, but too often, the dominant image of what has happened in Afghanistan has been shaped by bitter recriminations between parties that one might have hoped would find ways of working cooperatively. This has been in large measure because the outcomes of the statebuilding process in Afghanistan have been disappointing to the Afghan government, *and* to its internal critics, *and* to its international backers – and each, in order to satisfy its own constituencies, has sought to impute the bulk of the blame for failure to someone else. The result has been a set of impressions in the wider world that do not do justice to the complexity of the tasks that have been involved in statebuilding.

As far as the issue of hybridity is concerned, a mixed picture emerges. The failure to build the rule of law suggests that an approach making more use of pre-existing dispute-resolution mechanisms, especially if suitably modified, could mark a significant step forward. By contrast, the neopatrimonial system of executive power highlights the risk of combining the old and the new, with bureaucratic structures accentuating the pathologies of patronage and networking. However, there is another lesson here. The adverse effects of neopatrimonialism were most likely not *intended* by those who promoted the adoption of a presidential system at the 2003–2004 Constitutional *Loya Jirga*, especially the United States; but they were hardly *unforeseeable*. Indeed, a number of briefing papers prepared for the Constitutional Drafting Commission warned of the dangers of a presidential system in Afghanistan (Rubin 2013, 149–163). Here, expertise was overwhelmed by political interests, and this is likely to be an enduring problem with institutional design in statebuilding exercises. Hybridity is not a phenomenon to be either universally condemned or universally venerated; rather, the implications of hybridity need to be appraised in specific contexts.

That said, there are three lessons from the Afghan experience that deserve to be highlighted. The first is that it pays not to be overly ambitious in statebuilding. Many of the problems of the Afghan transition arose because the Afghan government, but even more its international supporters, attempted to do far too much. While the UN initially highlighted the importance of a 'light "expatriate" footprint' (United Nations 2002, para. 98), the range of issues covered by the 2006 Afghanistan Compact proved dauntingly large (Rubin and Hamidzada 2007), and naturally created high expectations of what could be achieved. It is better to exceed low expectations than to create high expectations that are routinely disappointed. The second lesson is that one should not look for 'great leaders' to solve one's problems. The adoption of a strong presidential system did not lead to strong and coherent leadership; it resulted in manipulative neopatrimonialism and burgeoning corruption. President Karzai, sadly, proved to be a leader for the good times, and with the passage of time his limitations became all too obvious. But third, and most seriously of all, the Afghan case shows that it is very difficult to build an effective state when a neighbouring country, for its own geopolitical reasons, is intent on wreaking havoc on one's territory. For the best part of a decade, Afghanistan has been confronted by a creeping invasion from Pakistan. The failure to confront this effectively has not been a failure of the Afghan government or people. To deal with the threat posed by Pakistan's ambitions lies beyond their power. The blame for this festering sore lies squarely with the international community, and the consequences may yet be a harvest of despair.

References

Abi-Habib, Maria. 2011. "At Afghan Military Hospital, Graft and Deadly Neglect." *The Wall Street Journal*, September 3.

Ahmed, Azam. 2012. "For Afghan Officials, Facing Prospect of Death is in the Job Description." *The New York Times*, December 8.

Asia Foundation. 2004. *Democracy in Afghanistan: A Survey of the Afghan Electorate*. Kabul: The Asia Foundation.

Asia Foundation. 2012. *Afghanistan in 2012: A Survey of the Afghan People*. Kabul: The Asia Foundation.

Bach, Daniel C. 2011. "Patrimonialism and Neopatrimonialism: Comparative Trajectories and Readings." *Commonwealth and Comparative Politics* 49 (3): 275–294.

Barry, Michael. 2011. *Kabul's Long Shadows: Historical Perspectives*. Princeton: Liechtenstein Institute on Self-Determination at Princeton University.

Braithwaite, John, and Ali Wardak. 2013. "Crime and War in Afghanistan. Part I: The Hobbesian Solution." *British Journal of Criminology* 53 (2): 179–196.

Bratton, Michael, and Nicolas Van de Walle. 1994. "Neopatrimonial Regimes and Political Transitions in Africa." *World Politics* 46 (4): 453–489.

Call, Charles T., with Vanessa Wyeth, eds. 2008. *Building States to Build Peace*. Boulder: Lynne Rienner.

Chandler, David. 2011. "The Uncritical Critique of 'Liberal Peace'." In *A Liberal Peace? The Problems and Practices of Peacebuilding*, edited by Susanna Campbell, David Chandler, and Meera Sabaratnam, pp. 174–190. London: Zed Books.

Chandrasekaran, Rajiv. 2010. "Karzai Seeks to Limit Role of U.S. Corruption Investigators." *The Washington Post*, September 9.

Chayes, Sarah. 2006. *The Punishment of Virtue: Inside Afghanistan after the Taliban*. New York: Penguin Press.

van Creveld, Martin. 1999. *The Rise and Decline of the State*. Cambridge: Cambridge University Press.

Eckstein, Harry. 1992. *Regarding Politics: Essays on Political Theory, Stability and Change*. Berkeley: University of California Press.

Edelstein, David M. 2008. *Occupational Hazards: Success and Failure in Military Occupation*. Ithaca: Cornell University Press.

Edwards, Lucy Morgan. 2010. "State-building in Afghanistan: A Case Showing the Limits?." *International Review of the Red Cross* 92 (880): 967–991.

Eisenstadt, S. N. 1973. *Traditional Patrimonialism and Neopatrimonialism*. Beverly Hills: SAGE Publications.

Elklit, Jørgen, and Palle Svensson. 1997. "What Makes Elections Free and Fair?." *Journal of Democracy* 8 (3): 32–46.

Felbab-Brown, Vanda. 2013. *Aspiration and Ambivalence: Strategies and Realities of Counterinsurgency and State Building in Afghanistan*. Washington, DC: The Brookings Institution Press.

Ferguson, Adam. 1995. *An Essay on the History of Civil Society*. Cambridge: Cambridge University Press.

Filkins, Dexter. 2010. "With U.S. Aid, Warlord Builds Afghan Empire." *The New York Times*, June 5.

Foschini, Fabrizio. 2012. *The Commuter of Alisheng: Death of a Country District Governor*. Kabul: Afghanistan Analysts Network, 14 August.

Fukuyama, Francis. 2004. *State-Building: Governance and World Order in the 21st Century*. Ithaca: Cornell University Press.

Fukuyama, Francis, ed. 2006. *Nation-Building: Beyond Afghanistan and Iraq*. Baltimore: The Johns Hopkins University Press.

Fukuyama, Francis. 2010. "Transitions to the Rule of Law." *Journal of Democracy* 21 (1): 33–44.

Gardizi, Manija, Karen Hussmann, and Yama Torabi. 2010. *Corrupting the State? Or State-Crafted Corruption: Exploring the Nexus between Corruption and Subnational Governance*. Kabul: Afghanistan Research and Evaluation Unit.

Gill, Graeme. 2003. *The Nature and Development of the Modern State*. New York: Palgrave Macmillan.

Giustozzi, Antonio, and Niamatullah Ibrahimi. 2013. "From New Dawn to Quicksand: The Political Economy of Statebuilding in Afghanistan." In *Political Economy of Statebuilding: Power after Peace*, edited by Mats Berdal and Dominik Zaum, 246–262. New York: Routledge.

Giustozzi, Antonio, and Mohammed Ishaqzadeh. 2013. *Policing Afghanistan: The Politics of the Lame Leviathan*. London: Hurst & Co.

Goodhand, Jonathan. 2008. "Corrupting or Consolidating the Peace?: The Drugs Economy and Post-Conflict Peacebuilding in Afghanistan." *International Peacekeeping* 15 (3): 405–423.

Goodhand, Jonathan, and David Mansfield. 2013. "Drugs and (Dis)order: Opium Economy, Political Settlements and State-Building in Afghanistan." In *Local Politics in Afghanistan: A Century of Intervention in Social Order*, edited by Conrad Schetter, 211–229. London: Hurst & Co.

Goodin, Robert E. 1996. "Institutions and their Design." In *The Theory of Institutional Design*, edited by Robert E. Goodin, 1–53. Cambridge: Cambridge University Press.

Higley, John, and Michael G. Burton. 1989. "The Elite Variable in Democratic Transitions and Breakdowns." *American Sociological Review* 54 (1): 17–32.

Hilbink, Lisa. 2012. "The Origins of Positive Judicial Independence." *World Politics* 64 (4): 587–621.

Hynek, Nik, and Péter Marton, eds. 2012. *Statebuilding in Afghanistan: Multinational Contributions to Reconstruction*. New York: Routledge.

Ignatius, David. 2013. "A More Modern Afghanistan." *The Washington Post*, January 17.

Independent Joint Anti-Corruption Monitoring and Evaluation Committee. 2012. *Report of the Public Inquiry into the Kabul Bank Crisis*. Kabul: Independent Joint Anti-Corruption Monitoring and Evaluation Committee.

Integrity Watch Afghanistan. 2010. *Afghan Perceptions and Experiences of Corruption: A National Survey 2010*. Kabul: Integrity Watch Afghanistan.

Jenkins, Kate, and William Plowden. 2006. *Governance and Nationbuilding: The Failure of International Intervention*. Cheltenham: Edward Elgar.

Kaplan, Fred. 2013. *The Insurgents: David Petraeus and the Plot to Change the American Way of War*. New York: Simon & Schuster.

Krasner, Stephen D. 1999. *Sovereignty: Organized Hypocrisy*. Princeton: Princeton University Press.

Linz, Juan. 1990. "The Perils of Presidentialism." *Journal of Democracy* 1 (1): 51–69.

MacGinty, Roger. 2010. "Warlords and the Liberal Peace: State-building in Afghanistan." *Conflict, Security and Development* 10 (4): 577–598.

Maley, William. 1997. "The Dynamics of Regime Transition in Afghanistan." *Central Asian Survey* 16 (2): 167–184.

Maley, William. 2000. *The Foreign Policy of the Taliban*. New York: Council on Foreign Relations.

Maley, William. 2003. "Institutional Design and the Rebuilding of Trust." In *From Civil Strife to Civil Society: Civil and Military Responsibilities in Disrupted States*, edited by William Maley, Charles Sampford, and Ramesh Thakur, 163–179. New York: United Nations University Press.

Maley, William. 2006. *Rescuing Afghanistan*. London: Hurst & Co.

Maley, William. 2008. "Building Legitimacy in Post-Taliban Afghanistan." In *State Building, Security, and Social Change in Afghanistan: Reflections on a Survey of the Afghan People*, edited by Ruth Rennie, 11–26. Kabul: The Asia Foundation.

Maley, William. 2009a. "Democracy and Legitimation: Challenges in the Reconstitution of Political Processes in Afghanistan." In *The Role of International Law in Rebuilding Societies after Conflict: Great Expectations*, edited by Brett Bowden, Hilary Charlesworth, and Jeremy Farrall, 111–133. Cambridge: Cambridge University Press.

Maley, William. 2009b. *The Afghanistan Wars*. London: Palgrave Macmillan.

Maley, William. 2011a. "The Role of 'International Society' in State-Building: Lessons from Afghanistan." In *Enduring States in the Face of Challenges from Within and Without*, edited by Yusuke Murakami, Hiroyuki Yamamoto, and Hiromi Komori, 220–237. Kyoto: Kyoto University Press.

Maley, William. 2011b. "The Rule of Law and the Weight of Politics: Challenges and Trajectories." In *The Rule of Law in Afghanistan: Missing in inaction*, edited by Whit Mason, 61–83. Cambridge: Cambridge University Press.

Maley, William. 2011c. "Pakistan-Afghanistan Relations." In *Pakistan's Stability Paradox: Domestic, Regional and International Dimensions*, edited by Michael Clarke and Ashutosh Misra, 121–136. New York: Routledge.

Maley, William. 2012a. "Afghanistan in 2011: Positioning for an Uncertain Future." *Asian Survey* 52 (1): 88–99.

Maley, William. 2012b. "Surviving in a War Zone: The Problem of Civilian Casualties in Afghanistan." In *Protecting Civilians During Violent Conflict: Theoretical and Practical Issues for the 21st Century*, edited by Igor Primoratz and David W. Lovell, 231–250. Aldershot: Ashgate.

Meienberg, Martina. 2012. *Nation-Building in Afghanistan: Legitimitätsdefizite innerhalb des politischen Wiederaufbaus*. Wiesbaden: Springer VS.

Mettelsiefen, Marcel, and Christoph Reuter. 2010. *Kunduz, 4. September 2009: Eine Spurensuche*. Berlin: Rogner & Bernhard.

Migdal, Joel S. 1994. "The State in Society: An Approach to Struggles for Domination." In *State Power and Social Forces: Domination and Transformation in the Third World*, edited by Joel S. Migdal, Atul Kohli and Vivienne Shue, 7–34. Cambridge: Cambridge University Press.

Migdal, Joel S. 2001. *State in Society: Studying How States and Societies Transform and Constitute One Another*. Cambridge: Cambridge University Press.

Monsutti, Alessandro. 2012. "Fuzzy Sovereignty: Rural Reconstruction in Afghanistan between Democracy Promotion and Power Games." *Comparative Studies in Society and History* 54 (3): 563–591.

Murray, Tonita. 2011. "Security Sector Reform in Afghanistan, 2002–2011: An Overview of a Flawed Process." *International Studies* 48 (1): 43–63.

Oates, Lauryn. 2009. *A Closer Look: The Policy and Lawmaking Behind the Shiite Personal Status Law*. Kabul: Afghanistan Research and Evaluation Unit.

Ottaway, Marina. 2002. "Rebuilding State Institutions in Collapsed States." *Development and Change* 33 (5): 1001–1023.

Parkinson, Sarah. 2010. *Means to What End? Policymaking and State-Building in Afghanistan*. Kabul: Afghanistan Research and Evaluation Unit.

Pemberton, Jo-Anne. 2009. *Sovereignty: Interpretations*. Basingstoke: Palgrave Macmillan.

Poggi, Gianfranco. 1978. *The Development of the Modern State: A Sociological Introduction*. London: Hutchinson.

Raz, Joseph. 1979. *The Authority of Law: Essays on Law and Morality*. Oxford: Oxford University Press.

Reus-Smit, Christian. 1999. *The Moral Purpose of the State: Culture, Social Identity, and Institutional Rationality in International Relations*. Princeton: Princeton University Press.

Reynolds, Andrew, and John Carey. 2012. *Fixing Afghanistan's Electoral System: Arguments and Options for Reform*. Kabul: Afghanistan Research and Evaluation Unit.

Richmond, Oliver P., and Jason Franks. 2009. *Liberal Peace Transitions: Between Statebuilding and Peacebuilding*. Edinburgh: Edinburgh University Press.

Risen, James. 2009. "Afghan Killing Bares Karzai Family Feud." *The New York Times*, December 19.

Risen, James. 2012. "Intrigue in Karzai Family as an Afghan Era Closes." *The New York Times*, June 3.

Roberts, David. 2013. "Hybrid Polities and Post-Conflict Policy." In *The Routledge Handbook of International Statebuilding*, edited by David Chandler and Timothy D. Sisk, 94–105. New York: Routledge.

Rubin, Barnett R. 2002. *The Fragmentation of Afghanistan: State Formation and Collapse in the International System*. New Haven: Yale University Press.

Rubin, Barnett R. 2013. *Afghanistan from the Cold War through the War on Terror*. New York: Oxford University Press.

Rubin, Barnett R., and Humayun Hamidzada. 2007. "From Bonn to London: Governance Challenges and the Future of Statebuilding in Afghanistan." *International Peacekeeping* 14 (1): 8–25.

Rubin, Elizabeth. 2009. "Karzai in his Labyrinth." *The New York Times*, August 9.

Rumsfeld, Donald. 2011. *Known and Unknown: A Memoir*. New York: Sentinel Books.

Rynning, Sten. 2012. *NATO in Afghanistan: The Liberal Disconnect*. Stanford: Stanford University Press.

Saltmarshe, Douglas, and Abhilash Mehdi. 2011. *Local Governance in Afghanistan: A View from the Ground*. Kabul: Afghanistan Research and Evaluation Unit.

Sanger, David E. 2012. *Confront and Conceal: Obama's Secret Wars and Surprising Use of American Power*. New York: Crown Publishers.

Schetter, Conrad, ed. 2013. *Local Politics in Afghanistan: A Century of Intervention in Social Order*. London: Hurst & Co.

Schmeidl, Susanne. 2010. *The man who would be king: The Challenges to Strengthening Governance in Uruzgan*. The Hague: Netherlands Institute of International Relation *Clingendael*.

Shah, Taimoor, and Carlotta Gall. 2007. "Afghan Rebels Find Aid in Pakistan, Musharraf Admits." *The New York Times*, August 13.

Shahrani, M. Nazif. 1998. "The Future of the State and the Structure of Community Governance in Afghanistan." In *Fundamentalism Reborn? Afghanistan and the Taliban*, edited by William Maley, 212–242. London: Hurst & Co.

SIGAR. 2013. *Quarterly Report to the United States Congress*. Washington, DC: Special Inspector General for Afghanistan Reconstruction, 30 January.

Stapleton, Barbara J. 2012. *Beating a Retreat: Prospects for the Transition Process in Afghanistan*. Kabul: Afghanistan Analysts Network.

Suhrke, Astri. 2011. *When More Is Less: The International Project in Afghanistan*. New York: Columbia University Press.

Tadjbakhsh, Shahrbanou, and Oliver P. Richmond. 2011. "Conclusion: Typologies and Modifications Proposed by Critical Approaches." In *Rethinking the Liberal Peace: External Models and Local Alternatives*, edited by Shahrbanou Tadjbakhsh, 221–241. London: Routledge.

Tondini, Matteo. 2010. *Statebuilding and Justice Reform: Post-conflict Reconstruction in Afghanistan*. New York: Routledge.

Ullmann-Margalit, Edna. 1977. *The Emergence of Norms*. Oxford: Oxford University Press.

United Nations. 2001. *Letter dated 5 December 2001 from the Secretary-General addressed to the President of the Security Council*. New York: United Nations, S/2001/1154, 5 December.

United Nations. 2002. *The Situation in Afghanistan and its Implications for International Peace and Security: Report of the Secretary-General*. New York: United Nations, A/56/875, S/2002/278, 18 March.

United Nations. 2013. *Afghanistan. Mid-year Report 2013: Protection of Civilians in Armed Conflict*. Kabul: United Nations Assistance Mission in Afghanistan.

United Nations Development Program. 2007. *Afghanistan Human Development Report 2007. Bridging Modernity and Tradition: Rule of Law and the Search for Justice*. Kabul: United Nations Development Programme.

Uslaner, Eric M. 2008. *Corruption, Inequality and the Rule of Law*. Cambridge: Cambridge University Press.

Waldman, Matt. 2010. *The Sun in the Sky: The Relationship Between Pakistan's ISI and Afghan Insurgents*. London: Discussion Paper no.18, Crisis States Research Centre, London School of Economics and Political Science.

Wardak, Ali. 2004. "Building a Post-war Justice System in Afghanistan." *Crime, Law and Social Change* 41 (4): 319–341.

Wardak, Ali, and John Braithwaite. 2013. "Crime and War in Afghanistan. Part II: A Jeffersonian Alternative?." *British Journal of Criminology* 53 (2): 197–214.

Weidmann, Nils B., and Michael Callen. 2013. "Violence and Election Fraud: Evidence from Afghanistan." *British Journal of Political Science* 43 (1): 53–75.

Weingast, Barry R. 1997. "The Political Foundations of Democracy and the Rule of Law." *American Political Science Review* 91 (2): 245–263.

Wendle, John. 2012. "'Auschwitz-like' Afghan Military Hospital Investigation 'Delayed'." *The Telegraph* (London), July 25.

Wilder, Andrew. 2007. *Cops or Robbers?: The Struggle to Reform the Afghan National Police*. Kabul: Afghanistan Research and Evaluation Unit.

Wissing, Douglas A. 2012. *Funding the Enemy: How US Taxpayers Bankroll the Taliban*. Amherst: Prometheus Books.

Statebuilding in Afghanistan: a contradictory engagement

Astri Suhrke

Chr. Michelsen Institute, Bergen, Norway

This article lays out a critical perspective on statebuilding in Afghanistan after 2001, arguing that the massive international intervention had inherent contradictions which undermined the prospect of creating an Afghan-owned, liberal new order. Tensions related to the rentier-state condition, local ownership versus international control, and building peace while waging war are examined in detail. It follows from this analysis that the scaling-back of the international presence, now in process, is a necessary precondition for more accountable, autonomous, and sustainable statebuilding. The transition itself may be violent, with intensified competition for power and over new sources of rent. Yet it opens up new space for the Afghans themselves to re-establish a functioning and legitimate state, based on long-term bargains between elites and subjects and a measure of compromise among contesting ethnic and sectarian groups.

Introduction

Historically, states have developed through accumulation of capital, centralization and control over the means of coercion, and the enhanced power of rulers to access these resources by appearing to be legitimate. The key issue for internationally assisted statebuilding in Afghanistan was to what extent these three ingredients – capital, coercion, and legitimacy – could be effectively supplied from outside. On these issues, analysts were soon divided (Johnson and Leslie 2004; Rubin 2005; Suhrke 2006).

This article develops a critical perspective which contends that the statebuilding agenda for Afghanistan after 2001 contained an inherent contradiction. The aim was to build an Afghan-owned, liberal new order, but the principal instruments were heavy and intrusive external assistance. From this constellation of ends and means flowed three sets of tensions that seriously eroded the statebuilding project.

First, the massive aid-and-war economy created a rentier-state condition. Easy money discouraged the government from generating local capacity and slowed the development of a sustainable, Afghan-owned order. This feature in turn collided with aspirations for a democratic polity. With foreign patrons providing vital economic and military resources, the government had few incentives to develop long-term bargains with its own people. In this respect it was no different from previous Afghan governments that had also presided over rentier states; they all failed the democratization test. Moreover, the heavy and primarily Western nature of the foreign presence weakened the legitimacy of the government, thereby eroding a main pillar of the state and enabling the armed opposition to appropriate the traditional sources of legitimacy: Islam and nationalism.

Second, the dependence on external financial, military, and technocratic resources produced tension between what we can call 'ownership' and 'control'. International actors wanted a measure of control over their programmes and the reform agenda; national actors pressed for the same, in the name of the internationally sanctioned language of 'local ownership'. The tension, inherent in most aid projects, was magnified in Afghanistan by the large international presence and the high stakes involved. The tension worked like sand in the machinery of state-building. It drove the continuous tug of war over the modalities of aid, civil service appoint-ments, and elections – as well as how to deal with corruption, and how to fight (or negotiate with) the insurgents.

Third, tension stemmed from the conflicting imperatives of simultaneously waging war and building peace. Local militias were armed, and local alliances were made that undermined good governance and the establishment of a monopoly of force. Both principles are central to state-building. The military campaign waged by the US-led coalition forces generated additional ten-sions. Subject only to US or NATO commands, the growing number of foreign troops started to behave and look like an occupation force. Mounting civilian casualties, night raids, and deten-tions alienated Afghan 'hearts and minds'. That many more civilians were killed by anti-govern-ment elements was small consolation for the families affected.

The escalating violence in the second half of the 2000s had a multiplier effect on the internal tensions of the international project. The costs of the war to the US and its allies created demands for faster results and more controls that clashed with Afghan demands for 'ownership'. Short-term objectives trumped the long-term interests of good governance and statebuilding, further weakening the foundational legitimacy of the state. And so the vicious cycle became entrenched.

The critical analysis outlined above is anchored in a structuralist perspective. It differs, in this respect, from what was long a conventional interpretation, namely that an early and better-resourced intervention, and a more coherent strategy, would have made a difference (Maley 2006 and this volume; Rubin 2007; Rashid, 2008; Jones 2009; Paris, 2013). Belief in the power of a good strategy, of course, privileges the power of agency – even in an extraordi-narily difficult situation. By contrast, the argument in this article is that the Afghan context was not simply very difficult, requiring exceptional qualities of statecraft on both Afghan and inter-national sides; even a more coherent strategy would have been circumscribed by the inherent tensions generated by the massive intervention itself. By the same logic, a better-resourced inter-vention soon after 2001 would simply have produced earlier the tensions that appeared with full force later, when the surge in aid, troops, and consultants took place. The strength of this argu-ment becomes more evident through a closer examination of these tensions as they developed in the decade after 2001.[1]

Building the state

Capital

Of the three key ingredients of statebuilding, capital was plentiful in post-Taliban Afghanistan. The illegal drug economy generated income and foreign exchange, the value of which by mid-decade was commonly estimated at about half of the (legal) GDP. The other main income source, roughly of the same order of magnitude, was foreign transfers (IMF 2010). By the end of the decade, US assistance alone was in the order of USD 10 billion a year (USGAO 2009). From a statebuilding perspective, both sources of capital were problematic. The sheer size of the aid sector created extreme dependence, weak local ownership, and corruption. The drug sector represented a vast, illegal structure of power – a quasi-state of sorts – that under-mined the legitimacy of the state. With the international community firmly refusing to legalize poppy production, the drug wealth could not be harnessed by the state (although state actors were heavily involved in a private capacity). Functioning as a 'shadow economy' (Goodhand 2005), the drug sector provided life-saving income to farmers, sustained trading networks, and provided capital to enterprising political entrepreneurs. It also fed a political economy of crime, corruption, and violence that undermined an ideal statebuilding process based on provision of public goods and the protection of rights.

As for foreign aid, it was evident already by the middle of the decade that foreign donors were creating a rentier state unparalleled in Afghan history and nearly unique in the world of international assistance. Rentier states have several weaknesses that are widely recognized in the literature (North 1990; Bates 2001; Ross 2001; Bräutigam, Fjeldstad et al. 2008; Verkoren and Kamphuis 2013). Rentier rulers are unlikely to develop effective tax systems, accountability for spending patterns, or capable autonomous bureaucracies, or to invest in local productive enterprises. Most importantly from a political perspective, perhaps, is that where foreign aid is the main source of state income, structures of accountability are geared towards the donors, crowding out domestic institutions of democratic accountability. States heavily dependent on foreign aid are vulnerable to external shocks and likely to implode if rents suddenly cease. The Somalia of Siad Barre is a classic example; the same dynamic felled the last communist government in Afghanistan in 1992.

Despite these well-known weaknesses, and the fate of Najibullah (who lost power in 1992 after Soviet support dried up) being fresh in public memory, the post-Taliban order in Afghanistan soon acquired the features of a rentier state. Foreign transfers totally dwarfed domestic sources of revenues (on the order of 8:1), a situation that remained almost unchanged throughout the decade.

Building a rentier state

While exact aid figures are lacking, the main patterns are clear. In the beginning, aid flowed in at a relatively modest rate. In the first year after the invasion it was around USD 1.5 billion, mostly in humanitarian assistance. The volume then picked up, tripling to around USD 5 billion a year by mid-decade, and increasing to (in a conservative estimate) around USD 8 billion a year for the second half of the decade (GoA 2009; USGAO 2009).

By the standards of the day – which was before the 2003 Iraq war changed the scale of reconstruction costs – the first donor conference, in Tokyo in January 2002, was a success. A pledge of USD 5.1 billion was sizeable; in fact it was exactly the same amount planned by the World Bank and the European Commission for the reconstruction of Bosnia and Herzegovina after the 1995 peace agreement. That was a one-off commitment, and considered 'massive' (Hurtic, Sapcanin et al. 2000). In the case of Afghanistan, by contrast, donors agreed only two years after Tokyo to add another USD 5.6 billion for reconstruction, and subsequent biannual pledging conferences topped that amount.

The response indicated Afghanistan's special status in US strategy and Western public imagination. It was the 'good war', and the main front in the US-led 'war on terror'. It was also the place where the Taliban had cruelly suppressed women, blown up the giant Buddha statutes, and staged spectacles of public executions. Afghanistan was the home of the fabled *mujahedin* who had fought back the Soviets and, in much of the Western public discourse, a country with a whiff of Orientalist mystique. The aid organizations constituted a powerful lobby for more assistance. Afghan NGOs, which had rapidly grown in number, joined the large international organizations to call for additional funds to address the vast problems of destruction, dislocation, poverty, neglect, and abuse (see Goodhand, this volume). The objective needs were undisputed. Afghanistan had been one of the poorest countries in the world, even before it was stricken by prolonged violence and social dislocation starting in the late 1970s.

The inflow of aid, while modest on a per capita basis (as the aid organizations pointed out), nevertheless overwhelmed local absorptive capacity. The World Bank had warned early on that even aid flows in the relatively modest magnitude of USD 2.5 billion a year were 'very high' in relation to Afghanistan's GDP – a customary indicator of absorptive capacity, and equally of rentier status (World Bank 2004). To efficiently spend foreign aid at on the order of several billion dollars a year required an administrative infrastructure that was lacking in the early post-Taliban period. International aid organizations and consultants were consequently employed to manage the money flow; they soon formed the backbone of a virtual parallel administration. This did produce immediate results, although in the longer term it meant importing rather than building the capacity that could support a national statebuilding process.

There was also some intense lobbying on the Afghan side. In preparation for the 2004 donor meeting in Berlin, leading technocrats and reformers had worked with the World Bank and the UN Development Program (UNDP) to prepare a detailed framework for reconstruction assistance. The result, *Securing Afghanistan's Future*,[2] was a comprehensive seven-year plan for development, with a costing estimate of USD 28.5 billion in aid requirements. These massive infusions of aid were justified by what was described as a critical turning point in the postwar order. Unless the international community came forth with billions of dollars in fresh capital, Afghanistan would become a 'narco-mafia state', warned the finance minister, Ashraf Ghani; he dismissed the previous USD 5 billion pledged in Tokyo as 'peanuts' (Agence France-Press 2004).

The government's plea for heavy external funding can be understood with reference to Jean-François Bayart's theory of *extraversion* as a political strategy (Bayart 2000). Developed with reference to Africa, Bayart's thesis was that aspiring national elites deliberately invited relationships of external dependence in order to collect rent, which could be used to advance their position vis-à-vis rival groups at home. From this perspective, the Berlin conference was an opportunity for Afghan technocrats and reformers to stake their claims in shaping the country's future and, in the process, secure their positions vis-à-vis rivals at home – including the old guard of *mujahedin* and warlords. Favoured technocrats could draw on their support in the donor community to build powerful bureaucratic empires and related political constituencies, and they needed to do so before the international community shifted its attention to another international crisis area, above all Iraq. The minister of finance and the minister of the newly created Ministry of Reconstruction and Rural Development were especially well positioned in this regard. Both were technocrats who spoke the language of the donors and had gained their trust. Their ministries were selected for preferential treatment of upgrading and professionalization.

The quickening pace of aid in the second half of the decade reflected a growing sense of desperation in the US-led coalition and the donor community. The insurgency was growing, and so were problems of corruption, injustice, and an ineffective state; but external actors were caught in an 'investment trap'. With all that had been invested so far in terms of money, lives, and political prestige – even NATO's future was said to be at stake – the only option seemed to be staying the course and adding more. The sense of proportionality that was a well-known and accepted premise of aid was brushed aside. The importance of genuine local ownership that had framed the initial plans for a light footprint was gone. The only donor adjustments were new twists in strategy: a new office to oversee local governance, a new office to deal with corruption, and so on. Even the American analyst Barnett Rubin, whose magisterial political history of Afghanistan (Rubin 1995) had examined the problems of previous Afghan rentier states under Daoud (1970s) and the communists (1978–92), now emphatically called for more aid (Rubin 2007).

The rentier state in operation

While statistics are incomplete, the post-2001 state seemed to dwarf previous rentier states in Afghan history (Rubin 1995; Kipping 2010). Foreign aid financed around 90% of all official expenditure in post-Taliban Afghanistan during most of the post-invasion years, declining only slightly towards the end of the decade (World Bank 2011).

Foreign funds covered the basic functions of the post-Taliban state – including salaries or salary support for senior civil servants and salaries for the army and police – as well as most development expenditure. Two-thirds of all aid money was spent directly by donors through sub-contractors of their choice. Afghan authorities had no control over these funds and did not have full information about their magnitude and purpose. This so-called 'external budget' dwarfed the government budget. The arrangement was an extreme expression of the principle of 'shared sovereignty', advocated in some academic and aid circles as a means to rescue 'failed states' and reduce corruption in post-conflict countries (Krasner 2004). Yet it signalled a first-order dependence on external donors that mocked the declared policies of local ownership and made basic state functions subject to the variable interests and funding capacity of foreign donors.

A second feature of the Afghan rentier state was its self-perpetuating dimension. While international consultants had been ubiquitous soon after 2001, a new class of skilled Afghan government officials had come into being by the end of the decade. Known as 'the second civil service', or dual public sector, it depended on heavy salary support from donors. By early 2010, donors paid an estimated USD 45 million a year in salary support to some 6600 Afghan officials in key administrative positions. The main supporters were the World Bank, the United States, the United Kingdom, and the UNDP (SIGAR 2010a, 2010b).

The large aid inflows set in motion a negative spiral that affected reconstruction and capacity building. With existing institutions unable to handle large and multiple contracts, corruption increased; this led to more fiduciary controls and slower budget execution, which in turn generated demands for more aid and consultants in order to produce results. The trend peaked with the US-led surge in 2010 in both the military and the civilian sector. While the budget execution of some ministries around mid-decade had been around 40–50%, by the end of the decade it had slowed to around 25% for the Afghan-administered budget as a whole (IMF 2010). The overall result was heightened bureaucratic activity that meant a lot of work for technical advisers and consultants of all kinds, while in the countryside ordinary Afghans were still waiting for the peace dividend. One donor response to this problem was to increasingly work around the central state by targeting the local level. However, this created other problems, related to accountability, coordination, and duplication of structures.

The most direct way of reducing financial dependence would have been to increase domestic revenue, as the international financial institutions had consistently urged the government to do. Yet by the end of the decade, revenue collection had grown only marginally, from 5% to 8% of GDP (IMF 2010). The problem of domestic revenue mobilization was not exclusively a result of the rentier condition. Early Afghan statebuilders had recognized the challenge. As Abdul Rahman Khan had lamented in the late nineteenth century,

> One quarter of the money which is rightly mine, I get without trouble; one quarter I get by fighting for it; one quarter I do not get at all; and those who ought to pay the fourth quarter do not know into whose hands they should place it. (Gregorian 1969, 142)

Then as now, the main problem was the weak grip of the central state on the provinces where wealth was created, in particular provinces astride the central trading routes, where local rulers jealously guarded the customs collections and other sources of revenue on behalf of their own patronage networks as much as the central state (Mukhopadhyay 2011). Some of these strongmen (such as Gul Aga Sherzai) had been recently empowered by the US military to help fight Islamic militants; others were favoured by foreign donors for apparent administrative effectiveness (Muhammad Atta). The conflicting imperatives and lack of central direction in donor policies were again evident. With these constraints, it is noteworthy that the Ministry of Finance could point to any increase in tax collection at all during the second half of the decade.

Corruption

Rentier states are not necessarily corrupt, but recent studies (Dalgaard and Olsson, 2008) show that states with very high levels of foreign aid are also likely to have high levels of corruption. Corruption in Afghanistan had caused concern already by mid-decade; during the second half it became 'pervasive, entrenched, systemic and by all accounts ... unprecedented in scale and reach' (USAID 2009, 4). A more recent study characterized corruption as 'a central feature of governance' (Verkoren and Kamphuis, 2013, 517). The Kabul Bank scandal is an extreme though illustrative case. Bank shareholders and managers siphoned off around USD 900 million from funds deposited by the US government to pay the salaries of Afghan security forces. A subsequent investigation concluded that 'the Kabul Bank case is the outcome of an organized criminal activity and of a bad financial sector regulatory system in Afghanistan' (MEC 2012, 21).

Spectacular corruption was hardly surprising, given that the country's wealth originated primarily from two sources: an illegal drug economy that required protection, and a vast and sudden influx of external transfers from aid agencies and foreign militaries. The money flow simply overwhelmed the country's social and institutional capacities to deal with it in a legal and socially acceptable manner. The wide-spread perception among many Afghans that the international presence itself entailed diverse forms of corruption contributed to an acceptance of illegality. Multiple subcontractors, high overheads, and large sums spent by donors in numerous and seemingly impenetrable ways through the 'external budget' appeared as so many ways for outsiders to enrich themselves on Afghanistan's misfortune.

The inflows created an aid-and-war economy, with an atmosphere of easy money that encouraged permissive strategies, reinforced by the prospect that the boom would not last. Huge contracts created a bidding frenzy among Afghans as well as international companies. The US Department of Defense, for instance, authorized work contracts in Afghanistan for USD 11.5 billion in two years alone (2007–09) (SIGAR 2010a, 2010b). National contingents of the International Security Assistance Force (ISAF) had discretionary funds for intelligence or development to 'win the hearts and minds' of the people. Discretionary funds available to US military commanders in 2010–11 alone were estimated at USD 1.5 billion (Public Intelligence 20101/11). The huge international presence meant funds were flowing in multiple directions: for rent of properties and lease of land for bases; for military construction; for the hire of private security companies, and private militias, and sundry services. Donors tried to reduce corruption primarily through monitoring, liberalization procedures, and capacity building, and through greater scrutiny on their own side. Yet the diversity of funds and channels used by donors contributed to an opaque fiduciary environment, and within Afghanistan, security constraints increasingly made on-site monitoring of projects difficult.

The magnitude of corruption in post-Taliban Afghanistan severely distorted the statebuilding venture. Corruption reinforced the rentier state and all its problematic features. The dynamic was simple. Political access gave privileged entry to bidding for contracts or obtaining a government licence to businesses that served the international presence. Windfalls from contracts financed politics of patronage that further enhanced the power and status of the agents involved, and bought further access. In this cycle, incentives were structured only one way: to perpetuate the system. In the provinces, political access to foreign militaries generated huge incomes for key strongmen and their families, typically financing blatant misuse of power. ISAF commanders accepted the distorting effects as the unavoidable local costs of fighting a war (Aikins 2010).

Corruption also undermined the internal as well as the external legitimacy of the government, something it could badly afford in the midst of a growing war. Widespread disenchantment with corrupt and abusive authorities in the sub-national administration limited support for the government and played into the hands of the insurgents. Afghans almost uniformly ranked corruption as a major problem (Integrity Watch/Afghanistan 2010), and many Afghans questioned a social order where the newly rich flaunted their wealth while economic and physical insecurity dominated the life of many (Asia Foundation 2010).

Political functions and dysfunctions of the rentier state

Conflicts over ownership and control were embedded in the rentier state. The foreign patrons tried to establish a thick network of controls, through oversight in administrative and fiduciary matters and political appointments; joint rules for reconstruction and statebuilding, as per agreements (e.g. the document agreed to at the 2006 London international conference on Afghanistan, called The Afghanistan Compact) and boards (e.g. the Joint Control and Monitoring Board); and funding a 'second civil service' (and topping up salaries), including 105 positions in the Office of the President. The 'external budget' was an instrument of more direct control.

On different levels and in many ways, Afghan political and administrative elites fought back in the name of 'local ownership'. Some did so openly – above all, former finance minister Ashraf Ghani, who in early and spectacular clashes with donors and UN organizations demanded that all aid money, including relief assistance, be channelled through his ministry. He was mostly rebuffed, but the issue remained a constant thorn in the aid relationship. All subsequent finance ministers kept pressing the issue, and gained support from some European donors as well as the World Bank. By the end of the decade, donors formally agreed in principle to channel 50% of their aid through the government.

Ownership-versus-control issues in explicitly political matters were focused on the Office of the President. In the first half of the decade, conflicts arose over individual appointments (of governors and senior police officers where ISAF troops were deployed, and of nominees to the Supreme Court) and over civil-service reform. Towards the end of the decade, conflict over fraud in the 2009 presidential elections took centre stage. Politically bruised from this fight and from a related struggle with the parliament, Karzai nevertheless re-emerged to consolidate his power. He continued to manage the appointment process to suit the calculus of patronage. Some governors considered corrupt, abusive, or incompetent were removed, only to be reappointed elsewhere. As Karzai's relationship with his foreign patrons worsened towards the end of the decade, and foreign (especially American) officials publicly rebuked him, Karzai became more dependent on a domestic base to sustain his position. He cemented relations with Northern Alliance leaders such as General Fahim, catered to Shia-minority constituencies, privileged notables from his own Popolzai lineage in local politics in the south, and paid even more attention to the appointments process (Parkinson 2010). Predictably, relations with donors soured further.

Similar tensions arose in judicial and legislative matters. Karzai used his powers of presidential pardon to interfere with the legal process in order to protect his own network, even if it meant crossing important donors. The case of Mohammad Zia Salehi was emblematic. A high-level adviser to the president, Salehi had been indicted for corruption in late 2010 with the aid of the US Drug Enforcement Agency and the FBI, which had trained the special Afghan investigative units that collected the evidence against Salehi. When Karzai ordered his attorney general to drop the case, US officials responded with great anger but an even greater show of helplessness. In legislative matters, Karzai likewise balanced contradictory interests to strengthen his domestic political networks. On the eve of the 2009 elections, for instance, he catered to conservative

Islamic and Hazara-minority interests by signing a Shia Personal Status Law that had been strongly denounced by Western governments and human rights organizations.[3]

Disagreement extended to matters of NATO strategy, relations with Iran and Pakistan, and negotiations with the Taliban. Since mid-decade, Karzai had criticized NATO strategies for inflicting heavy civilian casualties and relying on night raids, both of which created deep popular resentment. The tempo of criticism increased during the second half of the decade, imparting a strong nationalistic tone to the 2012 negotiations over the US military presence after the scheduled withdrawal of combat troops in 2014. Karzai also struck an independent tone in relation to the Taliban and relations with Iran. Already by 2010, analysts were speaking of a U-turn in the president's policy (Rashid 2010).

External funding of 105 staff positions in the Office of the President clearly did not translate into control. Karzai and other elite members of the rentier state fought their patrons with a combination of partial compliance, resistance, and evasion. They were able to do this because the international project formally celebrated 'local ownership' and because the statebuilding project was premised on conditions of sovereignty that entailed formal Afghan autonomy in the constitutional exercise of judicial, legislative, and executive powers. The fact of mutual dependence buttressed this autonomy. Afghanistan's political-strategic significance to NATO created bargaining power. With so much invested in the country, the US-led coalition could not credibly threaten to withdraw support unless the government fully cooperated.

Importantly, Afghan elites did not seek to influence their international patrons through long-term political institution building at home, such as strengthening political parties (see Giustozzi, this volume) or the parliament. Instead, the political and technocratic elites that formed the core of the rentier state engaged in short-term survival strategies. One strategy was to maximize political space for autonomous action by exploiting the many disagreements among donors, for instance regarding the external budget; the importance of merit appointments versus accepting local strongmen as allies in fighting the insurgency; approaches towards judicial reform; and (towards the end of the decade) negotiations with the Taliban. A second approach was to develop short-term bargains with other elite representatives, whether tribal notables, local commanders, former *mujahedin* leaders, or religious leaders, in order to create political capital on particular policy issues and possibly longer-term support if and when foreign assistance was reduced. Karzai's appointment management was an expression of this strategy. A third approach was to accumulate capital. Capital could be used to trade favours, buy armed followers, or obtain political support for the present or for future contingencies, quite apart from the personal benefits of material gains.

The preference for personalized survival strategies over long-term institution building was partly a function of the rentier state. Assured of foreign support by donor promises of long-term commitment, Afghan leaders had few incentives to develop long-term, institutionalized bargains with their subjects. This orientation was reinforced by a 2005 election law that penalized the development of political parties. There was also the general effect of elections to shorten the time horizons of national and provincial elites. But the penchant for short-term survival strategies also reflected the origins of the post-2001 regime.

Having come to power as a result of the US-led intervention, the post-Taliban elites were diverse, representing exiles, technocrats, and various *mujahedin* factions. None (except a few ex-communists and the wing of Hezb-i-Islami that operated in the legal political arena) had a background in conventional political parties or experience in mobilizing people for social change.

The contrasting behaviour of the last communist government in Afghanistan, under President Najibullah, is interesting in this regard. A rentier ruler, though of smaller magnitude, Najibullah responded to Soviet preparations for withdrawal in 1986–87 not only by seeking a short-term bargain with local leaders; he also tried to revive the Communist Party and make it more acceptable by promulgating a new constitution (1989) that recognized Islam, universal human rights, foreign investment, and a neutral foreign policy, and permitted multiple political parties. This response was consistent with the regime's origin in a political party (the People's Democratic Party of Afghanistan) based on a theory of social change through popular mobiliz-ation and centralized leadership. Najibullah had joined the party's moderate faction already in 1965 and spent his whole professional life steeped in party politics. When his Soviet patron pre-pared to disengage, Najibullah tried to create a long-term bargain of a different kind with the Afghan people and Afghanistan's neighbours. He lasted for a while, but – faced with the with-drawal of Soviet subsidies and flat refusal by the insurgents and their foreign sponsors to nego-tiate – he lost out.[4]

Coercion

The second constitutive element of statebuilding – coercive force in the service of the central state – was initially provided by international forces. ISAF made an essential contribution in the early years after 2001 by providing the coercive power necessary to protect the capital, estab-lish the apparatus of the central state, and enforce the political rules for access to power at the central level. In this respect ISAF and, indirectly, the US-led invasion force (Operation Enduring Freedom, OEF), formed the military muscle for the implementation of the transition agreement adopted in Bonn. Yet an inability to create a monopoly of force was the Achilles' heel of the statebuilding venture from the outset, and it became more pronounced over time.

The elusive monopoly of force

The challenge to the state's attempt to establish a monopoly of force came initially not from the Taliban but from a profusion of nominally friendly, armed groups existing in a legal grey zone. Some were part of the Northern Alliance forces that had joined the American forces during the invasion. They had a formal structure, appeared in the international project under the name of the Afghan Military Forces, and were slated for demobilization and reintegration after 2001. The Disarmament, Demobilization and Reintegration (DDR) programme started late (2003), and did not include the militias working with the US-led coalition. As such, the programme laboured from the beginning in the shadow of the ongoing military campaign of the US-led forces to crush the Taliban and al-Qaida.

Another programme for the 'disbandment of illegal armed groups' (DIAG), was launched in 2005, targeting the many armed factions that had remained and indeed had grown. This pro-gramme also had difficulties. Many armed groups claimed quasi-legal status and had powerful patrons – local strongmen, factional leaders, and later some members of the new parliament. The programme was run by the Ministry of Interior, some of whose officials were also patrons of armed factions (Sedra 2008 and this volume). In 2006, the US military command started to re-establish local militias (Lefèvre 2010). Intended as a short-cut to boost Afghan mili-tary power to fight the growing insurgency, the initiative opened yet another avenue for armed groups or local commanders to gain a powerful patron (see Hakimi, this volume). When the DIAG programme was ended in 2008, the UN estimated some 1800 armed groups (with perhaps 120,000 members) remained (UN 2008).

To Afghan and international human rights activists, empowering the militias was arguably the single most important flaw in the whole international project. It also cut into the foundation of the new state. Regardless of their value in the war against militant Islamists, the militias had a negative impact on the statebuilding venture. They represented a clear reversal of the early transition policy of disarming irregular combatants and illegal forces in order to permit the state to establish a legitimate monopoly of force.

In political terms, however, the early DDR programme served a critical purpose in the postwar transition by helping key military leaders shift into the political arena without their armed followers. Leaders of the armed factions that had formed the Northern Alliance moved into important positions in the national or sub-national administration as ministers, governors, or senior advisers. Political life had its rewards. The leader of the main Tajik armed faction, Mohammed Fahim, was appointed defence minister, and his close associate, Bismullah Khan, became chief of staff of the new Afghan National Army. Uzbek general Dostum was initially a deputy minister of defence, before moving on to other positions; Hazara leader Muhammad Mohaqiq was deputy chairman of the Interim Administration; and so on. For mid-level commanders and their cadres, however, the programmes had little to offer and indirectly stimulated the growth of militias and the illicit economy.

The Afghan National Army

The importance of establishing a national army was recognized by all parties to the Bonn Agreement (Afghan Government 2001). At first, the build-up of the Afghan National Army (ANA) was slow, reflecting a modest investment and high attrition rates. The total force level in 2005 was only 22,000 men. Then things changed. Goals were progressively revised upward, to just under 200,000 by 2010 (US Army 2010). By any measure, it was an extraordinarily fast expansion – driven initially by the growing challenge from the insurgents, and then increasingly by NATO's emphasis on an Afghanization of the war that would permit a drawdown of its own combat forces.

The rapid expansion raised questions about the quality of the new army, related to high illiteracy rates, brief training, intra-army ethnic tensions, and ultimately both fighting effectiveness and political loyalty (Giustozzi 2009). Other issues arose from the ANA's dependence on the United States. US forces had already started training and equipping the new army in 2003. By mid-decade, the US funded over half of the government's defence budget, including salaries, logistics, training, construction of recruiting stations, rehabilitation of hospitals, construction of garrisons in the south-east and the south, the establishment and operation of four regional ANA commands (Kandahar, Herat, Gardez, and Mazar-e-Sharif), and the formation of the central Army Corps of three infantry brigades in Kabul. By the end of the decade, military aid rose sharply. US agencies requested a total of USD 7.5 billion for fiscal year 2010 to build the ANA, almost double the amount actually spent on the ANA in the previous year (USGAO 2010). Funding was mostly channelled through the external budget, which gave the US additional discretionary power. The US in effect determined the size and composition of the Afghan army, although force ceilings were formally decided in cooperation with the Afghan government and other allies.

The funding structure highlighted problems of sustainability. Without very substantial donor funding, the Afghan government could not possibly maintain an army this size. There were also other security forces to be funded, including the national police (ANP), which increasingly had taken on a paramilitary function. The ANP relied heavily on donor funding as well, initially drawing on a multilateral trust fund (Law and Order Trust Fund for Afghanistan, LOTFA), but by the end of the decade primarily US bilateral funding. The World Bank was repeatedly drawing attention to what it regarded as disproportionately large expenditures on security, warning that it could bankrupt rather than support the statebuilding process (World Bank 2004) (Byrd and Guimbert 2009).

The military's role in domestic politics – and, more broadly speaking, the kind of state being built – was another matter of long-term concern. For all its shortcomings, the ANA was a far stronger institution than the main civilian branches of the state, above all the judiciary, the parliament, and parts of the executive branch. There were general reasons for this. Building an army is comparatively easier than building, say, a judicial system, a point noted in a frank assessment by the UN mission in a mid-decade report to the Security Council which highlighted the relative strength of the Afghan Army (UN 2005). Developments since then showed little evidence of great strides in institution building on the civilian side, particularly in the institutions charged with oversight of the military. By contrast, the United States and its NATO allies invested heavily in building up the army.

The imbalance suggested the possibility of a strong military role in politics, perhaps along the lines of Pakistan, or in ways that would recreate Afghanistan's past experience. Although the Afghan military in modern times has not seized and retained political power at the central state level, it has twice executed coups that paved the way for regime change. Army factions played a significant role in both the overthrow of the monarchy in 1973 and the events that led to the April revolution in 1978. Whatever form a strong military role in politics might take, it would be contrary to the declared policy of the UN and the international community of establishing a post-Taliban state founded on democratic processes.

Legitimacy

Statebuilding, as history has amply demonstrated, is a highly conflictual process. In Afghanistan, previous efforts to strengthen the central state invariably courted confrontation with vested interests, above all in the form of local tribal authorities, large landowners who were faced with demands for taxes and manpower, and religious leaders who guarded their role in administering justice. Statebuilders who had modernizing visions of radical reform in social, economic, legal, and educational structures met additional resistance and, invariably, political defeat, as happened to King Amanullah in the 1920s, President Daoud in the 1970s, and the Communist Party (People's Democratic Party of Afghanistan) in the 1980s.

Statebuilding with an ambitious modernizing agenda places great demands on the three foundational pillars of capital, coercion, and legitimacy. Of these, legitimacy is particularly valuable because it facilitates non-coercive compliance by generating normative support. In modern history, feats of successful statebuilding have usually had a public purpose, often couched in nationalistic terms, that lent legitimacy to the venture. That was above all the case in the two classic statebuilding achievements in the non-colonized world: the Meiji Restoration in Japan in the late nineteenth century, and the creation of Turkey out of the ruins of the Ottoman Empire in the early twentieth century. In both cases, the statebuilding project was designed to strengthen the state *against* foreign threats. Nationalism and anti-foreign sentiments provided the principal glue and justification for reforms; the foreign threat also gave the aspiring reformers strong incentives to embark upon change despite the risks and costs involved. While many of the reforms were Western-inspired and used Western technical assistance, national leaders were truly 'in the driver's seat', as the current expression would have it.

Sources of legitimacy in internationally assisted statebuilding

In post-2001 Afghanistan, as we have seen, statebuilding was largely designed and financed by outside sources. At the same time, the agenda was socially transformative in intent, arguably equal to or exceeding that of previous Afghan reformers, the communist governments included. As before, resistance formed along two main axes. Centre–province relations were shaped by the interest of local power holders in maintaining or increasing their autonomy from the centre, but also in gaining a greater share of power at the centre and influencing national policies. At the centre, the main concern was to extend state control over the provinces in order to extract resources and influence local administration and politics. Centre–province relations were partly cast in terms of identity politics, a result of the greater political saliency of ethnic identity after the civil war in the 1990s, when Tajik, Uzbek, Hazara, and Pashtun militias had subjected 'the other' ethnic populations (but also some of their own) to vicious violence (Hakimi and Suhrke 2013) . A second and more consistent line of opposition to the modernizing agenda came from conservative, traditional, and religious leaders, particularly in ex-*mujahedin* circles, who feared that many of the intended reforms would undermine their status and power, as well as changing Afghan society in un-Islamic ways.

In this contested situation, what were the sources of legitimacy for the new political order? The question went beyond the legitimacy of particular individuals such as Hamid Karzai; it concerned the broader edifice erected with much international support to replace the Taliban regime in order to reform and develop Afghan society.

The main justification for the new order was to establish at least a minimally effective state out of the chaos left by revolution, invasion, and civil war. This was implicit in the popular aspirations for peace and security that followed the fall of the Taliban, captured in surveys, public opinion polls, and much anecdotal information. The broader rationale was laid out in the preamble to the 2001 Bonn Agreement, where the Afghan parties expressed their determination to 'promote national reconciliation, lasting peace, stability and respect for human rights' and embraced 'the principles of Islam, democracy, pluralism and social justice' to guide the future political order. The international project was formally premised on these ideals as well, and validated in UN resolutions that endorsed the Bonn Agreement and authorized multilateral security assistance.

By implication, a state that provided a measure of security, justice, basic social services, and 'good governance' would carry its own source of legitimacy. That belief was increasingly expressed in the international aid community and other supporters of the government, as well as among Afghan reformers. The problem with a utilitarian source of legitimacy, however, is that it exerts no normative force merely by virtue of its ideational existence; to cash in on its legitimacy potential, the state has to actually deliver. The same applies to elections. To legitimize a political contest, elections have to be seen as reasonably free and fair.

On the whole, the Afghan state did not deliver. True, significant strides were made on the educational and health fronts. Many people prospered, particularly in the northern and central regions, and some individuals became fabulously rich and powerful. Yet the government and its international supporters failed to provide the basic elements of human security in many parts of the country; failed to halt the growing abuse, corruption, and incompetence in public administration; failed to stem the mounting insurgency and the perception that the international forces were responsible for excessive or unjustly inflicted violence; and failed to provide a political exit from the war. The liberal democratic vision initially promoted by international and Afghan reformers and supported through numerous governance projects was overshadowed by the daily realities of violence, inequality, and corruption, and was fading even in the declaratory policy of donors. Whatever legitimacy was bestowed in this way by the first presidential and parliamentary elections, it seemed lost in the violence and fraud that marred the second round in 2009 and 2010 (van Bijlert 2009; Worden 2010). The point was recognized by international actors, who started to speak of 'good enough' governance as the more realistic goal.

That left religion and nationalism as possible legitimizing ideologies. The only Afghan governments to have openly discarded both – the communists – did not survive long. The post-Taliban authorities were careful to recognize the centrality of Islam in law and society in the new constitution and other instruments of authority, but the uneasy balance between state and religion that has shaped the history of modern Afghanistan resurfaced and was sharpened by the reform agenda, particularly in the legal sector (Suhrke 2011). The relationship between the Karzai government, its foreign supporters, and Afghan religious authorities remained complicated and at times strained. Invoking Islamic modernism to legitimize the Western-supported order was certainly possible, but difficult – the insurgency had appropriated its militant forms and fought to expel the US-led forces, while internationally the West and militant Islam were locked in a wider war. Nationalism was difficult; given the state's heavy dependence upon international capital, consultants, and foreign military forces to survive, it could not credibly invoke nationalism as a legitimizing ideology. The only effort in this direction was the government's consistent accusation of Pakistani support for the insurgents, which possibly gained it some nationalist credentials.

For some Afghans, the promise of a liberal order remained the principal source of legitimacy for the post-Taliban order. For others, legitimacy was linked to utilitarian values, in particular the ability of the regime to provide individualized benefits in the form of protection, political positions, and economic resources. Vast networks of patronage delivering such benefits in return for political support became a principal safety net for the governing elites on both national and sub-national levels. While helping to sustain the regime and the political order it represented, the patronage system was a fragile and fickle source of legitimacy. It depended on continued access to resources through the aid-and-war economy. In centre–province relations, moreover, there was a catch: the means disbursed by the centre to buy loyalty also strengthened the ability of local strongmen to act independently (Sinno 2008).

Conclusions

The interpretation of international engagement presented here assumes that statebuilding, by and large, must be driven by national forces if it is to be sustainable and ensure a measure of domestic accountability. This does not mean, of course, that international assistance is superfluous or merely counterproductive. Rather, it is a question of proportionality and autonomy. By the former is meant a degree of assistance that can be absorbed without creating parallel administrations, huge corruption, sudden distortions in local power relations, and the dysfunctionalities of a rentier state. The latter denotes the relative ability of the recipient to define the priorities of assistance. These are hardly radical propositions; they are at the core of the contemporary language of statebuilding and peacebuilding, which celebrates 'local ownership', 'absorptive capacity', and the locals' being 'in the driver's seat'. In practice, however, these sound and widely recognized principles were massively violated by international donors and the coalition forces in Afghanistan. The reasons had to do with the particular significance attached to the country after the 9/11 attack on the United States, and – over time – the felt need of the US-led coalition to protect what already had been invested in terms of money, lives, and prestige.

A decade of escalating violence and limited achievements on the statebuilding front forced the international coalition to undertake a modified retreat. Most foreign combat troops are scheduled to be withdrawn by 2014, while continued development aid and technical assistance are promised. If the analysis in this article of the international involvement during the past 10 years is correct, this scaling-back is a necessary precondition for a more accountable, autonomous, and sustainable statebuilding process in Afghanistan.

The transition will undoubtedly be difficult and marred by violence. The process of defining the Afghan state will continue and, as with most statebuilding processes, is likely to proceed with an element of violence. There are also particular conflicts associated with the legacy of an aid-fuelled rentier state with a large foreign military presence. The transition to reduced dependence on the US-led coalition will invite fierce competition among the local stakeholders and their foreign supporters for access to power. There will be fierce competition over new sources of rent, such as minerals exploitation, that might replace the easy aid money of the past. The failure to date to negotiate an end to the insurgency will complicate the transition and invite further violence.

Yet the withdrawal of most foreign combat troops will probably take some of the wind out of the sail of the insurgents, although regional powers may intensify efforts to establish their own zones of influence. More fundamentally, a less intensive and intrusive foreign presence overall will open up space for Afghans to deal with the challenges of re-establishing a functioning state based on long-term bargains between elites and subjects as well as compromises among contesting ethnic and sectarian groups. In this perspective, the transition appears as a precondition for starting the process of creating internal legitimacy for the Afghan state and hence a more viable statebuilding process.

Notes

1. For a book-length discussion, see Suhrke (2011).
2. A government/International Agency Report. Prepared for International Conference, March 17–April 1 2004. Available at www.effectivestates.org/Papers/Securing%20Afghanistan's% 20Future.pdf
3. For the first time in Afghan history, the 2004 Constitution (available at http://www.afghanembassy.com. pl/cms/uploads/images/Constitution/The%20Constitution.pdf) recognized the legal status of the country's religious minority by granting courts the right to apply Shia jurisprudence in family matters where both parties are Shia. Conservative Shia clerics captured the process, preparing a draft law in 2006 that was bitterly criticized by liberal Shia scholars as well as by reformists and women's organizations. The law had detailed and restrictive provisions on the rights and obligations of women. It allowed child marriage, limited the woman's custodial rights to the children in case of divorce, restricted the wife's freedom to leave the house, and detailed her sexual obligations. The law generated widespread protest, but Karzai signed off on a slightly modified version in early 2009. See Suhrke (2011, 206–211).
4. Najibullah survived under UN protection in Kabul until 1996, when the Taliban entered the city and murdered him. For a critical reappraisal that questions whether Najib's fall was 'inevitable' after the withdrawal of Soviet subsidies, see Steele (2011 and this volume).

References

Afghan Government. 2001. Agreement on Provisional Arrangements in Afghanistan Pending the Re-establishment of Permanent Government Institutions. 5 December 2001. http://www.afghangovernment. com/AfghanAgreementBonn.htm

Agence France-Press. 2004, March 26. "Afghanistan to ask for 27 to 28 billion dollars at Berlin conference." Report. http://reliefweb.int/report/afghanistan/afghanistan-ask-27-28-billion-dollars-berlin-conference

Aikins, M. 2010. "Last Stand in Kandahar." The Walrus (Canada). http://walrusmagazine.com/articles/ 2010.12-international-affairs-last-stand-in-kandahar/

Asia Foundation. 2010. "Afghan Public Opinion Poll." http://www.asiafoundation.org/news/2010/11/asia-foundation-releases-2010-afghan-public-opinion-poll/

Bates, R. H. 2001. Prosperity and Violence: The Political Economy of Development. New York: W. W. Norton.

Bayart, J.-F. 2000. "Africa in the World: A History of Extraversion." African Affairs 99: 217–267.

van Bijlert, M. 2009. AAN Election Blog No. 23: How Much are we Expected to Believe? Kabul: Afghan Analysts Network. http://aan-afghanistan.com/index.asp?id=265. 2009.

Bräutigam, D., O.-H. Fjeldstad, et al., eds. 2008. Taxation and Statebuilding in Developing Countries. Cambridge: Cambridge University Press.

Byrd, W., and S. Guimbert. 2009. Public Finance, Security, and Development. A Framework and an Application to Afghanistan. Washington, D.C.: World Bank. Policy Research Working Paper.

Dalgaard, C-J., and O. Olsson. 2008. "Windfall Gains, Political Economy and Economic Development." Journal of African Economies 17 (AERC Supplement 1): 72–109.

Giustozzi, A. 2009. "The Afghan National Army. Unwarranted Hope?" *The RUSI Journal* 154 (6): 36–42.

GoA. 2009. *Donor Financial Review*. Kabul: Islamic Republic of Afghanistan, Ministry of Finance.

Goodhand, J. 2005. "Frontiers and Wars: The Opium Economy in Afghanistan." *Journal of Agrarian Change* 5 (2): 191–216.

Gregorian, V. 1969. *The Emergence of Modern Afghanistan. Politics of Reform and Modernization, 1880-1946*. Stanford: Stanford University Press.

Hakimi, A., and A. Suhrke. 2013. "A Poisonous Chalice: The Struggle for Human Rights and Accountability in Afghanistan." *Nordic Journal of Human Rights* 31 (2): 201–223.

Hurtic, Z., A. Sapcanin, et al. 2000. "Bosnia and Herzegovina." In *Good Intentions: Pledges of Aid for Postconflict Recovery*, edited by S. Forman and S. Patrick, 315–366. Boulder, Colo.: Lynne Rienner.

IMF. 2010. "Islamic Republic of Afghanistan: Sixth Review." Country Report No. 10/22. Washington D.C.: International Monetary Fund.

Integrity Watch/Afghanistan. 2010. *Afghan Perceptions and Experiences of Corruption. A National Survey*. Kabul: Integrity Watch/Afghanistan.

Johnson, C., and J. Leslie. 2004. *Afghanistan. The Mirage of Peace*. London: Zed.

Jones, S. G. 2009. *In the Graveyard of Empires: America's War in Afghanistan*. New York: W.W. Norton & Co.

Kipping, M. 2010. *Two Interventions. Comparing Soviet and U.S.-led State-building in Afghanistan*. Kabul: Afghan Analysts Network.

Krasner, S. D. 2004. "Sharing Sovereignty: New Institutions for Collapsed and Failing States." *International Security* 29 (2): 85–120.

Lefèvre, M. 2010. *Local Defence in Afghanistan. A Review of Government-backed Initiatives*. Kabul: Afghanistan Analysts Network.

Maley, W. 2006. *Rescuing Afghanistan*. London: Hurst & Company.

MEC. 2012. *MEC's Recommendations Analysis Report*. Kabul: Independent Joint Anti-Corruption Monitoring&Evaluation Committee.

Mukhopadhyay, D. 2011. "A View from the Provinces". Unpublished paper.

North, D. C. 1990. *Institutions, Institutional Change, and Economic Performance*. Cambridge: Cambridge University Press.

Paris, R. 2013. "Afghanistan: What Wrong?" *Perspectives on Politics* 11 (2): 538–548.

Parkinson, S. 2010. *Means to What End? Policymaking and State-Building in Afghanistan*. Kabul: Afghanistan Research and Evaluation Unit.

Rashid, A. 2008. *Descent into Chaos: The US and the Failure of Nation Building in Pakistan, Afghanistan, and Central Asia*. New York: Viking.

Rashid, A. 2010. It is Time to Rethink the West's Afghan Strategy *Financial Times*.

Ross, M. 2001. "Does Oil Hinder Democracy?" *World Politics* 53 (3): 325–361.

Rubin, B. R. 1995. *The Fragmentation of Afghanistan: State Formation and Collapse in the International System*. New Haven, CT: Yale University Press.

Rubin, B. R. 2005. "Constructing Sovereignty for Security." *Survival* 47 (4): 93–106.

Rubin, B. R. 2007. "Saving Afghanistan." *Foreign Affairs* 86 (1): 57–78.

Sedra, M. 2008. "The Four Pillars of Demilitarization in Afghanistan." In *Afghanistan, Arms and Conflict. Armed Groups, Disarmament and Security in a Post-war Society*, edited by M. Bhatia and M. Sedra, 119–157. London and New York: Routledge.

SIGAR. 2010a. *Actions Needed to Mitigate Inconsistencies in and Lack of Safeguards over U.S. Salary Support to Afghan Government Employees and technical Advisors*. Washington, D.C.: Office of the Special Inspector General for Afghanistan Reconstruction (SIGAR).

SIGAR. 2010b. *DOD, State and USAID Obligated Over 17.7 Billion to about 7,000 Contractors and Other Entities for Afghanistan Reconstruction During Fiscal Years 2007-2009*. Washington, D.C.: Special Inspector General for Afghanistan Reconstruction.

Sinno, A. H. 2008. *Organizations at War in Afghanistan and Beyond*. Ithaca: Cornell University Press.

Steele, J. 2011. *Ghosts of Afghanistan*. London: Portobello Books.

Suhrke, A. 2006. *"When More is Less: Aiding Statebuilding in Afghanistan"*. Bergen, Chr.: Michelsen Institute. Report. Available at http://www.cmi.no/publications/publication/?2402=when-more-is-less

Suhrke, A. 2011. *When More is Less. The International Project in Afghanistan*. London and New York: Hurst&Co and Columbia University Press.

UN. 2005. *Report of the Secretary-General on the Situation in Afghanistan and its Implications for International Peace and Security*. New York: United Nations. S/2005/183.

UN. 2008. *Report of the Secretary-General on the Situation in Afghanistan and its Implications for International Peace and Security.* New York: United Nations. S/2008/697.

USAID/Afghanistan. 2009. *Assessment of Corruption in Afghanistan.* Kabul: USAID.

US Army. 2010. US Army Times.

USGAO. 2009. *Afghanistan: Key Issues for Congressional Oversight.* Washington, D.C.: United States Government Accountability Office.

USGAO. 2010. *The Strategic Framework for U.S. Efforts in Afghanistan.* Washington, D.C.: United States Government Accountability Office. GAO-10-655R June 15, 2010

Verkoren, W. and B. Kamphuis. 2013. "Statebuilding in a Rentier State: How Development Policies Fail to Promote Democracy in Afghanistan." *Development and Change* 44, (3): 501–26.

Worden, S, 2010. "Afghanistan: An Election Gone Awry." *Journal of Democracy* 21 (3): 11–25.

World Bank. 2004. *Afghanistan. State Building, Sustaining Growth, and Reducing Poverty.* Washington, D.C.: The World Bank.

World Bank. 2011. *Transition in Afghanistan: Looking Beyond 2014.* Washington, DC: The World Bank. http://siteresources.worldbank.org/INTAFGHANISTAN/Resources/AFBeyond2014.pdf

Contested boundaries: NGOs and civil–military relations in Afghanistan

Jonathan Goodhand

Department of Development Studies, SOAS, University of London, UK

In recent years there has been a growing focus in academic and policy circles on the changing roles of military and civilian actors in the context of multi-mandate peace and stabilization operations. This focus on 'civil–military cooperation' (CIMIC) and the related notion of the 'security–development nexus' reflect changed thinking about the causes of (and solutions to) to wars and insecurity, the role of external actors, and the balance between 'hard' and 'soft' forms of intervention. This article explores the civil–military interface in Afghanistan, focusing on the changing role of NGOs and specifically their growing but troubled relationship with externally promoted statebuilding and counterinsurgency. A recurring theme in the article is that of contested boundaries; CIMIC has been the site of intensive 'boundary work' in which NGOs and the military seek to negotiate or contest where boundaries are drawn and who has the power to draw (and police) them.

Introduction

In recent years there has been a growing focus in academic and policy circles on the changing roles of military and civilian actors in the context of multi-mandate peace and stabilization operations.[1] This focus on 'civil–military cooperation' (CIMIC) and the related notion of the 'security–development nexus' reflect changed thinking about the causes of (and solutions to) to wars and insecurity, the role of external actors, and the balance between 'hard' and 'soft' forms of intervention. This article explores the civil–military interface in Afghanistan, focusing on the changing role of NGOs and specifically their growing but troubled relationship with externally promoted statebuilding and counterinsurgency. A recurring theme in the article is that of contested boundaries; CIMIC has been the site of intensive 'boundary work' in which NGOs and the military seek to negotiate or contest where boundaries are drawn and who has the power to draw (and police) them. Whilst the most salient boundary in the CIMIC debate is the divide between the military and the civil (or humanitarian), in practice this cannot be separated from a range of other interrelated boundary disputes that are legal, ethical, territorial, political, social, and institutional in their nature.

A focus on boundaries exposes underlying power relations and what is at stake in such demarcation disputes. This approach is at odds with mainstream policy narratives on intervention and liberal peacebuilding, which tend to ignore or blur boundaries in order to hide the asymmetries of power and resources involved – the vocabulary of *integration*, *cooperation*, *inclusivity*, and *cohesion* dissolves boundaries and assumes common interests and values. Bridging concepts such as *human security*, *social capital*, and the *conflict–security nexus*[2] are sufficiently open-ended and systematically ambiguous as to enable very different actors with different sets of interests to sign up to them. Whilst an emerging literature on hybridity[3] and friction[4] between the exporters and importers of liberal peacebuilding has been useful in highlighting and problematizing the external–internal divide, there has been less analytical work that focuses systematically on the internal boundaries dividing the complex assemblages making up the liberal peace. Even critical accounts of the liberal peace tend to stress the processes of convergence between the various agents of liberal peacebuilding. For example, Duffield (2007, 91), writing about NGOs from a Foucauldian perspective, describes the 'drawing together of the plurality of autonomous aims represented by Western states, recipient governments and aid agencies in a shared web of mutual interests and overlapping objectives'. A focus on the 'boundary encounters' engendered by NGOs' engagement in CIMIC provides a vantage point for studying how different sets of material, institutional, and political interests shape policies and programmes on the ground. Final outcomes are the result of complex processes of mediation, brokerage, boundary maintenance, and transgression and are rarely those that were initially intended.

This article first provides some historical background on NGOs in Afghanistan. Second, it explores the ways in which the NGO–military interface has changed in the post-Bonn environment as a result of shifts in military and humanitarian doctrine and practice and evolving operational challenges on the ground. The focus is primarily on a subset of service-delivery relief and development NGOs. Negotiating the boundaries between the civil-humanitarian and the military-political has proved to be a contested process, particularly in the context of Provincial Reconstruction Teams (PRTs),[5] though in practice NGO–military interactions have varied greatly from area to area and between agencies. Finally we turn to some of the implications of the foregoing analysis in light of the 2014 transition involving the drawdown of International Security Assistance Force (ISAF) forces, when new sets of boundaries are likely to be negotiated and inscribed. How will NGOs position themselves in the new political landscape, and how constrained are they by the legacies of their engagement in statebuilding and counterinsurgency?

Fuzzy boundaries: NGO identities in Afghanistan

NGO is a catch-all term, which encourages analytical vagueness. Yet, like all labels, it 'does' something, and has discursive and material effects – including bids for legitimacy, gaining access to resources, mobilizing supporters, and so forth. Classical definitions of NGOs tend to assume clear boundaries which differentiate them from other types of organizations, but in practice these boundaries are often blurred and contested. This is particularly the case in Afghanistan, which is characterized by extreme institutional hybridity[6] and fluidity. The divisions between civilian and military actors, state and non-state, and for-profit and not-for-profit, are extremely fuzzy. NGOs are multifaceted organizations which can be many things at the same time and present different faces to different people – they may be simultaneously a formal, legal entity, an income generation project, a social network and an arena for competing factions (Hillhorst and Van Leewen 2003).

Boundaries between NGOs are also important, and similarly contested. Significant divisions referred to in this article are those pertaining to:

- *Location of headquarters and scope of operations*. This divides *international NGOs* (INGOs) – sub-divided into solidarity organizations like Afghanaid and the Swedish Committee for Afghanistan, that work exclusively in Afghanistan, and INGOs that operate internationally, such as CARE, Save the Children, Oxfam, etc. – and *Afghan NGOs* (ANGOs), many of which date back to the early 1990s. Some of the larger ANGOs employ hundreds of staff and command budgets of USD 1–10 million (Ayrapetyants et al. 2005).

- *Scope of activities.* There are *niche* NGOs that maintain a single-issue focus (e.g. International Crisis Group, Amnesty International, Medecins Sans Frontieres), and *multi-mandate* NGOs that pursue different goals and activities simultaneously (e.g. Oxfam, Care International).
- *Mode of engagement.* NGOs are variously involved in direct delivery, capacity building, advocacy, or some combination of these.
- *Neutrality.* Within the family of humanitarian NGOs there is a divide between *Dunantist* NGOs, who recognize the founding principles of the Red Cross, and *Wilsonian* NGOs, who see their role as an extension of, or compatible with, their country's foreign policy interests (Donini 2010).

Our focus here is on a subset of service-delivery organizations, within the formal NGO sector, that are part of a wider transnational assemblage funded largely by official donors and aid-giving Western publics. However, it is important to recognize two things. First, the boundaries noted above are largely drawn by aid actors themselves, largely in order to fulfil bureaucratic, technical, or funding criteria; they carry very little meaning to Afghan communities, who rarely differentiate between NGOs, or between NGOs and other international organizations. Second, many of the roles commonly attributed to NGOs are also played by a diverse range of actors in the 'grey' or 'shadow' political economy of giving and compassion (Donini 2010). This includes non-traditional donors such as China, India, and the Gulf states; Islamic charities and institutions; remittances from migrants and diaspora; kinship-based networks; politico-military structures; and private-sector organizations.[7] Although it is beyond the scope of this article to examine the institutions, networks, and funding flows associated with 'shadow humanitarianism' – much of which is entirely separate from and largely invisible to formal 'project society' – it is important to bear in mind that NGOs are only a small (though important) part of the story of welfare provision and protection in Afghanistan.

Histories, drivers, and legacies of NGOs' engagement in Afghanistan

Although NGOs have criticized the post-Bonn 'securitization' and 'politicization' of aid, these are not new phenomena.[8] The delivery of aid in Afghanistan has always been shaped by the security environment and by the politico-military agendas of external and domestic players. Western solidarity organizations during the *jihad* against the Soviets were conscious agents of politicization,[9] as have been several Islamic organizations.[10] The label 'NGO' has been a convenient cover for other sets of interests.[11] Periods of heightened external engagement have always brought out in sharp relief the tensions between Dunantist NGOs, which seek to insulate themselves from politics and follow Red Cross principles of neutrality, impartiality, and universality, and Wilsonian NGOs, which have been less reticent to align themselves behind the foreign policies of their governments and funders.

Ostensibly normative debates on independence and neutrality are often related to more prosaic concerns about material interests and institutional pressures. Changing aid markets and shifts in donor policies have played important roles in shaping the NGO sector in Afghanistan.[12] NGOs are part of a transnational industry which employs thousands of people and which responds to market pressures, leading to behaviour that is sometimes at odds with declared norms.[13] Western militaries are likewise shaped by market pressures,[14] and, as explored below, tensions between NGOs and the military can be partly attributed to competition for resources and legitimacy. NGOs and the military are thus deeply embedded in the Afghan political economy. They constitute important sources of rent (though the military's resources are far greater) that lubricate and sustain clientelist networks and that provide the start-up capital for local businesses (licit and illicit) and for launching political careers.

NGOs' engagement with the Afghan state has shifted over time. In the 1980s, many were consciously aligned with anti-state forces; in the early 1990s, the state all but disappeared, and NGOs and the wider UN humanitarian system saw themselves as a 'caretaker state'; during the Taliban period, the regime was seen as an illegitimate 'presumptive state authority' which had to be worked around.[15] This shifting engagement with the state is also reflected in the life trajectories of many Afghans who worked for NGOs. During the war years, NGOs provided an alternative career path for educated, middle-class Afghans, particularly following the post-*jihad* disillusionment with politico-military groups. After the Bonn Agreement, many of these individuals moved into high-level government positions, heading up key ministries including the Ministries of Rural Rehabilitation and Development, Education, Agriculture, and the Interior. Several continue to retain links with their former NGOs as advisors or consultants.

Although geopolitics and aid markets have been drivers of change within the NGO sector, this does not mean that other, less tangible factors, including declared norms and ideological orientations, are not important. Within the NGO sector there are strongly held beliefs about the means and ends of humanitarian action and its relationship with politics. Humanitarian 'minimalists' argue for fidelity to the Red Cross principles and drawing strong 'Maginot lines' between aid and politics (Barnett 2005). 'Maximalists', on the other hand, advocate a more expansive role for NGOs, involving the simultaneous pursuit of relief, development, human rights or justice, and peacebuilding or stabilization (Goodhand 2006).

Another arena in which the discourses, norms, and practices related to NGOs are crucially important is their reception and (re)articulation by Afghan society. Western NGOs have often encountered a deep-seated ambivalence from the Afghan population, particularly in rural areas, because they are perceived to be agents of Westernization and modernization. Political entrepreneurs such as parliamentarian Bashar Dost periodically tap into these long-standing anxieties to mobilize anti-NGO or anti-foreigner sentiments. If one views NGOs less as a separate sector than as a social formation, part of political and civil society, that has emerged and grown over the last 40 years, then the question is less about what NGOs have done than about how these organizations shaped, reflected, and embodied changes and contradictions, in a society undergoing tremendous stresses and transformations.[16] The ways in which NGOs have been vectors of change in Afghan society, as well as brokers of resources and ideas, have been little studied but constitutes a rich area for further research.[17]

The post-Bonn governmentalization of NGOs

As other contributions to this volume emphasize, the international footprint in Afghanistan became heavier over time. And the growth of this footprint – in military, political, and financial terms – has paralleled, and partly induced, a creeping governmentalization of NGOs. Reflecting a broader trend towards the economization of conflict termination (Goodhand 2010; Zyck 2012), aid was seen as a crucial adjunct of statebuilding and postwar stabilization (see Suhrke, 2011 and 2013, this volume). Since the Bonn Agreement there has been a year-on-year increase in funding for reconstruction and development. Some USD 30 billion was spent for humanitarian and development aid in Afghanistan between 2001–2012, although this figure is dwarfed by the estimated USD 243 billion spent on security (International Development Committee 2012). Reflecting this increase in funding, there was a rapid growth in the number of NGOs. In 1999 there were 46 registered international NGOs; by 2002 this had risen to 350. The growth has been largest in the Afghan NGO sector, though in financial terms INGOs are far more important.[18]

Although NGO politicization is not new in Afghanistan, as noted above, historically, aid organizations managed to maintain a degree of strategic and operational autonomy from Western governments. But after 2002, NGOs' room to manoeuvre became far more circumscribed. This is reflected in the changed focus of activities, with humanitarian action constituting a shrinking share of the aid budget and a decline in Dunantist NGOs and traditional humanitarian donors (Donini 2009).[19] This in turn is related to the politics of how intervention was framed, with there being strong vested interests to view Afghanistan not as a 'humanitarian crisis' but as a stabilization and 'early recovery' context.[20] The bulk of the funding to NGOs has come from governments engaged in the conflict, which, as explored below, skews priorities towards conflict-affected provinces and also induces Afghan scepticism of NGO claims of neutrality and impartiality.

Humanitarian action, reconstruction, and development are more crowded fields nowadays than they were during the Taliban period. There are many new actors from the military and private sector involved in activities previously seen as the preserve of the UN humanitarian agencies (such as the UNHCR, UNICEF, and the World Food Programme) or NGOs.[21] And most importantly there is an internationally recognized Afghan government, whose legitimacy is perceived to be linked to the provision of public services and welfare. Whilst some donors have funded NGOs in the belief that they contribute more broadly to 'civil-society development', in monetary terms, a narrower instrumentalist agenda of using them as vehicles for service delivery, either as contractors in government-led national programmes[22] or as direct implementers of reconstruction projects, has been far more significant.[23]

The changed political and funding environment has placed growing pressures on NGOs to work primarily as contractors, implementing government programmes or competing with the private sector for donor funding, in which the parameters are tightly defined.[24] This has contributed to the creation of a rentier civil society – in parallel to the rentier state and rentier political parties that Suhrke and Giustozzi, respectively, write about in this volume – which consists of bureaucratically amenable NGOs that deliver aid (Howell and Lind 2009). It has also exacerbated the problem of a dual public sector, in which a weak and unevenly funded state sector is undermined by a better-funded parallel international public sector composed of UN agencies, contractors, and NGOs.

The unruly and unregulated nature of the aid market has fed negative public perceptions of NGOs, who have been described by Afghans as 'cows that drink their own milk' and 'worse than warlords'.[25] Yet, in spite of this perception, the figures show that proportionately, NGO funding has been relatively limited. Donors such as the Department for International Development (DFID) have made a point of channelling most of their funds through the Afghan Reconstruction Trust Fund and have prioritized their relationships with the government at the expense of ties with NGOs and Afghan civil society (International Development Committee 2012).[26]

Bleeding boundaries: the fusion of counterinsurgency and development[27]

Changing military doctrine has been an important driver of the growing fusion of counterinsurgency and development.[28] This has occurred against the backdrop of, at a global level, declining inter-state conflicts and increased international involvement in civil wars, usually of the asymmetrical variety, which collapse the temporal and geographical boundaries of the battlefield and the distinction between soldier and citizen.

One manifestation of this trend has been the proliferation of field manuals and policy documents relating to counterinsurgency (COIN).[29] It is argued that COIN operations are primarily political rather than military struggles; they can be understood as competitions for governance, with the ultimate goal being less about killing the enemy than about 'out-governing' them (Kilcullen 2011). Therefore, winning the hearts and minds of the population (sometimes shortened to the unfortunate acronym WHAM) is seen to be the key to victory. This 'functional integration of destruction and development, of military and civil forces for the lasting transformation of societies' (Feichtinger, Malinoski, and Chase 2012, 3) can be understood as the rehabilitation of a concept of counterinsurgency first developed during the late colonial wars.

The re-emergence of this doctrine has been facilitated by a closer relationship between counterinsurgency, peacebuilding, and development experts, and a related convergence between the military and UN peacekeeping doctrine.[30] Development organizations have actively promoted a more expansive, security-related role for aid. As a USAID policy paper on CIMIC states, 'Development is a cornerstone of national security along with diplomacy and defence. Development is also recognized as a key element of any successful whole of government counter terrorism and counter insurgency effort' (USAID 2008, 1). Institutional restructuring has also enhanced integration, examples of this including the US government's Office of the Coordinator of Reconstruction and Stabilization (S/CRS) in the Department of State and the UK government's Stabilization Unit.

In Afghanistan there was a receptive audience for COIN. Provincial Reconstruction Teams – see below – were the vehicles for its initial operationalization; then ISAF expansion, which had the effect of catalyzing the insurgency, intensified efforts to roll out COIN, further blurring the line between the stabilization and combat missions of foreign forces (Suhrke 2012). When General Stanley McChrystal assumed command of NATO operations in 2009, he introduced new rules of engagement which led to a shift in the balance between the deployment of 'hard power' (or 'kinetics') and 'soft power', with the purported goal of protecting the population.[31]

According to COIN doctrine, defeating the Taliban requires better penetration of society by the state, more effective regulation of disputes, and the provision of public goods in the form of security, better governance, and development. These are areas in which NGOs supposedly have a comparative advantage, due to their close relationships with local communities, flexibility, speed of implementation, and high tolerance of risk. NGOs are therefore seen as important actors in helping stabilize unruly peripheries and re-legitimize the Afghan state.[32] Aid has accordingly 'followed the battle space' (Reiff 2010), with its geographical allocation being related less to a humanitarian or development logic than to the security concerns of donor nations. For example, 80% of USAID resources have been channelled to south and east (US Committee on Foreign Relations 2011), most of this for short-term stabilization rather than long-term development.[33]

Aid workers and soldiers were both advocates of a heavier and aid-led international footprint;[34] but by adopting such a position they increasingly transgressed the 'Maginot lines' that each had erected to maintain their distance from politics. For soldiers, COIN is based on a fundamentally different understanding of the relationship between war and politics. Classically, the use of armed force within a military domain seeks to establish military conditions for a political solution (Simpson 2012). Violence was therefore meant to clear the ground, to enable politics to take over. But COIN involves the use of armed force that directly seeks political as opposed to military outcomes (Simpson 2012). Just as aid workers have been uncomfortable with the so-called blurring of the lines – for an organization like the International Committee of the Red Cross (ICRC), the line is a legal one, involving the transgression of international humanitarian law – so have sections of the military.[35] Yet COIN advocates were in the ascendency, and associated with this was a drive to know Afghan society more intimately – what Gregory (2008) characterizes as the cultural turn within the military, or a 'rush to the intimate'. 'Human terrain teams' (HTT) are one manifestation of this thirst for cultural knowledge, to better penetrate, map, and 'know' the human geography of Afghanistan (see Hakimi and Wimpelmann, this volume). NGOs were also important information brokers – as the late Richard Holbrooke, then US special advisor on Pakistan and Afghanistan, noted in 2009, '90% of US knowledge about Afghanistan lies with aid agencies' (cited in Crombe 2011, 60).[36]

Hence, COIN breaks down boundaries traditionally erected by the military, creating a citizen–soldier hybrid that blurs the distinction between the 'political role of the citizen and the apolitical role of the soldier' (Stahl, cited in Gregory 2008, 21). Whether the HTT, NGOs, or soldiers make good ethnographers is another question, and the rapid turnover of staff (military and humanitarian) on short-term contracts probably militates against such a possibility. There have been a plethora of papers and reports by soldiers who have 'gone tribal', with breathless titles like *One Tribe at a Time* (Grant 2009) and 'The Fight for the Village' (Petit 2010), but in its more crass forms this military orientalism 'recycles old bigotry in the language of political correctness' (Porter 2009, 198).[37] This process of othering and objectification may represent another point of convergence between NGOs and the military: both tend to reify the local, celebrating 'the community' as a place of virtue, solidarity, and resilience.

A final and telling manifestation of the 'bleeding boundaries' between military and aid actors is the growing interchangeability of the concepts and language they deploy. The language of *humanitarianism, civilian protection, human rights*, and *good governance* is deployed by both soldiers and aid workers.[38] Both seek to ascribe meaning to their missions by using the language of ethics and morality, and in this sense they can be understood as battles for legitimacy – yet, as Surhke argues (this volume), these legitimizing tropes tend not to resonate with the wider Afghan population, particularly because of a failure to deliver on the rhetoric.

Provincial Reconstruction Teams and the 'insecurity–development' nexus

PRTs have been at the sharp end of debates and policies related to CIMIC, because this is where the clashing world views, policies, and practices of military and civilian actors interact in very concrete ways (see Sedra, this volume). In the end there were 26 PRTs, which were designed to spread a peacemaking effort without creating a large peacekeeping force – in other words, an ISAF effect without an ISAF presence.

Aid strategies linked to PRTs varied over time and between PRTs, and the relationship between aid and the military differed, for example, between an American and a Norwegian PRT.[39] NGOs' relationship with PRTs has also varied, along a continuum from 'principled non-engagement' at one end to 'active, direct engagement and cooperation' at the other (Shannon 2009).[40] However, PRT aid strategies have broadly been based on several interrelated assumptions: that the insurgency is driven by a range of grievances related to underdevelopment, poverty, and bad governance; that aid can act as a form of force protection by winning the hearts and minds of the population, thus generating acceptance or support for the military; that aid can play a role in extending the capacity and legitimacy of the Afghan state; and that international actors, the Afghan government, and the wider population share the same goals and understandings of security, development, and governance.

COIN, like statebuilding, is seen as a process of territorialization, involving the diffusion of power outwards from centre to periphery. This is captured in concepts and expressions such as 'clear, hold, and build', the 'ink spot' (or 'oil spot') strategy, the creation of Afghan Development Zones, and delivery of 'iconic projects'. All are based on the idea of a sequenced set of activities, starting with the employment of pockets of civil-military teams, then gradually expanding these locations by conducting 'pacification operations' in the surrounding areas.

Over time there has been a shift in the focus of the original PRT model from building the short-term legitimacy of the respective international forces to the assumption of an increasingly subordinate role to the local authorities (Wilton Park 2010). To some extent this is demonstrated in Farrell and Gordon's (2009) account of the UK's COIN strategy in Helmand between 2005– 2009, which examines in detail the shifts in thinking and practice and the associated interdepartmental manoeuvring. The authors argue that the initial strategy suffered from many of the flaws of the wider statebuilding project: essentially it was a top-down 'technocratic model' with a limited role for civilians. In effect, the military defined the operational objectives and priorities, and civilians were expected to provide a form of reconstruction 'follow-on force'.

The plan was subsequently redesigned in 2007 as the 'Helmand Road Map', which according to the authors was a more bottom-up initiative, the result of collaboration on the ground between military and civilian actors. In late 2008, the task force HQ and the PRT were merged in a combined Civil-Military Mission in Helmand (CMMH), led by a Foreign and Commonwealth Office 'two-star'. Military stabilization-support teams were established in key districts to extend the reach and durability of the 'civil effect'. An emphasis was placed on undermining the Taliban's influence rather than fighting their forces.

Whilst Farrell and Gordon do not gloss over the limitations of UK COIN strategy or the tensions between the different players assigned roles within it, many, particularly on the NGO side, would dispute their overall story of progress and learning. As Sherard Cowper-Coles notes in his book *Cables from Kabul* (2011), 'An army that is willing to fight and die must, almost by definition, be hugely optimistic, unquenchably enthusiastic … and, ideally, not too imaginative.' Over and over, the British ambassador is told by military briefers that, 'though challenges remain', progress is being made – in spite of the fact that the reality was always far grimmer.[41]

There is little systematic evidence to support the military's narrative about the pacifying effects of aid. In fact, the most extensive qualitative study on WHAM, conducted by the Feinstein International Center, refutes many of the assumptions and assertions underlying the doctrine (Fishstein and Wilder 2012). First, there appears to be no connection between under-development, poverty, and the insurgency: some of the poorest areas in the country are unaffected by the insurgency, whilst some of the more wealthy regions in the south and east are the main recruiting grounds for the Taliban. At the national level, the rapid deterioration of security occurred just at the time when development assistance peaked (Zyck 2012).

Second, there is little evidence that aid provision can be a decisive factor in building security or generating consent and support for the government or foreign military forces. This is backed up by quantitative studies on the relationship between development and security (Beath, Christia, and Enikolopov 2012; Keohler and Zurcher 2007). Conversely, there is a great deal of evidence that 'too much aid spent quickly with little oversight can be delegitimizing and destabilizing' (Wilton Park 2010, 2). Poorly conceived aid programmes may lead to elite capture at the local level, or exacerbate the problem of rentier statehood at the national level, feeding corruption and contributing to the legitimacy crisis of the state (see Surhke, this volume; Wilder 2009). Also, large cash injections in the form of reconstruction programmes may paradoxically incentivize instability, either by appearing to reward insecurity and penalize security (Zyck 2012) or as a result of the leakage of resources to groups aligned with the Taliban.[42] The accumulated evidence suggests that there is a paradox at the heart of COIN: the strategy depends upon the existence of a strong and reasonably legitimate state, yet COIN practices themselves undermine the possibility of such a development.

Third, there is some evidence that well-conceived aid programmes can contribute to reconstruction and development goals. And by doing so, such programmes may contribute to 'human security', though, as another study notes, only when there is a clear division of roles between military and development actors: 'Contrary to contemporary wisdom, it appears that humanitarian and development actors are more effective in enhancing security – and in demonstrating a peace dividend – when they are no longer required to abide by stabilization agendas' (Barakat, Deely, and Zyck 2010).

Fourth, there is little evidence that the military are better placed to implement development programmes, leading many to conclude that military resources would be more effectively spent on security-related activities, rather than reconstruction, in which civilian specialists have a comparative advantage. Ill-conceived Quick Impact Projects, 'slush funds' (including US Department of Defence use of Overseas Humanitarian Disaster and Civic Aid and the Comman-der's Emergency Response Program), and 'iconic projects' (such as the Kajaki Dam) have absorbed large amounts of money and time for limited or perverse effects. Projects are run in parallel with the government and may not be aligned to national development strategies. For instance, there have been cases of soldiers distributing infant formula which runs directly counter to Ministry of Public Health guidelines. Surges of cash in conflict-affected environments may have a range of perverse and distortionary effects on local markets, generate intense distri-butional conflicts, and create unrealistic expectations. Such programmes may also undercut the work and relationships developed over several years by NGOs in a particular area.[43]

Fifth, the Feinstein studies and a subsequent Wilton Park conference related to this research largely debunked the myth that the foreign militaries, aid actors, and the Afghan government share common goals related to security, governance, and reconstruction. Talk of *coherence* and *integration* cannot mask fundamental differences in world views and objectives.

Why then did COIN strategy retain its hold on the 'hearts and minds' of military strategists and policy makers for so long, in spite of the growing evidence that it does not work? One answer may be that it had more to do with winning the hearts and minds of foreigners, rather than Afghans. At the coal face, the doctrine provides military personnel with a strong justifica-tion and positive narrative for an extremely demanding and largely thankless task. And at the policy level, it provides a 'feel-good', humanitarian story line to increasingly sceptical Western politicians and publics about the goals and costs, in blood and treasure, of military inter-vention in Afghanistan. In 'population-centric' warfare the key target population may not be Afghans but those living in the West who need to be convinced of the validity of the struggle. In a similar vein to David Mosse's (2004) insight about development projects which fail because of a crisis of representation, failure or success in Afghanistan may be less about military results on the ground than the ability to sell a particular narrative to Western audiences.

Living with uncertain boundaries: the consequences for NGOs

Whilst recognizing that there are a number of different militaries operating in Afghanistan according to different mandates and rules of engagement,[44] NGOs have raised several concerns about the overall role and rules of engagement of foreign troops.

Most important has been the failure to protect civilians. In 2008, 39% of civilian casualties were caused by pro-government forces, though this had been reduced to 12% in 2009.[45] Air strikes, and night raids in particular, caused 'fear, distrust, and anger' (Nowhere to Turn 2010, 10), and undermined the proclaimed strategy of winning hearts and minds. With McCyr-stal's replacement by Patraeus in 2010, the rules of engagement appeared to shift back to a more kinetic approach.[46] Afghan NGO Security Office (ANSO) figures for 2012 showed that in spite of the increased ISAF presence, up to 2011 there had been six years of sustained growth in con-flict. Although there was a 24% decrease in violent incidents in 2012, a United Nations Assist-ance Mission for Afghanistan (UNAMA) report published in mid-2013 showed that the number of Afghan civilians killed or injured in the first half of the year had increased by 23% compared to the same period in the previous year.

Counterinsurgency strategies may influence societal perceptions of NGOs and consequently their ability to build trust and negotiate access with Afghan communities. Military practices and tactics have led to concerns that humanitarian action may be seen as a front for intelligence gath-ering.[47] These include coalition troops wearing plain clothes and driving in unmarked white vehicles[48] and US forces distributing leaflets to Afghan communities calling on them to produce information on al-Qaida and the Taliban or face losing humanitarian aid.[49] After concerted lobbying of the US government by InterAction and other groups, these practices decreased, though this did not allay NGOs' fears about a loss of humanitarian space and the blurring of boundaries between aid actors and the military.[50]

When NGOs are seen as extensions of a foreign military and supporters of an illegitimate state, they become legitimate targets in the eyes of the militants. For example, in conversation with a senior ICRC delegate, an anti-government tribal leader warned about the dangers of crossing the boundary between humanitarianism and politics: 'Know when so-called humanitarian action becomes a sword, or a poison – and stop there' (quoted in Terry 2011, 188).

NGOs' security and 'humanitarian space' were based on historical notions of independence, transparency, and a non-threatening posture. This 'acceptance approach' enabled some NGOs, such as Mercy Corps International, to retain a presence in the south for over 20 years (Pont 2011). But the social contract of acceptability between humanitarian agencies, communities, and belligerents appears to have broken down in some places (Donini 2009) – particularly where Taliban structures are more fluid and where there is a greater preponderance of younger, more ideologically inclined fighters from Pakistan (Jackson and Giustozzi 2012). However, the fact that UNICEF and the ICRC negotiated ceasefires with the Taliban to conduct vaccination days, and the ongoing behind-the-scenes negotiations between NGOs and the Taliban (see below), indicate that this space has not entirely closed.

Whilst 'saving strangers' was always a dangerous business in Afghanistan, attacks on aid workers showed a sharp upward trend from the mid-2000s. Concerns about the security of aid workers led to the formation of the ANSO in 2003.[51] In 2008, NGOs were involved in more than 170 incidents (up by 20% from 2007), in which 31 aid workers were killed, 78 abducted, and a further 27 seriously wounded, with Afghan staff taking the brunt of attacks (Donini 2009). It is also likely that incidents and threats are under-reported by field staff, who fear programmes will be stopped, and by senior staff, who fear donors will cut funding (Donini 2009). In the first three months of 2013, according to ANSO figures, there was a 63% increase in incidents affecting NGO personnel compared to the same period in the previous year. Not all these incidents are at the hands of the Taliban and their affiliates, and the COIN strategy of funding local militias in the name of 'community policing' (see Hakimi, this volume) has in some provinces *increased* insecurity for NGOs and local communities.

It is also important to note that NGOs' assertions about the 'blurring of the lines' are often based on similarly sketchy evidence, are sometimes self serving, and may not reflect the concerns of the NGO sector as a whole or the communities they work with. The assertion of a straightforward causal link between CIMIC and the increased targeting of aid workers does not go undisputed. Some contend that NGOs are primarily attacked because they are soft targets, not because attackers are unable to distinguish between NGO staff from Coalition forces (Karp 2006). Furthermore, a 2012 ANSO report notes that attacks on NGOs in the first part of 2011 can largely be explained by the growing geographical spread of the insurgency rather than direct targeting.[52]

Even so, NGOs have had to adapt to the growing insecurity in various ways. Bunkering down has been one strategy, with aid workers retreating into fortified compounds and travelling less, and when they do, moving in unmarked vehicles. Paradoxically, then, the post-2001 expansion of the aid industry has occurred alongside NGOs' growing withdrawal and remoteness from Afghan society (Duffield 2012). In practice, this is the opposite of the 'ink spot' strategy, as aid organizations manage risk through retrenchment. Becoming invisible is seen as the best guarantee of security (Donini 2009). Signboards, once the trademark of NGOs, have been taken down, and most no longer fly the flag outside Kabul (Donini 2009). International staff travel has been radically limited, which in effect has meant a transfer of risk to national staff and to Afghan communities who assume the responsibility for guaranteeing NGO safety in the field.

As a national staff member explained: 'I go to the field less and less. When I do, I wear dirty clothes. I leave my ID and mobile phone behind. I don't even take a notebook' (quoted in Donini 2009, 8). An increasingly remote-control engagement with their programmes has obvious implications for the quality of supervision, monitoring, and accountability. It also has costs in terms of NGOs' relationships with communities.

However, as noted earlier, the NGO sector is not homogeneous. Responses to the changing operating environment have varied widely, and there has been a clear dividing line over CIMIC between INGOs and ANGOs. ANGOs have tended to be more pragmatic in their engagement with PRTs and the military in general. None are purely humanitarian; most are multi-mandate NGOs, focusing primarily on service delivery and reconstruction. To a large extent, they cannot afford to adopt a 'principled' position by turning down funding from PRTs. As INGOs become more constrained by security concerns, there is increased pressure from donors, who are offloading money onto local organizations.[53]

Renegotiating civil–military boundaries

Therefore, NGOs have been forced to adapt to the adverse effects of 'bleeding boundaries'. But they have also engaged in efforts to renegotiate and sharpen the boundaries between civilian and military actors. Below the radar, there have been ongoing discussions between NGOs and the Taliban, in spite of government sensitivities. As stated by one agency head: 'Anyone who talks to the Taliban risks being PNG'd [persona non grata] but of course everyone talks to the Taliban anyway – how else would we work?' (quoted in Jackson and Giustozzi 2012, 6).[54] There have also been some higher-level initiatives to facilitate access, including an Agency Coordination Body for Afghan Relief and Development (ACBAR) joint-access strategy and a UN-led Access Working Group established in Kabul in 2010 (Benelli, Donini, and Niland 2012). Arguably, the task of developing a modus operandi with the Taliban has been made more difficult by the ISAF 'kill or capture' policy, which has denuded the mid-level leadership of the organization – who have been replaced by more ideologically oriented leaders. It is also important to note that as the ISAF drawdown unfolds, NGOs will face a growing challenge in how to negotiate with the Afghan security forces for humanitarian access.

Talks between NGOs and Western militaries have taken place in a more open and formalized setting, though frequently they have failed, from an NGO perspective, because of the power asymmetries involved. In Kabul in 2004, an NGO Civil Military Working Group was formed which involved regular meetings at the Ministry of Interior with the purpose of resolving operational issues and providing a channel for NGO concerns to be directed at the military, the Afghan government, and foreign donors (Karp 2006).[55] In 2008, this group approved a set of guidelines: 'The Guidelines for the Interaction and Coordination of Humanitarian Actors and Military Actors'.[56] But relations were strained, and with the rapid turnover of staff, both sides began to send low-level representatives. The working group became defunct by 2009.[57] At the international level, a number of CIMIC policy documents and guidelines have also been developed.[58] In spite of all these initiatives, there remains an underlying tension between civilian and military actors because of their different world views, identities, interests, and organizational cultures. Generally, NGOs have tended to argue for sharp boundaries and a clear delimitation of tasks, whilst the default position of the military is to blur or demolish these boundaries through integration.

Conclusions: transition and changing boundaries

Afghanistan has been an advanced laboratory for the militarization of aid through PRTs (Benelli, Donini, and Niland 2012). But the debate on civil–military cooperation has been ideologically driven and is consequently not very open to nuance or evidence-based discussion. This article has sought to explore some of the key debates relating to CIMIC, and the complex entanglements that have developed, linking aid actors with the military. It has critically scrutinized the idea that NGOs should be viewed instrumentally as part of the stabilization 'tool-box', and that as a corollary to this there should be greater strategic integration, joint planning, and programming. The encounter between NGOs and the military is not one of equals, and consequently there has been an asymmetric blurring of boundaries: transgression has largely been in one direction, and this is symptomatic of a wider process of governmentalization. NGOs have to some extent invited this encroachment by aligning themselves so readily behind the statebuilding/stabilization agenda and accepting the funding of occupying powers.

Many of the underlying assumptions behind COIN and CIMIC are flawed or unproven. This includes NGOs' claims about the deleterious effects of the 'blurring of the lines', as well as the military's claims about the assumed causal connection between underdevelopment and the insurgency; the potential for aid to win hearts and minds; and the belief in the shared objectives of foreign troops, development agencies, and the Afghan government. The 'human terrain' in Afghanistan is far more complex than the WHAM doctrine allows. The idea that consent and support can be 'bought' through the provision or withholding of aid, or that 'development' can short-circuit complex political and social processes, shows a lack of understanding of the Afghan political economy and also of the importance of non-material resources and the ways that legitimacy is won and lost in Afghan society.

An exploration of CIMIC and COIN doctrine reveals wider flaws and pathologies within the liberal peacebuilding enterprise. Far from being hegemonic or coherent, it is fractured and contested from within and based upon flawed premises and strategies. At the heart of COIN was a paradox – that its success depended on the existence of a strong, reasonably legitimate state and yet the strategy of channelling resources through bureaucratically amenable NGOs undermined the possibility of such an eventuality. In COIN and in many other areas of intervention, exogenous statebuilding was ultimately undermined by its own sponsors.

Looking ahead, NGOs are likely to become even more pivotal players in the future. As military forces are drawn down to meet the 2014 deadline and funding levels decline,[59] there will be a sorting process, leaving behind a core of the more committed and professional national and international NGOs. As Barfield (2012) notes, in 2002 the international community believed that the absence of a strong centralized state was the driver of insecurity and terrorism, yet by 2012 it was the existence of a corrupt, illegitimate central state that was seen as the core of the problem. There are signs that, given this re-evaluation of the Afghan state, some donors are turning their attention back to NGOs and civil society.[60] This is consistent with a shift in strategy towards supporting more expedient, cheaper, and local entities – whether they are local militias, like the Afghan Local Police, or Afghan NGOs and civil-society groups – as part of an exit strategy. The attacks by the Taliban in May 2013 on the offices of the ICRC in Jalalabad and the International Organization for Migration in Kabul are perhaps signs of even more difficult times ahead for NGOs. Some will interpret these events as the predictable outcome of a flawed COIN strategy, the legacy of which NGOs will have to grapple with over the coming years. A more optimistic reading of the situation is that a decreased foreign presence will open up spaces in which committed NGOs can redraw boundaries, renegotiate access, and rebuild trust with Afghan communities.

Acknowledgement

This article draws upon a combination of the author's previous experience as an NGO worker in Afghanistan and Pakistan, empirical research conducted on aid and NGOs during the Taliban and post-2001 period, and perusal of the relevant published and 'grey' literature. An earlier version of this article was presented at a conference organized by the Australian National University, 'Afghanistan: Civil-Military Lessons Learned – A Comparative Study'. I would like to thank Antonio Donini, William Maley, Deniz Kandiyoti, and two anonymous reviewers for useful comments on an earlier version of this article.

Notes

1. See for example Chandler (2010); Duffield (2007); Paris (2004).
2. See Duffield (2007); Luckham and Kirk (2013).
3. See MacGinty (2011); Boege et al. (2009).
4. See Millar, van der Lijn, and Verkoren (2013).
5. PRTs are civil-military units tasked with bringing about security and spearheading reconstruction efforts in the provinces.
6. Hybridity in this sense means blurred boundaries between state and non-state or formal and informal institutions. However, we are also interested in this article in a broader understanding of hybridity drawing upon the work of MacGinty (2011) and Boege et al. (2009), who use it to mean the composite forms of thinking and practices that result from the interactions between different actors, practices, and worldviews.
7. Although these institutions and networks are quite different from one another, they have all had a significant effect upon how Afghan communities survived and coped during the war years by performing a range of functions including channelling resources, managing risks, providing protection, generating employment, etc.
8. For writing on the history of NGOs and aid in Afghanistan see Atmar, Barakat, and Strand (1998); Borchgrevink and Berg Harpviken (2010); Baitenmann (1990); Donini (1996); Goodhand (2002, 2006); Marsden (2010); and Nicholds and Borton (1994).
9. See Baitenmann (1990) on the role of US advocacy organizations and cross-border NGOs. See also Donini (1996) and Goodhand (2002) on the pro-war positions adopted by many INGOs during this period. One infamous example was the English-language textbooks printed for Afghan refugees in which children learnt numeracy and literacy by counting AK-47s or dead Russian soldiers.
10. For example, the Al Rashid Trust, which allegedly operated training camps for Islamic militants.
11. During the 1980s, a number of NGOs were heavily influenced and in some cases colonized by the *mujahideen* parties. Furthermore, for Western donors, during the Cold War, an arm's-length subcontracting arrangement with NGOs was convenient, camouflaging the nature and scale of their involvement in cross-border operations. Subsequently, in the 1990s, increased donor funding for ANGOs led to the proliferation of 'briefcase' NGOs in Peshawar, a phenomenon that has been repeated in post-Bonn Kabul.
12. The availability of donor funding and specific policy initiatives have pushed the sector in certain directions. For instance, the shift in funding from refugee-related programmes in Pakistan to reconstruction efforts inside Afghanistan created strong incentives for NGOs to refocus on cross-border programmes from the early 1990s.
13. See Cooley and Ron (2002) for a discussion of the NGO sector as an industry that can best be understood through an analysis of market pressures.
14. Their increased involvement globally in peacekeeping and peace enforcement can partly be understood as a strategy to carve out a new role for themselves and justify continued investment in the armed forces in an environment, following the fall of the Berlin Wall, where there were strong pressures (at least initially) to reduce military spending in Western countries.
15. For example, the Strategic Framework Agreement for Afghanistan, adopted by the UN in 1998, effectively banned any form of aid for institutional development and capacity building (Duffield 2007).
16. For example, the NGO sector has contributed to the growth of a new Afghan middle class in urban areas, estimated by the World Bank to now constitute 10–15% of the population, somewhere between 2.75 million and 4.13 million Afghans (Kazam 2013).
17. See Wimplemann (2012) for one of the few attempts to set out such a research agenda. See also Monsutti (2012).
18. Over 1200 national and 301 international NGOs were registered in the country, according to the Ministry of Economy (MoE), in May 2010 (though it has been estimated that only 20% of this number are actually functioning NGOs) (IRIN 2010a). The Ministry of Finance reported 2400 local

and international organizations in February 2011, with NGOs generating over AFN 1.5 billion (about USD 33 million) of revenue for the treasury annually (IRIN 2011). According to Poole (2011), in 2009 only 0.5% of total aid was channelled through ANGOs whilst some 13.9% went to INGOs.

19. Notwithstanding the fact that the ICRC's budget for Afghanistan doubled in the post-Bonn period. However, the overall trend has been for a diminished role for Dunantist organizations and the expansion of multi-mandate NGOs or private-sector organizations able to handle large service-delivery programmes.

20. This resort to euphemism has a long history, going back for example to the wars of decolonization, which 'served as hothouses for the invention of euphemisms appropriate for wars of long-lasting occupation and transformation' (Feichtinger, Malinoski, and Chase 2012, 39).

21. These range from the military involvement in building hospitals to private-sector companies like DynCorp or DAI providing 'alternative livelihoods' or 'reintegration' programmes.

22. According to Cornish and Glad (2008), more than 80% of NGO activities are tied to government programmes.

23. Exceptions to this have been various civil-society consultations linked to key international events, including the Bonn process and the Afghanistan Compact. The Afghan Civil Society Forum was constituted in the wake of the civil-society consultation that ran in parallel with the Bonn conference (Borchgrevink and Berg Harpviken 2010).

24. For example, the US government relies heavily on commercial contractors. In FYs 2007–09, USAID provided about USD 3.8 billion to 283 contractors and other entities. Luis Berger International and DAI accounted for about USD 1 billion. The State Department's Bureau of International Narcotics and Law Enforcement obligated USD 2.3 billion for four contractors with DynCorp, accounting for more than 80% (US Committee on Foreign Relations 2011).

25. In 2005, partly to allay such concerns, an NGO code of conduct was signed by 90 national and international NGOs with the aim of setting high standards to ensure greater transparency and accountability as well as to improve the quality of services provided by NGOs. However, this has not prevented NGOs from becoming scapegoats for wider frustrations with Western intervention in Afghanistan, as shown by attacks on NGO offices during the May 2006 riots in Kabul.

26. According to an Afghan Ministry of Finance report (cited in IRIN 2005), out of USD 13.4 billion pledged between 2002 and 2004, only USD 3.9 billion was physically disbursed to the country by mid-2005. The same report indicated that only 9% of donor funding was given directly to NGOs, with 45.5% going to the United Nations, nearly 30% to the government, and 16% to private contractors.

27. The phrase 'bleeding boundaries' is taken from Roberts (2010).

28. See Miller and Mills (2010) on what they characterize as a 'military-industrial-academic' complex, comprised of warrior intellectuals and institutions like the RAND Corporation, the Centre for the Study of Terrorism and Political Violence at St Andrews, Kings College London, and the Carr Centre, Harvard University.

29. These include the UK military's 'Joint Military Doctrine Publication 3–40' (https://www.gov.uk/government/uploads/system/uploads/attachment_data/file/43332/jdp340guideweb.pdf); the US Army and Marine Corps 'Counterinsurgency Field Manual 3–24' (http://www.fas.org/irp/doddir/army/fm3-24.pdf); and the US Department of the Army 'Stability Operations Field Manual 3-07' (http://usacac.army.mil/cac2/repository/FM307/FM3-07.pdf).

30. For example, the 'Capstone Doctrine', which guides UN peace-support missions and identifies a core function as being to create a secure and stable environment, including strengthening the state's ability to provide security (UN DPKO 2008).

31. The extent to which there has been a substantive shift from the harder to softer dimensions of COIN is contested. McChrystal's replacement by General Petraeus in June 2010 led, many believe, to 'the gloves coming off' and greater use of air strikes, artillery, and Special Operations Forces raids.

32. As already noted, these pressures on NGOs are not unique to Afghanistan. In June 2003, in the aftermath of the fall of Baghdad, the administrator of the US Agency for International Development, Andrew Natsios, instructed an audience of NGO officials that if they wanted to continue to be funded by the US government they needed to emphasize their links to the government, and that if they were not willing to do this, he would find other NGOs or for-profit contractors that were (Reiff 2010).

33. Similarly, 25% of Canada's aid went to Kandahar, and one-fifth of DFID's funding to Helmand.

34. For example, in June 2003 more than 50 NGOs signed a letter requesting extension of the ISAF (ICVA 2003). See Suhrke (2012) for an analysis of the motivations for and dynamics around the increasingly heavy international footprint in Afghanistan.

35. In the words of Lieutenant General Sir John Kiszley of the British Army, 'Counterinsurgency calls for some un-warrior like qualities such as emotional intelligence, empathy, subtlety [and] political adroit-ness' (quoted in Jens and Smith 2010, 82). COIN may be seen as an aberration, or something that puts unnecessary constraints on soldiers' field of operations, and consequently they look forward to the opportunity of returning to 'proper soldiering' (Jens and Smith 2010, 82).

36. Two ANGOs with a strong focus on research and analysis that have been drawn upon by the inter-national community are the Tribal Liaison Office (TLO) and Cooperation for Peace and Unity (CPAU).

37. Lieutenant Colonel Petit's article 'The Battle for the Village' gives a flavour of this in his character-ization of the Afghan village: 'Villages are "insurgent camouflage". They are remote, culturally indis-tinguishable to outsiders, self-sustaining, and they provide nearly endless littoral nesting grounds for insurgents to roost in and operate from' (Petit 2010, 26).

38. In a Skype interview with a US Colonel in Kabul in November 2012, this author was struck by the similarities between his narrative and the language conventionally deployed by aid workers. The inter-view was peppered with phrases like 'understanding and moving with the people', 'ensuring govern-ance', 'providing goods and services', and 'connecting people to the government'. It was virtually indistinguishable from the justificatory language associated with the National Solidarity Programme.

39. See for example Strand (2010), who argues that the Norwegian PRT in Faryab ensured a clear division between military and civilian engagement and that there was an explicit strategy to integrate aid pro-vision through the PRT into the Afghanistan National Development Strategy and the Provincial Devel-opment Plan.

40. Shannon (2009) identifies four positions: principled non-engagement; arm's-length engagement; proactive, pragmatic, principled engagement; and active, direct engagement and cooperation.

41. See also Egnell (2011), who argues that an insular, conformist culture within the British Army and a misplaced belief in past counterinsurgency triumphs have militated against substantive learning and adaptation by the UK forces in Helmand.

42. For example, US contractors have hired armed militia groups to provide security who have been directly linked to the insurgency.

43. For example, in Badghis Province, one of CARE's local partners had started up a micro-loan business with interest rates of around 10% as part of a long-term community project. The PRT came in and set up a short-term-loans project with no fee, which brought people flocking to what CARE sees as a less sustainable option.

44. For example, in the north, ISAF troops were largely a peacekeeping force, whilst in the south they were increasingly drawn into and adopted a war-fighting posture. Between different national contingents there are different rules of engagement, and even within these contingents there are significant differ-ences. For example, Special Operations Forces come under a different command structure from the regular US Army. See Chandrasekaran (2012) on the conflicts between the US and UK militaries in Helmand. To complicate matters further, foreign intelligence agencies, particularly the CIA, follow different operating procedures which may often be at odds with the declared strategies and principles of the military.

45. According to UNAMA, there was a further 18% decrease in civilian deaths at the hands of ISAF/ANSF troops between 2009 and 2010.

46. See for example Boone (2011) on the brutalization of the war as a conscious strategy of US forces to provoke the Taliban into greater 'barbarism' and in so doing undermine their support amongst the population.

47. For example, a study for the ICRC notes that 'on several occasions, when arrests, bombings or poppy eradication occurred not long after ICRC staff had visited an area, the ICRC was accused of having passed information on to Coalition forces' (cited in Terry 2011, 175).

48. The picture is further complicated by the fact that not only military but also FBI, CIA, and US Drug Enforcement Administration officials dress in civilian clothing.

49. The leaflets were distributed in Zabul Province by US forces in 2004; see MacAskill (2004).

50. For example, in another incident which caused wide-spread concern amongst NGOs, US forces entered and took over the offices of Afghanaid in Kamdesh District, undermining the careful relations that had been established over several years in this conflict-affected district.

51. The ANSO was formed with European Community Humanitarian Aid Office and Swiss Agency for Development and Cooperation funding. It is hosted by ACBAR as an independent project, with offices in Kabul, Mazar-i-sharif, Herat, Jalalabad, and Kandahar. It provides security updates; daily alerts and location-specific advisories; organization and personal-security advice; analysis of security incidents; and coordination of security-related training (with RedR). In early 2011, the ANSO

registered as an NGO in the UK and was renamed the International NGO Safety Organization with the aim of replicating the ANSO in other countries.

52. The director of the ANSO stated in 2010, 'The armed opposition are in many cases acting more like a government in waiting and see a convergence of interests in maintaining NGO services' (cited in IRIN 2010b). Also, Taliban spokesman Qari Yusuf Ahmadi stated in March 2010 that the insurgents would ensure security for aid agencies in the areas under their control, provided that aid workers liaised with them (IRIN 2010c).

53. Interestingly, a Counterpart survey of Afghan civil society organizations found that security was not a priority concern for them.

54. The core document governing Taliban conduct is the *Layha*, first issued in 2006 and updated in 2009 and 2010. The revisions marked a discernible shift towards greater openness to aid organizations, though the extent to which policies laid out in this document were implemented in practice varied widely from area to area (Jackson and Giustozzi 2012). For a useful analysis of the content of the Layha from a legal and humanitarian perspective, see Munir (2011).

55. An informal analysis of the group in August 2005 found that it served as a channel for communication but was hampered by poor NGO participation and follow-up; that GOA participation was almost non-existent; that military rotation and sometimes indifference hindered the institutional development of the relationship; that different institutional cultures rendered exchanges 'somewhat challenging'; and that meetings focused on operational issues as opposed to larger policy considerations (cited in Karp 2006).

56. Can be accessed at: https://docs.unocha.org/sites/dms/Documents/Guidelines%20Afghanistan%20%20v.%201.0%202008.pdf

57. Subsequently, ACBAR developed a concept note submitted to the UN, ISAF, NATO, and the NGO community for a 'Contact Group' composed of a small number of NGO directors to meet with the ISAF deputy commander – a more informal concept, with lower expectations than the Civil Military Working Group – and the group began to meet, with a focus on preserving humanitarian space.

58. Several sets of guidelines have been produced and disseminated in order to clarify the roles of the military and civilian actors. These include international guidelines on CIMIC, most notably the Oslo Guidelines: The Use of Military and Civil Defence Assets in Disaster Relief (1994, updated 2006/07, available at http://www.refworld.org/docid/47da87822.html) and the MCDA Guidelines: The Use of Military and Civil Defence Assets to Support United Nations Humanitarian Activities in Complex Emergencies (March 2003, available at http://www.coe-dmha.org/Media/Guidance/3MCDAGuidelines.pdf).

59. Although generous pledges were made by donors at the Tokyo conference in 2012, the commitments still constitute a 35% decrease from current levels of aid.

60. One example of this is the DFID's creation of a large civil-society funding programme called in Dari 'Tawanmandi' [Strengthening].

References

ANSO. 2012. 'Quarterly Data Report. Jan 1st – Dec 31st 2012'. Kabul.

Atmar, H., S. Barakat, and A. Strand. 1998. "From Rhetoric to Reality. The Role of Aid in Local Peacemaking in Afghanistan." Report of a workshop held in York 12–15 June 1998, University of York, Responding to Conflict, BAAG, UK.

Ayrapetyants, A., et al. 2005. "Afghanistan Civil Society Assessment. Initiative to Promote Afghan Civil Society (I-PAC)." 3 June, *Counterpart*, Washington.

Baitenmann, H. 1990. "NGOs and the Afghan War. The Politicization of Humanitarian Aid." Third World Quarterly 12 (1): 1–23.

Barakat, S., S. Deely, and S. Zyck. 2010. "A Tradition of Forgetting': Stabilisation and Humanitarian Action in Historical Perspective." Disasters 34 (S3): 297–319.

Barfield, T. 2012. "Afghans Look at 2014." Current History 111 (744): 123–128.

Barnett, M. 2005. "Humanitarianism Transformed." Perspectives on Politics 3 (4): 723–740.

Beath, A., F. Christia, and E. Enikolopov. 2012. "Winning Hearts and Minds through Development? Evidence from a field experiment in Afghanistan." Policy Research Working Paper 6129, Washington: World Bank.

Benelli, P., A. Donini, and N. Niland. 2012. Afghanistan: Humanitarianism in Uncertain Times. Boston, MA: Feinstein International Centre, Tufts University.

Boege, V., B. Brown, K. Clements, and N. Nolan. 2009. "Building Peace and Community in Hybrid Political Orders." Journal of International Peacekeeping 16 (9): 599–615.

Boone, Jon. 2011. "Does the US Military Want Afghanistan to Get Even Nastier?." *The Guardian*. 8 December.

Borchgrevink, K., and K. Berg Harpviken. 2010. "Afghanistan: Civil Society Between Modernity and Tradition." In Civil Society and Peacebuilding. A Critical Assessment, edited by T. Paffenholz, 235–557. New York: Lynne Reinner.

Chandler, D. 2010. International Statebuilding. The Rise of Post Liberal Governance. London and New York: Routledge.

Chandrasekaran, R. 2012. Little America. The War within the War for Afghanistan. New York: Knopf.

Cooley, A., and J. Ron. 2002. "The NGO Scramble. Organisational Insecurity and the Political Economy of Transnational Action." International Security 27 (2): 5–39.

Cornish, S., and M. Glad. 2008. "Civil-Military Relations: No Room for Humanitarianism in Comprehensive Approaches." Security Policy Library, Norwegian Atlantic Committee, 5–2008.

Cowper Coles, S. 2011. Cables from Kabul: The Inside Story of the West's Afghanistan Campaign. London: Harper Press.

Crombe, X. with M. Hofman. 2011. "Afghanistan: Regaining Leverage" In *Humanitarian Negotiations Revealed. The MSF Experience*, edited by C. Magone, M. Neuman and F. Weissman, 49–68. London: Hurst.

Donini, A. 1996. "The Policies of Mercy. UN Coordination in Afghanistan, Mozambique and Rwanda." Occasional Paper no. 22, Thomas Watson Jr Institute for International Studies, Brown University.

Donini, A. 2009. "Afghanistan: Humanitarianism Under Threat." Briefing Paper, March 2009, Feinstein International Centre, Tufts University, Boston.

Donini, A. 2010. "The Far Side. The Meta Functions of Humanitarianism in a Globalized World." Disasters 32 (supplement S2): S220–237.

Duffield, M. 2007. Development, Security and Unending War. Governing the World of Peoples. London: Polity.

Duffield, M. 2012. "Challenging Environments: Danger, Resilience and the Aid Industry." Security Dialogue 43: 475–492.

Egnell, R. 2011. "Lessons from Helmand. What Now for British Counterinsurgency?" International Affairs 87 (2): 297–315.

Farrell, T., and S. Gordon. 2009. "COIN Machine: The British Military in Afghanistan." Orbis 53 (4): 665–683.

Feichtinger, M., Stephan Malinoski, and Richard Chase. 2012. "Transformative Invasions; Western Post-9/11 Counterinsurgency and the Lessons of Colonialism." Humanity Spring 3 (1): 35–63.

Fishstein, P., and A. Wilder. 2012. "Winning Hearts and Minds? Examining the Relationship between Aid and Security in Afghanistan." Feinstein International Centre, Tufts University.

Goodhand, J. 2002. "Aiding Violence or Building Peace?: The Role of International Aid in Afghanistan." Third World Quarterly 23 (5): 837–859.

Goodhand, J. 2006. Aiding Peace? The Role of NGOs in Armed Conflict. Boulder, CO: Lynne Rienner.

Goodhand, J. 2010. "Stabilizing a Victor's Peace? Humanitarian Action and Reconstruction in Eastern Sri Lanka." Disasters 34: s342–s367.

Grant, Maj J. 2009. One Tribe at a Time. A Strategy for Success in Afghanistan. Los Angeles: Nine Sisters Imports.

Gregory, D. 2008. "The Rush to the Intimate. Counterinsurgency and the Cultural Turn." Radical Philosophy 150: 8–23.

Hillhorst, T., with M. Van Leewen. 2003. "Grounding Local Peace Organisations. A Case Study of Southern Sudan." Journal of Modern African Studies 43 (4): 537–563.

Howell, J., and J. Lind. 2009. "Manufacturing Civil Society and the Limits of Legitimacy: Aid, Security and Civil Society after 9/11 Afghanistan." European Journal of Development Research 21: 713–736.

ICVA. 2003. "Afghanistan: A Call for Security (Joint NGO letter)." 17 June 2003. Accessed 7 August, 2013. https://icvanetwork.org/doc00000995.html

International Development Committee. 2012. "Afghanistan: Development Progress and Prospects After 2014." Sixth Report of Session 2012–13.

IRIN. 2005. "Afghanistan: New Code of Conduct to Regulate NGOs." 31 May, 2005. http://www.irinnews.org/report/28641/afghanistan-new-code-of-conduct-to-regulate-ngos

IRIN. 2010a. "In Brief: Licenses of 172 NGOs in Afghanistan Revoked." 11 May, 2010. http://www.irinnews.org/report/89089/in-brief-licences-of-172-ngos-in-afghanistan-revoked

IRIN. 2010b. "Analysis: Humanitarian Space Easing in Afghanistan?" 8 July 2010, http://www.irinnews. org/printreport.aspx?reportid=89776

IRIN. 2010c. "Afghanistan: Taliban stops targeting NGOs, humanitarian agencies." 10 July.

IRIN. 2011. "Pay your taxes, government tells NGOs." Accessed February 25. http://www.irinnews.org/ report.aspx?ReportID=92045

Jackson, A., and A. Giustozzi. 2012. "Talking to the other side. Humanitarian engagement with the Taliban in Afghanistan." Humanitarian Practice Group Working Paper, ODI, London, Dec., 2012.

Jens, D., and M. L. R. Smith. 2010. "Whose Hearts and Whose Minds? The Curious Case of Global Counter-Insurgency." Journal of Strategic Studies 33 (1): 81–121.

Karp, C. 2006. "Leading by Example. Australia's Reconstruction Task Force and the NGO Civil-Military Relationship in Afghanistan." Security Challenges' 2 (3): 1–8.

Kazam, H. 2013. "Afghanistan's Middle Class: What Will Happen To Us When the US Leaves'?" The Christian Science Monitor, August 2nd, 2013, Accessed August 6, 2013. http://www.csmonitor. com/World/Asia-South-Central/2013/0802/Afghanistan-s-middle-class-What-will-happen-to-us- when-the-US-leaves

Keohler, J., and C. Zurcher. 2007. Assessing the Contribution of International Actors in Afghanistan. Results from a representative survey. Governance in Areas of Limited Statehood. Governance Working Paper Series No. 7. Freie Universitat, Berlin.

Killcullen, D. 2011. "Deiokes and the Taliban: Local Governance, Bottom Up State Formation and the Rule of Law in Counter-Insurgency." In The Rule of Law in Afghanistan. Missing in Inaction, edited by W. Mason. Cambridge: Cambridge University Press.

Luckham, R., and T. Kirk. 2013. "Understanding Security in the Vernacular in Hybrid Political Contexts: A Critical Survey." Conflict, Security & Development 13 (3): 339–359.

MacAskill, E. 2004. "Pentagon Forced to Withdraw Leaflet linking Aid to Information on the Taliban." The Guardian, 6 May, Accessed November 25, 2012. http://www.commondreams.org/headlines04/ 0506-01.htm

MacGinty, R. 2011. International Peacebuilding and Local Resistance. London: Palgrave.

Marsden, P. 2010. Afghanistan: Aid, Armies and Empires. London: I.B. Tauris.

Millar, G., J. van der Lijn, and W. Verkoren. 2013. "Peacebuilding Plans and Local Reconfigurations: Frictions Between Imported Processes and Indigenous Practices." International Peacekeeping 20 (2): 137–143.

Miller, D., and T. Mills. 2010. "Counterinsurgency and Terror Expertise: The Integration of Social Scientists into the War Effort." Cambridge Review of International Affairs 23 (2): 203–221.

Monsutti, A. 2012. "Fuzzy Sovereignty: Rural Reconstruction in Afghanistan, Between Democracy Promotion and Power Games." Comparative Studies in Society and History 54 (3): 563–591.

Mosse, D. 2004. Cultivating Development. An Ethnography of Aid Policy and Practice. London: Pluto.

Munir, M. 2011. "The Layha for the Mujahideen: An Analysis of the Code Conduct for the Taliban Fighters Under Islamic Law." International Review of the Red Cross 93 (181): 81–102.

Nicholds, N., with J. Borton. 1994. "The Changing Role of NGOs in the Provision of Relief and Rehabilitation Assistance: Case Study Afghanistan." Working Paper no 74, ODI, London.

'Nowhere to Turn. The Failure to Protect Civilians in Afghanistan'. 2010. A Joint Briefing Paper by 29 Aid Organizations Working in Afghanistan for the NATO Heads of Government Summit, Lisbon, November 19–20, 2010, accessed from: Accessed November 25, 2012. http://www.oxfam.org/ sites/www.oxfam.org/files/bn-nowhere-to-turn-afghanistan-191110-en.pdf

Paris, R. 2004. At War's End: Building Peace After Civil Conflict. Cambridge: CUP.

Petit, B. 2010. "The Fight for the Village. Southern Afghanistan 2010." Military Review, May–June: 25–32.

Pont, N. 2011. "Southern Afghanistan: Acceptance Still Works." Humanitarian Exchange 49, HPG, ODI, 6–8.

Poole, L. 2011. "Afghanistan. Tracking Major Resource Flows 2002–2010." Briefing Paper. Wells, Somerset, UK: Global Humanitarian Assistance, Development Initiatives.

Porter, P. 2009. Military Orientalism. Eastern War Through Western Eyes. London: Hurst.

Reiff, D. 2010. "How NGOs Became Pawns in the War on Terrorism." The New Republic, 3 August.

Roberts, N. 2010. "Spanning 'Bleeding' Boundaries: Humanitarianism, NGOs and the Civilian-Military Nexus in the Post Cold War World." Public Administration Review, March/April, 212–222.

Shannon, R. 2009. "Playing with Principles in an Era of Securitized Aid: Negotiating Humanitarian Space in Post-2011 Afghanistan." Progress in Development Studies 9 (1): 15–36.

Shurke, A. 2011. When More is Less. The International Project in Afghanistan. London: Hurst Books.

Simpson, Emile. 2012. War from the Ground Up. Twenty First Century Combat as Politics. London: Hurst.
Strand, A. 2010. "Drawing the Lines: The Norwegian Debates on Civilian-Military Relations in Afghanistan." Noref Policy Brief, 8, June.
Suhrke, A. 2012. "Waging War and Building Peace in Afghanistan." International Peacekeeping 19 (4): 478–491.
Terry, F. 2011. "The International Committee of the Red Cross in Afghanistan: Reasserting the Neutrality of Humanitarian Action." International Review of the Red Cross 93: 173–188.
UNAMA. 2013. "Afghanistan Mid-Year Report 2013. Protection of Civilians in Armed Conflict." Kabul, Afghanistan, July.
UN DPKO. 2008. "United Nations Peacekeeping Operations. Principles and Guidelines." New York: United Nations Department of Peacekeeping Operations, Department of Field Support.
USAID. 2008. "Civilian-Military Cooperation Policy." July 2008, Washington.
US Committee on Foreign Relations. 2011. "Evaluating U.S. Assistance to Afghanistan." A Majority Staff Report prepared for the Committee on Foreign Relations, US Senate, One hundred twelfth congress, first session, 8 June.
Wilder, A. 2009. "A Weapons System Based on Wishful Thinking." Boston Globe, 16 Sept. Accessed August 7, 2013. http://www.boston.com/bostonglobe/editorial_opinion/oped/articles/2009/09/16/a_weapons_system_based_on_wishful_thinking/
Wilton Park. 2010. "Winning Hearts and Minds in Afghanistan: Assessing the Effectiveness of Development in COIN Operations." Report on Wilton Park Conference 1022.
Wimplemann, T. 2012. "How have Aid Organizations Transformed Afghanistan? Towards a Research Agenda." Draft workshop paper, unpublished.
Zyck, S. 2012. "How to Lose Allies and Finance Your Enemies: The Economization of Conflict Termination in Afghanistan." Conflict, Security & Development 12 (3): 249–271.

A tale of two retreats: Afghan transition in historical perspective

Jonathan Steele

Freelance writer, London, UK

NATO troops are leaving Afghanistan in 2014, a quarter of a century after Soviet troops ended their occupation. How comparable are the two retreats, and will Afghans suffer fighting and destruction similar to what happened when foreign troops last left? Mikhail Gorbachev, who took the withdrawal decision in 1985, felt the war had become an expensive stalemate. The USSR opted to base its exit strategy on diplomacy and the idea that the Afghan government should pursue peace talks with its armed opponents. This emphasis on negotiations differs from Obama's policy, which remains predominantly military and rejects compromise with the Taliban. Obama and NATO claim progress on the battlefield and argue that combat duties can safely be "transitioned" to newly trained Afghans. But most Afghans are gloomy. Although they do not expect Kabul to fall to the Taliban, they believe that the insurgents will capture large parts of southern Afghanistan. Many also fear that ethnic tensions will grow throughout the country, perhaps leading to conflict between warlords from the Tajik and Uzbek minorities and the Pashtun majority.

The phasing-out of the large-scale presence of foreign troops in Afghanistan in 2014 comes a quarter of a century after the withdrawal of Soviet troops at the end of a similarly uncomfortable adventure. For a reporter and analyst who covered both occupations, two questions are key. How different is NATO's retreat from the Soviet one in February 1989? And can Afghans expect their future to be brighter than what they suffered in the 1990s?

The Soviet withdrawal took place a little less than 10 years after the original invasion. It was not a disorderly affair. More than 100,000 soldiers pulled out in less than a year, a much faster retreat than the United States or Britain are making, though it was less of a problem logistically since the Soviet Union still existed and had a land border with Afghanistan. Troops could just drive home.

As with the Americans and NATO, the main motivation for the Soviet withdrawal was war-weariness, but it was dressed up in public, just as it is being dressed up in the West today. NATO bases its retreat on a transition of security responsibility to Afghans, and much play is made of the NATO-funded programme to build up and to train the Afghan army and police, who had reached a combined total of 340,000 people by June 2013. Afghan rather than NATO troops were taking the lead in combat operations in 92% of the country (NATO Media Backgrounder 2013). This allows the front-bench spokespeople of all three main parties at Westminster, the Conservatives, the Liberal Democrats and the Labour Party, to claim that the retreat is not just "cut and run". It is – in the jargon – conditions-based. The Afghan army is increasingly able to defend the country on its own, so NATO can withdraw. General John Allen, the outgoing commander of the International Security Assistance Force (ISAF), was euphoric in his speech to troops in Kabul in February 2013, as he handed the baton to his successor: "Afghan forces defending Afghan people and enabling the government of this country to serve its citizens. This is victory. This is what winning looks like" (Afghanistan News Center 2013).

Yet everyone knew that the main reason the ISAF was leaving Afghanistan differed from the official one. After 11 years, the American, British and other Western electorates were fed up with the huge cost of the war in money and soldiers' lives and dubious of constant claims that the war had been a success. The annual Pentagon Report on Progress toward Security and Stability in Afghanistan in December 2012 drove a coach and horses through the argument that the Afghan army could fight on its own (US Department of Defense 2012). It said that only 1 of the Afghan National Army's 23 brigades could operate independently without air or other military support from the United States and NATO partners (Bumiller 2012). It was hard to believe that in the next 2 years the 22 remaining brigades would improve to the point of being able to act independently.

Western politicians would do well to take a leaf out of the Soviet book. When Mikhail Gorbachev took power in the Kremlin in March 1985, he had serious misgivings about the war in Afghanistan, which he had inherited from his predecessors and which was not going well. In December 1979 the Soviet politburo had justified the intervention with a narrative that foreshadowed the arguments of President Bush and Prime Minister Blair in 2001. Afghanistan was in the grip of a vicious regime; there was an ethical imperative, as well as an essential national security interest, to replace it with a more liberal government. But good intentions do not guarantee successful outcomes, and the Soviet occupation had met greater military resistance than Soviet leaders expected. Nor was it as easy to bring about reforms in Afghan governance and traditional social practices as they had hoped. By 1985, the prognosis was bleak, and Gorbachev faced a situation that was similar to Barack Obama's dilemma in January 2009 when he was sworn in as US president at a time when Americans could see the war in Afghanistan was not going well. Obama had opposed the war in Iraq, which he rightly described as a war of choice, but he called Afghanistan a war of necessity. Gorbachev never trapped himself in such positivistic terminology. On the contrary, in his first public statement on the Afghan war, just under a year after taking office, in an address to the 27th congress of the Communist Party of the Soviet Union he called it "a bleeding wound" (Gorbachev 1986). His private view was equally clear. Documents released since the Soviet Union's collapse reveal what Gorbachev felt on his very first day in office. The Afghan leader, Babrak Karmal, had come to Moscow for the funeral of Gorbachev's predecessor, and Gorbachev warned him that Soviet troops could not stay forever. Any ideas of bringing socialism to Afghanistan had to be put off for the distant future. Karmal's strategy had to change. The two governments had to look for a political outcome for the long-running war. Gorbachev recommended that Karmal start to expand the base of his regime and unite all of Afghanistan's "progressive forces". It was an abrupt and blunt message, but it was to remain the corner-stone of the Soviet Union's Afghan policy for the next six years. War-fighting had to play second fiddle to politics.

How did Gorbachev reach this view? The Soviet Union was a highly controlled society with a censored media and no independent information outlets of any kind. Under Leonid Brezhnev and the elderly rulers who followed him, very little reporting about the war was permitted. The issue was taboo. So there was no public pressure on Gorbachev to end the intervention, as there has been for Obama. But it would be wrong to imagine there was no pressure at all. We know from the diaries of Anatoly Chernyayev, Gorbachev's closest foreign policy adviser, that the Central Committee and the newspaper *Pravda* were receiving what Chernyayev described as a "torrent of letters" from ordinary Soviet citizens. They complained that the war was unnecessary and a waste of resources and Russian lives.[1]

How much effect these Soviet citizens' complaints had on Gorbachev is hard to gauge. But he was also under pressure internationally. In addition to the regular United Nations votes condemning the occupation, the United States vigorously opposed it, as did Chinese leaders, who told Gorbachev there could be no normalization of relations as long as Soviet troops remained in Afghanistan. In short, the war was undermining Gorbachev's efforts to present himself as a new type of leader committed to detente and an end to the Cold War. All these factors resonated with Gorbachev's instinctive sense that the Afghan war was a stalemate that offered no benefits to Moscow. When he consulted his military advisers, they agreed that the war could not be won. He asked General Mikhail Zaitsev, the top Soviet commander in Afghanistan, to examine the options for victory. Zaitsev reported that it would depend on closing the border with Pakistan, and this would require at least a quarter of a million extra troops. He described this as unrealistic. Gorbachev consulted other advisers and a few months later took the matter to the Politburo, the top Soviet decision-making body, with a recommendation that they formally endorse his strategy of pushing for the earliest possible Soviet withdrawal.

That was October 1985, but it was not until April 1988 that the Russians launched the definitive withdrawal of all their troops. Why did it take so long?

It was not that the Soviet military opposed the decision or dragged their feet. With minor exceptions, they were fully on board with the politicians' drive to cut their losses and get out. Indeed, far from recommending a "surge" of extra troops, as the US military did when Obama became president, the Soviet military offered no objections when Gorbachev decided to signal his intention to end the deployment of all 115,000 troops in Afghanistan by announcing an initial reduction of 15,000 in July 1986. They felt victory was a mirage. As Marshal Sergei Akhromeyev told the Politburo in November 1986: "After seven years in Afghanistan, there is not one square kilometre left untouched by a boot of a Soviet soldier. But as soon as they leave a place, the enemy returns and restores it all back the way it used to be. We have lost this battle."[2]

The main reason for the delay in implementing the Soviet withdrawal was that Gorbachev wanted to give the Afghan political leadership time to develop a strategy of national reconciliation. They were supposed to do this by making overtures, to see if the armed opposition, the *mujahedin*, would accept local cease-fires and join the government. This would require a major change of policy by the *mujahedin* and their foreign backers, in particular Pakistan and the United States. Fortunately for Gorbachev, the international framework for an agreement already existed. Even while Brezhnev was alive, the Kremlin had begun to tell Western leaders it was willing to withdraw under the right conditions. The UN Security Council appointed a mediator to work with the four parties, the Soviet Union, the United States, and the governments of Afghanistan and Pakistan. The basic formula was that the Soviets would withdraw their forces in return for an end to outside aid to the *mujahedin*. Afghanistan would return to being an independent non-aligned state, and there would be international guarantees that its neighbours would cease all interference.

While Brezhnev and his elderly immediate successors were in power, the negotiations failed to make any headway, since both sides preferred to try to improve their military positions on the ground. The change came when Gorbachev acceded to power and accepted that the war had reached stalemate. The Afghan party leader, Babrak Karmal, resisted. A year went by with no progress, until Gorbachev arranged for Karmal to be replaced in 1986 by Dr Mohamed Najib, who was more willing to adopt a policy of national reconciliation. It then took another year and a half to reach an agreement with the United States and Pakistan. In the meantime, Soviet forces largely confined themselves to protecting Afghan cities and keeping the main roads between them open. Soviet commanders were anxious to avoid any perception of defeat, so they continued to use helicopter gunships and fighter-bombers to try to block *mujahedin* infiltration from Pakistan and the build-up of *mujahedin* forces. But they no longer went on large-scale offensives as they had done in the early years of the war.

Some US politicians and analysts have argued that it was Reagan's supply of Stinger missiles to the *mujahedin* that led to the Soviet retreat. The Hollywood film *Charlie Wilson's War*, made in 2007, is based on this idea. With this shoulder-held weapon, a *mujahedin* fighter could bring down a Russian helicopter; this turned the tide of war. It is an exciting boys-with-toys notion, but it is a myth. Gorbachev's decision to withdraw from Afghanistan was made more than a year before the first Stingers were delivered to the *mujahedin*.

During the two-and-a-half years between the decision to leave and the start of the pull-out, the Soviet Union did what it could to build up and train Afghan forces. So there are some similarities with current NATO strategy. But the big difference is that the Soviet leadership never made this so-called "transition" the corner-stone of its policy, as NATO governments are doing. Building up Afghan forces was intended mainly to reassure the Afghan leadership that it was not being abandoned. Dr Najib, although more committed than Babrak Karmal had been to compromise with the *mujahedin*, was not at all happy with the Soviet decision to withdraw. He did everything he could to delay the process, in part because his efforts at appealing to *mujahedin* leaders for a political settlement were being undermined by Pakistan and the United States. They expected Najib's government to collapse as soon as the Russians left, and they saw no reason to prop it up.

Najib was particularly upset at the final terms of the agreement which the Soviet Union signed with the Americans in Geneva in April 1988. The original formula, that Russian troops would leave in return for an end to outside aid to the *mujahedin*, had been uncontested for years. But at the last minute the Reagan administration announced that this was unbalanced. If the Russians were going to continue sending weaponry and fuel to the Afghan army after their troops had left, then it was unfair not to allow the rebels to go on getting help. At one level it was a legitimate point, but to the Kremlin it came as a shock. It basically meant that the Soviet Union would be withdrawing its troops and getting nothing in return. It was even more of a shock to Najib. At a meeting with Gorbachev in Tashkent, he desperately pleaded for the Soviet leader to reject the US demands. But Gorbachev was in no mood to compromise. By this time he was heavily engaged in his perestroika reform process in the Soviet Union. The first rumblings of nationalism were starting to be heard inside the Soviet Union, in Kazakhstan, Armenia and the Baltic republics. He was involved in a whole host of negotiations with the Americans on nuclear arms control, and did not want a major clash with them over the Geneva talks on Afghanistan. Afghanistan had become a sideshow. Gorbachev told Najib that the decision to withdraw was irreversible and that it would be just 10 months until the last Soviet soldier left the country. The news was bitter, but Najib had to swallow it. So too did Eduard Shevardnadze, the Soviet foreign minister, who turned out to be the most hawkish member of the Politburo. Even after signing the deal on the Kremlin's behalf for a total withdrawal, he advised Gorbachev that 15,000 troops ought to stay behind in Afghanistan to boost Najib's regime.

The actual retreat did not go smoothly, as Rodric Braithwaite has explained in his magisterial book on the Soviet occupation, *Afgantsy* (2011). The main highway for the Soviet drive home from Kabul went close to the Panjshir Valley, the heartland of the powerful Tajik *mujahedin* commander, Ahmed Shah Massoud. In order not to create any provocations that might delay the Soviet retreat, Massoud had ordered his men not to fire on the departing Soviet convoys. He even negotiated a temporary cease-fire with General Valentin Varennikov, one of the top Soviet commanders. But the Soviet Defence Minister, Dmitri Yazov, and other hawks in Moscow disliked Massoud, not least because they feared his troops could quickly topple Najib's regime as soon as the Russians left. They were itching for a final punch at the man who had humiliated them so many times in the first years of the occupation. Najib urged them to act. In January 1989, less than a month before the deadline for all Soviet troops to leave, Soviet aircraft and artillery gunners launched a series of massive strikes on Massoud's forces in what was code-named Operation Typhoon. The attacks lasted for three days and caused an unknown number of civilian casualties. Massoud described the onslaught as cruel and shameful. General Sotskov, the Soviet military adviser in Kabul who opposed the attack, summed it up in stark terms: "Almost ten years of war were reflected as if in a mirror in three days and three nights of political cynicism and military cruelty" (Braithwaite 2011, 290).

On 27 January 1989 the Soviet withdrawal resumed, and by 15 February it was all over. Before turning to NATO's retreat, a brief recapitulation is helpful.

First, the Soviet withdrawal was motivated by an assessment that the war could not be won. The high cost of the war in lives and treasure played a major role, but one can presume that if the war had been moving towards victory the Kremlin would have considered it a reasonable and worthwhile price to pay. The crucial factor that prompted the withdrawal was the realization that there was no light at the end of the tunnel and no victory to be had. Second, this analysis was shared by the military commanders on the ground as well as the politicians in the Kremlin. The top brass offered no opposition to the policy laid down by the civilian leadership, nor was there any demand for a "surge" in Soviet troops to try to knock the enemy back, the one minor exception being Operation Typhoon, the three-day assault on the Panjshir Valley a few days before the withdrawal was completed.

Third, the withdrawal was to all intents and purposes total. After February 1989 a few para-troopers remained at the Soviet embassy in Kabul to guard it. Some Soviet specialists continued to operate the Afghan forces' most sophisticated equipment and train Afghans in its use. A few special forces remained in the northern provinces, close to the Soviet border, acting as intelligence spotters and occasionally taking aggressive action. There are no figures, but these residual forces probably numbered in the low hundreds. This is very different from NATO's initial plan to keep over 10,000 troops in Afghanistan after 2014 as a deterrent to the Taliban and a confidence-boosting measure for the government in Kabul. (In June 2013, a row over US support for the opening of a Taliban office in Qatar led to President Hamid Karzai suspending talks with the US over the size and role of residual NATO forces. In return, the US began to study the option of withdrawing all forces after 2014. At the time of writing, no decisions had been taken.)

Fourth, although the Soviet leadership trained, supplied and funded the Afghan forces, no effort was made to proclaim that progress in this field was the justification for the withdrawal, or that the Russians were able to pull out because Afghan forces had reached a high enough degree of strength and efficiency to permit a transition of security responsibilities.

Fifth, the justification for Soviet troops to leave, or what could be called the cover for the retreat, was political rather than military. Gorbachev argued that Dr Najib had started a process of national reconciliation which was designed to lead to a political settlement to end the war.

One final point needs to be made about the Soviet experience. It is sometimes argued that the Russians invaded Afghanistan because of concerns about the stirrings of Muslim resistance to communist rule in the neighbouring republics of Soviet Central Asia. It is further argued that their retreat was motivated by similar fears; in other words that the Soviet occupation of Afghanistan was fuelling Muslim resentment in Kazakhstan, Uzbekistan and the other southern republics and that a good way to reduce it was to withdraw. But there is absolutely no evidence to support these arguments. Nowhere in the transcripts of Politburo discussions or a wealth of other Kremlin papers does any leader refer to the issue of a Muslim resurgence in the Soviet Union. Furthermore, a high proportion of the Soviet conscripts who were sent to Afghanistan came from the Central Asian republics. Had there been any concern in Moscow that they would be infected by fundamentalism, the Soviet military would presumably have sent Russians, Ukrainians and

Balts instead. On the contrary, the Kremlin was confident that the people of Central Asia were largely secular and moderate, with no interest in the vision of creating Islamic states.

The withdrawal of NATO forces takes place in a very different context. Unlike the Russians who decided the war could not be won, Obama and Cameron and their top brass never deviate from a recital of progress on the battle-field. They may describe it as "fragile", "gradual", or even "still reversible", but the message is always that NATO and its Afghan allies must crack on and keep the progress going. It could be that this optimism is for public consumption and that privately they know the war is hopeless. I have sometimes heard junior officers in the British Army expressing very gloomy views about the war. A considerable number have chosen to leave the army. But at senior level, there seems to be a sincere perception that things are improving. Take the experience of Sherard Cowper-Coles, who served as ambassador in Kabul and later as the foreign secretary's special representative for Afghanistan and Pakistan. Few British civilians have had as many private conversations with a string of different British commanders in Afghanistan. In his entertaining book *Cables from Kabul*, Cowper-Coles (2011) recounts anecdote after anecdote about British generals' unwavering view that the Taliban were losing.

A similar delusion is prevalent within the American military elite. In the summer of 2011, a leak revealed that CIA analysts had assessed the state of the war, district by district, and reached the conclusion that it was stalemated. But their view was countered by General David Petraeus, the outgoing US commander in Afghanistan, as well as General John Allen, who was taking over from him. They each added a note to the CIA report to say they disagreed with the intelligence agency's findings (Ignatus 2011).

Obama behaved in similar fashion. When he announced in June 2011 that he would start withdrawing troops the following year, he boasted to the American public, "We are starting this drawdown from a position of strength. The tide of war is receding" (Obama 2011). Five months later, the CIA description of the war as a stalemate had won support from the other 15 US intelligence agencies. The annual National Intelligence Estimate for 2011 declared that any gains made from the surge of extra US troops over the last two years were unlikely to be sustainable because of pervasive corruption and incompetence among Afghan government officials and the tenacity of Taliban fighters operating from safe havens in Pakistan (Landay and Youssef 2012). There is truth in their perception, though it carries a strong whiff of putting all the blame on Afghans and Pakistanis for what is essentially an American failure.

By mid-2013, there was still no evidence that the tide of war, in Obama's phrase, was really receding. The United Nations Assistance Mission reported a 23% rise in the number of civilian casualties over the first 6 months of the year compared to 2012, with the majority caused by the increased use of improvised explosive devices (IEDs) (UNAMA 2013). In February, the ISAF reported that the number of Taliban attacks in 2012 was exactly the same as in 2011. Their findings were particularly embarrassing for the ISAF because only a month earlier it had announced that Taliban attacks were down by 7% in 2012. Leon Panetta, the outgoing defence secretary, greeted the alleged drop with a triumphant boast: "Overall the Taliban are losing" (Burns 2013). A month later, the ISAF sheepishly explained there had been a clerical error and the number of Taliban attacks had remained steady after all. With egg still on their face, the ISAF announced shortly afterwards that they would stop publishing statistics on Taliban attacks.

The picture was no different when Taliban strength was examined geographically rather than arithmetically. The United Nations Mission in Afghanistan has an independent take on what is happening in the country. It reported in the summer of 2012: "In the southern, southeast and eastern regions of Afghanistan, entire districts and in some cases, almost entire provinces are, to varying extents, controlled by Anti-Government Elements" (UNAMA 2012, 16).

If unfounded optimism is the hallmark of current Western military and governmental thinking on Afghanistan – a far cry from Soviet realism – then a second major difference in the two retreats is their scale. The Russians continued to pump weapons, supplies and huge sums in aid to the Afghan government after 1989, just as the Americans plan to do after 2014; on the other hand, the troop withdrawal was to all intents and purposes total. This allowed Najib's government to present itself as fully sovereign. In contrast, if NATO keeps forces in Afghanistan after 2014, this will maintain the image, and reality, of an occupation. As long as there are several thousand foreign troops in the country, the Kabul government will find it hard to make a convincing case that it is truly independent. The Taliban will almost certainly continue to refuse to negotiate with it.

Obama's line on negotiations differs sharply from Gorbachev's. Although the US president occasionally pays lip service to the notion of a political settlement, his priority is predominantly military. In a few places, American and Afghan commanders have contacts with insurgent forces to discuss cease-fires, but these are limited and local. They are not publicized as a key element in Washington's exit strategy, which continues to trumpet the enhanced capabilities of the Afghan security forces as justification for the US retreat. In terms of his own electorate, the strategy of handing combat responsibility to Afghans may be good politics for Obama. In Afghanistan, it is a recipe for continuing the war, only with Afghans rather than Americans or British doing the killing and the dying.

What, then, is the best estimate of what will happen as Western troops pull out? Can lessons be learnt from Dr Najib's experience in 1989, when he found himself without foreign troops?

Dr Najib had taken some precautions once he saw that the Soviet departure was unstoppable. He changed his name to Najibullah to give it a more Islamic flavour. He also changed the national flag to add more green, the traditional colour of Islam. But these cosmetic changes were hardly going to be enough to win *mujahedin* support, and some Soviet officials expected his army to collapse quickly. "We're not going to be able to save Najibullah anyway", Anatoly Chernyayev, Gorbachev's foreign policy adviser, told Shevardnadze in a phone call in January 1989 (Braithwaite 2011, 289). In Washington, officials were eagerly looking forward to regime change. Peter Tomsen was a senior State Department official, and his book *The Wars of Afghanistan* (2011) is one of the best insider sources on the American relationship with the *mujahedin*. In March 1989, Tomsen was appointed US special envoy to the *mujahedin*. "We expect the resistance will soon be in Kabul and you will have the inside track to be our next ambassador", his boss told him (Tomsen 2011, 266).

I was one of the many Western journalists who flocked to Kabul as the Russians pulled out. We found Western governments doing all they could to create panic. They ordered their diplomats to leave, citing the risk of a collapse of law and order. The British chargé managed to get himself filmed by a TV crew pulling down the flag in the embassy compound and telling the reporter he was not sure whether he would even get to the airport safely before the storm broke. But if he and his Western colleagues really thought the *mujahedin* were about to capture the city, why not watch it and be on hand to work with their friends, the new rulers? In reality, the withdrawal order was just one more step in the long propaganda war that the West ran against the Soviet occupation (and Soviet foreign policy in general) as part of the Cold War.

With the Russians gone in spite of his desperate pleas for them to stay, Najibullah sought to exploit the new situation by presenting himself as a proud nationalist. "We only took help from one infidel. The other side has taken help from several infidels",[3] he told a group of tribal elders. What he meant was that the *mujahedin* had been aided by the United States, Britain, China and other non-Muslim countries, while he had needed only the Russians. Shown on TV, the elders remained impassive and inscrutable. A few days later he received me for an interview. At 43, Najibullah was a strong, broad-shouldered man who lived up to his nickname, the Ox, except that he had soft hands and long fingers more suitable for a piano player. He described himself as a nationalist, not a communist, and said he wanted good relations with East and West. At one point he even criticized the Soviet military presence in his country as a "diktat". It was a remarkable word, given that he still relied heavily on Moscow's help, but the aim was to project himself to his compatriots as a man who stood up to foreigners. Geoffrey Howe, Britain's foreign secretary, had recently called on Najibullah to resign. I asked Najibullah for his reaction. "If Howe made such a proposal and I resigned, wouldn't that be interference in Afghanistan's internal affairs? We've released ourselves with so much difficulty from one diktat, and now you're trying to impose another one on us", he replied (Steele 2011, 136). It made him sound like some kind of liberator.

But then, Hamid Karzai behaves in a similar way. To Washington's annoyance, the Afghan president regularly criticizes US policy and military activity, particularly when civilians are killed. He has even accused US troops of colluding with the Taliban. It is the classic dilemma of the client: dependent yet at the same time defiant.

Najibullah's effort to make a virtue out of the absence of any foreign troops in Afghanistan achieved some success. It persuaded a few local fighters that, as the Soviet infidels had left the country, *jihad* was no longer necessary. As a result, some commanders reached cease-fire agreements with the government. Najibullah also used money to persuade others to stop fighting. But the leadership of the largest *mujahedin* groups remained firmly committed to overthrowing him. Only the Shia groups were willing to cease fire, while just one of the seven main Sunni leaders, Pir Gailani, had started talks with Najibullah's people. The rest wanted military victory. With triumph imminent (as they saw it), the rivalries between the Peshawar-based factions intensified. Not only did they fail to co-ordinate their activities on the battlefield but there were armed clashes between them. The fundamentalist groups led by Gulbuddin Hekmatyar and Jalaluddin Haqqani (whose forces are still in action on the battle-field, this time against the Americans and the Karzai government) made a major mistake. They launched a battle to capture the city of Jalalabad, only 30 miles from the Pakistani border. The attack had Pakistan's support, but for guerrillas to launch a frontal attack on a conventional army is always risky. They were badly beaten and lost hundreds of men. They also committed a public relations blunder, and a war crime, when they executed 70 captured Afghan government soldiers. The atrocity had the effect of making the government army more determined to resist.

Victory in Jalalabad gave Najibullah a huge boost. Peter Tomsen recalls it as a disaster for US policy (Tomsen 2011, 279) and explains how hard he had to fight to maintain covert US assistance to the *mujahedin* and overcome resistance in the State Department. But he was successful, and he explicitly confronts one of the oldest of Afghan myths (Tomsen 2011, 454). This is the claim that the West walked away from Afghanistan after the Russians left. It is constantly repeated by US and British officials, as well as media commentators, usually in the context of saying "We have learnt the lesson and we won't do it again." In fact, Western government funding for civilian projects in *mujahedin*-controlled areas during the Soviet occupation had been minimal. Most aid consisted of military supplies, and this continued unabated for three more years. So too did US efforts to undermine Najibullah's attempts to hold peace talks with the *mujahedin*, particularly with the moderates who supported the return of the exiled king.

When Najibullah eventually fell in April 1992, it was not because the *mujahedin* were capturing territory and advancing on Kabul. The reason was that the Russians stopped sending him arms, cash and fuel. Yeltsin had supplanted Gorbachev. There was regime change in Moscow, and the new government had lost interest in supporting old Soviet clients. Angola and Cuba, too, found themselves cut off. In Afghanistan, as supplies dried up, Abdul Rashid Dostum, an Uzbek and one of the key government generals in the north of the country, switched sides and joined Massoud's Tajik *mujahedin*. Other generals defected, and the Afghan army quickly fell apart. Against most predictions, Najibullah had survived in power for more than three years after

Soviet troops left. During that time, Kabul continued to remain largely immune from attack. For many of today's residents of Kabul, at least those of a certain age, those years were the best they have ever known. There was security, and some development, and none of the humiliation which goes with seeing foreign troops and contractors rumbling down your streets and forcing traffic to the side.

What signposts does all this offer for the coming years? Will the Kabul government be able to survive? I spent two weeks in Kabul in November 2012, discussing these questions with a variety of Afghans, some who supported the current government, but most who were independent. I found the general mood to be apprehensive at best, gloomy at worst. The least pessimistic were well-educated young people whose adult lives had coincided with the relative stability of the last decade in the capital. But even they shared the expectation of a sharp worsening in the economy as the tens of thousands of jobs that depended on the foreign military and diplomatic machine disappear. They realized that money for aid projects and for support to Afghan non-governmental organizations would wither. The new rich were getting their money or their families to Dubai and other Gulf states. Many Kabulis were putting their houses on the market so as to acquire the cash to leave. Used-car agents reported more sellers than buyers.

What of the politics? Will there be compromise, collapse, or continuing conflict? By compromise I mean a peace agreement that provides the Taliban with a share in power at national and provincial levels. Very few Afghans see any prospect of that as long as the Taliban maintain that they will not negotiate with the Kabul government.

Karzai's mandate as president runs out in the spring of 2014. Some analysts have speculated that he will declare a state of emergency so as to prolong his rule, but Karzai has repeatedly promised to leave on time. Others believe that one of his two brothers will run for office. Whoever emerges as the strongest candidate for the 2014 elections (whether they are part of the Karzai family or not), the next government is likely to resemble the present one: a coalition of powerful Tajiks and some anti-Taliban Pashtun. The Taliban will probably be no more willing to negotiate with it than they are with Karzai.

The only powers that could alter this are Pakistan and the United States. There is a widespread feeling in Kabul that Pakistan holds the key. If Pakistan were to alter course and support a negotiated end to the war, the landscape would change. Pakistan would then put pressure on the Taliban leaders whom it hosts and urge them to come to the table with a reasonable set of demands. The Afghan High Peace Council thought they detected Pakistani movement in this direction in the autumn of 2012 when they persuaded Pakistan to release some two dozen Taliban leaders from prison. Around the same time, the High Peace Council produced what it called a peace process road map to 2015.[4] It was a surprisingly radical document that called for taking the Taliban off the various international terrorism lists and making it safe for their representatives to travel to meet negotiators. But it was later reported that about half the freed leaders returned to the insurgency. Moreover, the Taliban rejected the road map and repeated their long-standing refusal to talk to the Afghan government. Another negative sign was a statement from Pakistan's Ulema Council, the country's highest religious authority, in February 2013. It had been due to join its counterpart, Afghanistan's Ulema Council, at a meeting in Kabul where both sides would condemn suicide bombing and call on the Taliban to embrace negotiations. Instead, Maulana Tahir Ashrafi, the chairman of Pakistan's Ulema Council, pulled out of the meeting and issued a statement praising the Taliban's fight against the US and the Afghan government as *jihad*. His colleagues followed suit.

Hopes were raised with regard to a change of heart in Islamabad after Nawaz Sharif won the May 2013 elections. During the campaign, he had supported the idea of Afghan peace talks. But in his first months in office he did little to seriously promote them. The same was true of the United States, though there were two brief flurries of excitement. Early in 2012, the Obama administration seemed to have agreed to release five Taliban leaders from the Guantanamo Bay detention camp and support the opening of a Taliban office in Qatar, where preliminary talks could be held with US diplomats. But the release was blocked in the US Congress, and it took more than a year before Washington agreed to let the Taliban open the office; but this also turned out to be no breakthrough. When Karzai raised objections, the US delayed sending any officials to talk to the Taliban in their newly opened villa.

What of the second scenario – the collapse of the Afghan government after 2014? If that means a Taliban military victory and the fall of Kabul, few of the people I spoke to expected it. Although the Taliban were strong in the southern and eastern provinces, the so-called Pashtun Belt, they were not thought to be strong enough to capture Kabul. What people in the capital felt was more feasible was a resurgence of the armed struggle between warlords which they suffered between 1992 and 1996.

I spoke to Hanif Atmar, who served in Karzai's two administrations, latterly as interior minister until 2010. He is one of the few members of the new elite who has inside experience of the Najibullah period. He still refers to the late president as Dr Najib. He outlined the contrast with two decades ago. "Once Soviet troops were gone", he told me, "there was no justification for *jihad*. There was an imperative for defending the homeland. Dr Najib had a powerful party which held people together, and there were functioning state institutions. He had a better-equipped army than the current one and a sizeable air force, while we have little today." If Karzai is weaker than Dr Najib, then so too in Atmar's view are the Taliban. He believes they have less support in the rural areas than the *mujahedin* did. In 1989, and indeed throughout the Soviet occupation, resistance came from Tajiks and Hazaras as well as from Pashtun, whereas the Taliban are overwhelmingly Pashtun. There is little armed resistance to the ISAF and the Kabul government from other ethnic groups today.

The main danger, as Atmar saw it, came from the continuing significance of ethnic identity in Afghan politics, including in the Afghan army. The Tajik and Uzbek leaders of the old *mujahedin* factions still control private militias and dominate key units in the army. "The Afghan National Security Forces have not been built to resist factional and ethnic influences. Generals are not appointed on merit, but retain loyalty to factional interests", Atmar said. The point was well illustrated in February 2013 in a BBC Panorama report on the Afghan National Police in Sangin in Helmand. The police are fully armed and operate from fortified bases, almost on a par with army troops (BBC 2013). In addition to the woeful incompetence, drug-taking and reluctance to fight which the programme showed, it was noticeable that the bulk of the troops were Tajiks from northern Afghanistan. They did not know the local area or speak Pashto. In many ways they were just as foreign as Western troops. But whereas US and British troops are retreating in good order, the Tajik units in the Afghan National Army and Police would probably retreat in a rush.

So the most likely scenario after 2014 is that the government will lose more and more territory in the Pashtun Belt as the Taliban and Hezb-i Islami, the other main insurgent group, move in. This seems to underline the futility of all the effort the US and Britain have put into Helmand and Kandahar over the last six years. Take Wardak, a province just 40 miles from Kabul. The Taliban have stepped up assassinations of government officials and anyone associated with Western-supported non-governmental organizations there. They moved into the province's northern districts after the Americans abandoned their forward operating bases and pulled back towards the provincial capital, Maidan Shahr. Hundreds of families also fled there.

Mirwais Wardak runs an NGO called the Peace Training and Research Organization, which conducts regular surveys of rural Afghans. As his name suggests, he originates from Wardak province. In a report prepared in July 2011, when it was already clear that the ISAF would be ending its activities within the next few years, he wrote, "On the ground we are already seeing the response from both local communities and insurgent elements as the battle for territory and tangible assets increases. Political manoeuvring is increasing across the country and existing power holders appear to be consolidating their own.... Far from bringing unity, the current trends appear to be encouraging increasingly uncompromising positions vis-a-vis ethnicity and political parties, and tension is growing" (PTRO 2011).

As the ISAF withdraws, the balance sheet of the American and British military's record is far from glowing. Karzai shocked the British government in February 2013 when he said, in a *Guardian* interview, "In 2002 through 2006, Afghanistan had a lot better security. When we had our own presence there, with very little foreign troops, schools were open in Helmand and life was more secure" (Guardian 2013). A similar point had been made to me in Kabul by an engineer, Sayed Jawed, a Helmandi who has worked on archaeological restoration in the province for many years. He spoke of British and American failures in Helmand in elegiac terms. "After 2002 people were waiting eagerly for development. Even between 2004 and 2006, Lashkar Gah and central Helmand were safe and there were no Taliban. But the Brits and Americans came with a military face, using helicopters and tanks that reminded people of the Russians. Instead of spending money on education and women's rights in central Helmand they were flying to remote areas to combat the Taliban. They lost hearts and minds and now you cannot buy them", he said. "When the Brits and Americans leave, the Taliban will establish themselves in the weakest areas and the Afghan National Army won't have the ability to stop them." He is not even sure whether the army will be able to protect Lashkar Gah, the provincial capital, or Gereshk, Helmand's second-largest town.

No one can be sure how the security landscape will change over the next year or two. But it is a safe bet that as US and British troops withdraw, the Taliban will move forward. In some rural districts, local elders may make deals with the Taliban to accept their rule. In others there may be cease-fires between the Taliban and the national army. In yet others, fighting will continue. In Afghanistan, all war is local. After trillions of dollars of tax-payers' money have been spent and thousands of US, British and Afghan lives have been lost, Afghanistan will end up hopelessly fractured.

But one thing will be different this time. In Moscow, when their army's retreat was over, almost every Russian politician accepted that it had been a disaster to use ground troops in a foreign country's civil war. In Whitehall and Westminster, a similar view of the West's latest Afghan experience is not yet the norm.

Acknowledgements

This essay is based on my Anthony Hyman Memorial Lecture, given at the School of Oriental and African Studies, London, 7 March 2013. For the Soviet occupation, I relied on Soviet officials' diaries and memoirs, transcripts of Soviet Politburo documents released after the fall of the USSR in 1991, and material gathered during my four reporting visits to Kabul in the 1980s for the *Guardian* newspaper, London. My analysis of the NATO occupation is based on several visits since 2001, including an embed with British forces in Helmand in 2010. I was in Kabul most recently in November 2012. A fuller account of my work on Afghanistan is available in my book, *Ghosts of Afghanistan: The Haunted Battleground* (2011).

Notes

1. Quoted in the George Washington University National Security Archives: http://www2.gwu.edu/~nsarchiv/NSAEBB/NSAEBB272/Doc%202%201985-04-04%20Chernyaev%20Diary.pdf
2. http://www2.gwu.edu/~nsarchiv/NSAEBB/NSAEBB272/Doc 5 1986-11-13 Poliburo on Afghanstan.pdf

3. Contemporaneous notes taken by Steele's translator from Najibullah's TV speech, quoted in Steele (2011, 134).
4. Text available at http://www.foreignpolicy.com/files/121213_Peace_Process_Roadmap_to_2015.pdf

References

Afghanistan News Center. 2013. 10 February. Available at http://www.afghanistannewscenter.com/news/2013/february/feb102013.html

BBC. 2013. "Panorama: Mission Accomplished? Secrets of Helmand," broadcast BBC One, Monday 25 February. http://www.bbc.co.uk/news/world-us-canada-21547542

Braithwaite, R. 2011. *Afgantsy*. London: Profile Books.

Bumiller, E. 2012. "Pentagon Says Afghan Forces Still Need Assistance." *The New York Times*, December 10. http://www.nytimes.com/2012/12/11/world/asia/afghan-army-weak-as-transition-nears-pentagon-says.html?_r=1&

Burns, Robert. 2013. "Officials confirm attacks by Taliban not down after all: Coalition says it erred in reporting drop of 7%." *Boston Gobe*, February 27. http://www.bostonglobe.com/news/nation/2013/02/27/taliban-attacks-not-down-after-all/8TJLPXiWl8tRoqBxAKUJtJ/story.html

Cowper-Coles, Sherard. 2011. *Cables from Kabul*. London: HarperPress.

Gorbachev, Mikhail. 1986. "Political Report of the CPSU Central Committee to the 27th Party Congress." Moscow: Novosti Press Agency Publishing House.

Guardian (The). 2013. Hamid Karzai interview: full transcript. February 4. http://www.theguardian.com/world/2013/feb/04/hamid-karzai-interview-full-transcript?INTCMP=SRCH

Ignatus, D. 2011. "Can Petraeus handle the CIA's skepticism on Afghanistan?" *The Washington Post*, September. http://articles.washingtonpost.com/2011-09-01/opinions/35272935_1_david-petraeus-centcom-commander-cia-analysts

Landay, J. S., and Nancy A. Youssef. 2012. "Intelligence report: Taliban still hope to rule Afghanistan." *McClatchy*, January 11. http://www.mcclatchydc.com/2012/01/11/135574/intelligence-report-taliban-still.html#.UgTOJFOLosk

Nato Media Backgrounder. 2013. Afghan National Security Forces, June, http://www.nato.int/nato_static/assets/pdf/pdf_2013_06/20130604_130604-mb-ansf.pdf

Obama, B. 2011. "Remarks by the President on the Way Forward in Afghanistan." Washington, DC: The White House Office of the Press Secretary. http://www.whitehouse.gov/the-press-office/2011/06/22/remarks-president-way-forward-afghanistan

PTRO (Peace, Training & Research Organisation). 2011. *Conflict Analysis of SCA activities in Afghanistan*. http://www.ptro.org.af/images/stories/ptro_docs/Conflict%20Analysis%20of%20SCA%20activities%20in%20Afghanistan.pdf

Steele, Jonathan. 2011. *Ghosts of Afghanistan*. London: Portobello.

Tomsen, P. 2011. *The Wars of Afghanistan: Messianic Terrorism, Tribal Conflicts, and the Failures of Great Powers*. New York: Public Affairs.

UNAMA (United Nations Assistance Mission in Afghanistan). 2012. Afghanistan – Mid-Year report 2012, Protection of Civilians in Armed Conflict. July. Kabul.

UNAMA. 2013. Afghanistan – Mid Year Report 2013: Protection of Civilians in Armed Conflict. July. Kabul. http://unama.unmissions.org/LinkClick.aspx?fileticket_EZoxNuqDtps%3d&tabid_12254&language_en-US

US Department of Defense. 2012. *Report on Progress Toward Security and Stability in Afghanistan*. www.defense.gov/news/1230_Report_final.pdf

March towards democracy? The development of political movements in Afghanistan

Antonio Giustozzi

War Studies Department, King's College, London, UK

Although the post-2001 period in Afghanistan has been hailed as a return to an earlier process of democratic opening that was interrupted in the early 1970s, a comparison of the development of political movements up to 1978 and then after 2001 highlights important differences. Until the late 1960s, Afghan political parties were mainly focused on influencing a supposedly enlightened leadership towards faster modernization of the country. Their disillusion was beginning to push them towards the development of forms of organization which could mobilize sections of the population on their behalf, even if tentatively so. Little comparable effort was noticeable after 2001, when parties big and small, seemed intent mainly on securing a position from which to develop a following based on the distribution of patronage. It could be argued that the availability of resources on a large scale following international intervention in 2001 drove the Afghan political system in a direction quite different from the path which was initially embarked upon in the 1960s.

Introduction

This article focuses on two interrelated aspects of political movements in Afghanistan. The first concerns their efforts to reach out to the wider population, using their organizational development as an indicator of that intent. If there has been a 'march towards democracy' in Afghanistan, we should expect to find traces of it in the organizational structures of political movements. The second aspect is the source of organizational models and the extent to which they are adapted to local circumstances. In other words, the article analyses the degree of success that the import of 'political technology' had in the Afghan context.[1] Political movements may lack the tools required to mobilize widespread support or rely on less-than-optimal tools. It is not a foregone conclusion that a political movement would naturally and quickly develop adequate organizational tools. Political movements may suffer from insufficiently developed organizational structures, but also from hypertrophic ones, or simply from inadequate structures dictated by external ideological influences and by the inability to adapt imports to local circumstances or to specific constituencies. The inability to develop organizationally is, therefore, only one aspect of the problem; political movements may also aim too high in their organizational development.

The process of developing such tools is long and tortuous and often unsuccessful, as the analysis and comparison in this article of pre-war and post-2001 developments shows. To borrow from Astri Suhrke's (2011) recent book, perhaps 'more' can be 'less' in relation to the exporting of political technologies to host countries. Arguably, political movements which fail to adapt imported political technology to the context where they operate show that they are less interested in mobilizing grass-roots support than in attracting external support. This article, therefore, tries to establish where Afghan political movements have been situating themselves along the continuum from 'grass-roots mobilization' to 'reliance on external support'. Although this article features a general discussion of the organizational development of political parties in Afghanistan, it is particularly concerned with the debate and policies of the liberal and progressive parties – expressions of the educated middle class, which political scientists tell us should develop into the backbone of the democratization process (Moore 1966). The key question posed by this article is: Was the inclusion of competitive elections in the 2001 Bonn Agreement (United Nations 2001) the resumption of a path lost in the 1960s, or the result of ideas and practices of post-conflict reconstruction imported to Afghanistan from abroad?

Despite the focus on elections and democratization after Bonn, comparatively little analytical work has gone into studying political parties in Afghanistan. This article aims to partially fill this gap by providing an overview of the organizational development of Afghan political movements, in chronological order, starting from their very origins in the early twentieth century. The next section discusses the first overt signs of radicalization among political movements in the 1940s and 1950s, in a context where parties and movements were still mostly focused on influencing a purportedly enlightened leadership towards faster modernization of the country. This is when the debate about reaching out to the wider population started. In the 1960s and 1970s, the pattern of political-party development bifurcated. The elite started showing some interest in political parties, and experiments started to develop 'chain of transmission' structures which could have helped improve the efficiency of government. At the same time, among the political intelligentsia, the debate about 'reaching out' was still going on and becoming more sophisticated, relying increasingly on imports of political technology from abroad. After exploring these debates and actual changes in political organization, the third section turns to post-2001 developments in the organization of political parties. The conclusion draws a comparison between the pre-1978 and the post-2011 developments, highlighting important differences with respect to how political parties related to the wider population.

Arguably, political movements exist mainly for one or more of the following purposes:

- Representing interests
- Mobilizing support for a particular agenda or leadership
- Coming together for collective action of peer groups
- Connecting government and population – that is, acting as the 'chains of transmission' of directives from top to bottom, but also as 'feedback mechanisms' from the bottom to the top, allowing the leadership to remain informed about the feelings of the base and of the general population

To achieve these purposes they can use a varying set of strategies, of which electioneering is just one. Depending on its aims and strategies, a political movement faces the challenge of organizing in the way most appropriate to further them. A political movement purely dedicated to representing interests may not require a very sophisticated structure. In Gunther and Diamond's (2003) framework, the elite-based party represents a model well adapted to this purpose, as it emerged in Europe during the eighteenth and nineteenth century. As this paper will show, however, the 'circles' which are the form of organization of elite-based parties can also be adopted by moderate opposition and non-elite groups, as long as their main concerns are to represent interests and to lobby on their behalf. It is also worth asking whether representing interests and lobbying require a party format per se; a political movement might not feel the need to form a party at all, but remain an informal political network.

The Gunther and Diamond model also struggles to account for 'chain of transmission' parties, which are unsatisfactorily lumped together with other 'elite-based parties'. 'Chain of transmission' parties are focused on the purpose of transmitting orders from top to bottom, as in a government bureaucracy. Typically, they operate in one-party regimes, or in regimes where little serious political competition exists (and hence mobilizing support is not a priority). They have to be distinguished from clientelistic organizations, whose purpose is instead to mobilize support. This article will discuss several examples of 'chain of transmission' parties in Afghanistan.

Undoubtedly, the ways political movements structure themselves are not just dictated by their aims. As Duverger (1981) famously argued, parties adapt to their constituencies. Liberal parties, for example, were shaped through this adaptation to make middle-class participation attractive. Imposing a Leninist model of organization on a constituency of farmers would (and did) turn out to be very difficult, as that model required a disciplined and regimented membership, historically the product of mass industrialization. However, it has to be stressed that such adaptation only takes place through trial and error, or even an evolutionary process wherein parties which do not adapt to potential constituencies simply perish (Mingst 2008). Political movements often shop around for organizational models, imitating each other or taking inspiration from foreign countries; but the success of imitation is always dependent upon adapting a model to varying circumstances.

Early origins: from enlightened courtiers to conspirators

The origins of political movements in Afghanistan can be traced back to the small 'circles' (or as the Anglo-Saxon world calls them, 'clubs') of the intelligentsia and the more educated section of the aristocracy that King Habibullah (r. 1900–1919) tolerated around the court. The two circles which formed initially (Ikhwan-e Afghan [Afghan Brotherhood] and Jan-nesaran-e Islam [Islamic volunteers for sacrifice] – to which some authors add the so-called *ghulam-bachagan* [group of courtiers' sons]) were the victims of a bloody crackdown in 1909 (Ruttig 2006). In 1911, reformist circles were allowed to reorganize. These small circles were mostly busy trying to lobby the king, first in favour of a constitution and later in favour of entering the First World War on the German-Turkish side (with the aim of reclaiming Pashtun lands taken over by the British). His son and successor, Amanullah, was initially much closer to these groups, and as a young man he had even joined one of the largest, Anjuman-e Seri Jawanan-e Afghan (Secret Association of Young Afghans).

The Jawanan-e Afghan had their moment of glory from 1919, when Amanullah became king following the assassination of his father, King Habibullah. However, with a membership of a few hundred, the Jawanan-e Afghan was not in a position to provide Amanullah with much more than advice and a chain of transmission and feedback with the country's small educated middle class. Moreover, once he was in power, the support base of the Young Afghans started fragmenting. A group of aristocrats led by Nadir Khan, who had earlier sympathized with the Jawanan, drifted away. They judged Amanullah's reforms too radical and disliked the pro-Turkish inclination of the new monarch. Others left as the reforms proceeded. In 1928, Amanullah tried to turn the Jawanan into a more structured political organization, Istiqlal wa Tajadud (Independence and Modernization), in order 'to gain the support of the masses for his reform' (Marwat 1997, 175), but the effort never took off. Amanullah's own tendency to micromanage and his disinclination to rely on allies and collaborators emptied the new party of much of its intended meaning. In any case it was too late, as the civil war which brought down Amanullah was about to start (Marwat 1997; *Afghanistan Past and Present* 1982). By 1929, Amanullah was out of power and with the support of key tribes Nadir Khan had replaced him.

Throughout this phase, the political circles did not feel the need for a mass base; they were betting everything on their ability to lobby more or less enlightened despots towards modernizing a conservative society. Hence the 'club' model described by Duverger was a suitable model of political organization.

The 1930 *Loya Jirga* [Grand Council] showed significant support for the pro-Amanullah elements, with republican sentiment also going strong, while resistance by the Jawanan-e Afghan continued for some time in the shape of a terrorist campaign. Although small in scale, that was the first example of 'armed struggle' inspired by a political movement in Afghanistan (as opposed as to a local community revolting against Kabul) (Marwat 1997).

The underground activities of the so-called 'Republicans'[2] and the Jawanan lapsed because of the repression that followed the 1934 assassination of King Nader Shah by a sympathizer of King Amanullah. However, their activities resumed in 1939, as dramatic events in Europe excited public opinion in Afghanistan as well. Afghanistan's growing contacts with the outside world and its economic difficulties probably both contributed to this re-emergence of the political opposition. Most of the activity of the underground Jawanan-e Afghan during this period was through the press, to which their secret members contributed extensively; the same was true of the 'Republicans'. This was a first step towards reaching out to wider sections of society, namely the educated class which had begun developing in Habibullah's time (Marwat 1997; Boyko 2010). However, the progressive reformers did not even try to establish a base among the wider population. The reason is probably that following the 'conservative revolution' which had overthrown Amanullah in 1929 they had little faith in the possibility of mobilizing support for the cause of progress and modernization among the villagers.

The 1940s–1950s: from moderate to radical reformism

The decision of Prime Minister Shah Mahmud to try reconciliation with the liberal opposition in 1946, when he set free all the incarcerated supporters of Amanullah, created a new environment in which political movements had an incentive to adopt new tools to reach out to the public. Initially, the remnants of the Jawanan and of the 'Republicans' shifted towards collaboration with the government in order to promote reforms and modernization. Developments in the region (the independence of India-Pakistan; Iran's reforms) also contributed to a revival of enthusiasm for reform (Marwat 1997). Wish Zalmiyan [Awakened Youth] formed initially as a coalition of political circles gathering intellectuals, state officials, and businessmen around a liberal agenda of reform.[3] In 1948, the coalition of circles gave itself a programme and started organizing regular meetings. It was the main expression of the growing dissatisfaction with the absolute monarchy and, at the same time, of the new perceived opportunities to engage with the government (Saikal 2004).

This new phase of reform saw attempts by members of the elite to co-opt or exploit the new liberal groups which were emerging and, more generally, to consider the advantages that the establishment of a political party could bring to the different factions of the establishment. The infighting within the royal family was a major factor in accounting for this opening to the middle class. The leading innovator within the ranks of the royal family, Prince Daud, established a link with Wish Zalmiyan, using Pashtun nationalism as the main bait to attract them to his side. In 1950, facing resistance, he also launched his own party, sometimes referred to as Hezb-e Demokrat-e Milli (National Democratic Party) but better known as Klup-i Milli or National Club (KM from now on), as a more amenable alternative to a Wish Zalmiyan reluctant to allow Daud the kind of control he wanted (Farahi 2004).

The KM never tried to hide its establishment-party character; indeed, it was popularly known as the 'Ministers' Party'. The party tried to coerce the MPs to join, but a hard core of 11 opponents of the government, mostly linked to Wish Zalmiyan or its splinter groups, refused. Its provincial branches were led by the governors, or in any case government officials. Despite the incentives and the coercion, the KM did not grow to match even the size of the already modest membership of Wish Zalmiyan. By 1951, in Kabul, where it sucked in a number of high-ranking government officials, the KM counted on 260 members, while all the provincial branches of Kandahar, Herat, Mazar-e-Sharif, and Balkh lagged far behind, the largest of them having just 40 members. The party never had much vitality and did not produce even a single periodical publication; outside government circles, it attracted only a few members of Kabul University's student union and some members of Wish Zalmiyan. Finally in 1953 even the KM was shut down, by Daud, when he was appointed prime minister (Boyko 2000).

The liberal circles campaigned actively in the relatively free 1949 elections and overall elected around 50 members of parliament; Wish Zalmiyan elected 5, who then proceeded to gather another 11 around themselves in a National Front inspired by Mossadeq's example in Iran (Ruttig 2006 and 2011). Their membership remained in the low hundreds, so they did not develop mass-membership structures. They must therefore have relied on the political networks of prominent members to reach out to notables and other opinion makers around the country. In 1948, as political debates started intensifying, Wish Zalmiyan had already started fragmenting, as some more radical circles left over its collaboration with sectors of the establishment. The moderates continued to prefer lobbying the government for reform, hoping that an enlightened despot would accept their advice. The radicals started looking around for ideas on how to mobilize wider support for their cause, to increase pressure on the monarchy.

It is important to point out that the split occurred along ethnic lines, with most Shiite and Tajik circle leaders going their own ways, to form Hezb-e Khalq (People's Party) and Hezb-e Watan (Fatherland Party), respectively. In the north of Afghanistan, another group, Ittehad wa Taraqi (Unity and Progress), started forming separately among Uzbeks, with an Uzbek ethno-nationalist agenda, and after the end of the parliamentarian experiment reportedly started drifting towards the idea of an armed uprising. Perhaps this tendency towards ethnic alignments derived from the reliance on personal networking for political mobilization – the circle leaders tended inevitably to network among their ethnic kin. Wish Zalmiyan, too, increasingly adopted an agenda centred on Pashtun nationalism. We can also see this ethnic drift as a result of the first efforts to seek a mass base for these parties, even if the numbers getting mobilized remained pretty small: at the peak of its organizational power, Wish Zalmiyan had 816 members in 9 cities. The 'circle' or 'club' organization remained the standard for this period (Ruttig 2006).

It is also worth mentioning the emergence of the first Islamic political organizations during this period. Seyyid Ismail Balkhi was the first to start proselytizing, mostly among Shiites, with some kind of Islamic Republic in mind, already in 1943, although his party Irshad (Exortation) only formed a few years later. Shortly afterwards, Mawlana Faizani, the founder of Hezb-e Tawheed (Unity Party), started doing the same among Sunnis. Both were relying on their personal religious networks to reach out to people (Edwards 2002; Ruttig 2006). Little is known of these parties, but they cannot be described as 'Islamist' in the sense now common among political scientists, of political movements arguing for the political leadership of secularly educated Muslims as opposed to the leadership of clerics.

With the government crackdown of 1952, Prime Minister Shah Mahmoud brought the short liberal phase to an end. Such was the monarchy's fear of political parties that it did not even want to keep the KM in existence (Marwat 1997; Boyko 2000; Iskandarov 2004; Ghobar 2004 (1967); Ruttig 2006).

The 1960s–1970s: 'Government parties' without the approval of the ruling elite

From 1963 onwards, divisions within the royal family once again allowed political parties to organize openly as the king, Zahir Shah, opted to launch what would become known as the decade of democracy and sacked his cousin, Prime Minister Daud (Marwat 1997). Even after the 1964 constitution recognized the right of political parties to exist, their fate was to linger in limbo, without a party law which would have regulated their registration, role, and functioning. When the parliament turned out to be difficult to control and unable to deliver the desired results after the 1965 elections, the ruling elite increasingly resorted to manipulating the electoral process. Even for the first elections of 1965, the government invited or encouraged trusted individuals to run for seats which could be vulnerable to a challenge from the opposition.[4] The ruling elite might even have seen elections as an attempt to calm critics of the system, while buying time for important decisions to come – but it developed cold feet as numerous and vocal radical groups appeared (Ruttig 2013).

This attitude had important consequences. The political movements avoided committing themselves fully to an electoral strategy, and their organizational policies remained fluid – while the 'government parties', which some key allies of the monarchy were trying to organize, were themselves left stranded, never being given access to the resources which could have allowed them to build large clienteles. Among the forces aligned with the establishment, several attempts to launch parties took place, including Wahdat-e Milli (National Unity), Hezb-e Qanun-e Asasi (Party of the Constitution) and Hezb-e Ittehad-e Milli (National Unity Party) (Dupree 1971c; Marwat 1997; Farahi 2004; Iskandarov 2004; Rishtya 2005).

Nor did other attempts under the monarchy to form governments (or in any case 'moderate' parties) get very far. The case of Maiwandwal and his 1966 Hezb-e Mutaraqi Demokrasi (Progressive Democratic Party) was a noteworthy one, in that it tried to go a bit farther than just positioning itself as a recipient of government patronage to be redistributed. It was meant to be a reformist ('social democratic') group, gathering educated people around a pro-Western agenda; it recruited mainly government officials but also liberal reformists who had been with Wish Zalmiyan. It was characterized by strong support for the monarchy, moderation, and sympathy for the US in foreign policy and at home. Maiwandwal had been one of the rising stars in the Afghan political scene since his tenure as prime minister in 1965–1967. His performance as a reformer had been impressive compared to his predecessors, but the monarchy was particularly keen to prevent the rise of a political organization which could appeal to local elites, as opposed to the small and isolated progressive and Islamist parties based among the nascent intelligentsia. For many within the royal family, Maiwandwal represented a more immediate threat than the more radical but marginal groups. Once Maiwandwal left the government, the party lost many of its members (Marwat 1997; Farahi 2004; Iskandarov 2004). This was the most consistent experiment in the formation of a moderately progressive party, but it ended with Maiwandwal being murdered and his supporters dispersed after Daud's return to power in the 1970s.

After the establishment of the republic in 1973, a group within President Daud's inner circle also started thinking in terms of establishing a 'government party', in opposition to the pro-Soviet leaning of many in the Daud government in its early years. The leading figure in this effort was Sayed Waheed Abdullah, who with the help of a number of prominent supporters of Daud effectively launched the Hezb-e Enqelab-e Milli (HEM, Party of the National Revolution) in 1976. Daud's attitude to the party was ambivalent. In the internecine fight among supporters of Daud, Daud increasingly leaned on the group gathered inside the HEM. Despite high-sounding statements, however, he never invested significant resources in it or tried to develop it into an effective 'chain of transmission' (Sharq 2000; Slinkin 2003).

The HEM was conceived as a component of a party-state framework presided over by the president of the republic. One of its key roles would have been to select the future president, but it never achieved a mass base, nor did it work particularly hard to achieve one. Its activities consisted mostly in meetings within the ministries of interior, foreign affairs and frontier affairs. In practice, it was organized around a few leading personalities, who relied on their personal contacts and efforts to recruit more followers (Farahi 2004).

With the partial exception of Maiwandwal's, these parties did not really try to propagandize or to reach out to society; most members were government officials who were primarily trying to further their own careers within the government. By contrast, more radical groups had greater incentives to seek out support outside the government and the ruling elite. This combined with frustration with the monarchy's policies among important sections of the middle class, creating fertile ground for new forms of political organization and mobilization; and these were imported from abroad, chiefly from Iran, the Soviet Union, Egypt, and Pakistan, with some contributions from China and Western Europe as well.

The 1960s–1970s: from circles to cells

Until 1965, the mostly leftist and liberal circles proliferating around the country were all organized in more or less the same way: small discussion groups (*mahfel*) in the cities, gathering to determine what to do, to discuss theoretical texts, and to debate the issues of the day. About 30 such *mahfel*s existed in the early 1960s, only among the ranks of the pro-Soviet left (Bulatov 2003). At the centre of each was usually a charismatic intellectual. These groups had mostly originated in the old liberal circles of the 1940s–1950s; in some cases the continuity is obvious as the leading figures were the same. In other cases, it was more a matter of taking inspiration from Wish Zalmiyan and the other groups. While some genuinely liberal-democratic discussion groups continued to exist, the new generation of intellectuals was attracted by more leftist ideas. A contradiction soon emerged between their radical aims and the organization they were relying on to achieve those aims. Nur Mohammad Nur, who ran for Parcham [Flag] in the 1969 elections in Kandahar and later became a close associate of President Karmal in 1980–1986, recounts how he had to meet the elders in the villages, using his family connections, in order to carry out his campaign.[5] The *mahfel* could only rely on the members' personal networks to reach out to the population, which meant being dependent on the good will of these elders. And such good will was not often extended, given the increasingly radical agenda of these groups and the government's efforts to lobby the elders against the reformers. The debate over the organizational aspect of politics therefore became a crucial one at this stage. The members of these circles were becoming gradually aware that the *mahfel* was not a viable form of organization, as far as mobilizing wider support went.[6]

The Marxist literature imported from Iran, the Soviet Union, and Pakistan introduced the 'cell' to the Afghan intelligentsia, part of which decided to build a party around this notion. In the absence of an industrial society and the discipline that it brings with it, the cell as a form of organization could have only a limited audience in Afghanistan. It did not even particularly suit the very intelligentsia which enthusiastically adopted it, even if it did allow for a rather effective infiltration of government institutions in order to influence government policy. Initially, none of the pro-Soviet leftists envisaged a conquest of power through the cell organization. They advocated a 'national democratic' coalition, bringing together reformist elements of the elite, of the merchant classes, and of the intelligentsia, with whatever support the tiny working class could provide. (There were about 40,000 factory workers at the beginning of the 1970s.) The only significant portion of society which the cell as a mode of organization suited turned out to be the armed forces; as we shall see, the consequences would be far reaching. (*Aktual'nyi*, 48).

When in 1964 the various leftist circles started discussing the formation of a national party, other sources of influence and inspiration were present. On the left, a number of *mahfel*s were influenced by Maoist literature. Among these Maoists a discussion was going on concerning the formation of a proper Communist Party, with revolutionary aims. It is not clear, however, whether the organizational implications of such a move were clear to those debating the issue. Another influential personality who gathered *mahfel*s around his person was M.G. Ghobar; his was the most moderate of all these groups, rejecting any reference to socialism or to ideas imported from the Soviet Union. Yet another *mahfel* leader, whose ideas were not dissimilar from Ghobar's, was Siddiq Farhang. In the end, a pro-Soviet majority of *mahfel*s coalesced in the launch in 1965 of Hezb-e Demokratik Khalq (HDKh, the People's Democratic Party). The HDKh started establishing party organizations throughout the country, spreading from the cities where *mahfel*s had already been present, to the towns and the district centres, and then to some of the villages. The *mahfel*s were formally abolished, and the cell-based party structure became the adopted model; one can see here an external ideological influence, as well as a reflection of the uncertain legal status of all Afghan political parties.[7]

However, the *mahfel*s did not really disappear. Party leaders were chosen from among the *mahfel* leaders, and factions within the party existed informally, often coinciding with the old *mahfel*s or coalitions of those. The party soon started fragmenting again into rival factions. The two main ones (Khalq [People] and Parcham) were in fact coalitions of old *mahfel*s; smaller factions, like that of Tahir Badakhshi, who left the party in 1968, often consisted of a single *mahfel*.[8]

At the other end of the political spectrum, the Islamist movement was beginning to take its first steps, aiming to counter leftist mobilization, particularly on the Kabul University campus. The organization and constituency of Islamists and leftists were therefore remarkably similar: circles (called *halqa* [circle] by the Islamists) bringing together students and teachers. Even if, unsurprisingly, the Islamists were particularly strong in the theology faculty, they were soon recruiting effectively in the technical and sciences faculties as well. From 1970, the Islamists spread their recruitment efforts to the high schools in Kabul, and then in the provinces, and adopted the cell organization (*hasta*). In the Islamist organization, however, the circles were left in place, as an intermediate layer between the cells and the so-called *hauza* [district], an organizational layer, which in turn was connected to the central committee or, in the case of the provinces, to regional and provincial councils. The nature of the *halqa*, however, changed from the original discussion groups into a component of a hierarchical structure incorporating the heads of a number of cells. At about the same time, they also started organizing themselves as a national political movement and looking for ways to mobilize people beyond the educational system, including government officials. Like the leftists, the Islamist activists would contact neighbours and colleagues at work and in education and slowly try to politicize them, eventually revealing themselves as members of a political movement (Olesen 1995; Edwards 2002).

As the model of parliamentary politics was rapidly becoming discredited, political organizations also started splitting over the stance to take towards it. Centrists and some of the leftists continued to hope that parliamentary politics would eventually resume its path. They were preparing themselves for the 1973 elections – which never took place, because of Daud's coup, as we shall see below. However, the radical left (Khalqis, Maoists) and the Islamists either never had any faith in parliamentary politics or were losing it by 1970 (Bulatov 2003; Saikal 2004).

The transition from monarchy to republic following Daud's coup in 1973 did not represent a sea change per se in terms of political organization. In fact, the republic had a distinctly monarchical character, with Daud seemingly very solidly at the top. Again Daud displayed mixed feelings, at best, towards the option of relying on political parties as institutions capable of managing state–society relations more effectively than a patrimonial system, not to speak of the role of parties in the selection of the elites. Daud's prompt separation from the reformist groups in 1953 should already have intimated that in 1973 he saw the political organizations which were emerging in those days more as a vehicle to achieve short-term aims (the conquest of power, getting the modernization programme to take off) than as a way to restructure the political system (Saikal 2004).

For some time after the coup, the leadership of Parcham seems to have believed that it could propose itself for the role of 'government party'. Daud initially collaborated with the Parchamis. About half of the members of Daud's first cabinet were linked to Parcham, according to Marwat (1997), although according to Soviet sources just three were actual members. Even before they started being purged in 1975, however, they never came close to playing the role of 'chain of transmission' between government and society which they would have liked (Marwat 1997; Slinkin 2003; Iskandarov 2004).

Daud's repression of other political parties (and from 1975 onwards of Parcham as well) prompted a debate within the opposition parties and movements over the merits of intensifying recruitment within the army, as a safeguard against a violent crackdown. Having seen (and helped) Daud repress the Islamists, the leftists soon started fearing that they would be receiving the same treatment.[9] The cell structure served them well in infiltrating the government and the armed forces.

Unable to influence the elite as much as they had hoped to, the middle-class-based political movements intensified their efforts to spread influence among the rural population or the lower classes. The left achieved some success in organizing factory workers; Parcham recruited them in Shiberghan, and a small splinter faction of the HDKh called Guruh-e Kar [Labour group] did so in Mazar-e Sharif and Pul-e Khumri, but according to a Russian source, 80% of workers' mobilization was the result of Maoist activities (Bulatov 2003). In any case, the working class was tiny, so even a greater degree of success would not have significantly altered the situation (Bulatov 1997).

Bitter debates over ideology, organizational forms, and personalities ravaged the pro-Soviet left, the Islamists, and even more so the Maoists, reducing their threat to the regime and making them unable to respond effectively to the repression unleashed against them under Daud's republic. The main debate concerned such options as infiltration of the armed forces, a popular uprising, or a guerrilla war as the best way to bring down the government. All of these were tried at different stages by the Maoists and the Islamists, with little or no success until 1978. Only later, when the international environment changed, did some of them become seriously viable (Giustozzi 2010; Ibrahimi 2012). Members of Badakhshi's *mahfel*, which splintered from the HDKh in 1968, toyed with the idea of dispatching activists to the villages, and to some extent even did so; they believed that educated activists living in the villages as teachers and doctors could gradually mobilize the rural population. In 1975, these groups, influenced by the 'new left' in the 1970s, experimented with organizing an uprising in a few districts of north-eastern Afghanistan, but failed (Mansur 1992; Plastun 2002; Iskandarov 2004). The Maoists of the Guruh-e Enqelab-e Khalqha-ye Afghanistan (Revolutionary Group of the People of Afghanistan, one of the main Maoist splinters) adopted the same policy of dispatching cadres to the villages, but the results were disappointing; eventually, many cadres, tired of life in the villages, decided to go back to the cities (Piovesana 2012).

The only groups that in the late 1960s and early 1970s found a clear focus for their organizational efforts were Parcham and, even more so, Khalq. Reinvigorated by the inclusion within its leadership of the young and dynamic Hafizullah Amin, the leadership of Khalq increasingly started seeing the army as the most likely vehicle to power and 'revolution'. Although the party would theorize about the army as an acceptable revolutionary force only later, Amin seems to have developed his ideas in this regard much earlier, perhaps even before being appointed by the leadership in charge of developing recruitment within the army ranks. After the Khalq's Saur military revolution in 1978, he would argue that the officers and soldiers of the army were the sons of the peasants and as such were handing power to the HDKh in the interest of the working classes. Whatever one might think of the merit of Amin's idea, that was a plan of action, and he implemented it effectively. In the late 1960s, the army organization of Khalq was almost non-existent (much smaller in any case than Parcham's), but in the following years Amin was very successful in attracting officers to the party.[10]

In sum, the efforts of political movements to reach out to the wider population took the path of underground organization, influenced by imported ideologies and by the disinclination of the ruling elite to give them the space to operate legally.

Political movements post-2001: patronage reigns

The Bonn Agreement was drafted by the UN in interaction with the Afghan delegations (Suhrke 2011, 164). Its first draft did not mention elections at all; they were inserted only later, after a suggestion made by the Iranian representative at the talks, endorsed by other international participants, in particular the Americans (Dobbins 2008). The inclusion must have pleased many UN officials, even if Brahimi (the Special Representative of the UN Secretary General) himself had doubts about the viability of free and fair elections in the prevailing conditions (Suhrke 2011).

The succession of conflicts and civil wars between 1978 and 2001 had radically changed the political landscape. A range of political organizations, some new and some with roots in the small groups active in the 1970s, emerged in 2001–2002 as major players on the political scene, not least because they commanded large armed constituencies. Alongside them, unarmed political parties also tried to reorganize. These were either successors to the old and fragmented HDKh, or small organizations which claimed to be liberal and democratic (Giustozzi 2007, 2009 and 2011). Although there was significant monarchist representation, democratic and progressive political groups played hardly any role in the formulation of the Bonn Agreement, having been excluded (after having been invited initially) (Ruttig 2009). What drove the Afghan groups in Bonn to graciously accept the idea of elections as a tool to regulate the selection of the post-2001 elites after the initial transitional phase is not known with certainty; however, the fact that the proposal came from an Iranian delegate might have contributed to reassuring them about their future ability to manage the process; they probably viewed elections as a rather innocuous way to keep the international community engaged. Whatever the case, the electoral process was taken seriously by most Afghan political factions, which soon started actively competing to achieve a good show in the various electoral rounds.

In this sense it can be argued that although the electoral process was neither fully free or fair, it was not a mere farce either, as there was a degree of competition, despite the many manipulations. Indeed, the acceptance of competitive elections reached the point where we may speak of 'electoralism' (defined as a view which holds that 'free elections are a sufficient condition of democracy'; see Linz and Stepan [1996, 4]). Exchanges of the author with party leaders, cadres, and activists in 2003–2011 suggested that few of them, even among the new 'democratic' parties, understood the demands of Western-style competitive elections in terms of institution building and voters' rights (see below). Accepting the electoral process became a way to signal acceptance of if not support for international intervention in Afghanistan; those who rejected the latter rejected elections as well. This applied not only to the Taliban but also to much of the hard left (mostly Maoist groups), which often split over participation in the elections.[11]

Like his predecessors up to 1978, President Karzai in 2002–2010 showed little interest in institutionalized political organizations as an aid to running the country. Karzai seldom hid his distrust of political parties. The Hezb-e Jamhuri-ye Afghanistan (Party of the Republic) was launched by sympathizers of Karzai in 2006, with the understanding that he would endorse it and turn it into a major pillar of his 2009 presidential campaign. The party was mainly run by moderate academics and a number of ministers, sometimes of dubious reputation; it attracted some support in its early days, probably because it was seen as likely to become a privileged source of government patronage. However, after some initial indications of interest, Karzai refused to join the party and distanced himself from it. The party leadership reacted by muting its support for Karzai and the government. Interest in the party rapidly petered out. Its initiator, Ismatay, an old pro-democracy activist, died, and in the end the party played no role whatsoever in Karzai's 2009 campaign.[12]

Moreover, Karzai did not just abstain from getting involved in the formation of a nationwide political organization, but actively worked (with American support) to prevent the formation of strong national political parties and kept the influence of organized political factions within the parliament limited (Wilder 2006; Elliot 2009; Suhrke 2011).[13] All this of course reminds us of the 1960s, when the royal family similarly tried to slow down the development of political parties. In addition, the political settlement at the base of the post-2001 system remained fragile, as external intervention dramatically altered the internal balance of forces but was not expected to last indefinitely or to favour particular groups and factions forever. This fragile political settlement and the weak or absent institution building notwithstanding, international endorsement of the electoral process as key to the selection of the political elite proved strong enough to focus the organizational efforts of mainstream parties and networks towards fighting elections. Their intent, however, appears to have been more to win legitimacy in the eyes of international actors than to do so in the eyes of the Afghan population, as will be seen below. For instance, individuals close to Dostum, the leader of Junbesh-e Milli-ye Islami (National Islamic Front, see below), refer to how keen he was to maintain good relations with the American embassy and how his support for the transition from violence towards electioneering was largely determined by this type of consideration.[14]

The mainstream organizations

The best-funded and largest political movements were all derived from the military organizations which had fought in the civil wars. They aimed at gaining leverage vis-à-vis Karzai and his inner circle, as well as a vis-à-vis foreign donors and military forces, in the expectation of a rebalancing of the distribution of the spoils at the centre (Giustozzi 2007, 2009). In both cases, but particularly in the latter, participating in elections appeared to be a good way to demonstrate their political relevance, as well as their willingness to play by the rules set out in Bonn.

Among the post-2001 parties, the most intense organizational effort was evident in Junbesh-e Milli-ye Islami (National Islamic Front), the party of General Dostum, which from 2002 to 2006 created village, district, and provincial organizations, mainly in the north-west of Afghanistan. The effort was to a large extent patronage-driven, as the party was dependent on Dostum's funds and foreign support to maintain the structure, and never rolled out a fee-raising and membership-card system to fund itself, despite the existence of plans to do so. Junbesh's popularity, mainly among Uzbeks in the north but also numbers of Tajiks and Turkmen, derived in part from its role in extending patronage. However, the party also acted as a vehicle for representing interests in northern Afghanistan, advocating greater representation in the state machinery and in the government for Turkic-speakers, as well as language rights and regional (northern) interests (Giustozzi 2009; Peszkowski 2012). These residual ideological and representation-of-interest concerns showed in the organizational eclecticism of the party:

- a patronage network based on notables directly connected to the leadership and running for election or recommended for appointments in the state machinery
- councils gathering notables at the various levels, with a sprinkling of party cadres at the highest (district and provincial) levels, the intent clearly being to represent local interests
- a militant branch (Jawanan-e Junbesh [Junbesh Youth]) gathering activists and intent on mobilizing the youth

From 2006 onwards, this patronage-oriented structure suffered from the failure of the party to successfully lobby with the central government to secure sufficient resources for redistribution. As a result, it entered a state of decay and lost much of its functionality. Even the more activist-based Jawanan-e Junbesh had to curtail its activities and reduce staffing levels dramatically. A resurgence in the activities of the Jawanan was noticed in 2012, probably following a new flow of funds from donors to General Dostum (Giustozzi 2012).

Similarly to Junbesh, Haji Mohaqeq's Hezb-e-Wahdat Islami-e-Mardum [Islamic Unity Party of the People], toyed with the idea of representing Hazara ethnic concerns and interests, and invested more effort in organizational development than its rivals, but once marginalized from the state apparatus and therefore from most sources of patronage, it faced a phase of organizational decay ('Political party assessment' 2006). Neither Junbesh nor Mohaqeq's Wahdat, however, responded to the patronage cut-off with a new focus on grass-roots mobilizations, opting instead for a variety of efforts to reopen patronage channels in Kabul or abroad (Giustozzi 2012).

The moderate Islamist Jami'at-e Islami (Islamic Society) also developed its organization somewhat after 2001, although more slowly than Junbesh. In practice, the party continued relying on a number of connected political networks to operate, feeding them with abundant patronage, but it also started opening offices and recruiting cadres to organize electoral campaigns and to advertise its presence; like Junbesh and Wahdat, the party therefore started taking on a representational role. The party offices, which existed in many districts in northern Afghanistan, were expected to operate as a chain of transmission, informing the local notables of the position of the party and hearing views from them. It is not clear to what extent this was effectively done, but such offices might have helped the fragmented leadership of the party assess what the mood was among its followers in the districts. The tendency of Jami'at to increasingly position itself as representing the interests of the Tajik minority might have been influenced by the party offices' picking up this type of grievance from the grass-roots (Giustozzi 2012 and 2009). Other 'mainstream' parties, such as Harakat-e Islami (Islamic Movement), also produced their mix of patronage distribution and representation of interests (International Crisis Group 2013).

The organizational development of the branch of Hezb-e Islami led by Faruqi and Arghandiwal was similar to that of Jami'at, except that it started even later (the party only managed to register in 2005) and had access to much more limited patronage to boost the party machinery. The party started opening offices nationwide.

Of all these parties it could have been said that 'vertical structures for communication, consultation and reporting are rudimentary' ('Political parties assessment' 2011). What is even more important to note is that while the network dimension of these political organizations was permanently active, the party structures described above (the offices) were active during periods of electoral campaigning, often closing after the elections.[15]

Political networks were built upon personal relations of various kinds. In the case of Jami'at or Hezb-e Islami, these were connections mostly developed through long years of battlefield comradeship. But the electoral system gave an incentive to prospective candidates to maintain and develop local connections:

> Political networks in rural Afghanistan are not strictly about resource or service provision. They are also about social relationships, marriages and religious obligations. (Coburn 2010, 4)

This was more obvious in the tribal areas of the country, although not exclusive to them. In areas where the accumulation of wealth in the hands of a few individuals had proceeded further, patronage dominated the formation of political networks to a much greater extent:

> MPs in Paktya are a part of tribal structures and in some ways are extensions of tribal networks into the central government, at least more so than in other areas. In Balkh, however, where Governor Atta Mohammed Noor is the dominant political force, an MP's ability to deliver resources is closely tied to that MP's relationship with him. One interviewee said: 'These days our environment is controlled by Atta. He is the only person. All of the MPs are controlled by Atta and they have a good relationship with each other. All of the high and beautiful buildings that you can see belong to them.' (Coburn 2010, 6)

So, even Jami'at and Hezb-i Islami members often cultivated local relations to the benefit of their electoral campaigns and, more generally, to spread their influence. Often these efforts trumped political ideology, particularly in the case of Jami'at, which attracted former leftists, particularly among Tajiks. Arguably, the coexistence of patronage practices and ideological or representative politics proved hard to sustain. Faced with party colleagues who made a quick and successful career by redistributing patronage, the more committed and ideological party activists soon faced demoralization and disenchantment. They started quitting politics altogether, or formed their own fringe organizations. An example of this with respect to Jami'at was the group of Hafiz Mansur, an Islamist intellectual who married political Islam and Tajik ethno-nationalism and eventually formed his own party after being disappointed with the corrupt ways of the mother organization.[16]

The 'democratic' parties

A host of smaller parties established themselves after 2001; these belonged to different political tendencies (mostly progressive or leftist, at least judging by their leaders) but had in common the aim of competing in the planned 2005 parliamentary elections (Ruttig 2006 and 2009; Larson 2009). In general, the way they organized was similar to the circles which had dominated the political scene in the 1960s, but some of these parties maintained the ambition to develop full-fledged party structures. A number of them sought advice about how to organize and campaign, either through individual contacts in foreign embassies or through the more systematic effort mounted by the National Democratic Institute (NDI), which started its activities in Afghanistan in 2003. The International Republican Institute was also active, but limited itself to developing the campaigning skills of the candidates.[17] The NDI provided training in election campaigning, election monitoring, campaign organization, and 'political party strengthening through 8 regional centres' ('Political party assessment' 2006, 2).

Few if any of these parties appear to have been proactive in developing the kind of grass-roots structures which would have allowed fund-raising (among other things), for example keeping records of active membership ('Political party...' 2006). This relaxed attitude towards grass-roots organization is symptomatic of a number of issues, ranging from the limited interest for representation through political parties to the poor economic conditions of most of the middle class. More importantly (from the perspective of this article), even the new parties generally appear to have been built on the expectation that, if successful, they would turn into patronage machines:

> Most of the members in party organizations expect the party to provide material benefits to its constituents, rather than viewing the party as an organization members need to support to realize their political and policy goals. It has also been widely reported that some parties are financed from

external sources or illegal sources, further inhibiting the growth of membership-based dues and fundraising. ('Political party...' 2006, 13)

The NDI itself recognized that most of the new and old parties' commitments to democracy and transparency might have been hollow, although it stated the belief that training and advice would help them overcome this problem. Although congresses were held by most of these parties, often this did not take place in an 'open, inclusive, and democratic manner', partly because parties mostly lacked accurate membership lists:

> The leadership of many parties developed a constitution solely to satisfy the requirements of the Political Party Law, without consulting party members in the drafting process or implementing the constitution's requirements after registration had been completed. ('Political party...' 2006, 13–14)

By 2010, the so-called 'new democratic parties' were floundering, having proved unable to obtain access to patronage resources or to establish solid roots in society (Larson; 'Political party...', 48). In practice, when the 'new parties' were operating at all in the rural areas they were resorting to the same practices as in the 1960s (reaching out to elders for support, or using their own social and political networks), or even those of their contemporary competitors like Jami'at-e Islami. A local cadre of one of the new parties admitted that he was contacting strongmen in the villages, including former militia commanders, to get voted in for the party in the 2010 parliamentary elections.[18] The Herat leader of another such party complained to the author in 2009 about the fact that Westerners had done nothing to help him and his party, despite their support for international intervention.[19] The difficult coexistence of patronage and ideological politics soon started dragging down the new parties as well, with the difference that these did not have the powerful patronage resources of mainstream parties. When the leader of Hizb-i Jamhurikhawan (Republican Party), one of the main new parties, obtained a job in the policy department of the presidency, the party lost much of its original dynamism.[20]

Is the drift towards patronage politics an indicator of a conscious Afghan resistance against ideological and representation-oriented political movements of any kind? The representation role that some predominantly patronage-based parties have been playing after 2001 has been discussed above. In addition it should be noted that there is evidence that radical parties have been recruiting heavily, in universities and high schools at least. For example, the illegal branch of Hezb-e Islami and its fronts are very strong in Nangarhar University and have a presence in all other universities (Giustozzi 2010). Hezb-ut Tahrir (Liberation Party, but in fact more akin to a proselytizing religious movement), which preaches the re-establishment of the Caliphate, has established strong positions in the pedagogical institutes of northern and north-eastern Afghanistan, and then in the high schools of these regions. It also has a presence in the universities.[21] On the left side of the political spectrum, the groups of activists found on the campuses were small in numbers and not very visible. In the provinces, it could well be that grass-roots activities belonged to Maoist groups rejecting the electoral politics carried out in the provinces.[22] This would seem to suggest that mobilizing support on a basis other than patronage was not altogether impossible. Therefore, other explanations have to be sought for the failure by both mainstream and 'new democratic' parties to do so, except in limited circumstances.

In the words of long-standing leftist activist Soraya Parlika, "To attract people you have to work hard, have public activities and offer them a future"[23] – which is exactly what the new parties largely failed to do. The activists had a weak presence in society, even in the university and colleges, where a natural constituency should have existed (Giustozzi 2010). The platforms of the new parties were bland – almost indistinguishable from one another – and attracted almost no attention, even if they passed the test of an international community anxious to marginalize radicals of all kinds.

Conclusion

The Afghan ruling elites have consistently been hostile to political parties as such, with the exception of the 1978–1992 period, when the HDKh tried to impose single-party rule. While this orientation is widely judged by analysts to have been a major mistake, it need not have impeded the development of political parties. After all, political parties in continental Europe did develop in an initially hostile environment; the result in most of Europe was political-party systems different from the North American or British ones, but not necessarily worse or weaker. Indeed, from the 1930s onwards a slow but steady tendency of Afghan political movements to develop roots beyond the educated class and the ruling elite has been noticeable. Although such efforts were not necessarily successful, we can see this string of failures as part of a process of trial and error, whereby parties and political organizations sought the right mix of ideological content and organization to build a wider constituency. This tendency accelerated considerably in the 1960s, as it gradually became clear that merely lobbying the government from the margins was not achieving much. Between the late 1960s and early 1970s the focus of the debate started shifting towards how to mobilize grass-roots political support. The failure of the government to deliver at least the basic guarantees of the rule of law drove much of that effort towards subversion, but that was not a foregone conclusion.

The post-Bonn phase of Afghan history could not simply have been the resumption of a pattern of development abandoned in the early 1970s. The environment changed dramatically because of the emergence of large, well-resourced, patronage-oriented, and armed political organizations like Jami'at and Junbesh. From the perspective of the smaller progressive and liberal parties, however, the situation had not changed that much compared to the 1960s. They were, once again, the junior players in the political system, even if it was no longer dominated by a centralized and rather cohesive state apparatus.

What is striking is that, after 2001, debates within the small progressive parties on how to mobilize support among the population were focused on either participating in the elections or distributing patronage. The only exceptions to this were some efforts to represent specific (mostly regional or ethnic) interests. This might not be surprising if it had been confined to the political organization that emerged out of the civil-war military factions, which in any case were quite discredited in 2002; but it affected even the old and new political parties with no armed wings. The predominant obsession of party leaders of all hues appears to have been how to secure a portion of the large patronage resources which suddenly became available with international intervention. Although a causal link cannot easily be established, it seems at least a plausible working hypothesis that the availability of plentiful patronage resources represented a major disincentive for the political movements to develop organizational tools for mobilizing society. This is not due to any incompatibility between the distribution of patronage and organizational development; it is due to the fact that developing a strong organization is a complex and time-consuming effort yielding only uncertain results. The work of party activists, to convince people to support a party or movement with the promise of long-term (but always uncertain) gains, is not an easy one. Buying votes on the basis of the distribution of patronage is much easier – as long as resources are available.

The premature focus on participation in the electoral process contributed negatively to political-party development by discouraging progressive and leftist parties from sponsoring radical causes or expressing deep popular grievances. Already for the 2004 elections these parties had without exception adopted moderate, hardly distinguishable platforms, which had little resonance beyond some middle-class circles. However, the grievances existed in vast sectors of the population, and they would be picked up by extremist groups, which had no interest in elections at all. 'Electoralism' was clearly imported into the Afghan political scene; there was little indication of any endogenous demand for elections as such in 2001–2002, and little understanding of the demands of free and fair electioneering. However, the intervening powers and international organizations turned the electoral process into the cornerstone of the political process and appear to have pushed Afghan political actors towards believing that their access to patronage resources would be determined by their acceptance of the new rules of the game. This might have made the endogenous development of organizational forms capable of mobilizing the population in the political arena even more difficult.

In addition, the Western disengagement from Afghanistan from 2011 onwards threatened the very foundations of the post-2001 system. As of this writing, sources of patronage are drying up fast, in a political system which might not even be able to fund its own elections without external support. Eventually, Afghan political parties will have to reconnect to their society, find solid constituencies, or perish; but this can only happen as a result of a major crisis.

Acknowledgement

This article is based on years of association with and exposure to party leaders, cadres, and activists from 2003 onwards. For a period, there was a systematic research effort covering political parties and organizations in the context of statebuilding in Afghanistan (Crisis States Research Centre, London School of Economics, 2009–2010), which was however aborted due to lack of funding. Overall, several tens of interviews were conducted in 2003–2012.

Notes

1. The term 'political technology' is used here as in French political science to indicate all modes of political organization and management. See Badie (1984). See also Badie (2000) on the role of intellectuals as importers of political technology.
2. There were reports of activities by anti-monarchy groups (hence the label 'Republicans'), but the name of this group is not known; it might not even have been an organized movement.
3. On Wish Zalmiyan's organization, see Boyko (2010).
4. See Rishtya's description of the electoral process (2005); see also Dupree (1971a and 1971b) and Tapper (1983).
5. Interview with Noor Ahmad Noor, Amsterdam, August 2006.
6. Interviews with former political activists in Kabul and the provinces, 2006–2010; Ibrahimi (2012).
7. Interviews with former political activists in Kabul and the provinces, 2006–2010; Marwat (1997); Bulatov; Iskandarov (2004); Ruttig (2006).
8. Interviews with former HDKh activists in Kabul, 2008–2009.
9. Interviews with former cadres of Parcham, the Netherlands, Kabul, and London, 2008–2010.
10. Bulatov (1997, 267 ff); interviews with former Khalqi and Parchami political activists in Kabul and the provinces, 2006–2010.
11. Meetings with activists and leaders, 2003–2011; personal communication with researcher Thomas Ruttig, August 2013.
12. Interview with a high-ranking official of Hezb-e Jamhuri Afghanistan, Kabul, October 2008; personal communication with Thomas Ruttig, August 2013.
13. Personal communication with a former official of an international organization based in Afghanistan, November 2012.
14. Interviews with Junbesh cadres, 2004–2009.
15. In Baghlan, for example, all the main party offices were closed down after the 2010 parliamentary elections (interviews with local activists and notables, September–October 2012).
16. Meetings with Mansur, 2009 and 2010; meetings with Jami'ati intellectuals, 2004, 2010, 2012; interviews with Uzbek intellectuals formerly linked to Junbesh, 2004, 2005, 2009; meetings with Hazara intellectuals, 2005 and 2010. On one occasion Mansur was reportedly beaten for his criticism by Jami'ati strongman Marshal Fahim.
17. Personal communication with NDI staff, Kabul, 2004, 2005, 2009. See also http://www.ndi.org/afghanistan and http://www.iri.org/countries-and-programs/middle-east-and-north-africa/afghanistan.

18. Communication with party activists in Kunduz and Baghlan, 2003–2004; meeting with a party activist, Herat, 2009.
19. Meeting with a local party leader, Herat, 2009.
20. Personal communication with Afghan activists, 2009.
21. Giustozzi (2010); interviews with Afghan intellectuals and party activists in northern and north-eastern Afghanistan, 2012.
22. This was the case of the north-east, for example (personal communication with an Afghan intellectual from Takhar, November 2012).
23. Interview with Soraya Parlika, Kabul, September 2009.

References

Afghanistan Past and Present, 1982. Moscow: Social Sciences Today.

Badie, Bertrand. 1984. *Le développement politique*. Paris: Economica.

Badie, Bertrand. 2000. *The Imported State*. Stanford: Stanford University Press.

Boyko, Vladimir. 2000. "The Origins of Political Parties in Contemporary Afghanistan in the Light of New Archival Data." *Central Asia Journal* 46: 189–205.

Boyko, Vladimir. 2010. *Vlast' i oppositsia v Afganistane*. Moscow: Oriental Institute.

Bulatov, Yu. A. 1997. *Narodno-demokraticheskaya partiya Afganistana*. Dissertation. Moscow: MID.

Bulatov, Yuri A. 2003. *Narodno-demokraticheskaya partiya Afganistana*. Moscow: MGIMO.

Coburn, Noah. 2010. *Connecting with Kabul: The Importance of the Wolesi Jirga Election and Local Political Networks in Afghanistan*. Kabul: AREU.

Dobbins, J. F. 2008. *After the Taliban*. Herndon: Potomac Books.

Dupree, Louis. 1971a. "Comparative Profiles of Recent Parliaments in Afghanistan." *AUFS South Asia series* XV (4): 1–18.

Dupree, Louis. 1971b. "Afghanistan Contineus its Experiment with Democracy." *AUFS South Asia series* XV (3): 1–15.

Dupree, Louis. 1971c. "A note on Afghanistan: 1971." *AUFS field reports, South Asia Series* 15 (2): 1–35.

Duverger, Maurice. 1981. *Les Partis politiques*. Paris: Seuil.

Edwards, David B. 2002. *Before Taliban: Genealogies of the Afghan Jihad*. Berkeley: University of California Press.

Elliot, Ashley. 2009. "Political Party Development in Afghanistan: Challenges and Opportunities." Paper presented at the 'Policy Options for State-Building in Afghanistan' event, SAIS, 18 April 2009.

Farahi, Abdul Ghaffar. 2004. *Afghanistan During Democracy & Republic*. Peshawar: Area Study Centre.

Ghobar, Ghulam Mohammad. 2004 (1967). *Afganistan dar masir-e tarikh*. Teheran: Jangal.

Giustozzi, Antonio. 2007. "Afghanistan: Political Parties or Militia Fronts?" Chapter 8 of *Transforming Rebel Movements After Civil Wars*, edited by J. de Zeeuw, 179–204. Boulder: Lynne Rienner Publishers.

Giustozzi, Antonio. 2009. *Empires of Mud*. London: Hurst.

Giustozzi, Antonio. 2010. *Between Patronage and Rebellion: Student Politics in Afghanistan*. Kabul: Afghan Research and Evaluation Unit.

Giustozzi, Antonio. 2011. "Armed Politics and Political Competition in Afghanistan." In *The Peace in Between: Post-War Violence and Peacebuilding*, edited by Astri Suhrke and Mats Berdal, 153–172. London: Routledge.

Giustozzi, Antonio. 2012. *The Resilient Oligopoly*. Kabul: AREU.

Gunther, Richard, and Larry Diamond. 2003. "Species of Political Parties: A New Typology." *Party Politics* 9 (2): 167–199.

Ibrahimi, Niamatullah. 2012. *Ideology Without Leadership: The Rise and Decline of Maoism in Afghanistan*. London, Berlin: AAN.

International Crisis Group. 2013. *Afghanistan's Parties in Transition*. Bruxelles: International Crisis Group.

Iskandarov, Kosimsho. 2004. *Politicheskie partii i dvizheniya Afganistana vo vtoroi polovine XX veka*. Dushanbe: Irfon.

Larson, Anna. 2009. *Afghanistan's New Democratic Parties: A Means to Organise Democratisation?* Kabul: AREU.

Linz, Juan, and Alfred Stepan. 1996. *Problems of Democratic Transition and Consolidation*. Baltimore: John Hopkins University Press.

Mansur, Hafiz. 1992. *Panjshir dar duran-e jihad*. Peshawar.

Marwat, Fazal-ur-Rahim Khan. 1997. *The Evolution and Growth of Communism in Afghanistan (1917–79): An Appraisal*. Karachi: Royal Book Co.

Mingst, Alexander. 2008. "Evolutionary Political Economy and the Role of Organisations." Andrassy Working Per Series No. XXII, Budapest.

Moore, Barrington Jr. 1966. *Social Origins of Dictatorship and Democracy*. Boston: Beacon Press.

Olesen, Asta. 1995. *Islam and Politics in Afghanistan*. London: Curzon.

Peszkowski, Robert. 2012. *Reforming Junbesh*. Berlin: AAN, 2012.

Piovesana, Enrico. 2012. *Sholayi*. Reggio Calabria: Città del Sole (Kindle edition).

Plastun, Vladimir N. 2002. *Evolutsiya deyatel'nosti ekstremistskikh organizatsii v stranakh vostoka*. Novosibirsk: Sibirskii Khronograph.

"Political Parties in Afghanistan: A Review of the State of Political Parties After the 2009 and 2010 Elections." 2011. Washington: NDI.

"Political Party Assessment Afghanistan." 2006. Washington: NDI.

Rishtya, Sayed Qassem. 2005. *Afghanistan: The Making of the 1964 Constitution*. Lausanne: Publi-Libris.

Ruttig, Thomas. 2006. *Islamists, Leftists and a Void at the Center*. Berlin: Adenauer Foundation.

Ruttig, Thomas. 2009. "Afghanistan's Democrats: From Underground to Marginalization." In *Afghanistan, 1979–2009: In the Grip of Conflict*, 102–104. Washington: The Middle East Institute.

Ruttig, Thomas. 2011. *Afghanistan's Early Reformists*. Berlin: AAN.

Ruttig, Thomas. 2013. *How it all Began*. Berlin: AAN.

Saikal, Amin. 2004. *Modern Afghanistan*. London: Tauris.

Sharq, Hassan. 2000. *Bare-foot in Coarse Clothes*. Peshawar: Area Study Centre.

Slinkin, Mikhail F. 2003. *Oppositsia i vlast' (60–79-gg XX v.)*. Symferopol: Krim.

Suhrke, Astri. 2011. *When More is Less*. London: Hurst.

Tapper, Richard. 1983. "Ethnicity and Class: Dimensions of Intergroup Conflict in North-central Afghanistan." In *The Conflict of Tribes and State* in Iran and Afghanistan. London: Croom Helm.

United Nations. 2001. Agreement on Provisional Arrangements in Afghanistan Pending the Re-establishment of Permanent Government Institutions. http://www.un.org/news/dh/latest/afghan/afghan-agree.htm

Wilder, Andrew. 2006. *A House Divided? Analysing the 2005 Afghan Elections*. Kabul: AREU.

The dynamics of informal political networks and statehood in post-2001 Afghanistan: a case study of the 2010–2011 Special Election Court crisis

Timor Sharan

University of Exeter, UK

This article focuses on the 2010–2011 Special Election Court crisis, which serves as a microcosm of the broader post-2001 political network dynamics in which opportunistic practices of bargaining and the instrumentalization of identities have emerged as key features of Afghan politics. Post-2001 international state-building has produced a 'network state' where the state and political networks have become co-constitutive in state-building. This has produced the democratic façade of a state, underpinned by informal power structures and networks. In light of this analysis, a successful international exit from Afghanistan and post-2014 state survival may depend as much on the political stability of the empowered networks as on the strength of the Afghan National Security Forces and the outcome of the ongoing reconciliation and negotiation with the Taliban.

Introduction

The results of the 2010 parliamentary election triggered a prolonged crisis in Afghanistan's Wolesi Jirga (Lower House) which came to be known as the Special Election Court (SEC) crisis.[1] The SEC crisis set into motion a fierce battle between competing political networks within and beyond the Wolesi Jirga which, at its height, brought the country closer to the brink of inter-network war. The conflict was between two opposing camps, namely President Karzai's network and the ad hoc Support for Rule of Law (SRL) coalition led by Zahir Qadir. The establishment of the SEC and its decision to disqualify 62 sitting MPs (one-fourth of the Wolesi Jirga) for fraud was seen by many analysts as a direct attempt by Karzai and his network clienteles in the judiciary and the executive to manipulate the election outcome in their favour. The SRL, a coalition of several smaller anti-Karzai political networks, was formed in the Wolesi Jirga against these attempts. It succeeded in declaring the court illegal, passed a vote of no confidence for the attorney general and the Supreme Court judges, and at one point proposed that the president be impeached. The crisis ended a year later when a compromise was reached between the two camps in which just 9 of the 62 sitting MPs were replaced.

Much academic and policy work on state-building in Afghanistan has addressed the role and impact of the attempts to build formal state institutions (Ottoway and Lieven 2002; Ghani, Lockhart, and Carnahan 2005; Rubin 2006). This paper offers a different analytical framework, one that is grounded in the analysis of informal political networks in constituting the post-2001 state (cf. Giustozzi 2007; Coburn 2011b). It shows how competition and conflict between political networks over the state has shaped the very nature of governance and statehood in Afghanistan since 2001. From this perspective, the 2010–2011 Special Election Court crisis serves as a microcosm of these network dynamics. The crisis provides a useful window through which to explore the power dynamics of political networks in post-2001 Afghanistan and their impacts on statehood. Political networks are understood as *distinct open-hierarchical structures whose members are interdependent on each other's power and resources for political outcomes in an informally structured and continuously renegotiated arrangement.* They are seen as modes of organization that engage in pooling resources and collective action and cooperating to serve as a means of governance. Political networks are treated here as units of analysis having their own structural characteristics, modes of conflict resolution, and bases of legitimacy. Although these political networks are hierarchically assembled, each 'network node' pursues her or his own interests and is able to exit the network at any time. In fact, the strength of political networks lies in their weak ties (Granovetter 1974). Except for Hizb-i-Islami, the seven Sunni and eight Shia main former Afghan *mujahedeen* groups (known as *tanzim*s) were essentially network forms of organization – political networks (as discussed in the second section). After 2001, the former *mujahedeen tanzim*s underwent a process of restructuring in terms of their organizational capacity, internal structure, and power relations (see Giustozzi, this volume). They have further splintered into smaller sub-networks, whilst new ones have emerged with stronger links to international state-building. Elsewhere I have shown how these *tanzim*s came to constitute and transform the post-2001 state following the Bonn Conference power-sharing arrangement (Sharan 2001; Sharan and Heathershaw 2011). There I highlighted that the state and political networks have become undistinguishable from one another in post-2001 state-building, wherein the established networks masquerade *as* the state. This article, building upon these previous studies, sheds further light on how the dynamics of political networks have influenced statehood and post-2014 political stability.

I begin by addressing the role of political networks in international state-building. Given the empirically-based focus of this study, this paper does not attempt to exhaust the theoretical discussions in the field. The second section provides a descriptive background to the 2010–2011 Special Election Court crisis and the events surrounding it. The following two sections explore the opportunistic practices of bargaining and exchange and the consequent instrumentalization of identities as the key aspects of political network dynamics. In the final section, this paper suggests that a 'network form of state' is emerging, aided by the legitimacy granted by internationally sponsored state-building. It concludes by suggesting that a successful international exit from Afghanistan and the post-2014 state's survival depend upon the political stability of the empowered political networks as much as on the strength of the Afghan National Security Forces and the outcome of the ongoing reconciliation and negotiation with the Taliban.

Political networks and international state-building

The liberal approach to peace-building has been criticized for failing to realize that post-conflict liberalization would engender further local inter-elite battles while failing to tackle the root causes of conflict (Paris 1997; Duffield 1999). Stedman (1997) defined the role of non-cooperative elites in the implementation of peace settlements as that of 'spoilers', and advocated the strategies that international 'custodians of the peace' can adopt to induce, socialize, or coerce these elites into cooperation within or subordination to the terms of the political settlement. Since then, leading figures have argued that the post-conflict state must be constituted through strong formal institutions to contain local inter-elite competition (Chesterman 2004; Paris 2004). In recent years, Richmond (2011) and MacGinty (2011) have brought our attention to the contextual role of local endogenous actors and their power relations with international state-building in producing a local–international hybrid peace. Similarly, Barnett and Zürcher (2009) argued that existing approaches are too focused on international actors, treating domestic politics as 'constraints', thus failing to incorporate fully the preferences and strategies of local actors and so ignoring domestic politics. In their recent work comparing Afghanistan with

Tajikistan, they argued that cooperation with an accommodating elite and conflict with 'spoilers' are the two least likely outcomes for an international peace-building mission, out of a total of four possibilities. They argued that state and sub-national elites are often able to protect factional interests whilst retaining a veneer of stability for international consumption – an outcome of 'compromised peacebuilding'. A further option is that of 'captured peacebuilding', where 'state and local elites are able to redirect the distribution of assistance so that it is fully consistent with their interests' (Barnett and Zürcher 2009, 24–25).

This paper shares Barnett and Zürcher's concerns, yet starts from the position that post-conflict elites must be understood first and foremost with respect to the political network and the hierarchical authority structure that they both constitute and represent. Local politics cannot be reduced to an analysis of elites and their orientation for or against an internationally mediated political settlement. In a post-conflict setting as in Afghanistan, where state institutions and structures have been eroded or effaced following civil war, international intervention and state-building find themselves reliant upon local political networks to reassemble and transform the post-conflict state and its modern institutions.

In *Organizations at War in Afghanistan and Beyond* (2008), Sinno made a compelling argument that ethnic groups, classes, civilizations, religions, and nations do not engage in war or strategic interactions; rather, organizations do. Armed conflicts in places like Bosnia, Rwanda, Sierra Leone, Sudan, and Afghanistan were in essence conflicts between political organizations, despite exhibiting ethnic, religious, and even class components. Sinno reasoned that engaging in conflict requires the performance of a number of essential processes, such as coordination, mobilization, and the manipulation of information, that cannot be implemented by amorphous entities (e.g. civilizations, ethnic groups, or the masses); however, organizations that represent different community interests and groups can perform these functions. In this light, *tanzim*s were at best network forms of organization (political networks) because of their open-hierarchical structures. Sinno characterized them as highly decentralized and continuously renegotiated arrangements wherein field commanders provided their loyalty, support, and assistance to a party in return for the resources necessary to maintain their resistance activities. These *tanzim*s were able to build extensive webs of connections during the civil war with tribal chiefs, village mullahs, commanders, and community leaders to coordinate actions and achieve objectives (Roy 1990). Sinno (2008) explored how differences in the organizational structure of *tanzim*s affected their war-fighting capabilities. Hizb-i-Islami's hierarchically organized structure – along with its close relationship with Pakistan – meant that it had a more effective mobilizing support system in attracting funds and weaponry from Western and Arab countries than other *tanzim*s. However, the more decentralized networks of other *tanzim*s like the Jamiat-i-Islami were more effective on the ground during the anti-Soviet insurgency. The *tanzim*s' network structure and their mode of operation made them a formidable resistance force against the Soviet intervention and were ultimately responsible for their success.

International intervention in post-2001 state-building 'rented peace' by making bargains with former *tanzim* leaders and commanders who had helped defeat the Taliban (temporarily) in reassembling and transforming the state within an existing war economy. The Bonn political settlement divided the state administration and its resources among the rival *tanzim* commanders based on their military strengths (Jalali 2003; Sharan 2011). The Bonn conference gave legitimacy to this power structuring because of the agreed logic of a 'light-footprint' approach to state-building (Strand, Harpviken, and Suhrke 2004). In the post-2001 period, the former Mujahedeen *tanzim*s have further splintered into smaller sub-networks whilst new ones (such as the Karzai political network, explained below) have emerged with stronger links to international state-building in the early years of intervention.[2] Between 2002 and 2005, Karzai and his largely Western-educated Pashtun technocrats skilfully used their positions in the internationally sponsored state and their access to state resources to co-opt some of the key former *mujahedeen* elites into their network and coercively remove others from their state positions (Sharan 2011). The difference here was clearly international support, which shifted decisively in favour of Karzai and his network clients, thus fomenting the 'network conflict' that came to dominate the post-2001 international state-building. Since 2005, the power balance between different networks has shifted away from the technocrats and royalists and back to the jihadists.

The Special Election Court (SEC) crisis in the Wolesi Jirga must be seen within the wider context of the continued power dynamics between rival political networks. The Wolesi Jirga is a forum in which to observe network dynamics in action. It functions as an excellent 'assembling point' for political networks and their clienteles, outside the state administration, through which they maintain and expand their power and interests. It has become a strategic 'network-building arena' connecting the centre with the periphery – linking state officials, network leaders, local power brokers, community leaders, and licit and illicit commercial networks at the local, national, and international levels. As shown below, it provides protection, security, and employment for political networks and their key members. Key network leaders such as Mohammad Mohaqeq (former minister of planning and a former northern commander of the Wahdat-i-Islami *tanzim*), Yonous Qanooni (former minister of interior and former commander of the Jamiat-i-Islami *tanzim*), and Haji Zahir Qadir (leader of the powerful Jabbarkhel Ghilzai sub-tribe), who were effectively purged by Karzai (Sharan 2011), have found protection in the new House. It is estimated that over 50% of the new Wolesi Jirga members are former *mujahedeen* network elites (Hussaini and Niazi 2010). The following section provides a brief historical background for the crisis, highlighting the key networks involved and the roles played by their clienteles.

The Special Election Court crisis: background

The final result of the 18 September 2010 parliamentary election was a major setback for the Karzai political network. Some of Karzai's network nodes in the south, where Karzai's support was considered high, were either unable to win votes or were disqualified by the Independent Electoral Complaints Commission (IECC). These included his first cousin Hishmat Karzai in Kandahar. In addition, not a single Pashtun candidate from Ghazni Province was elected because of the low turnout among the Pashtun population (Ruttig 2010).[3] Fraud, vote rigging, and insecurity further reduced the Karzai network's vote bank. The IECC, the organization responsible for election complaints, received more than 3000, with significantly higher levels of ballot stuffing, voter fraud, collective voting, and intimidation in the Pashtun south (Bijlert 2011b). Insecurity and Taliban threats meant that one-fourth of polling stations in the south and south-east, where Karzai's political network influence was considered to be greater, were closed (Bijlert 2011b). The Independent Election Commission (IEC) ultimately disqualified 1.5 million ballots, an estimated one-quarter of the total votes cast, and disqualified 27 winning candidates for electoral fraud – many of them part of Karzai's Pashtun political bases (Bijlert 2011b).

Immediately after the announcement of the election results, the attorney general's office and the Supreme Court – the heads of both organizations being members of the Karzai network – demanded a recount and accused the IECC of bias (see Table 1 for a timeline of events). At the same time, Karzai ordered the IEC to hold a new round of elections in Ghazni Province to reflect the ethnic composition of the province. (In Ghazni, the Hazara-ethnic candidates, with overwhelming participation, had won the 11 quota seats for the province, further reducing Karzai's influence in the south.) Many analysts considered this an attempt by Karzai and his clienteles to change the election outcome in their favour. On 1 December 2010, in retaliation, the IEC certified the final election results. The Author's ethnographic fieldwork has revealed that the IEC's decision was motivated by international donor support. However, it was difficult to verify

Table 1. Timetable of events.

18 September 2010	Parliamentary election.
24 November 2010	The IEC announces results for 34 provinces (all except Ghazni): 1.5 million votes are disqualified and 27 candidates are disqualified.
24 November 2010	The attorney general's office and the Supreme Court demand a recount and issue arrest warrants for three IEC staff members.
1 December 2010	In retaliation, the IEC certifies the final election results.
21 December 2010	Karzai issues a decree forcing the creation of the Special Election Court.
26 January 2011	Karzai agrees to inaugurate the Parliament if, in return, MPs allow the SEC to prosecute those found to have committed fraud.
23 June 2011	The SEC issues its verdict disqualifying 62 sitting MPs.
25 June 2011	MPs pass a vote of no confidence against the attorney general's office and the Supreme Court judges.
5 July 2011	MPs propose impeaching the president.
10 August 2011	Karzai backs down and issues a decree forcing the IEC to have the final say.
21 August 2011	The IEC announces the list of nine MPs to be replaced.
3 September 2011	The nine new MPs are sworn in under armed protection. The opposition calls it a coup.

the accusations that the head of the IEC, Fazal Ahmad Manavi, had links to the opposition. The attorney general's office issued an arrest warrant for three IEC staff members, one of high rank, accusing them of orchestrating mass fraud (Ober 2011). With advice from the Supreme Court, Karzai issued a decree to set up a Special Election Court (SEC) to reinvestigate the IEC's list of disqualified candidates and other fraud cases. Eventually, on 26 January 2011, under intense pressure from international donors and disgruntled candidates, Karzai made a deal with the elected members to promptly inaugurate the Parliament if, in return, the MPs agreed that the SEC could implement any criminal cases identified by the court.

Six months later, on 23 June 2011, the crisis resurfaced when the SEC issued its decision to disqualify 62 sitting MPs, one-quarter of the Wolesi Jirga. Two days later, in response, the Wolesi Jirga passed a resolution denouncing the creation of the SEC as illegal. This was followed by a vote of no confidence against the attorney general's office and the chief judges of the Supreme Court. To coordinate these efforts, an ad hoc coalition called Support for Rule of Law (SRL) was established. At one point, MPs even discussed the possibility of impeaching the president. After two months of political manoeuvring, discussed below, and failing to generate enough support through bargains and exchange, Karzai and his team backed down, issuing a decree giving the IEC the final authority to resolve the crisis. Ten days later, in a compromise, the IEC announced that it had decided that only 9 of the 62 MPs should be disqualified (Bijlert 2011c). In his interview with the BBC's Persian Service on August 2011, the head of IEC, Fazal Ahmad Manavi, confirmed that he was under a lot of pressure from circles within the government: 'We had to take this decision on the basis of some *faysalahaye siyasi* [political agreements]. The nine disqualified MPs were either relatively unknown or seem to have lacked sufficiently strong backing from powerful political networks, whereas the new MPs seem to have had the necessary connections (Bijlert 2011c). At least four of them were former jihadi commanders with links to powerful individual-network power brokers.[4] On 3 September 2011, with the presence of heavily armed police and army, the nine new MPs were sworn in, while the opposition SRL coalition members were literally imprisoned in their office, unable to enter the parliament building. The SRL coalition leader, Haji Zahir Qadir, characterized it as a 'coup d'état' against the Parliament.[5] The next section seeks to identify some of the main types of clients which both the Karzai and SRL networks relied on.

The power dynamics of political networks

The Karzai political network

It seems that the Karzai network were quick to activate key nodes such as ministers, governors, and ethno-regional power brokers to reassemble an ad hoc political network around the crisis, strengthening their position. Ethnographic fieldwork and interviews with dozens of key informants reveal an interesting picture of how Karzai's network operated around a number of influential state officials. These were Humayoon Azizi, the minister for parliamentary affairs; Hazrat Omar Zakhiwal, the minister of finance; Sadeq Modabber, the head of the Office of Administrative Affairs (Karzai's office); Rahmatullah Nabil, then director of the National Directorate of Security; and Asadullah Khaled, the minister for border, tribal, and ethnic affairs. Utilizing state resources, they negotiated bargains and exchanges to co-opt MPs. Although difficult to substantiate and fully confirm, the picture drawn suggests that during the crisis the minister for parliamentary affairs functioned as 'liaison officer', making deals inside the Parliament. The finance minister sanctioned the extra patronage payment to the head of the Office of Administrative Affairs, who then distributed the agreed sums to the co-opted network leaders.

Several informants highlighted the key roles played by Rahmatullah Nabil and Asadullah Khaled in employing state coercive powers to threaten and intimidate opponents. Some opposition and independent MPs publicly claimed during parliamentary hearings that they had been warned that if they did not support the SEC's decision, their families, relatives, and even tribal colleagues would risk losing their state positions. It is widely reported in the Afghan media (Hakimi 2011) and confirmed by several senior persons in the president's office that some ethno-regional power brokers, including Abul Rasul Sayyaf and Mohammad Mohaqqeq, have been receiving an extra monthly security budget for up to 60 bodyguards, as well as other expensive gifts such as armoured cars, for their support. In the tribal south, Asadullah Khaled played a role in co-opting and intimidating MPs and tribal leaders. At the community level, he warned those community leaders involved in business that their access to state services as well as to legal and illegal commercial networks would be significantly constrained if they did not support the SEC's stance. As a regional human rights commissioner in Kandahar noted:

> In Kandahar, Khaled and Ahmad Wali Karzai [Karzai's brother, who was assassinated in mid-2011] have intimidated Achikzai and Noorzai elders over their support for the Wolesi Jirga. They run their own prison, so if they do not follow them, especially those least well connected, they could lose their businesses, state positions, and access to the drug economy.[6]

Another group which provided clients to Karzai in the Wolesi Jirga included influential network leaders who acted as power brokers. These elites are not separate from the two state networks mentioned above but overlap with them at certain moments. During the crisis, these power brokers were instrumental in connecting Karzai, as the top patron, with MPs in Parliament. The Hizb-i-Islami, under the leadership of Abdul Hadi Arghandiwal, proved to be the most loyal and the biggest bloc to support the Karzai decision, with over 30 members as part of the Sabah parliamentary group in the Wolesi Jirga.[7] The former leader of Hizb-i-Ettihad, Abdur Rab Sayyaf, was another influential power broker who provided the networking skills needed for Karzai to build his support in the Wolesi Jirga. Since 2001, Sayyaf has become Karzai's central connecting node in the House. Twice he stood for the position of speaker of the House to represent the Karzai group; both times he fell short by only a few votes. In addition to these ethnic-Pashtun power brokers, Karzai obtained the support of other ethno-regional power brokers in the Parliament. Both Sadeq Modabber (head of the Office of Administrative Affairs) and Mohammad Mohaqqeq (leader of the Wahdat-e-Mardom group) provided support amongst the Hazara MPs. The latter publicly took an anti-Karzai stance, while privately he bargained with Karzai to provide clients.

In the post-2005 Wolesi Jirga, political network patrons have exercised some degree of control and hierarchy over their clients by establishing Parliamentary Groups (PGs). The provision for the formation of parliamentary groups was established in the first year of the Wolesi Jirga in 2005 as a formal mechanism to encourage greater efficiency and organization in plenary discussions. *De jure*, a PG must have at least 21 members and be inclusive of all ethnic, religious and gender groups. The head of the PG has the advantage of attending the Wolesi Jirga executive meetings to decide parliamentary agendas. *De Facto*, ethnographic fieldwork in some PG headquarters uncovered that the PGs are at best a form of patronage network centred around key political network leaders such as Abur Rab Sayyaf, Mohammad Mohaqqeq, Sadeq Modabber, Haji Zahir Qadir, Karim Khalili and Abdul Hadi Arghandiwal. Each parliamentary group has an office/guesthouse close to the Wolesi Jirga where they host visitors, financially sustained and politically led by competing leaders. Various factors contribute to Mps' decision to join a PG including financial gains, political influence, ethnic and tribal affiliations, and legal and illegal business interests. A female MP asserted:

> In the first month of the Wolesi Jirga, Haji Zahir Qadir [head of the Peace Caravan PG and the leader of the Support for Rule of Law coalition] approached me to join his group. He told me that he knew that I live in a rented house. He offered me 2000 US dollars per month if I joined his group.[8]

Financial funds are one of the central contributing factors to the survival of a political group. Wafaey and Larson (2010) found that the main reason for the disintegration of Khat-i-Sehum (Third Line) and some other earlier non-legacy/jihadi PGs was the lack of funds as well as internal divisions along identity-based rifts. For powerbrokers, the political and financial return is high (discussed in the next section), especially at moments of trading favours like electing a new Speaker or voting to approve a minister. Sabah, Etemad and Dawat were the three main PGs that seem to have provided Karzai with the necessary client-base during the crisis. The patron of these groups, Abdul Hadi Arghandiwal (the current Minister for Economy), Sadeq Modabber (the head of Office of Administrative Affairs) and Abdur rab Sayyaf are considered to be close allies of Karzai in the post-2001 period.

Support for the Rule of Law political network

The main opposition network in the Wolesi Jirga was the ad hoc Support for Rule of Law coalition. The SRL was formed immediately after the Special Election Court's decision to disqualify 62 MPs. While some MPs genuinely joined the SRL to defy the court's decision (which they considered as undermining the integrity of the Wolesi Jirga), others joined for fear that they might be either disqualified or accused of vote rigging. Whatever the reasons, the following MP's justification captures the dominant rhetoric used for constituency consumption at the time: 'The creation of the SEC, putting pressure on the IEC to change the election result, failure to nominate candidates for ministerial posts, and ignoring Wolesi Jirga resolutions are some of the systemic actions by the president designed to undermine the Parliament.'[9] The court's decision had affected the votes of two-thirds of parliamentarians, who weren't sure whether a criminal case would follow. It is not clear how many MPs initially signed up for the SRL; estimates varied from 140 to 180 (out of 249). As the crisis dragged on and it became clear that no criminal case would follow, the number fell substantially, especially after the compromise decision to disqualify only nine MPs.

The most powerful central node in the SRL, around whom other dispersed anti-Karzai networks assembled, was Haji Zahir Qadir. He was the leader of the largest opposition PG, Peace Caravan, estimated to have around 40 MPs. Haji Zahir Qadir's background is revealing. He belongs to the powerful Arsala family, one of the most influential, affluent, and prominent families in the eastern region. As the son of Haji Abdul Qadir, the most famous Pashtun jihadi commander among the Northern Alliance and former governor of Nangarhar (assassinated in 2002), he held influential roles in Nangarhar, including head of the border police. In 2005, Karzai, in an attempt to marginalize him in Nangarhar Province, exiled him to Takhar Province as the head of the border police there, installing his close ally Gul Agha Shirzai as the strongman in the region (Mukhopadhyay 2009). Since 2009, he has established himself as a national figure in Kabul in opposition to Karzai. During and after the crisis, the Karzai network made several attempts to discredit him and his family by accusing him of being involved in drug smuggling, kidnapping, and corruption. In January 2012, months after the crisis, he was elected the first deputy speaker of the Wolesi Jirga, winning 140 votes and further consolidating his power in the House. In 2013, the minister of finance, a close ally of Karzai, accused Haji Zahir Qadir of smuggling flour worth USD 269 million from Pakistan. The next day, in response, Haji Qadir declared to parliamentarians that he had more than USD 350 million in his bank account, reminding them how he had financially maintained them during the crisis (National Radio Television of Afghanistan, 2013).

The SRL succeeded in building a powerful network against Karzai. It managed to draw support from some state officials, power brokers, and tribal elders who either were disillusioned with Karzai's corrupt practices or felt betrayed by Karzai's past false promises. Amongst these was Dr Abdullah Abdullah, Karzai's main opponent in the 2009 presidential election. Following his defeat in the election, Abdullah was quick to capitalize on his 30% voting bank by establishing the Coalition for Change and Hope. A number of influential MPs who are also members of Dr Abdullah's Coalition played a key role in the SRL coalition. Another leader who supported the SRL, albeit privately, was the second vice-president, Karim Khalili. Given Khalili's formal position as the second vice-president as well as his influence within the Wolesi Jirga as the patron of the Saday-e-Adalat (Voice of Justice) PG, his support provided confidence among the opposition. One explanation for his objection to the SEC could be that he knew that the SEC would reduce his clientele in the Wolesi Jirga, especially when Karzai demanded a re-election in Ghazni Province. Almost all of the elected MPs in Ghazni were members of Khalili network.

The SEC crisis highlights two mutually reinforcing network practices as key features of post-2001 Afghanistan: (1) opportunism and bargains; and (2) the instrumentalization of identities.

Network practices

Opportunism and bargaining

The SEC crisis provided an excellent occasion for opportunism and bargaining. A patron–client practice is an exchange relationship, of some private and personal nature, where players have reciprocal needs and expectations but unequal power and status (Johnson and Dandeker 1990). This relationship is a dyadic one, characterized by unequal status, reciprocity, and personal contact that is arranged hierarchically (Scott 1972). Piattoni (2001, 17–18) argued that the best-resourced 'buyer' in a client–patron network is usually a political actor close to government resources, most often to the incumbent authorities. The available evidence suggests that Karzai has been maintaining an expensive and expansive patronage system in Parliament, with payments made to MPs for passing bills or for securing approval for the appointment of a new minister. During the crisis, the bargaining took place with multiple actors and layers of patronage, offering power brokers bargains in exchange for their skills to buy loyalty and support. Most bargains were made for financial gain; however, political privileges were also considered. Offers of government positions, state contracts, licences and gifts were wide-spread. Although one cannot estimate the amount of financial reward offered to extend patronage, it was certainly extensive.[10] As one MP summarized it:

The jihadi leaders, ministers, and governors would attend MPs' houses to make deals. These offers could include anything, really, from a simple bribe, to covering the expenses of their guest-houses, to offers of gifts like cars, and to installing their family members in key positions. This is obviously negotiated and decided.[11]

Another MP highlighted the expanding nature of these patronage practices, stretching beyond Afghanistan's key players to include regional and international countries:

This is a crisis of those who sold themselves in exchange for toman [Iranian currency], for kaldar [Pakistani currency], for dollars and pounds. They have put the country into *lilam* [bidding]. They will divide it further and gradually sell parts of it.... Tell me, if you do not have an agenda, bring in your *mohra* [nodes] and stay committed like a man. The House has become a *buzkashi* [goat-pulling] ground; whoever possesses more power and money abuses it.... Tell me, is this the nation's House, Mr Karzai's House, or Mr Manavi's [head of the Independent Election Commission] House? Is this the House of *zorgoya* [despots], or the House of Iran, Pakistan, or other embassies?[12]

This is also confirmed by other studies. In Noah Coburn's (2011) study of the political economy of the Afghan Parliament, an informant reported to her that one power broker, usually considered of only moderate importance, 'paid one car or US$10,000 for each vote he could convince MPs to give to [a certain more influential MP]; [this influential leader] then gave this amount back to him' (Coburn 2011, 15). She also found that in some cases power brokers invested their own money, knowing that they could get a higher return later from the patron.

Interviews with several senior officials at the Ministry of Finance and other line ministries indicate the extent of appropriation of public resources for personal gain. In 2010, the Presidential Palace accounted for the highest amount of illegible budget (unaccounted-for money) spent in the country, at around USD 300 million, followed by the Parliament, at around USD 50 million (Office of National Budget, 2011). Although it is difficult to establish how this money is being spent, one could plausibly surmise, based on key informants' statements, that a substantial part is spent to buy loyalty and make bargains. The two statements below, by senior officials at the Ministry of Finance and the Office of Administrative Affairs, reflect the overall level of bargaining that became entrenched in post-2001 Afghanistan.

I cannot tell you exactly how this money is being spent but we are constantly under pressure by the presidential office and the minister [of finance] to provide money.... Definitely most of this money is being channelled illegally as extra payments to key individuals. This is not something new. But this is having serious consequences. This year the World Bank, under the Afghanistan Reconstruction Trust Fund, cut 70 million of our funds.[13]

Similarly, another senior official noted:

The OAA [Office of Administrative Affairs] is Karzai's right arm. Do you know why he has more than 100 unofficial advisers? It is just a title. From the tribal elder in Uruzgan to those who claim that they are opposed to him, like Mohaqqeq and Dostum, all are on his payroll. They are all part of the system. People call it a mafia, but as someone who has worked in [...] department, I can tell you it is a functional system they created for themselves.[14]

These statements point to the nature of statehood and governance that is being propagated by this system of payment and the promise to buy loyalty. Of course, this does not include other unaccounted-for money that Karzai and his clients receive from neighbouring countries. In 2009, Karzai publicly admitted to receiving suitcases of money from neighbouring countries for his office expenses.[15] He also confirmed in 2013 having received payments from the US intelligence services for the past 10 years – 'ghost money' that 'came in secret and left in secret', which he claimed to have spent on his office expenses.[16]

The vote of confidence for the ministers of finance and interior on 19 February 2012, during the SEC crisis, is another telling example of opportunism and bargaining. Reportedly, a few days before the vote, the ministers had made deals with the power brokers and their associated MPs.

What followed is best described by Kandahar MP Abdul Rahim Ayubi who arrived in the Wolesi Jirga the day after the vote covered with chains in protest, accusing some MPs and the Wolesi Jirga's executive committee of making deals.

> They pre-planned the vote of confidence to make deals, and once the bargain had been achieved they hastily closed the issue. They prevented MPs from asking questions, especially those who had evidence against the ministers. I have evidence that implicates ministers with some MPs over corruption and bribes. Why would ministers visit MPs' houses the night before the vote? Why would directors of customs, provincial governors, police chiefs, and the attorney general get involved and lobby for ministers? Today, I have come to Parliament in chains to protest against such practices and to honour the dignity of this house.[17]

State officials are not the only ones who provide financial and political deals. During the SEC crisis, following rumours that Azizi Bank had gone bankrupt, MPs scheduled an inquiry session to investigate the bank's financial state. Compelling evidence suggested that the bank had been involved in illegal and corrupt business practices. As the day of the inquiry approached, tensions intensified. Amazingly, on the day itself, despite most MPs' earlier rhetoric of corruption and mismanagement, the MPs voted overwhelmingly not to further investigate the bank's financial dealings. Some MPs complained that deals had been made and that some of them were threatened and intimidated by network nodes within the administration linked to the bank. As one MP put it:

> I fear for my life. Azizi Bank has threatened me on many occasions. We have evidence that 450 million dollars was transferred to Dubai for purchasing property; not a single penny has returned. The bank has also been involved in corruption in the oil business.[18]

Most MPs interviewed pointed out that if the investigation had gone ahead it would have exposed and implicated MPs and a wide network of top officials. In 2010, investigation into the corruption of the largest bank in Afghanistan, Kabul Bank, revealed that the bank officials had bribed the Wolesi Jirga before they had won the bid to process government staff salaries. Of the total estimated USD 75 million dollars in bribes paid by the bank, a substantial part had gone to MPs. Evidence shows that the bank had became an 'unofficial arm of the Karzai government', helping corrupt elites transfer money to offshore accounts (Bijlert 2011a). On the list of 200 people involved in receiving irregular loans from Kabul Bank were 103 former MPs, several governors, and some ministers (Bijlert 2011a). Both Azizi Bank and Kabul Bank expose the complexity and extensiveness of the connections across Afghanistan's political, financial, and administrative institutions and structures. This illustrates how some of these political networks cut across formal and informal, public and private, and licit and illicit structures of power, expanding their political and economic interests right under the nose of international statebuilders. A more detailed study of *illegality* as a key aspect of post-2001 Afghan politics is urgently needed but is beyond the scope of this paper.

The reason for the intensification of MPs' deal making lies in the political economy of the Wolesi Jirga. The political economic explanation is that the new parliament has provided the necessary political protection needed for most politician-turned-businessmen to maintain themselves within the system (Coburn 2011a, 2011b). In his study of the political economy of the Afghan parliament, Coburn found that the role of business transactions has become more important in terms of political financing, protecting their resources and preserving business monopolies of corrupt networks (2011a, 2011b). He found that MPs not only have to cover the cost of maintaining an office, staff, and other expenses, they also have to fulfil a number of traditional political obligations for their constituencies, including providing a place for constituents to stay while visiting Kabul, attending weddings, providing expensive gifts, offering food on feast days, and fulfilling religious obligations such as paying for a religious figure to recite the Quran. The current monthly salary of an MP is around USD 2000. The state also pays for two bodyguards and an assistant. It seems that bargaining and exchange is a practical strategy that allows MPs to function. Several MPs highlighted how some MPs have incurred debts to be elected. As one MP said, 'Some MPs have borrowed a lot of money to come to Parliament, so they have to make deals to pay for their debt.'[19] Another sarcastically complained that the crisis had failed to create more opportunities for deal making: 'Since the start of this crisis and the fact that not many laws have been passed or new ministers introduced, MPs have not made any deals, so they have become desperate.'[20] In fact, these bargains and opportunistic practices are not considered corruption but rather a survival strategy that has become normalized in an environment of uncertainty, elite distrust, and malfunctioning state institutions.

Opportunism and bargaining in Parliament is a reflection of wider local expectations and practices. Coburn (2010) found that people saw their MPs first and foremost as part of the local patronage networks. Prior to the election, in many places, he found competition taking place among different local power brokers and political-economic and identity networks over who to send to Parliament. Once in Parliament they are expected to help provide services, including securing jobs and business contracts, helping local power brokers to grab land, and even providing exemption from exams, through their state connections (Coburn 2010). Such high expectations put MPs in a difficult situation. This is evident from one MP's reply when asked for his reason for joining the Karzai network: 'They are the dominant network. They are in power. If I do not establish a close relationship with them, how could I resolve my people's [constituents'] problems when they come to Kabul?'[21]

Instrumentalization of identities

Opportunistic practices of bargaining and exchange were mutually reinforced with the politicization of identities, especially along ethnic lines, which was another key characteristic of the Special Election Crisis. Bhatia and Sedra (2007) and Wimmer and Schetter (2003) have shown that in the post-Bonn state-building era, politics has become centred on the politicization of ethnic differences. Sharan and Heathershaw (2011) highlighted how, in moments of contestation like the 2004 and 2009 presidential elections, network elites politicized identities along tribal, ethnic, and regional lines to mask their opportunistic practices of bargain and exchange. As the quote below reflects, the Wolesi Jirga has become a key venue for daily instrumentalization of identities.

> Another main issue for the current conflict in the Wolesi Jirga is the tribal, ethnic, and linguistic fanaticism of the House. Whenever there is a serious issue to be discussed or voted on, it takes an ethnic line. Even open-minded and independent MPs adopt such lines.[22]

However, as the SEC crisis shows, ethnic divisions can be understood as a form of political network competition over the state, rather than a battle over primordial identities. From the very beginning, the crisis took an ethnic dimension, starting with the demand by the Karzai network for re-election in Ghazni Province to reflect the ethnic composition within the province. Although Karzai's primary concern might have been simply to try to expand his network within his southern constituency, the rhetoric he used to justify his demand was couched along ethnic lines. In return, the Hazara political network leaders, including the second vice-president, expressed their strongest objection, partly to safeguard their gain and partly to please their ethno-regional constituencies. Mohammad Mohaqqeq, the leader of the Wahdat-e-Mardom network, publicly situated the crisis within a historical context as yet another attempt by the Pashtun leaders to marginalize the ethnic Hazaras, while privately he was making deals. Within the environment of a complex 'ethnic security dilemma' (Kaufmann 2000, 441) represented by these leaders in post-2001 state-building, ethno-regional leaders could claim to defend and protect particular ethnic groups.

Many Afghan analysts saw the crisis as simply an extension of the power struggle between the Pashtun-dominated government represented by Karzai and the Tajik-dominated opposition represented by Dr Abdullah, who stood against Karzai in the 2009 presidential election. Others saw it as a rivalry between the Hizb-i-Islami and Jamiat-i-Islami *tanzims* dating back to the civil war. Such simplistic accounts are widespread across Afghanistan, as the following quote illustrates.

> Unfortunately ethnicity is rooted and institutionalized in Afghan politics. Ethnic conflict has increased in the new Parliament, particularly between the Pashtuns and Tajiks. During the crisis, the Pashtun MPs supported the government line, while the Tajiks supported the opposition.[23]

On the face of it, one could make a crude analysis that the Sabah parliamentary group representing the Hizb-i-Islami, and Sayyaf's Dawat network in the Wolesi Jirga, both predominately Pashtun, supported Karzai during the SEC crisis, while the majority of ethnic-Tajik MPs joined the opposition. The instrumentalization of identity-based division was one of the key strategies employed by political networks to conceal their practices of bargain and exchange. The SEC crisis reproduces this pattern. A more detailed analysis suggests that network power brokers and their associated MPs were skilful in portraying the events during the crisis as arising from ethnic tensions to conceal their back-room deals.

Statehood and intervention in post-2001 Afghanistan

The Special Election Court crisis highlights a number of important characteristics of emerging post-2001 statehood and governance in Afghanistan. The crisis suggests that a 'network form of state' is emerging as part of the internationally sponsored post-2001 state-building process. Since 2001, political networks have become indistinguishable from the state. The state is constituted *as state* by its appreciation of informal exchange: political networks have formed an internationally supported government which enacts statehood through a system of patronage and opportunism. The state has provided a framework for inter-network competition, compromise, and accommodation, made manifest in identity-based divisions, patron–client relations, and the appropriation of public resources for personal gain. Indeed, the state itself has exacerbated this problem as it provides the primary incentive structure – outside of the drug trade – for inter-network conflict. The subsequent instrumentalizations of identity-based divisions are not isolated acts of strongman choice for self-enrichment but have become an instrument to achieve the purposes of political networks. These mutually reinforcing network practices are in fact essential to the survival of the networks and hence of the Afghan state itself. Thus, the nature of state-building in contemporary Afghanistan contains multiple layers of contradiction, 'progressing' to build a schismatic state riven by political networks and fostering profiteering and opportunism.

The liberal peace formal institutions that were built with hundreds of millions of dollars in international aid money have become an instrument of manipulation by political networks, who use state capacities of coercion and administration to legitimize their actions and to strengthen their influence within the state. The state and political networks are undistinguishable from one another; the empowered networks masquerade *as* the state. The members of the Wolesi Jirga see certain levels of connection within and outside the state as necessary for them to be able to operate within an environment of managed uncertainty and opportunism, developed as the result of practices of bargaining and the instrumentalization of identity-based divisions. This goes beyond the analysis offered by Larson (2010), who saw the MPs as deliberately concealing their intentions and remaining publicly ambiguous. For instance, MPs' ability to politically manoeuvre within complicated formal state institutions as well as informal local societal power structures and licit and illicit business networks is a determining factor in their survival. A high-ranking IEC employee in the north once explained how he had manipulated election data in favour of a candidate who had initiated the contact.[24] The motive for the IEC staff member was to get closer to Governor Atta Mohammad Noor's lucrative illicit business network through the candidate. Another MP, from Kandahar Province, explained how he had strategically set up a team of campaigners who could provide him with access to state institutions in the province to win the vote:

> In Kandahar, Karzai's brother is the king. The entire province is divided between three main power brokers, who made deals before the election on who to send to the Wolesi Jirga.... The people in my district asked that I stand in the election. I set up a team in Kandahar whose one half was working within the government and the other half outside. This helped me get elected against the power brokers.[25]

Where does the post-2001 network state stand in its relations to the ongoing international intervention and state-building? Given the main focus of this paper on power dynamics among local political networks, there was little discussion of the role of international state-building; however, this is not to suggest that international interveners were or are passive players. In the immediate international intervention in 2001, what enabled political networks to regain power was indeed the intervener's strategy of 'renting peace', where they made bargains with former *mujahedeen tanzims* to help constitute and reassemble the state (Sharan 2011). From then on, the unintended consequences of international state-building's financial support and conferred legitimacy further enabled political networks and their elites to consolidate power. Scott's (1998) logic of 'authoritarian high modernism' seems relevant to the international state-building project. International interveners were able to impose political and economic agendas and institutions inherent to liberal peace such as elections, rule of law, property rights, and the Parliament on local political networks. However, as Scott (1998) reminds us, such grand schemes in modernization are commonly subverted as much as they are implemented, and this subversion often takes place under the noses of the international statebuilders. What they failed (and are still failing) to understand was that such grand schemes fail because they overlook local knowledge and power dynamics. From the very outset, the international interveners in Afghanistan overlooked the historically grounded stubbornness of the informal practices that had dominated Afghan politics throughout its modern state formation. The post-2001 outcome is a combination of 'compromised peacebuilding' (Barnett and Zürcher 2009), where political networks are able to protect their interests whilst preserving a veneer of stability for international consumption, alongside 'conflictual peacebuilding', in which the Taliban continue to violently contest the whole basis of the post-Bonn settlement. This outcome is not a 'sovereignty paradox' (Zaum 2007), where the means (international intervention) contradict the ends (national sovereignty). As the case of Afghanistan reveals, once the concept of the state is freed from the 'territorial trap' (Agnew 1994, 54), we can see that international intervention generates a network state rather than the ideal of a vertically organized and territorially encompassing sovereign entity. This outcome is an unintended consequence of the international interveners' poorly constructed strategies and actions, and one that is not necessarily in their interests.

At its present stage, whatever the outcome, the circulation of discourses legitimizing the Afghan state and state-building are essential to maintain and justify international engagement. Privately, key donors often do criticize the consolidation of the network state and its daily practices in Afghanistan; publicly, however, they have little option but to justify the outcome. During the 2010–2011 SEC crisis, the US and its allies privately backed and supported the Independent Election Commission's decision to overrule Karzai's attempt to remove 62 sitting MPs, but arguably they could not do much in the face of a strong Karzai network intervention. The depiction of a senior foreign affairs official is revealing about Karzai's relation with international intervention, at least since the 2009 presidential election:

> Karzai has taken everybody hostage: the Americans, the UN, the Afghans, even the opposition. Imagine him sitting in the driver's seat of a suicide-bombing car, accelerating. He tells the Americans, If you put pressure on me, I will explode myself and you get conflict and instability; he tells the Afghans, If I leave, the country will slip back to 1990s civil war; and he tells the opposition that if they plot against him he will destroy the current system and expose their corruption and illegal businesses.[26]

Conclusion

In this paper, I have examined the power dynamics of political networks during the Special Election Court crisis and their network practices of patronage, opportunism, and identity manipulations, shedding light on the nature of statehood and governance in post-2001 Afghanistan. The crisis suggests that competition and conflict among political networks have produced a 'network state', in which competing political networks readily utilize state resources and international patronage to expand their interests. The success of the Support for Rule of Law coalition in standing firm against the Karzai network's authoritarian advance during the crisis and even forcing them to back down from removing the 62 sitting MPs further strengthens the argument that we must consider the fundamental role and power of political networks in post-2001 Afghanistan.

This insight has policy implications for the ongoing NATO-led withdrawal from Afghanistan and political stability in the post-2014 period. Drawing on this study's findings, a successful international exit from Afghanistan and the post-2014 state's survival would be contingent on the stability of the empowered political networks that currently constitute the Afghan state as much as on the strength of the Afghan National Security Forces and the outcome of ongoing reconciliation and negotiation with the Taliban, the two key foci of the current international exit strategy. Political networks are a source of conflict and violence but also of peace and state survival. Both peace and violence in the post-2014 period will have less to do with the outcome of the current ongoing international military effort than with how power dynamics among rival political networks play out and how they reorganize themselves. At the time of this writing, negotiations were ongoing between various rival political networks to choose a candidate in the 2014 presidential election to guarantee their post-2014 interests. In the Karzai-led camp, there is discussion about the candidacy of Abdur Rasul Sayyaf, a powerful jihadi strongman who is close both to Karzai's team and to some of the former Northern Alliance *mujahedeen* networks. In the so-called opposition camp – comprised of various coalitions of political networks including the National Front (led by Ahmad Zia Masood, Mohammad Mohaqeq, and Rashid Dostum), the National Coalition (led by Dr Abdullah Abdullah), and the Support for Rule of Law coalition (led by Haji Zahir Qadir) – discussion on a common candidate continues.

Whatever the outcome of these negotiations and the candidates selected, I contend that the Afghan state is likely to survive the post-2014 period more or less in its current form because the power dynamics of political networks have locked them into a complex bargaining and exchange system, such that any attempt by political networks to destabilize the status quo would essentially undermine their deeply entrenched and intertwined political and financial interests. Empowered political networks have benefitted impressively within the post-2001 system that they helped to build with the intention of guaranteeing their long-term interests. A reduction in external resource flows (e.g. military contracts and aid programmes) will affect the magnitude of exchange and bargaining but arguably will not weaken their relative abilities to buy loyalty, given their control over the Afghan economy (both licit and illicit). While instability can increase the likelihood of violence, it can also decrease it if violence is so destabilizing that it threatens to destroy the system as a whole. It is possible that the current intensification of political tensions and the rhetoric of threat and fear (e.g. relapse into civil or ethnic war) preferred by political networks are meant more for constituency consumption in the generated moment of uncertainty and ambiguity, as opposed to being a real sign of the potential for violence as portrayed by daily news headlines.

However, this argument depends on two key external factors. First, the proposed international military presence in Afghanistan – the present negotiation over the US military camps in the country – must continue, to curb the 'bad neighbour' effect. In the 1990s, neighbouring countries supported political networks competing against each other, which led to a decade of civil war. Second, international aid must continue to sustain the Afghan state, especially the Afghan National Security Forces, which number around 300,000. After all, the Soviet-backed regime only collapsed in 1992, when the Soviets stopped supporting the regime financially, three years after their military withdrawal (Steele, this volume).

Acknowledgements

I am indebted to many people for making this research possible, especially to Qayoom Suroush for his help and support in the data collection. I benefited immensely from his knowledge and assistance. I am also thankful to John Heathershaw, Mark Sedra and Jonathan Goodhand for their comments and suggestions.

Notes

1. This research is based on the author's extensive ethnographic fieldwork during his Ph.D. study in Afghanistan between March 2011 and June 2012. Participatory observation in the Wolesi Jirga was supplemented with more than 40 interviews with key political informants, including MPs, network leaders, power brokers, international donors, government officials, and parliamentary group members. Indirectly, this research benefitted from the author's four years of professional work experience in Afghanistan, where he worked for several research and policy organizations, including the Afghanistan Research and Evaluation Unit, the Department for International Development (DfID), and USAID. To ensure interviewees' safety, the author has kept them anonymous.
2. From the major former *tanzim*s, the Jamiat-i-Islami has fractured into several smaller networks around key personalities such as Dr Abdullah Abdullah, Marhsal Qaseem Fahim, Yunos Qanooni, Ismail Khan, and Atta Mohammad Noor. The Wahdat-i-Islami has splintered into four smaller networks around Karim Khalili, Mohammad Mohaqeq, Qorban Ali Erfani, and Mohammad Akbari. Even the Hizb-i-Islami is now divided into two major networks: those who are part of the current government led by Arghandiwal; and those centered around Gulbuddin Hekmatyar, who are involved in the current insurgency war. Junbish is the only network that has not yet seen major division.
3. In 9 of the 19 districts in Ghazni, no votes were cast at all.
4. The new MPs were Hamidullah Tokhi, former Zabul governor and a former Hizb-i-Islami commander in Gereshk; Moallem Mirwali, from Helmand, who is close to the attorney general, Aloko; Guli Pahlawan, former rival of General Dostum in Faryab; and Ahmad Khan, the notorious former Junbish *tanzim* commander and former governor of Samangan.
5. Author interview, 4 September 2011.
6. Author interview, 12 June 2011.
7. Hussaini and Niazi (2010) identified the Hizb-i-Islami and its Sabah parliamentary group as the most coordinated network in the House.
8. Author interview, 8 September 2011.
9. Author interview, Kabul MP, 10 September 2011.
10. Accusation made by several MPs during the author's ethnographic observation in the House on 24 August 2011 and confirmed at the end of the session with several MPs.
11. Author interview, male Kandahar MP, 18 July 2011.

12. Author interview, female Kabul MP, 5 September 2011.
13. Author interview, Kabul, 4 December 2010.
14. Author interview, Kabul, 21 April 2012.
15. 'Hamid Karzai admits office gets "bags of money" from Iran.' *The Guardian.* http://www.guardian.co.uk/world/2010/oct/25/hamid-karzai-office-cash-iran.
16. 'With bags of cash, C.I.A. seeks influence in Afghanistan'. *New York Times*, 28 April 2013. http://www.nytimes.com/2013/04/29/world/asia/cia-delivers-cash-to-afghan-leaders-office.html.
17. Tolo News, 20 February 2012. http://www.youtube.com/watch?v=HYopiK4q2dA.
18. Author interview, Kabul MP, 16 July 2011.
19. Author interview, Kabul MP, 24 August 2011.
20. Author interview, Panjshir MP, 24 August 2011.
21. Author interview, Ghazni MP, 29 August 2011.
22. Author interview, female Kabul MP, 25 June 2011.
23. Author interview, Ghazni MP, 26 June 2011.
24. Author interview, Mazar-e-Sharif, 30 March 2012.
25. Author interview, Kandahar MP, 30 June 2011.
26. Author interview, Kabul, 12 July 2011.

References

Agnew, J. 1994. "The Territorial Trap: The Geographical Assumptions of International Relations Theory." *Review of International Political Economy* 1 (1): 53–80.

Barnett, M., and C. Zürcher. 2009. "The Peacebuilder's Contract: How External Statebuilding Reinforces Weak Statehood." In *The Dilemmas of Statebuilding*, edited by R. Paris and T. Sisk. London: Routledge.

Bhatia, M., and M. Sedra. 2007. Afghanistan, Armed Groups, Disarmament and Security in a Post- War Society. London: Routledge.

Bijlert, M. 2011a. "The Kabul Bank Investigations; Central Bank Gives Names and Figures." *Afghanistan Analyst Network*, May 2. http://www.aaaafghanistan.org/index.asp?id=1663

Bijlert, M. 2011b. "Untangling Afghanistan's 2010 Vote: Analysing the electoral data." *Afghanistan Analyst Network*, Briefing Paper (3).

Bijlert, M. 2011c. "A New Result for the Parliamentary Election?" *Afghanistan Analyst Network*, August 21. http://www.aan-afghanistan.com/index.asp?id=2032

Chesterman, S. 2004. *We, the People: The United Nations, Transitional Administration and Statebuilding.* Oxford: Oxford University Press.

Coburn, N. 2010. "Connecting with Kabul: The Importance of the Wolesi Jirga Election and Local Political Networks in Afghanistan." *Afghanistan Research and Evaluation Unit.*

Coburn, N. 2011a. "Political Economy in the Wolesi Jirga: Sources of Finance and Their Impact on Representation in Afghanistan's Parliament." *Afghanistan Research Evaluation Unit*, May 2011.

Coburn, N. 2011b. *Bazaar Politics: Power & Pottery in an Afghan Market Town.* California: Stanford University Press.

Duffield, M. 1999. *Global Governance and the New Wars.* London: Zed.

Ghani, A., C. Lockhart, and M. Carnahan. 2005. "Closing the Sovereignty Gap: An Approach to Statebuilding."' Working Paper 253. London: Overseas Development Institute.

Giustozzi, A. 2007. "War and Peace Economies of Afghanistan's Strongmen." *International Peacekeeping* 14 (1): 75–89.

Granovetter, M. 1974. "The Strength of Weak Ties." *American Journal of Sociology* 78 (6): 1360–1380.

Hakimi, A. 2011. "The Parliament Must Work to Institutionalise Democracy." *Bamdad News Agency*, Accessed June 7, 2013. http://www.bamdad.af/index.php/english/text/story/1298

Hussaini, A., and N. Niazi. 2010. "The Composition of the New Parliament." Report, February 2010. Kabul: *Kabul Centre for Strategic Studies.*

Jalali, A. 2003, February. "Afghanistan in 2002: The Struggle to Win the Peace." *Asian Survey* 43 (1).

Kaufmann, C. 2000. "Possible and Impossible Solutions to Ethnic Civil War." In *International Politics: Enduring Concepts and Contemporary Issues*, edited by A. Art and R. Jervis. New York: Addison-Wesley Educational Publishers.

Larson, A. 2010, September. "The Wolesi Jirga in Flux, 2010 Elections and Instability I." *Afghanistan Research and Evaluation Unit Discussion Paper.*

MacGinty, R. 2011. "Hybrid Peace: How Does Hybrid Peace Come About?." In *A Liberal Peace: The Problems and Practices of Peacebuilding*, edited by S. Campbell, D. Chandler, and M. Sabaratnam. London: Zed.

Mukhopadhyay, D. 2009. "Warlords As Bureaucrats: The Afghan Experience." *Carnegie Papers*, N 101. August.

National Radio Television of Afghanistan. 2013. Broadcast 15 May 2013, Accessed August 25, 2013. http://www.youtube.com/watch?v.nst8M0Ftec4

Ober, J. 2011. "Karzai's Court." *Foreign Policy, The AF-Pak Channel*. Accessed June 7, 2013. http://afpak. foreignpolicy.com/posts/2011/07/07/karzais_court

Office of National Budget Report. 2011. *Ministry of Finance*. http://mof.gov.af/en

Ottoway, M., and A. Lieven. 2002. "Rebuilding Afghanistan: Fantacy verus Reality." In *Policy Brief 12 (January)*. Washington, D.C.: Carnegie Endowmwent for International Peace.

Piattoni, S. 2001. "Clientelism in Historical and Comparative Perspective." In *Clientelism, Interests, and Democratic Representation: The European Experience in Historical and Comparative Perspective*, edited by S. Piattoni. Cambridge: Cambridge University Press.

Paris, R. 1997. "Peacebuilding and the Limits of Liberal Internationalism." *International Security* 22 (2): 54-89.

Paris, R. 2004. *At War's End: Building Peace After Conflict*. Cambridge: Cambridge University Press.

Richmond, O. 2011. "Resistance and the Post-Liberal Peace." In *A Liberal Peace: The Problems and Practices of Peacebuilding*, edited by S. Campbell, D. Chandler, and M. Sabaratnam. London: Zed.

Roy, O. 1990. *Islam and Resistance in Afghanistan*. Cambridge: Cambridge University Press.

Rubin, B. 2006. "Peacebuilding and State-Building in Afghanistan: Constructing Sovereignty for Whose Security?" *Third World Quarterly* 27 (1): 0–0.

Ruttig, T. 2010. "Ghazni's Election Drama – It's the System/" Afghanistan Analytical Network, December 2, 2010.

Scott, J. C. 1972. "Patron-Client Politics and Political Change in Southeast Asia." *The American Political Science Review* 66 (1): 91–113.

Scott, J. C. 1998. *Seeing Like a State: How Certain Schemes to Improve the Human Condition Have Failed*. New Haven: Yale University Press.

Sharan, T. 2011. "The Dynamics of Elite Networks and Patron–Client Relations in Afghanistan." *Europe Asian Studies* 63 (3): 1109–1127.

Sharan, T., and J. Heathershaw. 2011. "Identity Politics and Statebuilding in Post-Bonn Afghanistan: The 2009 Presidential Election." *Ethnopolitics* 10 (4): 297–319.

Simonsen, S. 2004. "Ethnicising Afghanistan? Inclusion and Exclusion in Post-Bonn Institution Building." *Third World Quarterly* 25 (4): 707–739.

Sinno, A. K. 2008. *Organizations at War in Afghanistan and Beyond*. Cornell: Cornell University Press.

Stedman, S. J. 1997. "Spoiler Problems in Peace Processes." *International Security* 22 (2): 5–53.

Strand, A., K. B. Harpviken, and A. Suhrke. 2004. "Conflictual Peacebuilding: Afghanistan Two Years After Bonn." *CMI Report 4*. Chr Michelsen Institute.

Wafaey, H. and A. Larson, A. 2010. "The Wolesi Jirga in 2010: Pre-election Politics and the Appearance of Opposition." Afghanistan Research and Evaluation Unit.

Wimmer, A., and C. Schetter. 2003. "Putting State-formation First: Some Recommendations for Reconstruction and Peace-Making in Afghanistan." *Journal for International Development* 15 (5): 525–539.

Zaum, D. 2007. *The Soverign Paradox: The Norms and Politics of International Statebuilding*. Oxford: Oxford University Press.

Order, stability, and change in Afghanistan: from top-down to bottom-up state-making

Andreas Wilde[a] and Katja Mielke[d]

[a]Institute of Oriental Studies/Chair of Iranian Studies, University of Bamberg, Bamberg, Germany; [b]Centre for Development Research, Department of Social and Cultural Change, University of Bonn, Bonn, Germany

This article presents findings from long-term empirical fieldwork and archival research into current and historical patterns of governance in north-eastern Afghanistan, conducted between 2006 and 2009. Despite the long civil war, striking continuities have been found in the make-up and functioning of the local social order. Patron–client relations, eldership, and related practices of mediation are crucial structuring principles of rural society. They have dominated Afghan politics over centuries and still do today. Viewed from a long-term perspective, this continuity, related patterns of representation, and the role of middlemen and brokers suggest a certain degree of stability, in contrast to the popular perception of instability and disorder in this country. Whilst in the past the expansion of the state relied on tacit agreement between government administrators and local elites, resulting in state-making from above, the war broadly changed actors, regimes, and coalitions, but not the underlying mechanisms of the social order. Hence, today, the failure of the current state-building project can be attributed to the fact that the effects of these mechanisms are insufficiently recognized and grasped by Western actors and state-builders. We argue that local Afghan actors have captured the intervention from below. Instead of state-building, we are dealing here with state-making dominated by patronage networks.

Introduction

Afghanistan is popularly perceived as a symbol of disorder and anarchy. It is seen as an ungoverned territory,[1] the site of a clash of cultures, and a place of struggle between good and evil, us and them. For more than three decades it has come to signify instability and disorder. Contrary to this view, we want to argue that Afghanistan as a country, with its diverse social communities, displays a high degree of order and always has. The kind of order or stability we have in mind is not tied to government or socio-economic welfare. We suggest, instead, that stability manifests itself through social relationships that inform the social practices, discourses, and mental cognitive realms of the Afghan population. This is at odds with prevailing understandings of stability and order which find expression in overly simplified dichotomies: the mirroring of chaos or disorder versus order; war or anomie (Merton 1938) versus peace; and development versus backwardness.

The following analysis attempts to leave this bias behind and to seek an alternative way of looking at Afghanistan and understanding its inherent political dynamics, before the war and at present. By introducing the idea of social order as the structuring principle for all human agency and social organization, which never ceases to exist but rather changes its institutional and normative contents, we intend to avoid simplistic dichotomies (Mielke, Schetter, and Wilde 2011).

The aim of this article is to illustrate the continuity of structuring principles of social order in today's north-eastern Afghanistan and to trace the course and limits of social change. We argue that popularly perceived crises described in terms of anomie, disorder, war, etc. by politicians, journalists, and the global public do not signify a total breakdown of social life or socio-economic activities. Instead, the actors and groups investigated rely on institutional coping mechanisms which are structured by and constantly restructure their world-views and actions. From this vantage point, order never ceases to exist. In the Afghan context of 'disorderly violence' and civil war, commonly perceived as signs of a power vacuum, armed conflict should be seen as a structural concomitant of the same power-driven mechanisms that persist in times of peace. They are grounded in the same particular world-views and cognitive frames of the local population, manifest in personal network and patronage practices.

The exploration of the main argument builds on two pillars. Given both authors' distinct research projects and methodological approaches,[2] the first part draws upon Persian chronicles and secondary sources on local and regional history. From the fragmentary picture provided by historiographical works, we proceed to the results of oral history and narrative interviews to capture the 'world-views' and mental orientations of respondents in the rural society of Afghanistan's north-east.[3] The long-term historical perspective is next complemented with insights about shifts in representation patterns within rural communities since the late 1970s. The role of local representatives in co-opting rural development interventions and the appropriation of state-provided resources by a small stratum of elites is used to point out the currently prevalent negotiated state-making[4] from below. Afghanistan's 30 years of war, conflict, and foreign intervention commonly engender an overemphasis on actors and regime-change dynamics and the formation of new alliances. Yet, the question of how the new elites position themselves and act is generally neglected. The clarification of this question requires long-term empirical field work at the village level and taking account of historical patterns of local-level governance. Drawing upon our experience, archival research, and fieldwork, we find a continuity of representation mechanisms such as patron–client ties, mediation, protection, and exchange of goods and favours.

The analytical concept of social order and the Afghan example

In most academic writings, order[5] is seen as a matter of degree, implying different levels of order on a wide spectrum, with absence of order at one (negative) end and the achievement of peaceful relations between individuals at the other (positive) end (Wrong 1979: 2, 20) – concluding, for example, that 'the more ... individual behaviour is collectively oriented, the higher the level of order' (Hechter and Horne 2003, 27). In contrast to this view, the analysis to follow proposes to apply 'social order' as a non-normative analytical concept. Instead of subscribing to a mere (normative) status description, the focus is on social order as structuring device which provides the frame and basis for all social interaction processes, the results of which depend on the interplay of social practices (institutions) and cognitive factors (world-view and moralities). Consequently, the heuristic focus of a social-order analysis lies in its processual dimension, constituted by the mechanisms and practices, including the discursive ones, which shape mundane social interactions. The outcomes are a function of the mutual interplay between these social practices and cognitive factors structured by power relations. Conversely, the assumption is that social order is influenced and restructured by these power-led processes and outcomes and constantly reproduces itself (Mielke, Schetter, and Wilde 2011)[6] – not without yielding generic effects in the form of social change. The argument of stability in social order will be unfolded in several steps. The historical section relies on an institutional analysis of patronage and mechanisms of reciprocity, including underlying world-views. The contemporary analysis is derived from long-term investigations into 'local governance'. Local governance, here, is understood as the mundane exercise of power which involves decision-making and -implementation processes within communities and concerning inter-community affairs, with the aim to realize peaceful coexistence and the provision of other collective goods in the local environment. This refers for example to the joint usage of everyday resources (i.e. their allocation, distribution, and accessibility), dispute resolution, and the provision of security. In the concluding remarks, the findings will be contextualized within the broader framework of the recent reconstruction and state-building project in Afghanistan.

While in academic writing on Afghanistan much attention has been put on regime change and coalition-building among political factions (Shahrani 2013; Ruttig 2013), for example on the dimensions of national and sub-national government (Nixon 2008a), structural continuities at the level of governance (in the sense explained above) are less often noticed. Others (Nixon 2008b; Barfield 2013) suspect drastic changes to have been caused as a result of the decades-long violent conflict and recent interventions. At the same time, and from the perspective of social order and local governance, political and especially social change at the community level is under-studied. The pooling of empirical material from two distinct research projects confirms the views of researchers who have underlined persistence and continuity in political patterns (Centlivres-Demont and Centlivres 2013; Geller 2009) and patron–client relations (Centlivres-Demont and Centlivres 2013; Sharan 2011), but also identify rentier logics (Verkoren and Kamphuis 2013) and the limited prospects for the current intervention's achieving its goal to 'develop' Afghanistan in the broadest sense (Suhrke 2012).

Patronage and mediation in local and regional history

According to Chabal and Daloz (1999), the institution of patronage is based on reciprocity and involves power asymmetries characterized by unequal status and access to resources. The patrons deliver social benefits and provide protection to their clients, while the latter owe their masters loyalty and political support (see Eisenstadt and Roniger 1980; Lemarchand and Legg 1972; Hall 1977; Weber Pazmiño 1991). As a social institution within a larger framework of social order, patronage is linked to mediation. As a rule, many leaders act as patrons and mediators at the same time. The intermediary is characterized by extraordinary negotiation skills and rhetorical expertise but also a multitude of personal contacts and relationships. Referring to the Afghan example, Glatzer (2005) argues that traditional power brokers had to be endowed with additional characteristics like personal wealth (either in land or livestock), good birth (indicated by pedigrees), a sense of responsibility, and personal charisma.

Although it is possible to follow the traces of local patrons and middlemen in Persian historiography, the written sources provide only scarce information about them. The chronicles do not usually provide information on their roles and duties; they just figure as *muysafid*s, *arbab*s, *rishsafid*s, *aqsaqal*s (lit. whitebeard, mediator), and *beg*s (title of former Uzbek rulers, today member of nobility), without individual names and characteristics. Their function can be only deduced from the contexts described in the texts. Power relations in the villages were of little interest; the authors mainly reported battles and the negotiations taking place afterwards. Here one pattern becomes obvious: acts of submission and tribute occur in exchange for recognition and protection. We learn neither about relations with their clients nor about their resources as outlined above. According to the *Tarikh-i ahmadshahi* (al-Huseini 1379/2000), for example, in 1750, Haji Bi Ming, the local ruler of Maimana, attended the Afghan king, Ahmad Shah Abdali, at Herat. He was accompanied by a group of unnamed 'whitebeards and notables' to solicit Ahmad Shah's assistance against the Bukharan ruler, Muhammad Rahim Bi (al-Huseini 1379/2000; McChesney 1991; Nölle-Karimi 2008). When in 1737 a Persian army marched on Balkh, the governor of Aqcha, 'Ata Beg, and some 'whitebeards and tribal leaders' collected a number of gifts and went to the Persian camp. Upon their arrival, they paid homage to the Persian prince, Riza Quli Mirza, and were granted robes of honour in return (Kazim 1990, 576).

The scenario described here, with a group of notables begging the protection of a superior ruler or commander to avoid destruction and massacre, is very common in the sources. Even in late-medieval times, 'the arrival of Timurid troops before the city targeted was followed by negotiations with the local nobility' (Nölle-Karimi 2008, 84). In 1737, Riza Quli Mirza besieged the city of Balkh, and after a while, a group of city elders signalled obedience by delivering gifts. The same happened shortly thereafter in Kunduz, where the town's elders received the customary robes of honour and a confirmation of their political status in return (Kazim 1990, 608–09).

Although providing similar pieces of information, nineteenth-century sources suggest logics of representation that differ slightly from place to place. In his historical review of social organization among the Tajiks of Badakhshan, Kussmaul explores nineteenth-century travelogues and describes the position of an *aqsaqal* or *rishsafid* as a kind of village head or mayor who acted as a representative of rural communities (1965). In Wakhan, for instance, the *aqsaqal* position was monopolized and inherited by the most influential families belonging to the military elite. In the principality of Sheghnan, an *aqsaqal-i mubarak* bore the title of *wazir* (minister) and administered the districts near the capital. Very often, the whitebeards were exempt from taxes. They acted at two levels: firstly, they were involved in the internal organization of rural communities, where they were responsible for the construction and repair of bridges, irrigation canals, etc.; and secondly, they participated in gatherings at the courts of regional and local potentates. Acting as mediators, they negotiated solutions in cases of conflict over land and water rights (Holzwarth 1980). A similar pattern of social organization can be found in the lowlands of Qataghan, between the Kunduz River and the Amu Darya, where the Uzbek settlements were likewise represented by *muysafids* or *aqsaqals*, who were responsible for the maintenance of the irrigation system, the organization of festivities and *buzkashi* (goat-pulling) games, weddings, etc. (Rasuly-Paleczek 1993). Even after the subjugation of the region by the Afghans during the 1860s, the governor, 'Abd al-Rahman Khan, relied on the support of the judge of Kunduz in his negotiations with the local population, because of the reputation the latter enjoyed among the people (Noelle 1997). In his *Rahnama*, Kushkaki gives lists of influential personalities of high standing who lived in Kunduz during the first decades of the twentieth century; among them are Ghulam Rasul Bay, Mulla Muhammad Amin, and Aziz Khan Mingbashi (1989).[7]

After the integration of the region into the Afghan state, the government confirmed local actors in their positions. But at the same time, their function appears to have changed. While the army was in charge of tax collection, the new administration relied on middlemen for the extraction of revenues and the recruitment of soldiers (Grevemeyer 1990; Noelle 1997). With regard to pre-1978 Afghanistan, the time before the outbreak of large-scale conflict, we encounter patrons and mediators in a variety of settings and situations. For example, in the time of Amanullah (r. 1919–1928), a more institutionalized system of brokerage became firmly established, with *arbab*s acting between the state administration and local villages. The *arbab*, also called a *qariya-dar* (government-confirmed village-official) or *malik* (village holder), was a locally appointed overseer and middleman for one or several villages. The *arbab* was responsible for the registration of births, marriages, and deaths with the government. After the appointment, the respective office bearers were confirmed by the Afghan state, receiving a certificate of authority (*wasiqa*) (see Barfield 1981; Azoy 1982; Centlivres and Centlivres-Demont 1988; Rasuly-Paleczek 1993). The status and mode of cooperation of those middlemen with the Afghan government were fixed by a series of laws and decrees, e.g. the law concerning the establishment of the Afghan administration, under which indigenous personalities became responsible for the organization of village and hamlet governance.[8] With Amanullah's reforms, the role of intermediaries recruited from the rural aristocracy was regulated in four fields: taxation, allocation of land, recruitment of soldiers, and common administrative acts (Grevemeyer 1990).

Simultaneously, the government followed a strategy that is commonly described as 'internal colonization' (Dupree 1973) by resettling Pashtun tribes from the south and the east, and refugees from Soviet Central Asia, in the vicinity of Kunduz and Khanabad, near Baghlan, and in Balkh (Shalinsky 1986).

Expansion of the state mediated by local brokers: the Qataghan land-reclamation campaign

At the beginning of the last century, the province of Qataghan (today Kunduz, Baghlan, and Takhar) witnessed a period of political and economic decline. The decay of the irrigation system caused a considerable reduction of the agricultural land, which virtually turned into swamp (Azoy 1982; Barfield 1981; Grötzbach 1990). Yet, with the enforcement of a settlement policy promoted by the central government at the beginning of the 1930s, the situation changed drastically.[9] From that time onward, the region underwent a fundamental transition from a backward, peripheral province to Afghanistan's 'economic engine'. The new settlement policy also caused a change in the ethnic composition of the population (Grevemeyer 1990; Grötzbach 1972). This development was based on a shift in regional policy by the governor, Sher Khan, who played a major role in initiating the campaigns for land reclamation and the improvement of the local infrastructure. Moreover, private companies and the Afghan National Bank (Bank-i melli-yi Afghan) financed and fostered industrial projects like the Kunduz Cotton Company in 1936–37 and the sugar factory in Baghlan in 1940.[10]

Sher Khan advanced his policy with the active assistance of local elders (kalan-i qawm or muysafid-i qawm) like 'Abd al-Karim Khan, 'Aziz Khan Mingbashi, and Wakil 'Abdarrasul. These prominent men of high standing were the leaders of the major ethnic communities in Kunduz and its vicinity. Especially after the introduction of the Pashtun settlers and the refugees from Soviet Central Asia, the potential for inter-community conflicts increased, calling for mediators to prevent anticipated escalations. A similar pressure for solutions pertained to the distribution of the newly reclaimed land, as well as to the water shares of the different stakeholders of the new irrigation canals. Elders like 'Aziz Khan participated in frequent consultations with the provincial government to discuss the canal digging and the extension of the road network.[11] The Afghan state financed these projects but relied for their implementation on local power brokers. Having been responsible for the recruitment of the workforce, the elders supervised the canal digging as well as the construction of small roads, in return receiving plots on the major irrigation canals.[12]

Since many of the ordinary peasants hesitated to buy land provided by the Afghan state for fear of exploitation by tax collectors, some of the elders purchased additional plots in the irrigated areas. The same thing happened after the reconstruction of Kunduz City and its bazaar, with its more than 900 shops and trade centres.[13] As a result, the elders of Kunduz came to constitute the stratum of influential landlords and bazaar traders. Both – the acquisition of land as well as bazaar shops and trade centres – were prerequisites to win new groups of clients: ordinary peasants living in villages outside of Kunduz at the margins of the irrigated area, as well as small-scale traders.[14] Another commercial sector affected by intensified patron–client relationships was the Kunduz Cotton Company. Many officials gained the status of middlemen, wielding a great deal of power and considerable influence on the local cotton market.[15]

With this combination of settlement policy and economic investment, the Afghan state not only established a firm hold on Qataghan, it was also able to tie the region into the orbit of governmental control, first and foremost by improving the communication lines between the province and the capital (Grötzbach 1972). On the one hand, this development coincided with the establishment of administrative structures visible in the increasing presence of the state administration (Grötzbach 1990). On the other hand, it resulted in the mushrooming of patronage networks that were built up by local intermediaries. In particular, their contacts with Sher Khan and other bureaucrats gave a boost to their reputations, which earned them a range of new followers at community level. This is evident in reports about close friendships and the preferential distribution of assets to influential senior elders who were able to distribute land and award share-cropping contracts with local peasants.[16] Initially, the government programme aimed at providing land to the landless, but this policy was undermined from the very beginning by the stratum of local power brokers (Grevemeyer 1990).

The improvement of administrative structures and the growth of patronage networks were interdependent. The networks of the local elders furnished the staff of the bureaucracy and the private companies based in Kunduz. The example of the mayor's or the *arbab*'s office illustrates that certain positions were monopolized by the main elders and their clan networks. For instance, the position of the mayor of Kunduz became hereditary and shifted for several generations between the families of four elders and their descendants.[17] The influence of these networks reached deep into the Kunduz Cotton Company, which had branches and ginning mills in many district centres, shuch as Imam Sahib, Khwaja Ghar, and Taloqan (Barfield 1981; Dupree 1973; Grötzbach 1972). In the course of time, the relatives of elders like 'Abd al-Karim Khan 'Arzbegi, 'Abdulrasul Wakil or 'Aziz Khan Mingbashi occupied key positions at the local level such as village officer, community elder, tax official, mayor of Kunduz, *mirab* (irrigation manager), supervisor of the local silos, and so on. Backed by extensive networks and contacts, they were able to mobilize their followers; the elders were soon regarded as patrons ready to support their clients.

By 1960, Qataghan had witnessed impressive economic and population growth due to the settlement policy of the Afghan government, the eradication of malaria, and the extension of the regional irrigation system. Due to the effective use the Afghan administration made of patron–client ties, Qataghan developed as Afghanistan's major agricultural and industrial zone prior to the outbreak of the Afghan conflict in 1978–1979 (Grötzbach 1972; Grötzbach 1990; Barfield 1981; Grevemeyer 1990).

Shifts in representation patterns within rural communities

While the historical overview has looked at patronage and mediation by elders at the more visible levels of local governance, i.e. provincial and district administrators and the big men in Kunduz City, the following sections are derived from empirical investigations into community-level hierarchies and governance.[18] In comparison with the time before 1978, 'traditional' elders (*arbabs*, *muysafids*, *mirabs*, etc.) have lost significance; new types of elders, most significantly 'commanders', have emerged and dominate the patterns of representation of local communities towards the outside world, including the central government, its local administration, and foreign development actors. Their authority partly rests on different power resources from the ones utilized by conventional elders of the past. Moreover, the significance of financial resources, in the overall context of venality that dominates public and private life, has altered dependency relations to large extent.[19]

The following section explores the shift of rural elites in the widest sense, i.e. of the designations of their titles, roles, and duties from 1978 until the late 1980s, a period that witnessed the militarization of the rural countryside. One difficulty in tracing elite change lies with the partial overlap of the roles and functions of *arbabs* and *muysafids* in village environments. As 'conventional' elders, both types of position holders, who were sometimes even from the same family, largely relied on the same power and legitimation resources (i.e. land property, material wealth, noble family, extended network relations, rhetorical skills, and charisma). In contrast to what has been described as the task of *arbab*s, i.e. mainly liaising between local communities and the government, the other 'conventional' elders such as *muysafids* and *rishsafids* would be consulted in decision-making and for conflict settlement not meant to be interfered with by the formal administration and become 'official'. With the onset of the Sawr Revolution and throughout the 1980s, the role of *arbab* as liaison person and 'tool of communication' on behalf of the government administration ceased, because the government had been declared 'the enemy' in the process of ideological mobilization of the Islamist parties. Oral histories of local community members who themselves or whose relatives never held the position of *arbab* indicate a generally unfavourable attitude towards *arbab*s already before 1978.[20] Many of the traditional local leaders, respected figures, and local elites (including some *arbab*s from traditional families) were murdered by government forces in the immediate aftermath of the April Revolution in 1978. Rural elites constituted by big landowners became labelled as *feodal* (feudals) (see also Grevemeyer 1990) in leftist propaganda campaigns and were targeted by the land-reform policy of the regime. Oral histories indicate that in particular traditional leaders of great clout, literate persons, Islamic scholars, and intellectuals in the provinces were victims of arrest and murder.[21] By the early 1980s, an entire stratum of traditional rural elites had vanished from the countryside. Those who were not targeted either took up arms and turned into commanders or organized support for the resistance during the 1980s. Some of the *arbab*s, like some of the *muysafid*-type conventional elders, became active in the resistance as commanders; a few found new roles as heads of newly established local farmers' cooperatives. By the time the commanders had established a military administrative hierarchy in the 1990s, *arbab*s had been replaced by village commanders and those at the district and provincial levels (*sar-i grup* and *amir*).

As the resistance waned and the individual commanders' interests – connected with the incentives and partial legitimacy they imparted to Najibullah's regime – became increasingly fragmented, the precondition for the evolution of a new type of elder was created. Reportedly, after the withdrawal of Soviet forces, those conventional elders who had taken up arms, become local resistance leaders (commanders), and organized defence, left the battlefield to become farmers, herders, Iran-migrants, and *muysafids* again. Others, who had made careers as commanders but had been ordinary peasants or labourers before that, continued as *mujahedin* and engaged in the civil-war economy that followed the fall of Najibullah's government. During the 1990s, the opinions and experience of conventional elders were largely disregarded in local governance affairs. Only with the onset and relative stabilization of Taliban rule in the north-eastern districts (e.g. in Chardara and Qal'a-yi Zal) did the *arbab* position gain new clout. Apparently, the Taliban administration intended to gain a foothold in local communities by requesting local elders to appoint a person as *arbab*. The appointments favoured whoever volunteered for the position, because 'good people at that time did not want to be *arbab*'.[22] The reinvention of the position by the Taliban seems to have discredited the status and role of *arbab* even further, in the sense that it lost its initially monopolistic gatekeeper function in liaising with the government. The multiplication in numbers of newly instated *arbab*s in places like Chardara District, where one *arbab* had been serving the district's 20 villages in Zaher Shah's time and where reportedly 40 to 44 had been appointed by 2006, has contributed to their overall decline in status and significance. An elder of Warsaj confirmed this idea, stating, 'We call everybody *arbab* today. He is a person in charge of a village. I am an *arbab*, the other elder as well.'[23]

In the Taliban era, the Taliban's practice of inquiring about a local commander's legitimacy in the eyes of his constituency limited the arbitrary influence of the local commanders. At the same time, the enforcement of speedy justice for conflict cases that had been simmering for years without progress or solution prior to the Taliban's presence in the north-east robbed 'convention-al' elders of their main (traditional) responsibilities and often made them appear redundant. On the one hand, the requests of local Taliban administrations to have *arbabs* appointed undermined the reputation of elders further, because in locals' eyes the Taliban themselves were hardly viewed as legitimate force; on the other hand, the *arbabs*' appointment boosted the legitimacy of the elder position and reconfirmed their role as mediators.

As result of the merging and partial overlap of the authority of elders and commanders over time, the situation during 2006–2009 was characterized by the coexistence of conventional and new ('novel') elders. Commanders had replaced traditional elders (sometimes as the same person) throughout the 1980s. Because they managed to monopolize power resources and offered the only source of rule enforcement, ordinary people turned to them for support and help in dispute resolution or decision-making. The commanders' legitimacy rested on their possession and active employment of arms, their ability to lead a group of follower-fighters, and their access to material and financial support. Similar to the elders' positioning at different socio-spatial scales (family, mosque community, *manteqa*,[24] etc.), the newly established chain of command was organized hierarchically from local commander to group leader and district or provincial commander. However, the system in place eventually foresaw the replacement of arbitrary commanders who showed bad conduct towards their local constituency. In such cases village elders appealed to the more senior position holder in the above-mentioned hierarchy. The evidence gleaned from the interviews indicates that the exchange of village-level commanders upon the request of the local residents in a particular community was common practice. Along a similar line, narratives about commanders, some of which were told by (ex-)commanders themselves, often suggested that they had been approached by the people and begged to be their commander. This occurred mostly during the time of the Taliban's advancement into the north-east.[25] Hezb-i Islami and Ettehad-i Islami commanders often took on these roles. If they more or less showed 'good conduct', that is, not exposing the local population to arbitrary violence and injustice, and possibly even trying to protect the people in their sphere of influence from oppression, they were perceived as stabilizing figures and enjoyed legitimacy.[26]

Interviews also revealed that commanders of different regimes were often offspring of the same family. A father who fought against Soviet army bases during the 1980s was typically succeeded by his son who was a commander of any of the fighting factions during the civil war. In some cases, becoming a commander was a survival strategy for defending oneself against looters. During the second half of the 1990s, a son was either with the Taliban on any of the Islamist parties' tickets, or with General Dostum or Ahmad Shah Ma'sud's forces in the north-east. With the undifferentiated US support for the Northern Alliance against the Taliban at the end of 2001, many of the local commanders in and around Kunduz were able to extend their influence and reconfirm their clout. Once the fighting was over, these influential commanders did not just return home, but used their resources to secure assets in Afghanistan's immediate post-war order. The so-called warlords occupied large areas of land illegally and used their deterrence potential to intimidate members of the ordinary population, not least through the collection of *'ushr*.[27] Only with the demobilization, disarmament, and reintegration (DDR) process that took off in 2003, during which they submitted their weapons to the police, did the pressure on local communities notably slacken. The evidence from Chardara shows how crucial a power resource the possession of guns was for a commander in maintaining his authority. Though most accounts state that DDR was very uneven und ineffective, here, after 2003, ordinary dwellers dared to voice contesting claims over land against one particular commander for the first time because they knew he had turned in his weapons. Similarly, the collection of *'ushr* ceased because of problems with enforcement and the need for former commanders to legitimize themselves by measures other than force in the mid-to-long term. With the ousting of the Taliban, the reshuffling of local positions, the subsequent formation of the transitional government, and the prospect of accessing government positions provided opportunities. In local parlance, commanders turned from being *ghair-i rasmi* (without official status) to occupying *rasmi* (officially assigned) positions in the government administration (see below). Nevertheless, several of these formerly significant commanders secretly sustained armed groups. By 2007 and at the latest 2009 they had already revived training camps in their area of influence, were actively re-arming, and started to rely again more strongly on relations with still-loyal commanders at the community level. As a result, local strongmen used the intermittent period of the last three to four years to position themselves and re-arm; today *'ushr* collection is again common.[28]

Today, in a nutshell, conventional elders are largely disrespected by influential community members who can support their own causes and interests, for example by paying money for 'justice' or by the threat of force. The conventional elders' reputation has suffered because of a visibly growing lack of enforcement capacities. The 'new' elders' legitimacy does not derive primarily from norms of seniority and heightened or special piety. Rather, they can rely on the support of armed followers and, in consequence, the threat of force, as a result of a former career as *mujahedin* (sub-)commanders during the shifting political alliances and regimes in the north-east over roughly the last 30 years. In addition, few 'new elders' have a background as refugees or returnees – either originating in refugee camps in Pakistan or Iran, or from labour migration in Iran or the Gulf states, or endowed with religious authority from education in Pakistan's *madaris* (religious schools). Their authority rests on different types of knowledge, because they have been exposed to various environments and experiences now of benefit to their home communities (especially at the interface with development agents; see below), or they have become religious scholars. Despite these new trends, now as then, within communities, elders are not appointed but derive their status always from conduct and behaviour over a certain period of time and their possession of material endowment (means for hosting and feeding guests, visiting government offices, or travelling to dispute sites) through different circumstances (e.g. inherited wealth, land, property, business, possibly war booty, etc.). This is true for novel and conventional elders alike. An elder of larger significance is likely to possess better access to higher-level decision-makers and persons of influence, whether they are government officials, armed strongmen, or NGO representatives, because of his reputation. The sources of the individual's reputation can include a long-term relationship, for example a kin-relation with the influential person, in question in case of a 'conventional' elder; a joint party belonging and history of fighting, for a 'novel' elder; having a good problem-solving capacity; or the ability to bring harmony and unity to the community and its conflicting factions. Also, over the last decade, legitimate eldership has become increasingly related to the cashing-in of development projects.

The mediation of rural development after 2001

Next, evidence from a detailed qualitative analysis of governance structures in five irrigation networks in three districts of Kunduz Province will be used to illustrate how local representation patterns have effectively co-opted rural development and reform projects.[29] The government of Afghanistan had approved a Strategic Policy Framework for the Water Sector in 2004 (MIWRE, 2004; Rivière 2005), which – besides the revision of the old water law and irrigation regulations – foresaw the introduction of water user associations at the watercourse level, in the framework of the adoption of the internationally fashionable 'integrated water resources management' paradigm (Rivière 2006). It revolved around the idea of river-basin management according to hydrological boundaries and the establishment of respective institutional management bodies, instead of managing water through conventional administrative arrangements manifest in district and provincial irrigation departments (Mollinga et al. 2009). With pilot canals chosen within the EU-financed Kunduz River Basin Programme, a German NGO was commissioned to work with irrigators' communities to implement efficiency-enhancing measures and in particular to overhaul the traditional management practices. The logframe prescribed the achievement of efficient community-based management of irrigation water. For this purpose, social mobilizers were sent to the communities adjacent to the watercourse to introduce the idea of water user groups and canal committees. Both were thought to serve as preliminary building blocks to prepare the later establishment of water user associations once the water law had been passed by Parliament (which eventually happened in 2009) and the foreseen organizational structures were legally valid (Mielke, Shah, and Abdullaev 2010; Wegerich 2010).

Traditionally, for the management of irrigation systems – i.e. primary, secondary, and tertiary canals that are diverted from the Kunduz River in different districts – irrigation users appoint a water manager (*mirab*). He is officially in charge of intake construction in spring, the establishment of rotation schedules that determine the water share depending on the location of the plots along the canal during times of water scarcity, canal maintenance and repair works during and after flood events, and the organization of labour and tools for such works. In practice, the *mirab* is appointed by a few large landowners, whose land is usually located in the upstream command area of the canal network. Consequently, the *mirab* acts on their behalf throughout his tenure, which in times of water scarcity means preferential irrigation of the upstream fields of particular persons and non-punishment of large landowners or their farmers who water their land illegally, e.g. by opening offtakes at night. The appointment of the *mirab*, which provides him with a decent starting salary from the richer landlords (and the opportunity to collect a regular salary from the water users for his efforts throughout the year at the end of his term), is expected to be matched by loyal service in the interest of these landowners. The *mirab*–landowner relationship represents power and dependency relations in rural Afghanistan which resemble those of clients and patrons, where the latter provide protection and income incentives in return for the loyalty of the former. This might seem reasonable enough, but it clearly infringes upon local norms that require that the *mirab* distribute water equally according to the rotation schedule and that he should be skilled in certain ways – i.e. possess literacy, knowledge, and experience with regard to farming and irrigation – or that he should own land on the lower part of the canal. The fact that the appointment of a person as *mirab* contradicted these customary specifications in four of five investigated irrigation systems during 2006–2007 (Mielke, Shah, and Abdullaev 2010) illustrates the existence of highly unequal de facto distribution practices.

As a result of NGO project activities at the watercourse level, 18 water user groups (WUGs) and four canal committees were set up by early autumn 2007. In four out of six irrigation networks, the most significant elders had taken over the WUG's head position and the WUG was registered carrying their name. These (new and old) elders combined several traits: they had a guesthouse, and possessed an authoritative position in their community, and thus could ensure visitors' security. Some were locally influential commanders and large landowners at the same time. This only cursory summary of representation patterns suggests that WUGs have been hijacked by local strongmen. Given that several WUGs were established between the head and tail ends of one canal, the *mirab* would also be the leader of one of the WUGs. However, in the highly contested watercourse realms – where NGO infrastructure activities were expected to commence in the near future – no *mirab* has been appointed chair of the canal committee. Furthermore, the *mirab* appointment for these canals became more politicized, because the interests of the rural elite (landowners who at times acted also as elders and/or commanders) in the potential benefits of construction were disproportionately higher. It urged local stakeholders to take anticipatory measures, like appointing a person as *mirab* who could be expected not only to ensure that their interests were served but also to take on the lead role in WUGs and canal committees.

In effect, the intended goal of establishing equity in the allocation and distribution of irrigation water through the introduction of innovative new local governance mechanisms (the IWRM paradigm with WUAs, etc.) fell prey to local interests. As a matter of fact, the customary representation patterns with their inbuilt inequalities were perpetuated and strengthened.

Similar patterns have been found in other community-based natural resource management projects in the north-east. Communities were created artificially by the local staff of development-project implementers (NGOs), and intervention target groups were defined in meetings of local NGO staff with community leaders. As previously argued, in north-east Afghanistan the impacts of rural development measures have been mediated by two groups of development brokers (Bierschenk, Chauveau, and Olivier de Sardan 2002): local representatives (old and new elders) on the one hand, and the community mobilizers, engineers, and translators of national and international NGOs on the other hand (Mielke 2013). They complement each other, due to the reconfirmation of their status and legitimacy, which rises (particularly for the elders) with the implementation of projects in their constituency. However, not all elders are able to deliver; their performance depends on their connectedness with higher-up patrons, their status, and their reputation. This perspective was reflected in various communities' complaints in 2006–2009 about not having 'good elders' or any elders at all, causing one pasture community to actually raise money and buy a government position for one of their elders, which they hoped would ensure their further access to governmental and development assets in the future.

Undermining the centre: state capture by patronage networks from below

If the realm of natural resource users and rural development is left behind and the view shifted to local–state relations, the same pattern of middlemen acting as gatekeepers, who mediate access to the local district government, partially the provincial authorities, but often also directly with patrons in government positions in Kabul, can be discerned. This is evident in the example of the recruitment practices of the holder of one of the key central-government agencies in Kabul. The person in question hails from one of three major valleys in a south-eastern district of Takhar Province and places relatives and clients in the broadest sense in prestigious positions all over the province and beyond. Between 2006 and 2009, the period when empirical evidence was collected, one brother was deputy in the upper house of Parliament, and nephews held offices in crucial local line departments, for example the Ministry of Rural Rehabilitation and Development, or the commandership of police, or as the provincial drug commissary. Furthermore, the official in question is very well embedded and connected with all sorts of influential families in his home district due to an extensive network of relatives and smart marriage arrangements. His power rests partly on his family background as offspring of a rich and respected landowning family; it was augmented by him being one of the main sub-commanders of Ahmad Shah Ma'sud in the area. As ambassador in Iran after 2001, he is reported to have helped 18 students from his valley get into Iranian universities by 2006. Moreover, it is said that more students from this particular valley are studying at Afghan universities than from all the other 15 districts of Takhar Province taken together. Local people consider him a patron who can always be called upon in times of need and emergency, as was the case in April 2007, when heavy landslides washed away dwellings in several villages of the valley.[30]

In many parts of the two investigated districts of Takhar, elders (both conventional and novel) could rely on direct ties with position holders in the central government in Kabul. Elders in other districts lacked access to high-level government authorities because they neither formerly belonged to the immediate sphere of influence of Ahmad Shah Ma'sud's Northern Alliance, nor had managed to establish relations with position holders in Kabul or at the provincial level based on other connections. For example, in Asqalan, an irrigators' *manteqa* in Kunduz District, water users lamented the lack of 'good elders' in comparison with Chardara, which was eventually indicated by the unequal number of projects and NGOs perceived to be directed to that area by the government.[31] Communities which lacked elders with higher-up patrons were found to be disadvantaged and only able to compensate for their lack of access with money, thereby responding to the high degree of administrative corruption among government officers. Alone, those communities which also lacked the financial means to bribe government officials (user communities investigated in Burka [Baghlan] and Qal'a-yi Zal) reportedly refrained from appealing to the district or even higher government authorities and did not possess the leverage to further their interests. As a consequence, they have been largely left out of rural development schemes and have seen hardly any integration into influential networks.

Given that local access to government departments and offices is largely dependent on personalized relationships with government office holders, the population of Warsaj and Farkhar (Takhar) greatly benefited from the Jami'at and Northern Alliance connections of their (former) commanders, evidenced by an above-average representation in government positions during 2006–2009 and until today. In Burka and the studied districts of Kunduz, single figures with the 'right' affiliation qualify as patrons, but never achieved the same degree of influence as former commanders from Warsaj and Farkhar. Forming the second and third tier of the former Northern Alliance military network, many figures from the upper part of Farkhar Valley and Warsaj made post-2001 government careers after being Northern Alliance commanders and sub-commanders throughout the 1990s. The collected data suggest that just as the top tier of government officials (the vice-presidents and many heads of ministries) were recruited from the so-called Panjshiri faction of the Northern Alliance as first tier, former loyalists and strongmen from Farkhar and Warsaj were recruited to second-tier positions in the new government after 2001, i.e. at the level of deputy ministers, or in charge of task forces and independent government commissions. As a cumulative effect, according to patronage logics and as illustrated with the example above, the second tier of big men in the Jam'iat and the Northern Alliance has penetrated all ranks of local government in Kunduz and Takhar, as well as central-government ministry posts, and subsequently taken control of subnational government throughout these provinces.[32]

Conclusion

A look at historical sources and the current situation highlights certain important continuities. Now as then, practices of patronage and mediation characterize the underlying mechanisms of social order. From a structural, long-term point of view these consistencies are evident, though veiled under a veneer of frequently shifting actor coalitions, regime changes, and foreign interventions. In pre-war Afghanistan, the expansion of the state administration was locally mediated and based on tacit agreement between the government and rural elites. Yet, state-making followed a top-down logic, driven by successive regimes' attempts to extend their rule. The events of 1978–1979 resulted in the revocation of the previous arrangement between state and local powerbrokers (Grevemeyer 1990). In spite of popular revolts, mobilization, and the actor-specific changes resulting from the war, reciprocity, patronage, eldership, and mediation remained the structuring principles of social power relations and governance. The rise of new elites, including the establishment of a new type of elder or representative, was facilitated by patron–client relations. At the same time, connotations of eldership changed significantly. Now other types of resources, especially financial assets, have gained importance. In non-Afghan contexts the replacement of network ties by these new resources (financial assets) would have the potential to alter patron–client relations; locally, however, they are solely invested in the building up of new dependency relationships by those who otherwise lack connections. Consequently, over the last decade, locally appropriated state-making processes from below can be observed. The resource flows provided by the political and military intervention in Afghanistan since 2001 have enabled the newly established elites to capture the Western-planned state-building agenda. In this manner state-making overlaps with and perpetuates the existing social order, along with its inherent power structures and local world-views. Hence, change is visible at the actors' level only, but not from a structural, governance-related point of view. Today, Afghan statehood is shaped by rent-seeking and patronage dynamics nourished by resource flows which are fed in by the international intervention. The common reading and understanding of the situation in Afghanistan through the lens of elites and regime change, and at the same time the neglect of historical and context factors, go hand in hand with the misconception of governance. Governance is all too often viewed through the prism of executive government. The visible changes at the surface of order, i.e. government change and the related reshuffling of personalized networks and implementation of new bodies (e.g. WUGs, WUAs, and canal committees) are mistakenly viewed as changes in governance; in fact they refer merely to the local-government dimension.[33] Moreover, they obstruct the short-term observer's ability to grasp the structuring principles of social order. As a result, the underlying local dynamics of patronage and mediation are insufficiently understood by interventionists and state-builders alike, and this has contributed to the current impasse in the Western state-building project in Afghanistan.

Acknowledgements

The authors would like to thank two anonymous reviewers for their helpful comments on a first draft of this article.

Notes

1. Only a few sources speak of Afghanistan (as a country) as being ungoverned or ungovernable – see for example "Fixing a Broken World" (*Economist*, 2009). Usually authors distinguish spatial entities within Afghanistan as ungoverned, and they mostly refer to the Afghanistan–Pakistan border region – see for example Mills (2009), Chalk (2007), and Windmueller (2009).
2. Both authors conducted their research between 2005 and 2012 in the framework of the Local Governance and Statehood in the Amu Darya Borderlands project of the Center for Development Research (ZEF), University of Bonn. Extensive field research at the village level was carried out in north-eastern Afghanistan between 2006 and 2009.
3. The fieldwork based on oral history interviews was conducted in April and May 2007 and from December 2007 to January 2008 in Kunduz and Imam Sahib. In line with social-anthropological research convention and to protect the respondents, names of people and small places are not given.
4. The term 'state-making' is preferred here over 'state-building' because it emphasizes the negotiation dimension of state control and the processes of its extension. It allows taking into account the partial willingness and acceptance of those who are subject to the extension of state control on the one hand, but also the domination of state structures 'from below' through the dominance of certain patronage networks. Accordingly, state-making has to be distinguished from the commonly referred-to state-building, as its outcome is not fixed and certainly differs from the ideal vision of the international intervention's state-building agenda. See also Agrawal (2001) and Mielke (2013).
5. In the social sciences, discourses on 'the problem of order' have been broadly dominated by two underlying notions. One associates order with a call for 'ordering' and stipulates order as the antipode of chaos, disorder, fuzziness, and violence. In contrast, according to constructivist notions (Berger and Luckmann 1966), order forms at cognitive levels in the observer's mind and thus implies subjective meanings. The two 'schools' are not mutually exclusive; nor does either represent a homogeneous

concept. In fact, viewed from a scientific-historical angle, both idealized notions can be interpreted in chronological order: as the first is affiliated with modernist scientific thinking, the second is attributed to postmodernism's post-structural approaches. Nevertheless, the latter does not necessarily escape a normative bias, as individual processes of 'ordering' are likely to make use of normative frameworks for orientation in everyday life. The identified overlap suggests that a multitude of 'phenomena of order' exist. While semantics provides for the existence of several parallel meanings of order in popular and academic accounts (Anter 2007), the binary distinction succumbs to the highly complex entanglements that structure social logics empirically.

6. For conceptual clarification, the interested reader is advised to refer to the above-mentioned working paper (Mielke et al. 2011). In the present article, patron–client relations and mediation are seen as institutions rooted in local world-views. The latter are constituted by norms such as reciprocity, seniority, eldership, generosity, etc. Both institutions (social practices) and world-views (cognitive frames) are assumed to resemble the structuring principles of contemporary rural society. In empirical practice, the distinction between institutions and what we summarize as 'world-views' is hard to trace, since the two categories overlap in their role of enabling and restraining social interaction. The category which has been termed 'world-view' encompasses the cognitive dimension of social order and thus relates to qualities of different sociological concepts linked to norms and values, e.g. shared mental models (Denzau and North 1994), Bourdieu's (1978) *habitus*, Esser's (2004) habits and frames, and Giddens' (1984) structuration.

7. Similar lists are provided for most of the other towns and settlements in north-eastern Afghanistan. For Imam Sahib, for instance, he lists Mulla Muhammad, 'Alam Wakil-i Uzbek, Mulla Taj Muhammad Wakil, Nek Muhammad Khan Mingbashi, Khwaja Muhammad Ja'far, Wat (Ata) Murad Mingbashi-yi Uzbek, etc. (Kushkaki 1989).

8. The law on the establishment of a national administration (*Nizam-nama-yi tashkilat-i asasi-yi Afghanistan*), issued in 1923, transferred responsibility at the hamlet and village level to local leaders and aristocrats. According to the taxation law (*Nizam-nama-yi malia*) issued in 1920, an elected village official (*malik* or *arbab*) had to cooperate with the revenue office. The decree regulating the taxation of livestock (*Nizam-nama-yi mal wa mawashi*, 1923, Art. 2) entitled four whitebeards (*muysafid*) to assist a tax commission in counting the livestock (Grevemeyer 1990).

9. Regarding the aspects and results of the resettlement policy, see Grötzbach (1972), Barfield (1981), Centlivres and Centlivres-Demont (1988), and Grevemeyer (1990).

10. Grötzbach (1972); Dupree (1973); Barfield (1981); Grevemeyer (1990). The cotton company became entirely nationalized in the era of Daoud Khan (Barfield 1981).

11. Interviews, 11 November 2007, Imam Sahib; 13 December 2007, Kunduz; 24 April 2007, Kunduz.

12. Interviews, 11 November 2007, Imam Sahib; 13 December 2007, Kunduz; 24 April 2007, Kunduz.

13. Down to the present, the descendants of the elders own a couple of shops and *karawan-saray*s in Kunduz City. For example, we find the Sara-yi Arzbegi and the Sara-yi 'Aziz Khan Mingbashi in the centre of town (interviews, 13 December 2007, Kunduz). Regarding the reconstruction of provincial towns across northern Afghanistan, see Grötzbach (1972; 1990).

14. Interviews, 13 December 2007, Kunduz; 26 April 2007, Imam Sahib; 19 November 2007, Kunduz. See also Grevemeyer (1990).

15. Barfield (1981) provided a detailed study on the working of the Spinzar cotton production system and the *ejaza* (lit. permission certificate; in the widest sense coupon) trade (139–148). For example, Haji Tawildar Jalil, a son of Mulla 'Abd al-Karim 'Arzbegi, worked as officer in the Spinzar Company (interview, 22 November 2007, Kunduz) and probably had a share in the *ejaza* trade.

16. Interviews, 24 April 2007, Kunduz; 1 May 2007, Emam Sahib; 22 and 24 November 2007, Kunduz; 10 November 2007, Imam Sahib; 12 December 2007, Kunduz. See also Note 18.

17. Interviews, 25 November 2007, Kunduz; 24 April 2007, Kunduz; 23 April 2007, Dasht-i Abdan; 11 December 2007, Imam Sahib; 13 December 2007, Kunduz.

18. Research for the following sections was carried out extensively over a period of 14 months in 2006 and 2007, complemented by a short-term research stay in 2009. Anthropological field research (participant observation, semi-structured interviews, participatory rural appraisal methods), oral-history interviewing, and life-history approaches were carried out in seven districts (Chardara, Qal'a-yi Zal, Warsaj, Farkhar, Burka, Ishkamish, and Kunduz) in the provinces of Takhar, Kunduz, and Baghlan. Given the limited space available, the insights presented here are derived from reflections on the qualitative interview data and can only be presented as extrapolations from observations.

19. Beyond venality there are also the extensive process of commodification of the war and the criminal economies (see Cramer and Godhand, 2002).

20. Interview, 4 June 2006, Qarayatim.
21. Interviews, 23 and 26 August 2006, Qal'a-yi Zal; 12 April 2007, Warsaj. See also Shahrani (1984) and Dorronsoro (2005).
22. Interview, 4 June 2006, Chardara. Reportedly, elders would introduce any volunteer to the Taliban administration in order to not be bothered further and to fulfil the request for appointment.
23. Interview, 12 April 2007, Warsaj.
24. A *manteqa* is a socio-spatial entity defined situationally from the perspective of the person belonging to it and referring to it. Often thought to be bounded by natural-geographical landmarks, it can be translated as 'area', 'village', 'valley', 'neighbourhood', or 'home'. See Favre (2005).
25. For example, in upper Asqalan, elders requested a former *mujahedin* commander to act as their 'Taliban-commander' (interview, 20 July 2007). In Burka, the heads of the *mir*-family (rural nobility) in Kokah Bulaq had an agreement with a Gujar commander who had fought jointly with them in the resistance against Soviet forces to act as Taliban commander for the Fulol Valley and 'save its population' from harm (interviews, 5 September 2007 and 26 March 2009).
26. This tendency was especially observed in field sites in Kunduz Province. It remains unclear to what extent it can be generalized, as the common narrative suggests that predatory commanders continue to operate in other areas. However, the perception of what 'predatory' signifies – either exploitative behaviour towards their own clients in their own zone of influence, or rivalry with other local commanders – needs further investigation.
27. '*Ushr* designates a tax on agricultural produce. It usually amounts to one-tenth of the harvest.
28. See Filkins (2012) for the example of Khanabad in Kunduz. By early 2013, '*ushr* was collected in all districts of Kunduz, as the author gleaned from interviews conducted for a different research study in February 2013.
29. The data were collected as part of the above-mentioned Ph.D. work by Mielke (forthcoming), which investigated local governance patterns for everyday natural resources in three distinct governance arenas (irrigation water, pasture land, and fuel wood).
30. Interviews, 19–21 April 2007, in communities of Takhar Province.
31. Interview, 11 June 2006.
32. As opposed to the first tier, which hailed mainly from Panjshir. In the first Karzai government, Dr Abdullah Abdullah, foreign minister, Yonus Qanoni, interior minister, and Muhammad Fahim, defence minister, emerged from the so-called Panjshiri faction of Jam'iat's Northern Alliance. The Panjshiri-dominated military arm of Jam'iat-i Islami captured Kabul in late 2001.
33. In pointing to the erosion of the old *arbab* system and the establishment of district councils by 2004, Barfield (2013) refers to drastic changes (e.g. the cession of local administration to the populace, new rural leaders, and the end of Pashtun dominance). He also acknowledges continuities, for instance conflict resolution outside Afghanistan's administrative framework (p. 123).

References

Agrawal, Arun. 2001. "State Formation in Community Spaces? Decentralization of Control over Forests in the Kumaon Himalaya, India." *The Journal of Asian Studies* 1 (60): 9–40.
Anter, Andreas. 2007. *Die Macht der Ordnung. Aspekte einer Grundkategorie des Politischen*. Tübingen: Mohr Siebeck.
Azoy, G. Whitney. 1982. *Buzkashi: Game and Power in Afghanistan*. Philadelphia: University of Pennsylvania Press.
Barfield, Thomas Jefferson. 1981. *The Central Asian Arabs of Afghanistan: Pastoral Nomadism in Transition*. Austin: University of Texas Press.
Barfield, Thomas Jefferson. 2013. "Continuities and Changes in Local Politics in Northern Afghanistan." In *Local Politics in Afghanistan. A Century of Intervention in the Social Order*, edited by Conrad Schetter, 131–144. London/New York: Hurst & Company/Columbia University Press.
Berger, Peter, and Thomas Luckmann. 1966. *The Social Construction of Reality. A Treatise in the Sociology of Knowledge*. Garden City/New York: Doubleday and Company.
Bierschenk, Thomas, Jean-Pierre Chauveau, and Jeanne-Pierre Olivier de Sardan. 2002. *Local Development Brokers in Africa. The Rise of a New Social Category*. Working Paper No. 13, Johannes Gutenberg University, Mainz, Department of Anthropology and African Studies.
Bourdieu, Pierre. 1978. *Entwurf einer Theorie der Praxis auf der ethnologischen Grundlage der kabylischen Gesellschaft*. Frankfurt a. Main: Suhrkamp.

Centlivres-Demont, Micheline and Pierre Centlivres. 2013. "The State, Intermediaries and 'Licit' Corruption. Local Politics in Northern Afghanistan in the Sixties and Seventies." In *Local Politics in Afghanistan. A Century of Intervention in the Social Order*, edited by Conrad Schetter, 111–129. London/New York: Hurst & Company/Columbia University Press.

Chabal, Patrick, and Jean-Pascal Daloz. 1999. *Africa Works. Disorder as Political Instrument.* Oxford et al.: International African Institute.

Chalk, Peter. 2007. "Case Study: The Pakistani-Afghan Border Region." In *Ungoverned Territories. Understanding and Reducing Terrorism Risks*, edited by Angel Rabasa et al., 49–76. Santa Monica, CA: RAND Corporation. http://www.rand.org/content/dam/rand/pubs/monographs/2007/RAND_MG561.pdf

Cramer, Christopher, and Jonathan Godhand. 2002. "Try Again, Fail Again, Fail Better? War, the State, and the 'Post-Conflict' Challenge in Afghanistan." *Development and Change* 33 (5): 885–909.

Denzau, Arthur, and Douglas C. North. 1994. "Shared Mental Models: Ideologies and Institutions." *Kyklos* 47 (1): 3–31.

Dorronsoro, Gilles. 2005. *Revolution Unending. Afghanistan: 1979 to the Present.* London: Hurst.

Dupree, Louis. 1973. *Afghanistan.* Princeton: Princeton University Press.

Eisenstadt, S. N., and Louis Roniger. 1980. "Patron-Client Relations as a Model of Structuring Social Exchange." *Comparative Studies in Society and History* 22 (1): 42–77.

Esser, Hartmut. 2004. *Soziologische Anstöße.* Frankfurt a. Main: Campus.

Favre, Raphy. 2005. "Interface between State and Society. An Approach for Afghanistan." Discussion Paper. Kabul.

Filkins, Dexter. 2012. "After America. Will Civil War Hit Afghanistan When the U.S. Leaves?." *The New Yorker*, July 9.

"Fixing a broken world. The Planet's most Wretched Places are not always the most Dangerous." *The Economist*, January 29, 2009. http://www.economist.com/node/13035718

Geller, Armando. 2009. "Warum (neue) Eliten in den Wiederaufbauprozess in Afghanistan involviert werden müssen: Ein Plädoyer für eine Strategie der Lokalismen." In *Strategisches versus humanitäres Denken: das Beispiel Afghanistan*, edited by Claudine Nick, 231–258. Zürich:vdf Hochschulverlag AG an der ETH Zürich.

Giddens, Antony. 1984. *The Constitution of Society. Outline of the Theory of Structuration.* Cambridge: Polity Press.

Glatzer, Bernt. 2005. "Konflikte und lokale politische Strukturen in Afghanistan." In *Unterwegs in die Zukunft. Afghanistan drei Jahre nach dem Aufbruch vom Petersberg. Grundlagen und Perspektiven deutsch-afghanischer Sicherheitskooperation*, edited by Claudia Gomm, 84–101. Berlin: BWV - Berliner Wiss. Verl.

Grevemeyer, Jan-Heeren. 1990. *Afghanistan: Sozialer Wandel und Staat im 20. Jahrhundert.* Berlin: Verlag für Wissenschaft und Bildung.

Grötzbach, Erwin. 1972. *Kulturgeographischer Wandel in Nordost-Afghanistan seit dem 19. Jahrhundert.* Meisenheim am Glan: Hain.

Grötzbach, Erwin. 1990. *Afghanistan. Eine geographische Landeskunde.* Darmstadt: Wissenschaftliche Buchgesellschaft.

Hall, Antony. 1977. "Patron-Client Relations: Concepts and Terms." In *Friends, Followers and Factions: A Reader in Political Clientelism*, edited by Steffen W. Schmitt, 510–521. Berkeley: University of California Press.

Hechter, Michael, and Chrstine Horne, eds. 2003. *Theories of Social Order. A Reader.* Stanford: Stanford University Press.

Holzwarth, Wolfgang. 1980. "Segmentund Staatsbildung in Afghanistan: Traditionale sozio-politische Organisation in Badakhshan, Wakhan und Sheghnan." In *Revolution in Iran und Afghanistan*, edited by Jan-Heeren Grevemeyer, 177–235. Frankfurt a. Main: Syndikat.

al-Huseini, Mahmud. 1379/2000. *Tarikh-i ahmadshahi* [Ahmad Shah's History]. Edited by Sarwar Humayun. Peshawar: Danish Khabaranduya tolana.

Kazim, Muhammad. 1990. *'Alamara-yi nadiri* [The Rare World-Embellisher]. Edited by Muḥammad Amin Riyahi, 3 vols. Tehran: Nashr-i 'elm.

Kushkaki, Burhan al-Din. 1989. *Rahnama-yi Qataghan wa Badakhshan* [The Guide of Qataghan and Badakhshan]. Edited by Manuchehr Sotuda. Tehran: Meyhan.

Kussmaul, Friedrich. 1965. "Siedlung und Gehöft bei den Taǧiken in den Bergländern Afghanistans." *Anthropos* 60: 487–532.

Lemarchand, Rene, and Keith Legg. 1972. "Political Clientelism and Development." *Comparative Politics* 4 (2): 149–178.

McChesney, Robert D. 1991. *Waqf in Central Asia. Four Hundred Years in the History of a Muslim Shrine, 1480–1889.* Princeton/New Jersey: Princeton University Press.

Merton, Robert. 1938. "Social Structure and Anomie." *American Sociological Review* 3.5: 672–682.

Mielke, Katja. forthcoming. "(Re-)Constructing Afghanistan? Rewriting Rural Afghans *Lebenswelten* into Recent Development and State-Making Processes. An Analysis of Local Governance and Social Order." PhD diss., University of Bonn, submitted in 2012.

Mielke, Katja. 2013. "Constructing the Image of a State. Local Realities and International Intervention." In *Local Politics in Afghanistan. A Century of Intervention in the Social Order*, edited by Conrad Schetter, 245–263. London/New York: Hurst & Company/Columbia University Press.

Mielke, Katja, Conrad Schetter, and Andreas Wilde. 2011. "Dimensions of Social Order. Empirical Fact, Methodological Concept and Boundary Notion." ZEF Working Papers 78.

Mielke, Katja, Usman Shah, and Iskandar Abdullaev. 2010. "The Illusion of Establishing Control by Legal Definition. Water Rights, Principles and Power in Canal Irrigation Systems of the Kunduz River Basin." In *Negotiating Local Governance. Natural Resources Management at the Interface of Communities and the State*, edited by Irit Eguavoen and Wolfram Laube, 181–209. Hamburg: LIT.

Mills, Greg. 2009. "Calibrating Ink Spots. Filling Afghanistan's Ungoverned Spaces." *RUSI Journal* 151 (4): 16–25.

MIWRE (Ministry of Irrigation, Water Resources and Environment). 2004. *A Strategic Policy Framework for the Water Sector.* Kabul: MIWRE.

Mollinga, Peter, et al. 2009. "Water, War and Reconstruction. Irrigation Management in the Kunduz Region, Afghanistan." In *Water, Environmental Security and Sustainable Rural Development. Conflict and Cooperation in Central Eurasia*, edited by Arsel Murat and Max Spoor, 21–48. London: Routledge.

Nixon, Hamish. 2008a. *Sub-National Statebuilding in Afghanistan. AREU Synthesis Paper Series.* Kabul: AREU.

Nixon, Hamish. 2008b. *The Changing Face of Local Governance? Community Development Councils in Afghanistan.* AREU Working Paper Series. Kabul: AREU.

Noelle, Christine. 1997. *State and Tribe in Nineteenth-Century Afghanistan. The Reign of Amir Dost Muhammad Khan (1826–1863).* Richmond: Curzon.

Nölle-Karimi, Christine. 2008. "The Pearl in its Midst. Herat and the Mapping of Khurāsān from the Fifteenth to the Nineteenth Centuries." Habilitation Thesis, University of Bamberg.

Rasuly-Paleczek, Gabriele. 1993. "Beg, Moyzafid und Arbab: Das politische System der Chechka Usbeken und der afghanische Zentralstaat." In *Studies in Oriental Culture and History. Festschrift for Walter Dostal*, edited by Andre Gingrich, Sylvia Haas, Gabriele Paleczek, and Thomas Fillitz, 89–105. Frankfurt a. Main: Peter Lang.

Rivière, Nicolas. 2005. "Linking Relief, Rehabilitation and Development Programme (LRRD) in Afghanistan. Water Sector Reform in Afghanistan (2001–2006)." Groupe u.r.d. (urgence, rehabilitation, développement).

Rivière, Nicolas. 2006. "Water and Irrigation Sector." In *Linking Relief, Rehabilitation and Development in Afghanistan. A Review Based on a Multi and Cross Sector Approach*, edited by Amélie Banzet, et al., 40–58. Groupe u.r.d. (urgence, rehabilitation, développement).

Ruttig, Thomas. 2013. *How It All Began. A Short Look at the Pre-1979 Origins of Afghanistan's Conflict.* Kabul: Afghanistan Analyst Network (ANN).

Shahrani, M. Nazif. 1984. "Causes and Context of Responses to the Saur Revolution in Badakhshan." In *Revolutions & Rebellions in Afghanistan*, edited by Nazif M. Shahrani and Robert L. Canfield, 139–169. Berkeley: University of California.

Shahrani, Nazif. 2013. "Centre-Periphery Relations in Afghanistan." In *Local Politics in Afghanistan. A Century of Intervention in the Social Order*, edited by Conrad Schetter, 23–37. London/New York: Hurst & Company/Columbia University Press.

Shalinsky, Audrey. 1986. "Uzbak Ethnicity in Northern Afghanistan." In *Die ethnischen Gruppen Afghanistans*, edited by Erwin Orywal, 290–303. Wiesbaden: Ludwig Reichert Verlag.

Sharan, Timor. 2011. "The Dynamics of Elite Networks and Patron-Client Relations in Afghanistan." *Europe-Asia Studies* 63 (6): 1109–1127.

Suhrke, Astrid. 2012. *When more is less. The international project in Afghanistan.* New York/London: Hurst.

Verkoren, Willemijn, and Bertine Kamphuis. 2013. "State-building in a Rentier State: How Development Policies Fail to Promote Democracy in Afghanistan." *Development and Change* 44 (3): 501–526.

Weber Pazmiño, Gioia. 1991. *Klientelismus. Annäherungen an das Konzept*. Zürich: ADAG.

Wegerich, Kai. 2010. "The Afghan Water Law. 'A Legal Solution Foreign to Reality?'." *Water International* 35 (3): 298–312.

Windmueller, Kirk. 2009. "State of Chaos. Security Threats from Ungoverned and Under-Governed Spaces." *Special Warfare* 22 (5): 19–21. http://static.dvidshub.net/media/pubs/pdf_8261.pdf

Wrong, Dennis H. 1979. *Power. Its Forms, Bases and Uses*. Oxford: Basil Blackwell.

The hollowing-out of the liberal peace project in Afghanistan: the case of security sector reform[†]

Mark Sedra

University of Waterloo, Ontario, Canada

Security sector reform (SSR) has been described as a linch-pin of the liberal state-building and peace-building processes in Afghanistan. The process was originally framed in accordance with the core liberal principles of the SSR model, prioritizing good governance, respect for human rights, sustainability, and democratic civilian control. However, as time passed and security and political conditions began to deteriorate on the ground, the process would gradually revert to a more conventional train-and-equip form, with its core liberal principles stripped away. The slide toward expediency experienced by the SSR process in Afghanistan demonstrates the deeply flawed manner in which the liberal peace project was advanced in Afghanistan. SSR donors became increasingly ambivalent about the human-security objectives of SSR, which were superseded by exigencies of the counterinsurgency, regional security, and domestic pressure for withdrawal. The Afghan experience has raised further doubt about the viability of the orthodox SSR model in conflict-affected countries, already the subject of significant critical debate.

Introduction

A close examination of the evolution of security sector reform (SSR) in Afghanistan points to a distinct pattern. The initial design and elaboration of the SSR agenda – as reflected in the rhetoric, policies, and programme documents of Afghan government and donor stakeholders – broadly conformed to the fundamental norms and principles of the SSR model.[1] Among those norms and principles are the SSR model's people-centred, human-security outlook; its emphasis on promoting good-governance precepts like transparency and accountability; its holistic vision, featuring a wide definition of the security sector beyond the security forces, including the justice system, informal structures, and civil society; and its prioritization of democratic civilian control and oversight. However, as the difficult ground-level realities of Afghanistan's transition – such as the lack of human and institutional capacity (amongst interveners as well as Afghans), the adverse security environment and fragmented power and political dynamics – began to challenge the fundamental assumptions of the orthodox model, the agenda began to fray and stray from these principles. Gradually, the liberal elements of the orthodox or 'ideal-type' SSR model that define and distinguish it from previous forms of security assistance were stripped away, leaving only a 'hard' security shell. The process still endeavoured to create 'Western-style' security and justice structures, but in a mediated, pared-down form, emphasizing coercive capacity and institutional technologies rather than liberal norms and principles. SSR became little more than a euphemism for more conventional forms of security assistance, a legitimating device to demonstrate the liberal credentials of the project. What was actually happening on the

---

[†]This article is based on multiple research missions to Afghanistan undertaken by the author between 2003 and 2010.

ground was a train-and-equip process driven by strategic donor imperatives and political inter-ests rather than the human-security needs of the Afghan population.

The short-term exigencies of the 'war on terror', which originally brought the US and its coalition partners to Afghanistan, always suffused SSR programming. Although less discernible at the beginning of the SSR process, the influence of the realist security agenda became more apparent as the country's security situation deteriorated. In other words, while illiberal and realist forms of intervention coexisted from the start with liberal technocratic reform initiatives, the former grew in scope and precedence at the expense of the latter as time went on.

The Afghan SSR process[2] has exposed the deep flaws in the orthodox SSR model and, by extension, the wider liberal peace project. Five main flaws in particular can be identified through analysis of donor policies and behaviour in Afghanistan: the prioritization of donor interests over recipient needs through the employment of a regime-centric rather than people-centric approach; the proclivity for apolitical, technical outlooks and approaches; a tendency to jettison the democratic principles of SSR and encourage illiberal practices and forms of be-haviour; a failure to develop an adequate understanding of the local context and adapt reforms to it; and a penchant for short-term approaches and lack of consideration for the long-term sustain-ability of reforms.

Afghanistan's SSR process diverges from all of the core principles of the orthodox SSR model, despite being implemented under its name. Since Afghanistan is widely accepted as a critical and challenging case of the application of SSR and the liberal peace project, and since domestic and external stakeholders presented SSR as an indispensible element of the post-Taliban transition, its deviation from SSR orthodoxy raises doubts about the viability and utility of the SSR concept itself. Afghanistan's SSR process has been unprecedentedly com-prehensive in scope, encompassing every aspect of the conceptual model and challenging it in virtually every conceivable manner. It is not that the issues and challenges presented in Afgha-nistan are absent in other conflict-affected countries; it is just that in other countries they are often less severe and do not tend to manifest simultaneously. The outcome of SSR in Afghani-stan may not provide a definitive verdict on the utility and applicability of the SSR model more generally, but it will offer insight on the ability of the model to overcome some of the more pressing challenges in conflict-affected environments.

Realist donor interests and regime-centric approaches

From the outset of Afghanistan's post-2001 transition, the SSR process was driven not by any human-security calculus, as stipulated by the orthodox SSR model, but by the objectives of the interveners, primarily the US. The intervention was motivated by the 'global war on terror' and has been geared to consolidate and even extend the gains that were made on the bat-tlefield, principally the ouster of the Taliban and the disruption and displacement of al-Qaeda. The liberal democratic principles underpinning SSR were largely window-dressing for this wider goal, a means to legitimate donor activities but not a prime motivating factor for policy and behaviour. The absence of a holistic approach to SSR, exemplified by the imbalances between 'hard' and 'soft'[3] security assistance, as well as the desertion of the human-security frame of reference, demonstrated the primacy of the Western security and political concerns underlying the SSR agenda.

Afghanistan's SSR process strayed from its people-centred focus, assuming a regime-centric approach, as reflected in the top-down, 'hard' security-oriented nature of the process. As Ayub, Kouvo, and Wareham (2010) argue, the wider reconstruction process has 'been top-down, focus-ing on strengthening the Kabul-based central government' and developing centralized security forces and judicial structures, rather than expanding service delivery at the local level. While the orthodox model displays a penchant for centralized, top-down reforms – in line with Western systems – it also recognizes the need for parallel action at the community level in the periphery to ensure that the population sees a security and justice dividend. The latter element of the SSR blueprint was conspicuously absent in Afghanistan, considering the traditional decentralization of political authority and the seemingly ingrained propensity for suspicion of centralized authority.

While this regime-centric approach, driven largely by donors' strategic interests, was always prevalent in some form during the post-2001 period, it became more transparent as the transition evolved, with liberal elements of the process gradually stripped away. The development of the Afghan National Police (ANP) provides a vivid example of the SSR agenda's shift from human-centric to regime-centric, driven by immediate NATO counterinsurgency (COIN) objectives. David H. Bayley and Robert M. Perito argue that the ANP has been trained as a paramilitary force, 'little soldiers who support or supplement military forces in offensive counter-insurgency operations' (2009, 3), rather than an instrument to protect people and communities. 'The police', as former Interior Minister Ali A. Jalali put it, 'have merely become an instrument of counter-terrorism and counterinsurgency' (telephone interview, 16 November 2006; see also Hakimi, this volume). The long-term dangers of a militarized police are not lost on Afghan officials. As one senior police general stated in 2009: 'When we have peace in the country, we will have problems' (interview, Kabul, 13 January 2009). The general was clearly concerned that a paramilitary police force that is more adept at military combat than at community engagement and that is unencumbered by oversight mechanisms and credible deterrents to abuse could be a threat to public security and state authority. Moreover, the factionalization of such a paramilitary structure could bolster non-state armed groups, undercutting the state monopoly of force. With this in mind, a 2011 US Senate report argued that the ANP's training curriculum and the balance between civilian police and military advisers 'needs to be adjusted to emphasize civilian police skills and the relationship between civilian police and their communities' (Cordesman 2009, 13). According to Bayley and Perito, 'the key contribution of local police forces . . . is to legitimate self-government by responding under law to the security needs of the individual citizens' (2009, 3). To make this contribution, the focus of training must be 'community service and crime prevention' rather than paramilitary capacity and the 'technical skills of law enforcement' (4). Bayley and Perito go on to explain (83–86) that in conflict-affected environments like Afghanistan, training should focus on imparting 'core' policing ethics – being available, being helpful, and being fair and respectful – epitomizing the people-centred approach that never materialized in Afghanistan. While the approach of Bailey and Perito may seem disconnected from the culture and history of security provision in Afghanistan and the surrounding region, it reflects the liberal, people-centred vision of SSR that was heralded as the fundamental goal of donor assistance but never actualized in practice.

While donors' strategic imperatives drove the regime-centric approach to SSR, it was embraced by many segments of the Afghan regime, particularly actors from the former Northern Alliance or United Front who were able to co-opt and even capture parts of the security architecture. They instrumentalized segments of the formal security sector to shield and extend their patronage-based networks and paint their domestic rivals as enemies of the state. Even President Karzai, while outwardly committed to the liberal principles of SSR, has consistently employed his influence over appointments in the security sector as a vehicle for neo-patrimonial politics and as a mechanism to limit the influence of local-level power brokers who are not compliant with his regime. This approach to appointments contradicts the donors' 'good governance' agenda. Local actors have adeptly manipulated the SSR process, which, despite its veneer of liberalism, has been driven predominantly by realist strategic calculus and Cold War–era 'hard' security thinking.

Part of the problem with the ANP training-and-mentoring process was that it was largely carried out by military personnel, who have a skill-set and mind-set entirely different from those of civilian community police. It would be odd to deploy police to train soldiers in combat tactics, but in practice the reverse, the use of soldiers to impart policing skills, is treated as acceptable. In 2009, there were just over 500 civilian police advisers, compared to more than 1000 military mentors focused on police development (Chilton, Schiewek, and Bremmers 2009).

In the haste to contain the insurgent threat to the Afghan regime and the international community, the SSR process neglected key efforts, like anti-corruption and human rights promotion, essential to improve the civilian population's experience of security and justice. The widespread tendency of the police to abuse their power and engage in predatory behaviour towards local communities has delegitimized them in the eyes of wide swathes of the Afghan population, undercutting the state's effort to expand its monopoly of force. Giustozzi and Isaqzadeh (2011, 16) note that according to the statistics of the Afghan attorney general's office, 18,276 police personnel (including 30 generals) were accused of being involved in 10,480 cases of misbehaviour (abuses of power and corruption) up to the first quarter of 2009–2010. This amounted to over 20% of the police force, a very high figure considering that 'it is unlikely that authorities have identified all the cases' (16). High levels of misconduct and corruption in the police force are especially problematic because 'corruption cases were rarely if ever pursued by the justice system, especially if they involved police' (US DoS 2011, 30). As a member of Parliament explained, 'People have lost faith in the police.... The police are the people who create Talibs, who create terrorists' (interview, Kabul, 10 April 2008).

The ANP's poor performance is a critical problem for state-builders and the wider liberal peace project because the police are the most visible representatives of the state to most Afghans. As the ANP's National Police Strategy attests, 'The ANP is, to many, the face of the Government' (MoI 2010, 7–8). When police are corrupt and predatory, they undermine the state's legitimacy. A UNAMA (United Nations Assistance Mission in Afghanistan) official summarized the problem in 2008: 'On a daily basis, people only interact with police, and it is the most corrupt institution in government.... With the government not taking action against corrupt police, it promotes the perception that it is government policy' (interview, Kabul, 8 April 2008). The National Police Strategy clearly acknowledges that corruption 'erodes the trust and confidence of our people which police must earn in order to be a valued institution' (MoI 2010, 8). This logic was not lost on Karl Eikenberry, the former commander of US forces in Afghanistan as well as US ambassador: 'Ten good police are better than 100 corrupt police and ten corrupt police can do more damage to our success than one Taliban extremist' (Doucet 2006).

Apolitical outlooks and deficits of political will

While SSR orthodoxy explicitly recognizes the political nature of the process, and there are few political environments more complex than Afghanistan's, the country's SSR agenda was typically framed and approached in a largely technical and apolitical manner. When SSR donors did seek to engage local political realities and invest political capital, they tended to do so in a clumsy and ill-considered manner geared primarily to achieving short-term tactical objectives. One prominent example of the maladroit manner in which donors engaged political realities pertaining to SSR was the issue of local ownership. In Afghanistan, the international community clearly selected owners on the basis of both expediency and shared interests and values. There were two sets of favoured 'local owners': the Tajik-led Northern Alliance that represented the main anti-Taliban grouping at the time of the US decision to invade Afghanistan; and the Western-oriented Afghan technocrats who had either returned from the West after the Taliban ouster or joined the government from the ranks of Western NGOs. These two categories of elites occupied places at opposite ends of the Afghan political field. Each faced significant legitimacy problems within Afghanistan – the Northern Alliance *jihadi* groups (often referred to as warlords) because of their human rights records and their role in wartime atrocities, and the Western-oriented technocrats either for abandoning the country altogether during the civil war for greener pastures abroad, or for taking jobs with 'alien' Western NGOs and agencies within Afghanistan. Relying so heavily on these particular local partners to advance reforms may have complicated efforts to imbue the process with broad-based legitimacy and ownership.

The Northern Alliance had a human rights record on a par with the Taliban, yet it represented the only capable Afghan military partner for the US and its coalition partners in 2001. The subsequent Bonn political process favoured a narrow ethnic-based faction of the Northern Alliance, the Panjshiri Tajiks,[4] facilitating its assumption of control over the principal 'power ministries' of the government – foreign affairs, interior, and defence – in the first Afghan Interim Administration. The Panjshiri faction used its control over the upper echelons of these ministries in the early days of the transition to extend its patronage networks deep within the state and security architecture, which allowed it to continue to exercise disproportionate power and influence even after later reshuffles brought greater ethnic parity to the cabinet. According to Robin Luckham (2003), such factionalization of the security sector and SSR process along ethnic lines is dangerous because 'when ethnic patronage is built into military, police and security bureaucracies, it corrupts them, weakens discipline, reinforces a sense of impunity and fosters public (and especially minority) distrust of the state itself' (22). In selecting local partners on the basis of military and political expediency the Western donors institutionalized a damaging ethnic imbalance in the security sector that contributed to the delegitimization of SSR.

The partnership between *jihadi* leaders and the US-led coalition moved beyond the overthrow of the Taliban and the establishment of the Afghan government. In areas with a Taliban presence, the US routinely supported local commanders to act as counterinsurgent proxies. According to one civil-society representative speaking in 2005, the US was supporting certain warlords in the south with financial stipends of up to USD 1600 per day for the use of their militias (interview, 9 November 2005). A commissioner of the Afghanistan Independent Human Rights Commission (AIHRC), Ahmad Nader Nadery, argued in 2012 that 'the United States embraced nearly any party that would oppose the Taliban, regardless of their human rights records' and political orientation (Nadery 2012). These actions reflected a blunt and expedient political strategy that did more to alienate parts of the Afghan political establishment and population than it did to build a stable reform constituency.

The other set of favoured local owners for Western donors were Afghan expatriate technocrats who returned from the West following the ouster of the Taliban or transitioned to the Afghan government from the employ of Western NGOs and international agencies. This group displayed a number of common characteristics: they spoke English, had achieved some level of education in the West, and tended to be secular in orientation. They quickly formed a narrow technocratic class aligned with Western priorities and interests, defined in opposition to the *jihadi*s. As a senior UNAMA official noted, 'Many Afghans say that technocrat Afghans are not real Afghans' (interview, Kabul, 6 April 2008). According to one member of Parliament, they have lost their connection to Afghanistan, and have their own self-interest, rather than the welfare of the country, at heart: 'They come with an empty bag. When it is full, they leave' (interview, Kabul, 12 January 2009). This group would be awarded some of the most prominent positions in the administration after 2001 and were granted salaries 'topped up' by donors. Moreover, the ministries and agencies they led typically received the lion's share of Western aid. Donors justified this inequity of funding with the mantra that they were 'rewarding good performers', which had more to do with the technocrat ministers' ability to speak English and master the jargon of international development and security than the quality of the governance and reform programming they presided over (interview, Senior Afghan government official, 8 November 2005). Rather than foster consensus and unity of purpose, Western promotion of the expatriate technocrat elites aroused resentment among *jihadi* and traditional elites. This approach not only fragmented the government politically, but also delegitimized many of the reform processes advanced by donors.

The technocrats – epitomized by Ashraf Ghani, former World Bank official turned finance minister – endeavoured to build domestic constituencies to gain the popular legitimacy they lacked and which the *jihadi* leaders and traditional aristocracy possessed to varying degrees. Such efforts, which had an air of artificiality, elicited mixed outcomes. Accordingly, viewing technocrats' endorsements of donor reforms as an indicator of strong Afghan ownership is questionable, as the technocrats themselves often lack a high degree of political legitimacy in Afghan society (see Goodhand and Sedra 2007).

The judicial-reform pillar provides a good example of the absence of local ownership in the Afghan SSR process. According to one donor official involved in judicial reform, Italy tended to view its lead-nation status for the pillar as a licence 'to make decisions for the Afghans' (interview, Kabul, 14 November 2005). The Judicial Reform Commission, created by the Bonn Agreement to oversee reforms, similarly sought to form and drive an external reform agenda outside the purview of the Afghan government. The commission was largely composed of 'Afghan expats making exorbitant salaries that were disconnected from realities on the ground', said the donor official. Indeed, a senior Italian official involved in judicial reform admitted in 2006 that the commission and many of the early coordination mechanisms in the area had been 'mainly forums for foreigners' (interview, Kabul, 22 June 2006). It was for this reason that the commission was dissolved in the fall of 2005. The judicial reform effort largely entailed the adoption of Western legal norms, precepts, and structures, with surprisingly little consultation with Afghan actors within either state or civil society. Ali Wardak explains that international efforts 'mainly focused on patchy "legal engineering" and quick fixes, and on meeting targets and the technical aspects of reform at the expense of its normative dimensions' (2011, 1310).

The objective of donors has often been more to put 'an Afghan face' on Western reforms, strategies, and processes than to identify and empower Afghan agency (Barno, Exum, and Irvine 2011, 2). This has rendered large parts of the security and justice architecture illegitimate in the eyes of many Afghans, who see them as foreign structures serving the needs of particular power holders, factions, and cliques rather than the population as a whole.

SSR activities were either directly imposed, with little effort to cultivate local ownership and build political consensus, or they were advanced on the back of alliances with particular elite constituencies, namely the Northern Alliance *jihadis* and the Western-oriented technocrats, who were not representative of Afghan society as a whole. The resultant weakness of local ownership, a key ingredient of SSR, can also be attributed to the absence of a sophisticated and nuanced political approach capable of navigating the complexities of this diverse and charged political environment and adapting reforms to it. The limited understanding of Afghan politics that informed donor political engagement left their interventions prone to manipulation and spoiler activity by local power brokers.

Undemocratic reforms and illiberal outcomes

The clearest sign that an SSR process has veered off track according to its own criteria is when it shows a willingness to compromise and suspend its foundational democratic principles, and even embrace illiberal practices, to serve short-term tactical objectives. The orthodox SSR model doesn't recognize the need for such trade-offs and in fact acknowledges that they can be dangerous, in that those illiberal practices could evolve into permanent features of the local security and justice architecture. In Afghanistan, such trade-offs were made routinely; the immense challenges to SSR prompted donors to push the democratic elements of the process to the side in favour of a more expedient 'hard' security train-and-equip strategy that could deliver immediate benefits to the COIN campaign. Stripped of its liberal democratic principles, the process could no longer be defined as SSR and risked embedding structures and systems that could entrench rather than root out numerous deep-seated problems of the troubled Afghan state such as corruption, abuses of power, and factionalization. Making such trade-offs in Afghanistan could be perceived as a corrective against the rigidity of the liberal SSR model, which seems to advocate one linear path to democracy and stability despite the plethora of trajectories histori- cally taken by Western states. In light of the messiness and unpredictability of post-war tran- sitions, flexibility would seem to be a virtue for Western state-builders and reformers – recognizing that most transitions feature some form of this paradox of illiberal liberalism, when illiberal measures are applied in the short term, ostensibly to pave the way for liberal out- comes over the long term. If these short-term trade-offs or compromises are indeed designed as part of an overarching transition strategy to achieve the broader liberal objectives of SSR, then they could be perceived as a necessary evil. In Afghanistan, however, they were never applied in such a manner. Tellingly, donor deferrals of liberal SSR principles in the name of tactical expe- diency were rarely accompanied by timetables delineating their reversal – the shift back from illiberal to liberal practices. Rather, they were constructed and implemented as ad hoc, mostly apolitical responses to immediate security and political crises, with their long-term implications largely an afterthought. Luckham (2003), in line with SSR orthodoxy, points out the dangers posed by the type of sequencing and prioritization of donor SSR programming in Afghanistan: 'Democratic accountability and the rule of law are not luxuries that can safely be postponed until order and security are restored; they are inseparable from it' (21).

In conflict-affected environments, particularly those featuring high levels of insecurity, it has proven difficult for security sector reformers, particularly when they hail from 'hard' security institutions like the military, to recognize and actualize the holistic vision of the SSR model. In a 2011 article, NATO Training Mission–Afghanistan (NTM-A) Commander Lieutenant General William B. Caldwell and NTM-A strategist Captain Nathan K. Finney laid out the goals of the programme to develop the Afghan National Security Forces (ANSF):

> There are three outcomes that we are interested in for the ANSF. First, that ANSF units are capable of doing in the field what they are trained to do. Second, that the people served by the ANSF have suffi- cient confidence in their security forces to take the necessary actions to promote stability and conduct their normal business (for example, engaging in commerce, children attending school). Finally, that the Afghan people are willing to resist attempts by insurgents to reassert themselves (providing actionable intelligence, refusing to support insurgent elements, and engaging in the political process). (Caldwell and Finney 2011, 76–77)

While the orthodox SSR model would dictate that the process prioritize efforts to guarantee respect for core human rights, ensure accountability to civilian authority, develop mechanisms to mitigate corruption, and provide a minimum level of transparency, these were not seen as key objectives of the NTM-A mission. The NTM-A struggled to balance the pragmatic and norma- tive demands of SSR in a politically unstable, conflict-affected environment. NTM-A officials would consistently argue that in the midst of an ongoing insurgency, the imperatives of winning the war, including providing police with military training and weapons to protect them- selves, took precedence over the normative considerations of advancing human rights, good gov- ernance, and the rule of law. Accordingly, the stated goals of the NTM-A were instrumental and pragmatic, to ensure that the security forces could resist the insurgency and create an enabling environment for stabilization and, eventually, political normalcy. It is worth noting that the

European Union Police Mission framed its engagement in the SSR process as a normative response to the pragmatic and realist NTM-A approach, an attempt to ensure adequate attention to issues of rights, governance, and justice through the institution of an SSR division of labour (see Gross 2009). However, the comparatively tiny scale of the EU engagement – the financial and personnel contribution was a mere fraction of that committed by the US – mitigated any balancing effect that was envisioned. While adherents to the liberal SSR model may point to the deleterious long-term ramifications of this unbalanced approach, the propensity of donors to circumvent SSR orthodoxy could be a sign that the SSR model is simply not viable in conflict-affected environments.

The successor to the Bonn Agreement, the Afghanistan Compact (2006), signed on 1 February 2006 at a conference in held London from 31 January to 1 February 2006, saw the end state of Western-supported military reform as 'a nationally respected, professional, ethnically balanced Afghan National Army ... that is democratically accountable, organized, trained and equipped to meet the security needs of the country and increasingly funded from Government revenue, commensurate with the nation's economic capacity'. Composed in consultation with international advisers, the compact better reflects SSR norms and principles, even if only at the level of rhetoric. By 2012, those principles had been largely abandoned by the NTM-A, with the fundamental goal of the process having shifted from creating a sustainable security and justice architecture meeting the human-security needs of Afghans to finding the minimum conditions for international troop withdrawal. This drastic shift in approach demonstrates the 'slide toward expediency' that occurred in Afghanistan, the transformation of the process from orthodox SSR into Cold War– era train-and-equip security assistance. The slide clearly showed the mixed and ephemeral adherence to the core democratic norms of the SSR project among key donors like the US, particularly once security and political conditions began to deteriorate.

There are numerous examples of the tepid commitment of SSR stakeholders to the democratic principles of the model. One of the core goals of SSR programmes is to establish legislative oversight of the security system, yet the area has received scant attention in Afghanistan's SSR agenda. For instance, while parliamentary committees on defence and internal security have been created to hold the security institutions accountable, these bodies lack the basic institutional and human capacity required to perform their duties.[5] Afghan parliamentary committees are typically assigned only one or two staffers and have not received the necessary training to fulfil the requirements of their mandate. These bodies often exploit their constitutional powers to call government ministers in front of their committees for questioning, but such hearings are typically geared towards political spectacle rather than informed debate. As one Western adviser to the parliament explained, such sessions involve 'a lot of political posturing, but little consistent understanding of why they are bringing the ministers in' (interview, Kabul, 10 April 2008). There is rarely any policy follow-up from such sessions, which lack an overarching policy perspective or goal. A prominent member of Parliament who served as the deputy of the Committee on International Affairs referred to them as 'useless' (interview, Kabul, 12 January 2009). Typical committee sessions start one hour late and last for only 30 minutes. The problem is, as the Western adviser noted, that MPs 'don't know their role in Parliament and don't understand their oversight function' (interview, Kabul, 10 April 2008). The executive branch also doesn't grasp the role of Parliament. As one parliamentarian who was a member of the Defence Committee explained, 'This government views oversight as an attack.... It has a combative relationship with Parliament' (Interview, Kabul, April 10, 2008)

Numerous legislators have complained that the Afghan Parliament would not be able to assume its legislative oversight role, as prescribed by SSR orthodoxy, without more aid and assistance (interviews, Kabul, 10 April 2008). From 2002 to 2008, only USD 8 million in total was dedicated to building the capacity of the entire Afghan Parliament, a paltry sum in light of the tens of billions of dollars spent to build the security forces (interview, Kabul, 10 April 2008). Since 2008, the US government, through programmes like the Afghanistan Parliamentary Assistance Program, has increased aid and endeavoured to 'strengthen the ability and capacity of members of parliament and secretariat staff to directly support parliamentary committees with drafting legislation, legislative research, rules of procedure, [and] conducting public hearings' (USAID 2011). It dedicated USD 41.1 million to the programme up until 2012, which many observers still see as insufficient to enable the Parliament to fulfil its oversight role in the security sector and beyond (SIGAR 2012, 102). Although the 2004 Afghan Constitution provides the executive and legislative branches of government with significant oversight powers and authority over the security sector, the degree of civilian democratic control and oversight exercised in practice has been limited.[6]

The democratic principles of the SSR model were sacrificed to expediency in the Afghan context. Reformers would argue that the adverse security and political environment in Afghanistan militated against the application of orthodox SSR, necessitating some short-term compromises. This argument confirms the non-viability of SSR in conflict-affected contexts, where such conditions are the norm, and the need for new assistance paradigms that can better address and adapt to such challenging environments. Such new approaches will undoubtedly be less normative, less overtly statist, less centralized, more modest in scale and scope, and more willing to engage non-state actors, structures, and norms. When it comes to the SSR model as it applies to conflict-affected contexts, a transition to a second-generation approach appears to be gradually materializing in response to the largely disappointing experiences in Afghanistan and elsewhere.

Insufficient local knowledge and lack of context in programming

In Afghanistan, the SSR process was based on a superficial understanding of Afghan history, politics, and society, contributing to numerous missteps and setbacks. Donors have been unable to adapt the SSR model to the local context, reflecting its lack of flexibility and ideologically hegemonic character. Security sector reformers' rhetorical endorsement of the importance of context notwithstanding, the application of universal templates is typically the order of the day, as the case of Afghanistan demonstrates.

An example of the lack of sophistication with which the SSR process engaged the local context can be found in its treatment of civil society, particularly Islamic actors. In Afghanistan, a devout Muslim country, the religious establishment is an important component of civil society, even though, like other segments of civil society and traditional authority, it was disrupted during the long civil war. Thomas Barfield notes how Islam 'permeates all aspects of everyday social relations, and nothing is separate from it.... Afghanistan is a place where the concept of Islamic politics is little debated, but only because its people assume there can be no other type' (quoted in Long and Radin 2012, 120). William Maley (2009) argues that a lack of sensitivity to the centrality of Islam in Afghan politics and society among Western state-builders, driven by their zeal to actualize the liberal vision of a division between church and state, has consistently antagonized and even alienated Afghans, setting back the state-building and SSR processes. 'The behaviour of Westerners in Afghanistan has shown a lack of sensitivity towards local customs', Vice-President Khalili claimed, speaking about both religious and traditional customs (interview, Kabul, 18 June 2006). It must be noted that Afghan power brokers have also displayed a tendency to instrumentalize Islam and notions of tradition to advance their narrow interests (see Hakimi and Wimpelmann, this volume). Islam is nonetheless deeply interwoven with the state and society, with the Constitution stating that no law can run counter to Islamic principles. Yet religious actors are rarely engaged in a constructive manner by donors in the security sector, particularly at the regional and community levels.

The judicial-reform process provides an apt example of this trend of failing to engage local-level religious leaders in the formal system. A survey of local religious figures in three key Afghan districts by an Afghan research organization, Cooperation for Peace and Unity, found that most were dissatisfied with the operation of the formal legal system and felt that they were not adequately consulted by the state. Even though many of these actors played a key role in adjudicating cases in the informal system, their involvement 'in the functioning of the [formal] legal system, or in its reform is very low'. The result of this absence of engagement is 'a widespread lack of trust [in] the district and provincial level courts' that has undermined reforms at the local level (CPAU 2007, 42). This may partially explain the widespread tendency to look to informal judicial structures to adjudicate disputes, and in some areas even Taliban justice mechanisms. Informal systems are surely no panacea for Afghanistan's troubled justice system and should not be romanticized as such (see Wimpelmann 2013 in this volume), but considering that the vast majority of Western aid is allocated to developing formal institutions of justice even though up to 80% of disputes are resolved in informal systems, it is clear that a significant gap exists between policy and reality (CPHD 2007).

In the area of police reform, Austin Long and Andrew Radin argue that the reliance on 'technocratic practices based on Western policing' has caused Western reformers to ignore the fact that in Afghanistan 'being a good Muslim is an integral part of being a good policeman' (2012, 114). They describe how 'US-funded police training remains overwhelmingly technocratic and poorly adapted to the particular context of Afghanistan, especially as the training does not emphasize the importance of Islam' (117). Indeed, a consistent grievance of the police and army has been the lack of mosques in training facilities, bases, and police stations. Police complain that 'patrolling and searching had overtaken prayer and mosque attendance as priorities' for police; this may be good for COIN objectives, but it can have the effect of 'separating the police from the citizens' (117, 124).

An international gender adviser in the Ministry of Interior Affairs suggested in 2006 that some liberal reforms could be made more palatable to Afghans if undertaken with Islamic sensitivities in mind (interview, Kabul, 24 June 2006). She noted that 'Afghans are reasonably open to bringing more women into the police, as long as it is in the framework of Islam.' The implication was that because gender-equality programming was, at times, advanced in a religiously and politically insensitive manner, it had aroused resentment and push-back.

Successful SSR, like any development or broader state-building project, depends on detailed and nuanced knowledge of the recipient country and its needs. In Afghanistan, the pressure to achieve rapid change after the fall of the Taliban regime seemingly overshadowed the need for knowledge accumulation, rigorous data collection, and analysis. The need for quick results precluded efforts to understand the Afghan context and tailor SSR efforts accordingly. As one senior European Union official remarked about SSR planning, 'Often in Afghanistan you are creating policy without the necessary data. The donor community has made pledges and contributions of funds without knowing what the needs are' (interview, Kabul, 13 November 2005).

Most external actors have based their reform efforts on the flawed assumption that a functioning state never existed in the country. Moreover, many security sector reformers assume that Afghanistan never had security forces capable of projecting power beyond the capital. Consequently, they have interpreted their task as building a security sector from scratch, on a blank slate, ignoring historical trends of state formation and traditional mechanisms for security and social order. Afghanistan's state-builders and security sector reformers have misunderstood both the nature of power distribution in Afghanistan and the historical foundations of the state. This dual misconception shaped the SSR process, decontextualizing and dehistoricizing it. An adviser to President Karzai said that SSR has been 'inhibited by poor donor understanding of Afghan history' (interview, Cambridge, UK, 10 February 2006), and a senior UNAMA official accused the main US body charged with advancing SSR, the Combined Security Transition Command–Afghanistan, of being an 'ahistorical institution' that 'always comes with a blank-slate approach' (interview, Kabul, 13 January 2009).

Almost five years into the reform process, an Afghan member of Parliament put the problem of SSR in Afghanistan succinctly: 'The West doesn't understand Afghanistan' (interview, Kabul, 16 June 2006). The result, as a UK Department for International Development (DFID) official put it, 'is a gap between what is possible in the context and what donor capitals think is possible' (interview, Kabul, 13 January 2009). The tendency of donors to view the current intervention and SSR process as a discrete or stand-alone episode of Afghanistan's recent history, rather than as part of a broader process of state formation and an outgrowth of a protracted conflict cycle with domestic, regional, and international dimensions, has distorted and undermined reform programmes. Western states seemingly ignore the fact that realizing the vision of the liberal state in Afghanistan is no less revolutionary than the reforms of the communist People's Democratic Party for Afghanistan or the Taliban brand of Islamization. All have aroused seismic political reactions from Afghan society, the aftershocks of which are still felt today. William Maley (2009) shows how state-building has played a Janus-faced role in recent Afghan history as both a driver of modernity and progress for some, and a disruptor of peace and social order for others.

A 2011 RAND Corporation report deriving lessons from security assistance in Afghanistan for the US military touched on the acontextual character of donor assistance and the ingrained proclivity to impose Western statist solutions:

> The case of Afghanistan ... shows that Western models for forces and ministries may not work in countries with very different societies, requirements, and resources. The ability to understand this fact and to derive reasonable plans for developing and fielding host-nation forces that take the unique context of the country into account will be a critical capability. (Kelly, Bensahel, and Oliker 2011)

Indeed, the orthodox SSR model, at least in theory, calls for SSR to be adapted to local contexts, not for local contexts to be transformed to resemble Western systems. Adapting the model to complex, non-Western, conflict-affected environments has nonetheless confounded reformers in Afghanistan. As one British soldier in Afghanistan stated in reference to police reform, 'Our biggest challenge is doing things the Afghan way.... The hierarchical system in the village community doesn't really allow our methods and process to work' (Kaphle 2012). There is surely no single Afghan way, and it is important not to valorize all that is local, given that many so-called 'traditional practices' are recent and artificial and have contributed to the country's instability. However, Afghanistan's state-builders and security sector reformers alike have too often strayed from indigenous knowledge and norms to import foreign and instrumentalized ideas and systems, based on superficial understandings of the local context, thereby creating unsustainable and fragile outputs.

Short-term planning and unsustainable reforms

The goal of SSR is to create a self-sufficient security system, not institutions dependent on external sources. With this in mind, surprisingly little has been done to practically address issues of reform sustainability in Afghanistan. The process has largely been driven by the short-term imperatives of addressing the insurgency and creating security conditions conducive for international military disengagement, rather than fostering the development of an autonomous security apparatus attuned to the human security needs of Afghans. In the SSR context, sustainability has economic, cultural, and political dimensions, but it is the economic dimension that best illustrates the sustainability dilemma in Afghanistan, where donor funding programmes have reinforced the country's historic position as a rentier client state, dependent on external revenue flows to maintain the integrity of its security sector.

The Afghan National Development Strategy states the problem simply: 'The international community has imported models of security forces that impose costs Afghanistan may not be able to sustain' (Islamic Republic of Afghanistan 2006). Even according to the most optimistic projections concerning the growth of Afghan revenue-generating capacity over the coming decade, the country cannot hope to cover its recurrent security expenditures, which in 2009–2010 represented roughly 200% of Afghan domestic revenues (General Budget Directorate 2012). This was actually a major improvement over the situation in 2004–2005, when security expenditures equalled almost 500% of domestic revenues and 23% of GDP (World Bank 2005). To put the latter GDP figure in perspective, the global average for defence expenditures hovers at roughly 4% of GDP (Rubin 2006, 181). One donor official stated, 'I can't envision when Afghanistan will not be dependent on international support' (interview, Kabul, 12 November 2005). In 2013, that view is still widely held in Kabul and donor capitals.

An examination of historical precedents in Afghanistan shows that when the state has been unable to pay its security forces, typically due to the withdrawal of foreign subsidies – whether British or Soviet – the security sector has collapsed and conflict has ensued. At its current fiscal trajectory there is a significant chance that this pattern could be repeated, as the inevitable downsizing of the international aid commitment to the country could create resource pressures that may again lead to the breakdown of the security sector and a resumption of civil conflict (see Sedra 2009).

The projected sustainment cost of the security forces at their ceiling of 352,000 is USD 5 billion to 6 billion per year, which is roughly equivalent to 25% of Afghanistan's GDP and 2.5 times total government revenue (Byrd 2012). As William Byrd (2012) states, 'Even with continuing rapid revenue growth over time, it will not catch up with projected security sector costs for a number of years, and there are very large demands on government revenues for civilian expenditures as well.'

According to Afghan government officials in 2010, it would be at least a decade before the country could fiscally sustain the Afghan National Army (ANA) by itself (GAO 2011, 32–33). The International Monetary Fund has projected that it will take the Afghan government until 2023 to raise revenues sufficient to cover its operating costs (the majority of which go to the army and police); until then, it will remain dependent on external funding (IMF 2010). The ANP alone will require an annual budget of USD 726.9 million to fund salaries, incentives, and food at its final strength of 157,000 (not including equipment costs), which would account for 57% of projected domestic revenues for fiscal year 2012–13 and 28% of the operating budget (SIGAR 2012, 76; MoF 2012, 4). To put this in a regional perspective, Afghanistan's per capita expenditure on the police (USD 21) is more than double the per capita expenditure of India (USD 10 as of 2009).[7]

There is wide acknowledgement of the sustainability problem facing the Afghan security sector, but few serious steps to systematically address it (Giustozzi and Sedra 2004). The gradual growth of the insurgency after 2006–2007 led to the jettisoning of plans to reduce the size of the force. Instead, it was massively expanded. On 11 June 2011, the Standing Security Committee of the Afghan government's Joint Coordination and Monitoring Board approved an increase of the ANSF's target strength to 352,000 (SIGAR 2011, 57). Warnings over sustainability, once presented with a high level of urgency, were ignored.

In 2012, NATO, in conjunction with the Afghan government, took initial steps to make the security sector more sustainable, announcing that the force ceiling for the ANSF would be lowered from 352,000 to 230,000. However, no timetable was offered for when the change would be completed, and according to Defence Minister Wardak, the final figure would 'be subject to revision based on the realities on the ground' and applied gradually (Shanker and Rubin 2012). This would lower the cost of sustainment from USD 5 billion or 6 billion per year to USD 4 billion, with the US expressing a willingness to foot USD 2.5 billion of the yearly bill (Byrd 2012). However, with the Pentagon trimming USD 500 billion from its budget over the coming decade, the US contribution may still be a tall order and subject to a decrease. Realistically, for its security architecture to survive, Afghanistan requires the type of long-term aid commitment that the US provides to Israel and Egypt, a prospect that is questionable. As Byrd (2012) explains, 'Fiscal analysis conducted by the World Bank indicates that Afghanistan will be unable to pay for the ANSF at anywhere near existing or targeted size and cost levels from domestic resources for the foreseeable future', a reality that 'would hold true even … at half the previous size and cost targets'. The SSR project's lack of sustainability in Afghanistan is so stark that it is difficult to envision how the sector could survive without indefinite Western support, creating a permanent rentier state.

Conclusion

According to almost any measure, security sector reform in Afghanistan has failed. Not only did it stray from the orthodox SSR model, it also failed to produce competent security forces on the basis of fundamental train-and-equip metrics. SSR has been stuck in a state of normative limbo, too transformative in its surface-level liberal vision to realize the core liberal principles of SSR, and not pragmatic and politically sophisticated enough to deliver major short-term tactical gains. SSR has consisted of two separate but parallel processes, one liberal and one realist, that rarely align and often clash. This is less a reflection of the type of liberal–local hybridity present in most SSR environments than an outgrowth of contradictory stakeholder interests and a concept unsuited to challenging conflict-affected environments. Donor SSR programmes may have been driven by calculated strategic imperatives like the 'war on terror' and the advancement of counterinsurgency objectives, but that does not mean that they were advanced in a politically informed or nuanced manner. For instance, even donor efforts to align with some Afghan power brokers in the south and east against the Taliban, as part of a broader proxy strategy, rarely considered local political and security impacts and implications, producing unexpected and often deleterious consequences.[8]

The typical response of many state-builders and security sector reformers in Afghanistan to the stalled SSR process has been a demand for more precise and textured metrics. The problem with SSR in Afghanistan, as this logic goes, is not that progress isn't being made, but that we don't have the right tools to measure it. For instance, 'the Obama Administration has developed about 45 different metrics to assess progress in building Afghan governance and security', and the UN utilizes a framework of comparable metrics to chart the transition (Katzman 2012, 34). Such measures are typically quantitative and reflect the pseudo-scientific, depoliticized, and decontextualized approach that donors have brought to SSR and state-building.

One need not look too deeply beneath the veneer of the SSR edifice in Afghanistan to detect its poor performance. A US official at the 2012 NATO summit in Chicago privately admitted to the New York Times that the Afghan military was 'a work in progress' and the police 'filled with drug users, thieves and "shakedown artists"' (Cooper and Rosenberg 2012). These bodies were supposedly the jewels of a decade of SSR, absorbing tens of billions of dollars in aid and the engagement of thousands of foreign advisers. It was also those forces that NATO assessed as sufficiently capable to be entrusted with safeguarding the country's fragile transition and protecting its vulnerable population beyond NATO's withdrawal in 2014.

Afghanistan's security sector reformers did not understand the country or seek to adapt the SSR model to its unique socio-cultural and political milieu after the Taliban were bombed out of office. One of the many crucial questions that the reformers did not pose was, as one senior UN adviser put it (interview, Kabul, 6 April 2008), what happens when you endeavour to abolish patronage and clientelism in a country where 'personal relationships supersede everything else'? The result may be, as one Afghanistan observer noted in 2003, a loss of 'institutional cohesion like in 1979' (interview, Bonn, 16 June 2003). In fact, that 'flawed patronage system could be the only thing that is feasible' in the present Afghan context (Ibid.). As a result, the advancement of the international community's technocratic SSR and liberal peace project may have only hastened the breakdown of existing social and political capital. In many ways, SSR was merely a façade. In the end, as the process evolved, donors' realist strategic interests, primarily the 'war on terror' and the advancement of COIN objectives, gained primacy over people-centred SSR orthodoxy.

Afghanistan presented immensely difficult conditions for SSR: an active conflict; high levels of corruption and criminality inside and outside the state; low levels of human and institutional capacity; the absence of a political settlement; divergent and often conflicting internal and external stakeholder interests; and a diversity of informal security and justice structures. The presence of just one of these factors is capable of derailing an SSR programme; the fact that all were present made the application of the orthodox SSR model virtually impossible. Afghanistan presented an exceedingly difficult case for SSR that nonetheless yielded important lessons for the model.

When the process began, donors broadly adhered to the orthodox SSR model, at least rhetorically. It treated Afghanistan as a blank slate upon which a 'Western-style' security sector could be built. However, as the security situation deteriorated and political dynamics frustrated reformers, the process shifted to more expedient train-and-equip modalities, stripping the model of the liberal elements that distinguish it from previous forms of security assistance. Train-and-equip assistance is more straightforward for donors; it can be easily measured and provided in compact, well-defined programme cycles. More importantly, the 'hard' security approach more directly satisfied the strategic and tactical interests of donors. As a part of this slide toward expediency, donors have also promoted some non-state structures and actors. But this frequently involved the instrumentalization and manipulation of informal structures, advanced without a crucial understanding of how local security and justice systems work. By 2012, the SSR process had been almost fully hollowed out, with issues like human rights and democratic civilian control secondary issues for reformers. The process was still seen by many as a key to Afghanistan's stability and the international exit strategy, but it was SSR in name only.

The orthodox SSR model places a high premium on local knowledge, something that the SSR programme in Afghanistan always seemed to lack. A RAND study on US security force assistance in Afghanistan aptly concluded, 'Without a firm grasp of the key facts and conditions in Afghanistan, security force assistance plans, however technocratically brilliant, will not succeed' (Kelly, Bensahel, and Oliker 2011, 86). This raises the question of whether the orthodox SSR model is in fact sufficiently intuitive and flexible to grasp and adapt to non-Western conflict-affected states like Afghanistan. On the eve of NATO's troop withdrawal from Afghanistan, set for 2014, the answer would appear to be that it is not.

Notes

1. A conceptual model outlining the key framing principles and implementation modalities for security-sector reform programmes has evolved since the emergence of the idea in the early 1990s and has been broadly endorsed by key Western donors and multilateral bodies like the United Nations and OECD. That model is reflected in key formative documents like the OECD's 2007 *Handbook on Security System Reform* (OECD DAC 2007) and the United Nations Secretary General's 2008 report on SSR (UNSG 2008).

2. At two Group of Eight security donor meetings, held in Geneva in April and May 2002, the Afghan SSR process was divided into five pillars and a multi-sectoral donor-support scheme was established. It allocated responsibility for overseeing each SSR pillar to a individual donor. The lead-nation system, as it came to be known, was structured as follows: military reform, US lead; police reform, German lead; demilitarization, Japanese lead; judicial reform, Italian lead; and counternarcotics, UK lead.

3. 'Hard' security assistance denotes activities to develop, restructure, or reform coercive security institutions like the army, police, and intelligence bodies. It focuses primarily on expanding the operational effectiveness of those institutions. 'Soft' security assistance, by contrast, refers to all activities addressing non-coercive structures, actors, and processes within the security and justice architecture. This primarily refers to efforts to expand and improve governance across the security system, to mainstream democratic norms like respect for human rights, and to support the transformation of justice and corrections institutions.

4. The Panjshiri Tajiks emanate from the Panjshir Valley, situated north of Kabul. Many of the top Tajik leaders of the Northern Alliance came from there, including Ahmad Shah Massoud. In April 2004, the valley became the heart of a new province called Panjshir. Afghanistan has 34 provinces.

5. The National Assembly, consisting of two houses – the Wolesi Jirga (House of People) and the Meshrano Jirga (House of Elders) – must approve all presidential appointments and wields the power of oversight over executive decisions. According to the Constitution of the Islamic Republic of Afghanistan (2004), 'Any commission of both Houses of the National Assembly can question each of the Ministers about specific topics' (Ch. 5, Art. 93). The Wolesi Jirga also has the authority, if it receives the support of one-third of the chamber, to directly question any member of the government. If the answers it receives are unsatisfactory, it has the power to enter a vote of no confidence in the government.

6. According to the 2004 Constitution, the president is the commander-in-chief of the armed forces and is responsible for 'appointing, retiring and accepting the resignation of and dismissing judges, officers of the armed forces, police, national security, and high-ranking officials in accordance with the law', including government ministers, the attorney general, the head of the National Directorate of Security, and members of the Supreme Court (Ch. 3, Art. 64). The presidency is thus the focal point for security policy in the country.

7. According to Giustozzi and Isaqzadeh (2011, 4), India spent USD 12 billion for its entire policing system in 2009, for a population of 1.2 billion. Afghanistan's population is estimated at 34 million.

8. See, for instance, the account by Fisher (2002) of US support of the Afghan warlord Bacha Khan Zadran.

References

Ayub, Fatima, Sari Kouvo, and Rachel Wareham. 2010. *Security Sector Reform in Afghanistan*. Brussels: The Initiative for Peacebuilding.

Barno, David W., Andrew Exum, and Matthew Irvine. 2011. *The Next Fight: Time for a Change of Mission in Afghanistan*. Washington, DC: Center for a New American Security.

Bayley, David H., and Robert M. Perito. 2009. *The Police in War: Fighting Insurgency, Terrorism and Violent Crime*. Boulder: Lynne Reinner.

Byrd, William. 2012. "Paying for Afghanistan's Security Forces During Transition: Issues for Chicago and Beyond." *Peace Brief 124*. Washington, DC: United States Institute of Peace (USIP).

Caldwell, William B., and Nathan Finney. 2011. "Building the Security Force that Won't Leave." *Joint Forces Quarterly* 62: 76–77.

Center for Policy and Human Development (CPHD). 2007. *Bridging Modernity and Tradition: The Rule of Law and the Search for Justice*. Kabul: CPHD.

Chilton, Scott, Eckart Schiewek, and Tim Bremmers. 2009. *Evaluation of the Appropriate Size of the Afghan National Police Force Manning List (Tashkil)*. Brussels: European Union.

Constitution of the Islamic Republic of Afghanistan. 2004. *Constitution of the Islamic Republic of Afghanistan*. (ratified January 26). Accessed 25 September 2013. http://www.afghanembassy. com.pl/cms/uploads/images/Constitution/The%20Constitution.pdf

Cooper, Helene, and Matthew Rosenberg. 2012. "NATO Agrees on Afghan Security Transition in 2013." *The New York Times*. May 2012.

Cordesman, Antony H. 2009. *Afghan National Security Forces: Shaping the Path to Victory*. Washington, DC: Center for Strategic and International Studies.

CPAU. 2007. *The Role and Functions of Religious Civil Society in Afghanistan: Case Studies from Sayedabad & Kunduz*. Kabul: CPAU.

Doucet, Lyse. 2006. "Afghanistan: A Job Half Done." *BBC News*. December 4.

Fisher, Ian. 2002. "Warlord Pushes for Control of Corner of Afghanistan." *New York Times*. August 6.

General Budget Directorate of Afghan Ministry of Finance. 2012. Accessed September 1. http://www.budgetmof.gov.af/

Giustozzi, Antonio, and Mohammad Isaqzadeh. 2011. *Afghanistan's Paramilitary Policing in Context: The Risks of Expediency*. Kabul: Afghanistan Analysts Network.

Giustozzi, Giustozzi, and Mark Sedra. 2004. *Securing Afghanistan's Future: Accomplishments and the Strategic Pathway Forward – Afghan National Army Technical Annex*. Kabul: Islamic Transitional State of Afghanistan.

Goodhand, Jonathan, and Mark Sedra. 2007. "Bribes or Bargains? Peace Conditionalities and "Post-Conflict" Reconstruction in Afghanistan." *International Peacekeeping* 14 (1): 41–61.

Gross, Eva. 2009. "Security Sector Reform in Afghanistan: The EU's Contribution." *Occasional Paper 78*. Paris: EU Institute for Security Studies.

IMF. 2010. *Islamic Republic of Afghanistan: Sixth Review Under the Arrangement Under the Poverty Reduction and Growth Facility, Request for Waiver of Nonobservance of a Performance Criterion, Modification and Performance Criteria, and Rephasing and Extension of the Arrangement*. Country Report No. 10/22. Washington, DC: IMF.

Islamic Republic of Afghanistan. 2006. *Interim Afghanistan National Development Strategy*. Kabul: Islamic Republic of Afghanistan.

Islamic Republic of Afghanistan Ministry of Finance (MoF). 2012. *Aid and Budget*. Issue 2. Kabul: Islamic Republic of Afghanistan.

Islamic Republic of Afghanistan Ministry of Interior Affairs (MoI). 2010. *Afghanistan National Police Strategy*. Kabul: Islamic Republic of Afghanistan.

Kaphle, Anup. 2012. "In Helmand, Training Afghan Local Police Is a Challenge." *The Washington Post*. February 11.

Katzman, Kenneth. 2012. *Afghanistan: Post-Taliban Governance, Security and U.S. Policy*. CRS Report for Congress 7–5700. Washington, DC: CRS.

Kelly, Terrence K., Nora Bensahel, and Olga Oliker. 2011. *Security Force Assistance in Afghanistan: Identifying Lessons for Future Efforts*. Santa Monica, CA: RAND.

Long, Austin, and Andrew Radin. 2012. "Enlisting Islam for an Effective Afghan Police." *Survival* 54 (2): 113–128.

Luckham, Robin. 2003. "Democratic Strategies for Security in Transition and Conflict." In *Governing Insecurity: Democratic Control of Military and Security Establishments in Transitional Democracies*, edited by Gavin Cawthra, and Robin Luckham, 3–28. London: Zed Books.

Maley, William. 2009. *The Afghanistan Wars*. 2nd ed. London: Palgrave Macmillan.

Nadery, Ahmad Nader. 2012. "Getting Human Rights Wrong Is not an Option", The AfPak Channel, *Foreign Policy Magazine*, May 17.

OECD DAC. 2007. *Handbook on Security System Reform: Supporting Security and Justice*. Paris: OECD.

Rubin, Barnett R. 2006. "Peace Building and State-Building in Afghanistan: Constructing Sovereignty for Whose Security?." *Third World Quarterly* 27 (1): 175–185.

Sedra, Mark. 2009. "The Army, From Abdur Rahman to Karzai." In *Viewpoints Special Edition - Afghanistan, 1979–2009: In the Grip of Conflict*, 83–87. Washington, DC: The Middle East Institute.

Shanker, Thom, and Alissa J. Rubin. 2012. "Afghan Force Will Be Cut After Taking Leading Role." *The New York Times*. April 10.

Special Inspector General for Afghanistan Reconstruction (SIGAR). 2011. *Quarterly Report to the United States Congress*. Washington, DC: SIGAR. July.

Special Inspector General for Afghanistan Reconstruction (SIGAR). 2012. *Quarterly Report to the United States Congress*. Washington, DC: SIGAR. April.

The Afghanistan Compact. 2006. *The Afghanistan Compact: Building on Success*. Accessed 25 September 2013. www.nato.int/isaf/docu/epub/pdf/afghanistan_compact.pdf

United States Department of State (US DoS). 2011. *Country Reports on Human Rights Practices for 2011: Afghanistan*. Washington, DC: US DoS.

UNSG. 2008. *Securing Peace and Development: The Role of the United Nations in Supporting Security Sector Reform*. Report of the Secretary-General. A/62/659-S/2008/39. New York: United Nations.

USAID. 2011. *Factsheet: Afghanistan Parliamentary Assistance Program (APAP)*. Kabul: USAID.

US Government Accountability Office (GAO). 2011. *Afghan Army Growing, but Additional Trainers Needed; Long-Term Costs not Determined*. GAO-11-66. Washington, DC: GAO.

Wardak, Ali. 2011. "State and Non-State Justice Systems in Afghanistan: The Need for Synergy." *Pennsylvania Journal of International Law* 32 (5): 1305–1324.

Wimpelmann, Torunn. 2013. "Nexuses of Knowledge and Power in Afghanistan: The Rise and Fall of the Informal Justice Assemblage." *Central Asian Survey* 32 (3): 10.1080/02634937.2013.835200

World Bank. 2005. *Afghanistan: Managing Public Finances for Development – Improving Public Finance Management in the Security Sector*. Washington, DC: World Bank.

Getting savages to fight barbarians: counterinsurgency and the remaking of Afghanistan

Aziz A. Hakimi

Development Studies Department, School of Oriental and African Studies, University of London, London, UK

This article focuses on the emergence and evolution of the Afghan Local Police (ALP), a pro-government militia supported by the US military in Wardak Province. The ALP and its previous incarnations have been justified, invoking notions of 'local solutions' and 'cost-effectiveness', as a politically convenient and culturally appropriate measure to supplement broader efforts to counter the insurgency and build up the regular forces. Inspired by the tribal policing concept of *arbaki*, ALP was envisaged as a short-term local defence force. But the programme has been controversial, and its impact in improving security questionable. In analysing the contestations between different actors involved in the programme, the article demonstrates that the US military's attempt to resuscitate 'age-old traditions' of self-protection proved difficult to realize and produced unforeseen and largely deleterious outcomes. It concludes that far from reflecting the needs of local villagers, ALP was a top-down imposition whose objectives were much narrower than the purported aim of protecting the local population in Wardak.

What inspired me was my first rotation here into Afghanistan, where I learned how to use the tribes and other ethnic groups to secure local and rural areas with small numbers of people.... I saw the power of this culture in protecting itself at the local level, which I believe is the secret to security in Afghanistan – at the district level and below. You can be very effective, but in a way that is traditional, and congruent with how they have protected themselves for hundreds of years.

General Donald Bolduc, Deputy Commander of Special Operations Forces in Afghanistan, and known as the godfather of the Afghan Local Police (*New York Times*, 20 May 2013)

We must work first and forever with the tribes, for they are the most important military, political and cultural units in that country. The tribes are self-contained fighting units who will fight to the death for their tribal family's honor and respect.

Major Jim Gant (2009, 4), Commander of ODA 316, United States Army special forces.

Introduction

The quotations above are illustrative of views that became increasingly prevalent in US military circles as the war against the Taliban showed few signs of victory.[1] These notions of the tribal traditions of local governance and self-defence have been invoked as part of the US counterinsurgency's tribal engagement strategy by selectively piggybacking on nineteenth-century colonial ethnography and subsequent anthropological and historical accounts of Afghanistan.[2] The

Afghan Local Police (ALP) programme, through which US special forces established self-defence forces in collaboration with local elders and government officials, was the culmination of a series of attempts to tap into and rejuvenate what were presented as enduring rural traditions of self-protection. The ALP was preceded by several other militia programmes, including the Afghan National Auxiliary Police, the Afghan Public Protection Programme (AP3), and the Local Defence Initiative. The ALP incorporated all previous militia formations under the Ministry of Interior and, at least in theory, subordinated them to the Afghan National Police command at the district and provincial levels.

However, in practice it proved difficult to revive traditions of self-protection that were based upon an idealized and reified vision of the past. This article shows how the US military struggled in the province of Wardak as local support proved elusive and many were quite unwilling to be left to defend themselves against Taliban insurgents. Instead of generating benefits for the wider population, the programme was largely about safeguarding US forces by using local fighters as cost-effective auxiliaries to fight the Taliban. The programme also provided security and financial benefits for local power brokers, including former *jihadi* commanders, who found employment for their militias, and senior government officials, who relied on ALP for protection. According to former militia commanders, the AP3, a precursor of ALP in Wardak, was used by US special forces for night raids and targeted killings against insurgents, and as such played a limited role in protecting the population.[3] The use of a defensive militia for combat purposes discredited the AP3, which was seen as an American tool used against some groups, whom the US considered enemies, while empowering other armed groups. In this sense, it was an attempt by an imperial power to mobilize tribal people in the defence of colonialism by 'getting savages to fight barbarians' (Duffield 2005, 141).

The first section of this article[4] provides a brief analysis of the shift towards the valorization of tradition and customary actors and institutions and its relevance to the object of this study. It sets the stage for a focused examination of the AP3 in Wardak. This is followed by a brief background of the ALP and its previous iterations, with a particular focus on the national level. The discussion then returns to Wardak to document the transition of AP3 to ALP. A short ethnographic account of an ALP inauguration ceremony in Sayedabad District in Wardak demonstrates that the ALP, like its predecessors, has involved intense negotiations and, despite reference to local ownership, eventually found little buy-in from the local people. I continue with the discussion of ALP in Wardak to elaborate on the final stages of the programme and the kind of legacy it left behind. In the concluding section, I argue that the case of ALP in Wardak highlights the real intent and outcome of US counterinsurgency and its externally driven, militarized version of state-building.

Tradition, self-reliance, and indirect rule

The emphasis on culturally appropriate, local, and informal actors and mechanisms as a solution to security and governance more broadly is not unique to Afghanistan, and reflects a wider shift in the literature and policy debates on peace-building and state-building.[5] The prominence given to customary institutions and non-state actors problematizes the dominant liberal notions of peace-building and state-building based on state sovereignty and monopoly on violence.[6] This is sometimes presented as a radical critique of interventionism. Yet, as Duffield reminds us, there are larger interests at play in protecting and cultivating tradition; 'securing the "traditional" and maintaining its cohesion', he argues, 'is essential for defending the "modern"'(2005, 148). Holding up 'Rousseau's "savage" or natural man' as 'the epitome of self-reliance', Duffield contends that 'self-re-production, and the natural resilience that this imparts, has long been axiomatic for people understood through the register of tradition, simplicity, backwardness and race' (146). He points out that 'native administration', the formalized indirect rule of Western colonies, was based on the assumption of self-reliance – that by being empowered 'by their own efforts in their own way', instead of having alien notions imposed on them, native people would be able to withstand the threats and lures of insurgent nationalism and other challenges to the imperial order (150). This cultivation of self-reliance, in Duffield's analysis, amounts to 'getting savages to fight barbarians'. The savage is invited to maintain his traditional, self-reliant ways of life and the coherence and continuity of his community as a defence against the barbarians who threaten the civilized world as a whole.

Similar to Duffield's formulation, the ALP programme claims to improve the self-reliance of local villagers as means of defending the post-2001 order against the threat of Taliban insurgency. As I show in the recounting of the ALP inauguration ceremony in Sayedabad District, in exchange for development's promise of bettering life and improving services, the local villagers were asked to defend society against the Taliban 'barbarians'. The deployment of development resources to build local security is central to US counterinsurgency doctrine (Goodhand, this volume; Kilcullen 2009; Dorronsoro 2011; Fishstein and Wilder 2012). For example, the 12 km road in Nerkh District (work began in the autumn of 2011) was approved by the US military as a means of driving a wedge between the local population, who were eager to get government services, and Taliban insurgents, who opposed it. The road, which was protected by the ALP, and other development services, like schools, played important roles in getting Hizb-e-Islami,[7] the military power in Nerkh, to break ranks with Taliban insurgents and mobilize local commanders to fight them, instead of jointly focusing on US forces.[8] In practice, as I recount below, the retrieval of the purported time-honoured traditions of Afghan tribes to defend themselves proved rather difficult to realize.

The Afghan Public Protection Programme – an experiment in local militias

Toward the middle of the decade, the security situation in most parts of southern and eastern Afghanistan had deteriorated considerably. By early 2008, the politically and strategically important province of Wardak had become a centre for the insurgency. As a result, the provincial capital, Maidanshahr, had become the focus of frequent insurgent attacks, while the government's influence barely extended beyond the governor's compound. Signs of insecurity had appeared in Wardak already in the lead-up to the 2004 presidential and 2005 parliamentary elections, mostly in the districts of Sayedabad and Nerkh. The politico-military environment in Wardak had been shaped over time by a range of armed groups dating back to the pre-2001 years of conflict. The early 1990s was a particularly violent period, when competition for power frequently degenerated into armed clashes between the different armed groups. For example, before the Taliban captured Wardak in the mid-1990s, factional rivalries between Hizb-e-Islami and Harakat-e-Inqilab-e-Islami,[9] two *mujahedin* parties, resulted in over 3000 deaths in and around Maidanshahr alone.[10] Political and military fragmentation continued as a result of power struggles among different *mujahedin* factions after the fall of the Taliban in November 2001. In these early years of the Karzai administration, Hizb-e-Islami regained some of its former military strength. However, the Taliban presence increasingly grew, its ranks included many former Harakat commanders. In a sense, the bloody power struggles between Hizb and the Taliban that have been raging on since 2010 in Nerkh mirror those in the early 1990s between Hizb and Harakat.

While Hizb initially enjoyed military superiority, its dominance gradually declined as the Taliban intensified their military campaign, and by end of 2008 most parts of Wardak had come under Taliban control. However, the district of Nerkh remained divided between the two groups. The security situation in Maidanshahr had deteriorated to the extent that in July

2008, after his appointment as governor of Wardak, when Halim Fidai travelled to Maidanshahr to assume his duties, insurgents were able to fire 15 rockets into the governor's compound on the day of his inauguration.[11] The insurgents had become so confident that they frequently carried out attacks against government offices located a few hundred metres from the governor's compound. Fearful of Taliban retaliation, civil servants hardly ever stayed overnight in Maidanshahr or the nearby districts, preferring to escape to the safety of Kabul.

In response to rising insecurity, the province became a testing ground for local governance and stability operations, which involved the formation of local defence forces as part of the US military's counterinsurgency efforts to bring stability to Wardak. In October 2008, Afghan and US officials began planning to establish a 1200-strong Afghan Public Protection Programme (AP3) force in four districts: Jalrez, Nerkh, Maidanshahr, and Sayedabad. The plan provided for between 100 and 200 guardians per district, but no more than a total of 1200 in the entire province, to be recruited by local *shuras*[12] and vetted by government institutions. In March 2009, the implementation of the AP3 began in Jalrez District.[13] By 2010, the AP3 had 1100 recruits. The AP3's mandate was a compromise, the product of competing interests and rationalities, including: the US military priority of defeating the Taliban, preventing insurgent attacks on government and NATO forces and protecting public infrastructure; attempts by local commanders to reinvent their militias and access state patronage; and President Karzai's attempts at regularizing foreign funded militias and centralizing the means of coercion and patronage (Perito 2009; Lefèvre 2010).[14] As a result, the AP3 from the outset faced many challenges in terms of recruitment, local buy-in, logistics support, and appropriation by local commanders.[15] The AP3 was funded by the US military, because European donors objected to payments to a paramilitary force. Initial recruitment among Hazaras in Jalrez began positively, but among Pashtuns the process moved very slowly, partly because Taliban insurgents intimidated local recruits, tribal leaders, and local power brokers. From the outset, there was therefore widespread scepticism about the programme – an attitude that was reinforced by the local people's bitter experience with militias in Wardak in the 1980s and early 1990s (Lefèvre 2010; HRW 2011). Subsequently, when Pashtuns joined the AP3, one particular sub-tribe with links to a local *jihadi* commander, Ghulam Mohammad Hotak, dominated the recruits. He took advantage of the initial problems in recruitment to accommodate hundreds of his armed followers in the AP3.

There are differing accounts of the extent to which the establishment of the AP3 was rooted in local demands. Governor Fidai claimed that elders in Wardak had requested the programme; yet in a two-day meeting in Kabul in October 2008, tribal elders, representatives of district *shuras*, and provincial council members opposed the formation of local militias and rejected a government declaration intended to demonstrate popular support for the initiative. Instead, local elders asked for the deployment of more Afghan National Army (ANA) and Afghan National Police (ANP) units in Wardak.[16] Many government officials were against the AP3 as well, notably the minister of defence, Rahim Wardak, on the grounds that support to local militias would undermine the Afghan National Security Forces (ANSF). In contrast, the minister of interior, Haneef Atmar, cautiously endorsed it, seeing the AP3 as a pragmatic solution to the problem of local insecurity. He explicitly linked it to the wider project of centralization and institutionalization, and therefore emphasized the need for central control and regulation of local forces. Furthermore, he envisaged the gradual replacement of private security companies with a Ministry of Interior guard force: the Afghan Public Protection Force. The model envisaged a government-controlled stop-gap measure, tied to the growth of the ANSF, whereby militia units would be demobilized or integrated into regular forces as the national army and police forces developed. This was a pragmatic way of building state power by extending control over existing armed groups and the means of violence.

Despite the lack of support from local elders and certain government officials, the US military and the Afghan government pushed ahead with the AP3's implementation. However, there was a wide gap between the theory and the practice, largely because the theory was based on an outmoded set of assumptions about the capacity of tribal leaders and local *shuras* to command the loyalties of local villagers. In practice, it was militia commanders who were the real power holders in post-2001 Afghanistan.[17] The lack of local support and Pashtun fear of retribution from the Taliban help explain why recruitment became difficult and remained largely limited to the Tajik and Hazara populations. After almost a year of limited progress, the US military and Afghan officials reached out to Ghulam Mohammad Hotak, former Taliban commander and one-time inmate of the US detention facility in Bagram (also known as the Parwan Detention Facility), to rescue the programme.[18] Hotak reportedly brought hundreds of his own supporters from Jalrez to the force, but after a few months of poor government support he quit the programme (Lefèvre 2010; HRW 2011).[19] Hotak came to bitterly regret his decision to join the AP3. Funding for the programme was always late, he said, and he himself had to buy basic supplies like food, vehicle fuel, and winter supplies, including heating for the force. As a result, he accumulated a large debt.[20] Many other local commanders also became heavily indebted because of late payments and inadequate logistical support, forcing them to dig into their own pockets to support their men – expenditures for which, allegedly, they were never properly compensated.[21] In addition, there was a regular shortage of weapons and ammunition. Despite Governor Fidai's repeated attempts to get the US military and the Ministry of Interior to intervene to address the emerging problems with AP3, he was largely ignored.[22] Because of inadequate support by the government, AP3 remained dependent on US special forces and was in turn relied upon for joint anti-Taliban military operations, including outside the province.

Although they were part of a plan that required additional US and Afghan forces to clear areas before the AP3 was deployed there to hold them, most AP3 units said they were used for clearing purposes, leading local commanders to describe AP3 forces as 'shields of meat' deployed to receive Taliban bullets.[23] Subsequently, many former AP3 commanders and senior government officials accused the US military of reneging on its promises to secure insurgency-affected areas *before* AP3 forces were deployed there.[24] In the absence of any clearing of territory, there was not much to hold. The new recruits, trained as a defensive and lightly armed force and with only three weeks of training, were ill prepared to fight a superior Taliban foe. Many ended up being used as frontline troops to fight the insurgents, resulting in significant losses in some parts of Wardak. One commander lost more than half of his men in just over a year.[25] Local commanders argued that the Americans simply contracted the war out to local villagers, while they adopted a bunker mentality and sat in their fortified bases, from the safety of which they watched as local armed groups clashed with one another.[26] Essentially, Afghan villagers were used as cheap and dispensable auxiliaries to fight America's war; the discourse about tribal traditions of self-protection appeared to be a mere fig leaf. Former minister Atmar echoed these views when describing the fate of AP3 recruits, who ended up being made 'scapegoats', blamed for the series of blunders committed by US military and Afghan government officials. In his words, members of the AP3 force were 'betrayed by their own sponsors'.[27]

Nationalization of US-supported local militias: the Afghan Local Police

As far back as 2005, local communities in southern and eastern Afghanistan had reportedly asked the central government to deploy additional police along the border areas with Pakistan to stem the tide of infiltration by insurgents and improve security in those areas. At the time, the Afghan government requested a quick expansion of the national police force, the ANP, but US and NATO officials refused to support the plan. This response led President Karzai to propose the idea of employing a community or local police force modelled on the tribal security practice known as *arbaki*, but the US did not support it at the time.[28] A proposal by the British prime minister, Gordon Brown, in December 2007 to increase support for community defence initiatives modelled on the *arbaki* tribal militias elicited a similar response from US military commanders in Afghanistan. For example, in January 2008, the commander of NATO forces, General Dan McNeill, described the British proposal as potentially disastrous, arguing that 'what we should not do is take actions that will reintroduce militias of the former power brokers' (quoted in Bruno 2008). His successor, General David D. McKiernan, also cautioned against arming tribal militias and providing support to warlords. However, as the situation deteriorated, the US military leaders appeared to have gradually changed their minds. In October 2008, the US secretary of defence, Robert Gates, argued that 'At the end of the day the only solution in Afghanistan is to work with the tribes and provincial leaders in terms of trying to create a backlash ... against the Taliban' (quoted in Bruno 2008).

From this point onwards, over the next few years, a number of initiatives to form local militias got underway. It is worth noting that as early as 2006, in spite of the objections cited above, the US military began supporting efforts to establish local militias. The first such joint US–Afghan initiative was the Afghan National Auxiliary Police (ANAP) programme (Jones 2012). The plan, approved in February 2006, provided for the recruitment of 11,271 men from 124 high-risk districts in 21 provinces, involving an additional 200–400 police officers per district. By July 2007, some 8300 ANAP members had received training in Helmand, Zabul, Kandahar, Farah, Uruzgan, and Ghazni, eventually reaching a total strength of 9000 men. ANAP was managed by the Ministry of Interior in collaboration with the US military command in Afghanistan. The force was widely criticized for empowering provincial power brokers and their private militias, and many of its participants were thought to be Taliban infiltrators (Perito 2009). ANAP was disbanded in May 2008.

The second major initiative involving the formation of local militias resulted in the AP3 in Wardak, as outlined above. In fact, planning and preparatory work for the AP3 had begun in October 2008. In parallel and at the same time as the AP3 was being rolled out in Jalrez District in March 2009, US commanders were exploring options to establish other small local militia units in southern and eastern Afghanistan. This became the Local Defence Initiative (LDI).[29] There was no role envisioned for the Afghan government in this process. It was an American programme, led by elite troops who were meant to embed themselves within Afghan communities.[30] At the time when implementation began, the LDI lacked the approval of President Karzai (US Embassy Kabul 2009).[31] However, when General Petraeus took command of the International Security Assistance Force (ISAF) in July 2010, he pushed for and succeeded in extracting a formal agreement from President Karzai to expand US military–backed militias.

President Karzai initially objected to General Petraeus's proposal to form local self-defence units to fight Taliban insurgents. The Afghan president was not necessarily against militias per se; his objection was more closely related to the role of US special forces and ensuring government control and oversight over these forces. One could also argue that the fight was over control of patronage. According to Afghan officials who were involved in the negotiations, they understood Petraeus's proposal to be influenced by his experience with the Sons of Iraq programme in Iraq. His proposal purportedly involved setting up small, local anti-Taliban armed groups, paid by the US military to work directly under US special forces command without links to any central government institutions – basically free-wheeling militias[32] – leading inevitably, Karzai believed, to *militia-sazi*,[33] the undermining of the ANSF, and ultimately the 'destruction of the state'.[34] Hence, Karzai refused to sanction General Petraeus's initial plan, insisting on the Afghan government's control of the process. The ALP was proposed as an alternative, which enabled the creation of thousands of 'local police' under the command of the Ministry of Interior.

The programme was officially authorized in August 2010, under the control of the Ministry of Interior, calling the militia members Afghan Local Police.[35] With the emergence of a state-sanctioned programme, most of the existing militias were gradually incorporated into the ALP, which became a seal of approval to legitimate and 'consolidate all known coalition and Afghan local self-defense force programs' (HRW 2011, 55). As a result of this agreement, it was hoped, the Afghan government would be able to assert greater control over the local militias supported by US special forces.[36] At the same time, it paved the way for the US military to expand its existing programme of support to local militias as part of its counterinsurgency strategy. The ALP and the simultaneous regulation of private security companies through the Afghan Public Protection Force were seen as instruments to assert Afghan sovereignty and centralize the means of coercion – although in practice this was more symbolic than substantive. Former minister Atmar characterized the twin initiative (ALP and the Afghan Public Protection Force) as an attempt to 're-nationalize security', firstly by ending the mandate of private security companies and secondly by reviving the tribal tradition of local policing known as *arbaki*.

Although it has a mixed record in terms of respect for human rights, the ALP, according to the United Nations Assistance Mission in Afghanistan (UNAMA), has in some contexts helped to improve security and reduce the presence of insurgents in areas where they are deployed (UNAMA and UNOHCHR 2012). In Wardak, however, the ALP had limited impact on security. As a key element of the US population-centric counterinsurgency, the ALP protects 5 million people, or 17% of the Afghan population, according to ISAF.[37] Apparently the ALP is so successful that the insurgents consider it their biggest threat, and as a result its members have been disproportionately targeted.[38] Other claims of the ALP's success include the programme's popularity among the local people, its accountability to the Afghan government and local elders, and cost-effectiveness – the ALP costs 40% less (per person, per year) in training and equipment than the national police.[39] These rationales have been deployed to justify plans to further expand the ALP programme, especially as more and more foreign troops exit the conflict and the burden of fighting is transferred to Afghan forces, including the ALP. However, while national buy-in had been secured, local support continued to prove elusive, as examined in the section below.

A call to arms goes unheeded

Despite its poor reputation, by summer 2010 the AP3 was transitioned into the newly approved ALP in Wardak. However, the problems inherited from AP3 were considered so serious that ISAF finally took steps in the winter of 2011 to address them. In the summer of that year, the Ministry of Interior had established new guidelines for the implementation of the ALP (MOI 2011). This led the US military to announce an ambitious plan to 'fix' ALP and 'redo it all over again' in Wardak according to the new guidelines.[40] The first step in reforming the ALP in Wardak involved the demobilization of 260 members of the force from Maidanshahr and Sayedabad who had earlier been transitioned into the ALP. They were demobilized because they did not meet the new ALP recruitment guidelines, which stipulated among other things that the ALP should be recruited from local villages through *shura*s and vetted by local elders and government institutions, and should report to the district police chief – this had not been the case with most AP3 units. Most of the recruits targeted by the demobilization campaign were from the provinces of Bamyan, Laghman, and Jalalabad, while some belonged to other parts of Wardak where the ALP had not yet been established. Most of them served guard duties in Maidanshahr and provided personal protection to provincial officials – who were not happy to have their personal guards dismissed as part of the reform process.

The partial application of the new guidelines to existing ALP sites then paved the way for the establishment of ALP units in other districts. However, the US military's attempts in the spring and summer of 2012 to expand the ALP to Wardak's insecure southern districts of Chak, Daimirdad, and Jaghatu petered out when the programme encountered similar problems as in the other districts. As explained below, the difficulty in expanding ALP to new districts had already been evident in February 2012, when Governor Fidai and US special forces tried to persuade elders in Sayedabad to 'give their sons' to the ALP. However, despite a lackluster response in Sayedabad, the US military seemed undeterred. Whilst the ALP programme emphasized that members should be recruited from local villages through *shuras* and vetted by local elders and government institutions, this proved difficult to put into practice, as illustrated in the ethnographic vignette provided below.

Americans go to Sayedabad in search of ALP recruits

A cold winter morning on 6 February 2012 in Wardak's Sayedabad District provided the setting for a US military 'information operations' ceremony organized by American special forces to launch the ALP programme in Sayedabad. They and their Afghan counterparts had come to Sayedabad to ask local elders to volunteer their sons to join the ALP, which they planned to establish in the district. In order to legitimize the process and give the appearance of an Afghan lead, they had brought along senior Afghan government officials from the provincial capital Maidanshahr, including Wardak's governor, Halim Fidai. As the officials entered, a small group of elders and young men got up to greet them. The room quickly filled to half its capacity as more villagers arrived in the hall. Local officials were obviously keen to put on a good show, and in their enthusiasm to make a positive impression, they had clearly coaxed local villagers from the vicinity of the district centre into attendance. The visiting officials also included the district governor of Sayedabad, provincial and district police chiefs, army commanders, and intelligence officers, in addition to a sizeable number of US special forces officers and soldiers. They, with their guns, ammo, and flak jackets, were occupying the other half of the meeting hall.

Once the officials and dignitaries had taken their places at the head of the congregation, the local villagers sat facing them in neat rows on the carpeted floor. Governor Halim Fidai, who unlike many of his counterparts was a trained religious scholar, had come to Sayedabad to deliver a message of deliverance to a people suspected of having strayed from the path of God, and of the government – the difference between the two not always being clearly differentiated by those in power. The government was reaching out to local villagers to give them a chance to save themselves from evil – the Taliban – by joining the ALP. Over the previous months, a number of reform initiatives, including the disarming and restructuring of existing ALP units in Maidanshahr and other districts, had been completed. The aim of this exercise was, ostensibly, to weed out ALP members who, in the past, had not been properly recruited according to the established guidelines, although some units were simply moved from one district to another. This was in preparation for the expansion of the ALP programme to new districts. Sayedabad was one of these districts.

Fazil Karim Muslim, a former Hizb-e-Islami commander and the district governor of Sayedabad, opened the meeting and spoke briefly, primarily to prepare the ground for governor Fidai's call to arms by reminding the audience that it was the duty of every Muslim to end *fitna* – i.e. discord or civil war in the Muslim community. The time had finally come to act, he emphasized, and the ALP was the instrument of their deliverance. Governor Fidai spoke next. He exhorted the old and young of Sayedabad to show courage and defy the Taliban by joining the ALP to protect their communities. After he had repeated this point a few times, finally, a man from the audience responded to the governor's call by saying, '*Da khpal tzan defa pa har cha farz da*' (the defence of one's self is everyone's obligation) – but he left unstated whether he meant against the Americans or the Taliban. Playing on a mix of tribal, religious, and nationalistic sentiments, the governor thanked this man, and further argued that once security had been established through ALP, there was no reason for foreign forces to stay in Afghanistan. In other words, the surest way to ensure the departure of American forces, whose night raids and air strikes in particular were major sources of popular angst, was for Afghans to stand up to Taliban and defeat them. 'This would be like killing two birds with one stone', the governor emphasized.

Shershah Bazoon, the head of the provincial council, spoke after the governor and stressed the material benefits of the programme by pointing out that other districts had acquired security, roads, and development thanks to ALP; it was now Sayedabad's turn. The ideological discourse, both religious and nationalistic, which had dominated the start of the meeting had now changed to a material discourse on the monetary and developmental incentives offered by an occupying power to poor Afghan villagers in exchange for agreeing to fight the Taliban. He then invited the elders gathered that day to play their part by joining the government and foreign forces to bring security to Wardak. The appeal to elders and local *shuras* for help in improving the government's reach and services to the country's rural population was a familiar trope, deployed by government officials to legitimize government interventions as well as to conceal their shortcomings. It also echoed the invocation of earlier patronage-based politics, which tied local power brokers to the central government and extended the government's authority using a system of indirect rule (Wilde 2013).

At the end of his speech, governor Fidai asked the participants to raise their hands to signify that they agreed with his proposal to form ALP units in Sayedabad. Initially only a few did so, at which point, encouraged from the sidelines by the commander of US special forces in Wardak, a US Army Lt. Colonel, the governor emphasized the point repeatedly until almost everyone had raised their hands. The governor, emphasizing the need not to repeat past mistakes – in reference to the post-Soviet period when the *mujahedin* engaged in internal struggles and prepared the way for the Taliban and al-Qaeda to take root – forced a show of hands in favour of the ALP. However, there still appeared to be little meaningful support for his suggestion, and an elder, Malik Azizullah, intervened to remind the audience how in the past, government-backed militias had created many problems for the people of Wardak. They retained memories of that period, he said, and still recalled the reign of terror in the late 1980s and early 1990s. He lamented that in spite of such warnings, the government went ahead and formed *arbaki* militias.[41] In his own village, he said, '15-to-20-year-old boys were employed in the *arbaki* militias and they didn't even consider me, a *malik*,[42] a man of means and reputation, a *saray*.[43] They made fun of a *spin ghirai*[44] like me.' This short, eloquent statement, delivered in a firm voice, directly challenged the provincial governor's request, and Azizullah then urged the governor and other officials to deploy regular army soldiers and policemen rather than repeating the mistakes of the past by arming local villagers with guns.

In the past, the AP3 had come under constant criticism on account of abuses committed by its members in Wardak. Most locals, therefore, remained sceptical of US military claims that this time round they would do things differently, starting with 'fixing' the AP3 and then expanding the ALP in Wardak. A prominent member of the provincial council, echoing the sentiments of his people, succinctly expressed the dilemma of most Wardakis when he pointed out that 'the people wanted more ANA and ANP, but the Americans forced the AP3 and ALP on them'.[45] Although the meeting ended with the US military officers and government officials somewhat disappointed at the outcome, the event was nevertheless declared a success by the organizers, while local villagers hurried back to their homes, in the hope of avoiding reprisals from the Taliban for taking part in the meeting.

As already noted, this call to arms can be described as 'getting savages to fight barbarians' (Duffield 2005). As Duffield argues, such calls to arms have a 'civilizational' purpose in the sense of attempting to provide a bulwark against threats to American empire and its local proxies in the central government. But this was difficult to sell to a highly sceptical and vulnerable public, with few believing the rhetoric of self-protection coming from a foreign army that held *shuras* with elders by day and attacked their villages at night. The initiative was presented as an attempt to restore Afghanistan to its allegedly harmonious traditions of the past.[46] The governor, far from holding to a vision of the state as an agent of modernity and bureaucratic efficiency, tried to sell the idea of tradition, self-reliance, and local security to a sceptical public of largely illiterate rural Afghans – ironically, the sorts of people the state habitually targets for its projects of high modernity (Scott 1998; Mitchell 2002). In this sense, it is 'a cheap and politically backward form of colonialism' (Duffield 2005, 144) and an example of 'decentralized despotism' (Mamdani 1996, 18), since the true objective of the project was not to bring representative democracy to the people but to govern native society through self-appointed local clients. This brief encounter, therefore, provided a small window into the world of US counterinsurgency in Afghanistan and its ill-conceived efforts to mobilize 'the tribes' in defence of American imperialism.

From promoting tradition to engaging in naked violence: ALP and its final pangs

In the early months of 2012, as the harsh winter gave way to spring, concerns over a new Taliban 'spring offensive' increased anxieties about security in Wardak. The US military–Afghan government attempts to 'fix' the ALP and expand it to new districts had produced few tangible results. Governor Fidai and his US special forces counterparts were now searching for a more dramatic solution to contain the insurgency and improve security.

Perhaps realizing that public opinion was coalescing against ALP, by the spring of 2012 governor Fidai had given up trying to 'fix' the ALP in Wardak. With pressure mounting ahead of the Taliban's spring offensive, he wrote to President Karzai on 12 March, pointing out that the ALP had not worked in Wardak and recommended that the 1600-strong ALP force be disbanded and replaced with 1000 regular police (at the time, Wardak had slightly more than 800 ANP personnel).[47] In his letter to President Karzai, Fidai pointed out that the ALP was not suitable for Wardak. Some of the reasons he noted were that tribal structures had been decimated by years of conflict; the tribes remained internally divided; and factional rivalries and conflicts among local power brokers ran deep. Most importantly, because the Taliban insurgency remained strong in most parts of Wardak and the government could not guarantee sufficient security, people generally feared for their lives and avoided a controversial programme like ALP. Therefore, in such a contested environment there was little support for a programme that risked exacerbating conflicts. Fidai suggested that a better alternative to the formation of local militias was the additional deployment of national security forces. Privately, several senior US military officers, as well as the political leadership in Kabul, had more or less come to the same conclusions as Fidai.[48] By late spring and early summer of 2012, the situation in Wardak had become so difficult that there were even serious suggestions that the US military arm Hizb-e-Islami as a proxy against the Taliban.[49] This strategy failed to materialize, possibly because of US objections and the unwillingness of key Northern Alliance power holders in Kabul to empower their historic rival in the process of fighting the Taliban. However, in May of that year, US forces in Wardak eventually admitted to carrying out joint military operations with Hizb-e-Islami forces against their Taliban enemies in Nerkh (Sieff 2012).

By early 2013, the US military's difficulties in improving security in Wardak entered a new phase. In February, allegations had emerged of abduction, torture, and extrajudicial killings by US special forces and 'secret' Afghan militia units associated with them in Wardak (Welch and Shalizi 2013). Provincial authorities claimed that around 700 families had been displaced as a result of insecurity created by the abusive actions of US special forces and their Afghan proxies.[50] In the reports that surfaced, attention was focused on Zekria Kandahari, an Afghan-American who, people in Wardak claimed, was the commander of the secret militia which carried out most of the abuses against civilians. The allegations prompted President Karzai to order all US special forces out of Wardak within two weeks.[51] In March, the US military began the withdrawal of its special forces from Nerkh (BBC News 2013). In their place, the government deployed Afghan special forces to work alongside regular Afghan army units to ensure security in Nerkh (Dozier 2013).

Subsequent investigations brought little clarity to what had taken place in Wardak, although President Karzai maintained a clear line accusing US special forces of committing these abuses, while the US military and ISAF continued to deny any involvement.[52] In July, Afghan government officials reported that Zekria had been recaptured (he had slipped away from US custody some months earlier). Wardak's history of irregular warfare, efforts to mobilize and expand the ALP, and continuing reports of shadowy collaboration between US special forces and local armed groups suggest that the province will continue to experience a dirty war and protracted insecurity. These local proxies working alongside the US military are rarely 'good guys' nominated by village elders and accountable to local *shura*s or the government. Rather, they are brutal men like Zekria Kandahari who as militia commanders have built fearsome reputations, often committing a litany of human rights abuses while in the service of the US military; and they remain unaccountable, despite clear evidence of abusive behaviour.

With the failure of ALP, the US in many respects reverted to an earlier phase of the conflict and tried to borrow lessons from US special forces' experience with the local militias of Northern Alliance warlords, a model of warfare which had successfully toppled the Taliban regime in late 2001. However, the human and political costs of the intervention were so great that the final stages of US military presence in Wardak left deep scars, and not only on the local population which had been subjected to the US military's violence; the episode also strained relations between the US and Afghan governments to the breaking point. The final legacy of the US military presence in Wardak was indeed a deeply contested one.

Violent practices and contested legacies

We now return to the 6 February meeting in Sayedabad. The 'information operation' ceremony for the Afghan Local Police ended just before lunch that day. US military helicopters took off from the Forward Operating Base Sayedabad and transported the government dignitaries and US officers back to the provincial capital, Maidanshahr. Over lunch, a local journalist covering the event on behalf of a US contractor told Governor Fidai that he was not hopeful that the locals in Sayedabad would agree to send their sons to join the ALP. The locals, he believed, were too intimidated to defy the Taliban and provide recruits to the ALP. He noted that most elders lacked power and had lost influence over the younger men. To reinforce the point, he evoked the words of Malik Azizullah, who had complained that morning about the armed men belonging to *arbaki* militias (the AP3) who did not even consider him a *saray* (a man) and made fun of him as a *spin ghirai* (white-beard). Most of them had come to the Sayedabad meeting in secret and refused to uncover their faces for fear of being recognized. He recalled that most elders were too scared to be interviewed on camera for TV clips; how unlikely, then, that they would find the courage to openly support a government-run militia programme backed by the US military.

Apparently, most people around the governor were fully aware of the danger the ALP programme posed to the people. They admitted privately that the main assumptions behind the programme, that traditional institutions and real elders exist in rural villages and that they are willing to support the government if the right incentives are provided, were deeply flawed.[53] Yet, everyone colluded in maintaining the façade of tribes, *shuras*, and elders, though in reality other forces had taken over the mantle of authority and power. The proponents of ALP have a tendency to argue that violent and abusive commanders do not represent the 'real' ALP. They insist that when the programme is properly implemented, ALP members are vetted by elders, bound to their communities, and answerable to the police chief in the district. But this line of argument ignores the fundamental reality that the programme serves as a conduit for a host of illegal armed groups, former insurgents, and proxies for US special forces (Van Bijlert 2013).

The justification for the ALP, promoted by, among others, General Bolduc (one of its founders) – that the programme is culturally appropriate, Afghan-led, less intrusive, and a more cost-effective response to the insurgency (Bolduc 2011) – is not supported by the research findings from Wardak. First, the ALP and its predecessors were top-down processes, opposed to the wishes of the local people and contradicted claims of local ownership. As the encounter in Sayedabad showed, external actors and Kabul-appointed representatives were often the main proponents of the idea of arming local militias in Wardak. Similar objections had been raised in 2008 when the government and US forces introduced the idea of the AP3 to local elders in Kabul; they wanted the ANA and ANP instead (Lefèvre 2010; HRW 2011). In tracing the genealogy of the post-2001 militias backed by NATO and/or the Afghan government, it is evident that the idea of forming local militias in Wardak did not emerge from the ground up; it was President Karzai and his ministers as well as US special forces and ISAF commanders who were at the forefront of efforts to arm local militias, and for reasons that had little to do with providing protection to the population.

Second, most Pashtun communities in insecure areas of Jalrez, Nerkh, and Sayedabad, and even parts of the capital, Maidanshahr, did not readily join local militias for fear of Taliban retaliation. This opened the way for a few entrepreneurial commanders (like Ghulam Mohammad Hotak) and their militias to capture the programme and arm their supporters; and when the demand exceeded the supply, hundreds of new recruits were brought from as far away as Bamyan, Samangan, Laghman, and Nangarhar.

Third, in terms of costs, the Afghan commanders and militias who took part in the programme paid a heavy price for their engagement, in financial and human losses as well as in loss of reputation.

Fourth, instead of reducing violence, the arming of local militias intensified factional power struggles, for example between Hizb-e-Islami and the Taliban in Nerkh, and increased the threat of reprisals from insurgents. Such policies of wholesale coercion and brutalization, it has been argued, have contributed to a dirty war that increases insecurity for Afghans and, in turn, further justifies arming local militias by foreign forces (Boone 2011).

Lastly, the ALP programme failed to improve security in the short or medium term. The end result in Wardak was a highly contingent and unstable political outcome. There were indications of a 'back to the future' scenario, whereby US special forces apparently relied on 'secret' militias outside the purview of the Afghan government in their efforts to contain the local insurgency – and left a string of dead, tortured, and disappeared civilians in their wake.[54]

The ALP in Wardak constitutes, in some ways, a microcosm of the dynamics of conflict in Afghanistan as a whole. Just as Western politicians invoke the image of Afghanistan as an unruly borderland, a front-line state in the war on terror, Wardak itself is positioned as the front line of the fight against the Taliban. Barbarians are needed by civilizations, and so too, it seems, by savages. Some Afghans profit from the new political economy of danger associated with the war on terror, as it is used to mobilize resources and support and to consolidate power. Many people have a lot to lose from the drawdown of NATO troops and a diminished foreign presence. As Keen argues, war may be less about defeating the enemy than about maintaining a system in which insurgents and counterinsurgents both accrue benefits (Keen 2012). A range of different actors and organizations accrue material or symbolic benefits from the ALP programme, and each fights to shape the process to its own advantage. This explains why, in spite of its evident failure, the programme persists, albeit in different forms. Keeping out the barbarians may be a lucrative business. Whether it works or not – and indeed whether there are, in fact, barbarians – are beside the point.

The call to arms in Sayedabad might be interpreted as a paradoxical attempt by the representatives of modernity and civilization to impose a traditional mode of governance on a tribal people. It reveals, in a nutshell, some of the contradictions and tensions surrounding external intervention in Afghanistan. At one level, the encounter appears to expose points of friction between the agents of pacification and order, represented by Afghan government officials and their US military backers, and the recalcitrant traditional elites of Afghan society, who may or may not hold sympathy for the Taliban insurgents, though the suspicion is always there. But the story is far more complicated, and in some ways the positions have been reversed. The governor, far from holding to a vision of the state as an agent of modernity and bureaucratic efficiency, attempted to sell the idea of tradition and local security to highly sceptical rural Afghans – ironically, the sorts of people the state habitually targets for its projects of high modernity. And yet the 'savages' resisted the offer of 'policing by tradition'; instead of escaping from the centralizing and modernizing influences of the state (Scott 1985, 1990), they insisted on inclusion within it.

The idea, popularized by American scholar Louis Dupree (1973), of a traditional Afghan peasantry erecting a metaphorical 'mud curtain' to keep the state at bay or to limit contact with the outside world no longer applies – if it ever did. The war appears to have changed Afghans' expectations of the state: many of the inhabitants of Sayedabad wanted more state, not less, though they wished for one that was legitimate and endowed with the capacity to provide security and a modicum of justice. This story is illustrative of the reasons behind the failures of counterinsurgency and militarized state-building interventions.[55] In fact, the US military and Afghan government's turn to patronage, tradition, and reliance on local clients and informal security forces is a very old strategy of power, echoes of which can be found in Afghanistan's history of indirect rule and brokering arrangements. However, there is a crucial difference between the organic emergence of new political orders in the absence of external intervention and the reality of coercion and imperial imposition by US special forces, counterinsurgency experts, and 'human terrain teams' attempting to social-engineer complex changes.

In summary, many local elders from different parts of Wardak demanded national solutions to the problem of insecurity and resisted attempts by proponents of counterinsurgency to lock them into indigenousness through the imposition of local traditions. However, Governor Fidai and the US military, in an attempt to secure the future, were reaching backwards 'to reconnect and rejuvenate earlier colonial modes of governing the world of peoples' by relying on local proxies to defeat the insurgency (Duffield 2005). In so doing, they inadvertently exposed the limits and contradictions of the 'cultural turn' in US counterinsurgency (Gregory 2008). In reality, after more than a decade of muddling through, the United States is leaving behind a violently transformed landscape peppered with local militias and

only loosely held together by short-term deals with local allies for whom violence and pre-
dation have become effective means of staying in power.

Notes

1. For a critical perspective on the history of Western interventions and their specific imageries of Afghanistan, see Hakimi (2012). Of particular note are the purportedly enduring 'tribal' and 'stateless'
notions of Afghanistan.
2. The tribal engagement strategy builds on the US military's experience with the 'Sunni Awakening' or
'Sons of Iraq' programme. In Afghanistan, President Karzai and the US military leadership hoped to
mobilize the tribes and create a backlash against the Taliban by building on tribal self-defence forces
known as *arbaki* (Bruno 2008). The *arbaki* concept then provided the model for US military–Afghan
government efforts in establishing local militias, which eventually culminated in the ALP. For analysis
of the *arbaki* tribal security system, see Osman (2008).
3. Interview with Mullah Aziz-ur-Rahman Siddiqi, former AP3 commander, 17 December 2011, Kabul.
4. The research for this article was conducted between September 2011 and June 2013 in Kabul and
Wardak through semi-structured interviews with a range of key informants, including Afghan officials
in Kabul, provincial governors and police chiefs, local elders, provincial council members, ANA, ANP,
and National Directorate of Security (NDS) personnel, serving and former ministers, ISAF and US
special forces officers, and journalists and civil-society activists. It was made possible by funding contributions from the Norwegian Ministry of Foreign Affairs and the United States Institute of Peace. The
research findings do not reflect the position or policy of the funding institutions.
5. For some useful literature on this point see Boege et al. (2009), Kilcullen (2009), MacGinty (2010),
Hagmann and Peclard (2011), Ahram (2011), Jones (2012), and MacGinty and Richmond (2013).
For a valuable critique of hybrid political orders, see Meagher (2012).
6. On liberal peace-building and state-building, see Ignatieff (2003), Fukuyama (2004), Paris (2004),
Thakur (2006), and Ghani and Lockhart (2009). For a critical perspective, see Chandler (2010),
Cramer (2006), Heathershaw and Lambach (2008), and Suhrke (2011).
7. Hizb-e-Islami was one of seven *mujahedin* parties based in Peshawar during the 1980s' anti-Soviet
jihad. Originally led by Gulbuddin Hekmatyar, after 2001 the party split into two factions. The political
wing operates legally from Kabul and is part of the Karzai government. The military wing is led by
Hekmatyar and is active in the insurgency.
8. Interview with Governor Halim Fidai, 11 December 2011, Wardak. According to Fidai, US commanders in Wardak had repeatedly asked him to intercede with local elders and Hizb-e-Islami commanders
in Nerkh to get them to stop attacking US forces and instead join them in fighting the Taliban. The US
military eventually admitted to joint operations between US forces and Hizb fighters in Nerkh against
the Taliban (Sieff 2012).
9. Harakat was led by Maulawi Mohammad Nabi Mohammadi, a conservative-traditionalist *jihadi* party
of rural mullahs from whose ranks many of the Taliban movement's leaders later emerged. Following
the death of its founder, the party has been led by Haji Mohammad Musa Hotak. Musa, a former
Harakat commander and Taliban deputy minister, is an MP and a senior advisor to President Karzai.
10. Interview with Governor Halim Fidai, 11 December 2011. Wardak.
11. *Ibid*.
12. Shura is an Arabic term which refers to a council or a consultative process. It is commonly used in Dari
and Pashto languages in Afghanistan. In Pashto-speaking regions, *jirga*, which is a Pashto term for an
ad-hoc gathering, mainly of tribal notables and local influentials, is considered the ideal type of consultative forum where key decisions are made and disputes are resolved. The Pashtun code of honour
known as *Pashtunwali* emphasizes resolving disputes through *jirga*, where the focus is on mediation
and compensation and not on meting out punishments.
13. AP3 'guardians' received 21 days of training, an AK-47 rifle, and a small quantity of ammunition. A
vehicle was provided for every 25 men. Individual pay was USD 170 per month, and sometimes not
paid for months.
14. Interview with Haneef Atmar, former minister of interior, 26 July 2012, Kabul.
15. Interview with Haji Mukhlis, former member of provincial council of Wardak, 1 January 2012, Kabul.
16. Mukhlis, *op. cit.*; Haji Janan, head of the provincial council of Wardak, 29 December 2011, Kabul.
For discussion of meetings between elders and government officials, see Lefèvre (2010) and HRW
(2011).

17. The shift in power from tribal leaders and the landed elite to a new class of violent entrepreneurs occurred primarily after the outbreak of the war in 1978. However, as Ghani (1978) showed, the centralization policies of Amir Abdul Rahman Khan from 1880 to 1901 'totally reshaped' the power of the tribal aristocracy and the religious establishment. Gibbs (1986) and J.W. Anderson (1978) argued that the decline in power and prestige of tribal chiefs (epitomized in the title of Anderson's seminal work 'There are no khans anymore') had begun prior to the outbreak of the war in 1978, partly because of changes in the agrarian economy and the monetization of the agricultural sector. For socio-political changes, especially the rise of a new class of military commanders after 1978, see Rubin (1995, 2000), Dorronsoro (2005), and Giustozzi (2009). Some tribal and religious (as well as urban and educated) elites also became commanders during the 1980s, as noted for example by Edwards (2002).

18. Interview with commander Ghulam Mohammad Hotak, 9 May 2012, Kabul; Governor Halim Fidai, 11 December 2011, Wardak.

19. Figures obtained in December 2011 show 350 ALP members in Jalrez District. A December 2012 US Department of Defense report mentioned a total figure of 576 ALP members in Wardak (USDOD 2012, 81).

20. Interview with commander Ghulam Mohammad Hotak, 9 May 2012, Kabul.

21. Interview with Mullah Aziz-ur-Rahman Siddiqi, former AP3 commander, 17 December 2011, Kabul.

22. Interview with Governor Halim Fidai, 11 December 2011, Wardak.

23. Interview with commander Mohammad Gul Torakai, 13 September 2011, Maidanshahr, Wardak.

24. Interview with Haneef Atmar, former Minister of Interior, 26 July 2012, Kabul; Governor Halim Fidai, 13 August 2012, Kabul.

25. Interview with commander Mohammad Gul Torakai, 13 September 2011, Maidanshahr, Wardak.

26. Interviews with Mullah Aziz-ul-Rahman Siddiqi, head of the Wardak *ulema shura* and former AP3 commander, 17 December 2011, Kabul and 3 March 2012, Wardak; Commander Mohammad Gul Torakai, 13 September 2011, Maidanshahr, Wardak; Ghulam Mohammad Hotak, 12 December 2012 and 9 August 2012, Wardak and Kabul.

27. Interview with Haneef Atmar, former Minister of Interior, 26 July 2012, Kabul.

28. Interview with President Hamid Karzai, 7 May 2013, Kabul.

29. For discussion of CDI and LDI militias, see Lefèvre (2010) and Jones (2012). It is worth noting that the AP3 was followed by a succession of other local militias, including the Community Defence Initiative (CDI) and Local Defence Initiative (LDI), Critical Infrastructure Program (CIP), Interim Security for Critical Infrastructure (ISCI), and Community-Based Security Solutions (CBSS). In addition, a number of Central Intelligence Agency (CIA) and US special forces–funded terrorist pursuit teams, such as the Kandahar Strike Force and the Khost Protection Force, and up to 70,000 private security guards, joined the ranks of local militias (Aikins 2012). For a detailed account of local militia formations since 2006, see *Counterinsurgency, Local Militias and Statebuilding in Afghanistan* (Goodhand and Hakimi forthcoming).

30. Interview with Col. Donald Bolduc, deputy commander of NATO Special Operations Forces, 15 November 2012, London.

31. Former minister Atmar criticized the LDI, calling it 'illegal' and in violation of a 2009 agreement between the Afghan government and the US military which had paved the way for the implementation of the AP3 in Wardak (and its subsequent planned expansion to other provinces, but this did not happen). Interview with Haneef Atmar, former Minister of Interior, 5 August 2012, Kabul.

32. Interview with Dr. Rangin Dadfar Spanta, national security adviser, 10 April 2012, Kabul.

33. A Dari term meaning the proliferation of militias.

34. Interview with President Hamid Karzai, 7 May 2013, Kabul.

35. Interview with Dr. Spanta, National Security Advisor, 10 April 2012, Kabul.

36. It is worth noting that the CIA and the US special forces continued to support the creation of local militias outside the ALP framework. Therefore, the agreement that gave birth to the ALP did not necessarily lead to a substantive centralization of the means of coercion. Interview with Aimal Faizi, presidential spokesperson, 7 May 2013, Kabul.

37. Interview with ISAF officials, 5 November 2012, Kabul.

38. Interview with Col. Donald Bolduc, Deputy Commander of NATO Special Operations Forces, 15 November 2012, London.

39. Interview with a senior adviser to ISAF commander General John R. Allen and the commander of US special forces in Wardak, 11 February 2012, Kabul.

40. Interview with the commander of US special forces in Wardak, 12 December 2011, Maidanshahr, Wardak.

41. The NATO- and government-backed militias were commonly referred to as *arbaki*, but the government and the Americans insisted that the ALP units should not be called *arbaki*. By *arbaki*, in this case, Malik Azizullah meant the AP3 militias.
42. *Malik* is a government-appointed local leader, generally a wealthy landowner. In his role as an intermediary, he is tasked with facilitating the interaction between local villagers and government officials in the district administration.
43. In Pashtun culture, telling someone that 'you are not a man', *saray-naye*, is a grave insult, basically questioning the person's manhood and ability to protect his property and household.
44. Pashto word for 'white-beard' or 'elder'.
45. Interview with Haji Janan, member of the Wardak provincial council, 29 December 2012, Kabul.
46. As Mamdani (2012) argues, the invention of native tradition was a precondition of indirect rule, which required the colonial regime to authenticate its local allies as 'traditional' and the society they ruled on behalf of the empire as 'tribal'. The ultimate aim was of course to rule 'tribal' society through colonially appointed 'traditional' leaders (Hopkins 2011), as happened for example in the North-West Frontier of India (Marten 2009).
47. Governor Halim Fidai's letter to President Karzai, dated 12 March 2012, on file with the author. In the letter, Fidai mentions a figure of 405 ANP personnel in Wardak, possibly referring only to ANP soldiers.
48. Interview with senior government officials and local journalists in Wardak, August 2012, Maidanshahr and Kabul.
49. *Ibid.*
50. Interview with Haji Janan, provincial council member, 17 April 2013, Maidanshahr, Wardak.
51. Karzai's national security adviser claimed that the order was meant only for Nerkh district and not the whole of Wardak. Interview with Dr. Spanta, National Security Advisor, 5 May 2013, Kabul.
52. Interview with President Hamid Karzai, 7 May 2013, Kabul.
53. Interview with the head of National Directorate of Security (NDS), 31 January 2012, Maidanshahr, Wardak.
54. Interview with Aimal Faizi, Presidential Spokesperson, 7 May 2013, Kabul.
55. For wide-ranging critique of state-building interventions in Afghanistan, see Heathershaw and Lambach (2008), Johnson and Leslie (2004), Giustozzi (2009), Goodhand and Sedra (2010), Suhrke (2011), Barfield (2010), Verkoren and Kamphuis (2013), and Edwards (2013).

References

Ahram, Ariel. 2011. "Learning to Live with Militias: Toward a Critical Policy on State Frailty." *Journal of Intervention and Statebuilding* 5 (2): 175–92.

Aikins, Matthieu. 2012. "Contracting the Commanders: Transition and the Political Economy of Afghanistan's Private Security Industry". Centre on International Cooperation, New York University.

Anderson, Jon. W. 1978. "There Are No Khāns Anymore: Economic Development and Social Change in Tribal Afghanistan." *Middle East Journal* 32 (2): 167–183.

Barfield, Thomas. 2010. *Afghanistan: A Cultural and Political History*. Princeton: Princeton University Press.

BBC News. 2013. "Nato Announces Afghanistan Wardak Agreement." *BBC*, March 20.

Boege, Volker, Anne Brown, Kevin Clements, and Ana Nolan. 2009. "Building Peace and Political Community in Hybrid Political Orders." *International Peacekeeping* 16 (5): 599–615.

Bolduc, Donald C. 2011. "Forecasting the Future of Afghanistan." *Special Warfare* 24 (4): 22–28.

Boone, Jon. 2011. "Does the US Military Want Afghanistan to Get Even Nastier?" *The Guardian*. December 8: 6.

Bruno, Greg. 2008. "A Tribal Strategy for Afghanistan". *Backgrounder*. New York: Council on Foreign Relations.

Chandler, David. 2010. *International Statebuilding: The Rise of Post-Liberal Governance*. London and New York: Routledge.

Cramer, Christopher. 2006. *Civil War Is Not a Stupid Thing: Accounting for Violence in Developing Countries*. London: C Hurst & Company.

Dorronsoro, Gilles. 2005. *Revolution Unending: Afghanistan 1979 to the Present*. London: C Hurst & Company.

Dorronsoro, Gilles. 2011. "Afghanistan: The Impossible Transition". Carnegie Papers. Washington, D.C.: Carnegie Endowment for International Peace.

Dozier, Kimberly. 2013. "Afghanistan Withdrawal: U.S. Leaves Nirkh, Key Base In Wardak Province." *Huffington Post*. March 30.

Duffield, Mark. 2005. "Getting Savages to Fight Barbarians: Development, Security and the Colonial Present." *Conflict, Security & Development* 5 (2): 141–159.

Dupree, Louis. 1973. *Afghanistan*. Princeton: Princeton University Press.

Edwards, David B. 2002. *Before Taliban: Genealogies of the Afghan Jihad*. Berkeley, California and London: University of California Press.

Edwards, David B. 2013. "Lessons on Governance from the Wali of Swat: State Building in Afghanistan." In *Beyond Swat: History, Society and Economy Along the Afghanistan-Pakistan Frontier*, edited by Benjamin D. Hopkins, and Magnus Marsden, 249–263. London: Hurst & Company.

Fishstein, Paul, and Andrew Wilder. 2012. "Winning Hearts and Minds? Examining the Relationship Between Aid and Security in Afghanistan". Feinstein International Center/Tufts University.

Fukuyama, Francis. 2004. *State-building: Governance and World Order in the 21st Century*. Ithaca, NY: Cornell University Press.

Gant, Jim. 2009. *One Tribe at a Time: A Strategy for Success in Afghanistan*. Los Angeles: Nine Sisters Imports.

Ghani, Ashraf. 1978. "Islam and State-Building in a Tribal Society: Afghanistan 1880–1901." *Modern Asian Studies* 12 (2): 269–84.

Ghani, Ashraf, and Clare Lockhart. 2009. *Fixing Failed States: A Framework for Rebuilding a Fractured World*. New York: Oxford University Press.

Gibbs, David. 1986. "The Peasant as Counterrevolutionary: The Rural Origins of the Afghan Insurgence." *Studies in Comparative International Development* 21 (1): 36–59.

Giustozzi, Antonio. 2009. *Empires of Mud: Wars and Warlords in Afghanistan*. London: Hurst & Company.

Goodhand, Jonathan, and Aziz Hakimi. forthcoming. "Counterinsurgency, Local Militias and Statebuilding in Afghanistan". United States Institute of Peace.

Goodhand, Jonathan, and Mark Sedra. 2010. "Who Owns the Peace? Aid, Reconstruction, and Peacebuilding in Afghanistan." *Disasters* 34 (1): 78–102.

Gregory, Derek. 2008. "'The Rush to the Intimate': Counterinsurgency and the Cultural Turn in Late Modern War." *Radical Philosophy* 150 (July/August): 8–23.

Hagmann, Tobias, and Didier Peclard, ed. 2011. *Negotiating Statehood: Dynamics of Power and Domination in Africa*. Malden, MA: Wiley-Blackwell.

Hakimi, Aziz. 2012. "The Changing Nature of Power and Sovereignty in Afghanistan." In *Sources of Tension in Afghanistan and Pakistan: A Regional Perspective*. Barcelona Centre for International Affairs (CIDOB).

Heathershaw, John, and Daniel Lambach. 2008. "Introduction: Post-Conflict Spaces and Approaches to Statebuilding." *Journal of Intervention and Statebuilding* 2 (3): 269–289.

Hopkins, Benjamin D. 2011. "Managing 'Hearts and Minds': Sandeman in Baluchistan." In *Fragments of the Afghan Frontier*, edited by Magnus Marsden, and Benjamin D. Hopkins, 49–74. New York: Columbia University Press.

HRW. 2011. *Just Don't Call It a Militia: Impunity, Militias and the Afghan Local Police*. New York: Human Rights Watch.

Ignatieff, Michael. 2003. *Empire Lite: Nation Building in Bosnia, Kosovo and Afghanistan*. London: Vintage.

Johnson, Chris, and Jolyon Leslie. 2004. *Afghanistan: The Mirage of Peace*. London: Zed Books.

Jones, Seth G. 2012. "The Strategic Logic of Militias". Working Paper. RAND Corporation.

Keen, David. 2012. *Useful Enemies: When Waging Wars Is More Important Than Winning Them*. New Haven and London: Yale University Press.

Kilcullen, David. 2009. *The Accidental Guerrilla: Fighting Small Wars in the Midst of a Big One*. New York: Oxford University Press.

Lefèvre, Mathieu. 2010. "Local Defence in Afghanistan: A Review of Government-backed Initiatives." AAN Thematic Report. Kabul: Afghanistan Analysts Network.

MacGinty, Roger. 2010. "Hybrid Peace: The Interaction Between Top-Down and Bottom-Up Peace." *Security Dialogue* 41 (4): 391–412.

MacGinty, Roger, and Oliver P. Richmond. 2013. "The Local Turn in Peace Building: a Critical Agenda for Peace." *Third World Quarterly* 34 (5): 763–783.

Mamdani, Mahmood. 1996. *Citizen and Subject: Contemporary Africa and the Legacy of Late Colonialism.* Princeton: Princeton University Press.

Mamdani, Mahmood. 2012. "What Is a Tribe?" *London Review of Books*, September 13.

Marten, Kimberly. 2009. "The Dangers of Tribal Militias in Afghanistan: Learning from the British Empire." *Journal of International Affairs* 63 (1): 157–74.

Meagher, Kate. 2012. "The Strength of Weak States? Non-State Security Forces and Hybrid Governance in Africa." *Development and Change* 43 (5): 1073–1101.

Mitchell, Timothy. 2002. *Rule of Experts: Egypt, Techno-politics, Modernity.* Berkeley: University of California Press.

MOI. 2011. *Ministry of Interior-Afghan Local Police Directive.* Kabul: MOI.

Osman, Tariq M. 2008. "Tribal Security System (Arbakai) in Southeast Afghanistan". 7. Crisis States Occasional Papers. London: LSE.

Paris, Roland. 2004. *At War's End: Building Peace after Civil Conflict.* Cambridge: Cambridge University Press.

Perito, Robert M. 2009. Afghanistan's Police: The Weakest Link in Security Sector Reform. 227 vols. Washington, DC: USIP.

Rubin, Barnett R. 1995. *The Fragmentation of Afghanistan: State Formation and Collapse in the International System.* New Haven, London: Yale University Press.

Rubin, Barnett R. 2000. "The Political Economy of War and Peace in Afghanistan." *World Development* 28 (10): 1789–1803.

Scott, James C. 1985. *Weapons of the Weak: Everyday Forms of Peasant Resistance.* New Haven and London: Yale University Press.

Scott, James C. 1990. *Domination and the Arts of Resistance: Hidden Transcripts.* New Haven and London: Yale University Press.

Scott, James C. 1998. *Seeing Like a State: How Certain Schemes to Improve the Human Condition Have Failed.* New Haven, CT: Yale University Press.

Sieff, Kevin. 2012. "Secret U.S. Program Releases High-level Insurgents in Exchange for Pledges of Peace." *The Washington Post*, May 7.

Suhrke, Astri. 2011. *When More Is Less: The International Project in Afghanistan.* London: Hurst & Co.

Thakur, Ramesh. 2006. *The United Nations, Peace and Security: From Collective Security to the Responsibility to Protect.* Cambridge: Cambridge University Press.

UNAMA, and UNOHCHR. 2012. "Afghanistan Mid-Year Report 2012: Protection of Civilians in Armed Conflict". Kabul, Afghanistan.

USDOD. 2012. "Report on Progress Toward Security and Stability in Afghanistan (December 2012)". Report to Congress. Washington, D.C.: US Department of Defense.

US Embassy Kabul. 2009. "Unconventional Security Forces – What Is Out There?" *Wikileaks*. November 12.

Van Bijlert, Martine. 2013. "Security at the Fringes: The Case of Shujai in Khas Uruzgan." *AAN*. April 6. http://aan-afghanistan.com/index.asp?id=3336

Verkoren, Willemijn, and Bertine Kamphuis. 2013. "State Building in a Rentier State: How Development Policies Fail to Promote Democracy in Afghanistan." *Development and Change* 44 (3): 501–526.

Welch, Dylan, and Hamid Shalizi. 2013. "Insight: Afghan Move Against U.S. Special Forces Tied to Abuse Allegations." *Reuters*, February 26.

Wilde, Andreas. 2013. "The Consistency of Patronage: Networks and Powerbrokers of the 'Arzbegi Clan' in Kunduz." In *Local Politics in Afghanistan: A Century of Intervention in the Social Order*, edited by Conrad Schetter, 59–75. London: Hurst & Company.

Nexuses of knowledge and power in Afghanistan: the rise and fall of the informal justice assemblage

Torunn Wimpelmann

Chr. Michelsen Institute, Bergen, Norway

This article explores Western attempts to strengthen mechanisms of informal justice in Afghanistan. It traces the origins and evolution of an 'informal justice assemblage': the constellation of specific expert discourses, institutional practices, and strategic considerations that made it possible and plausible that Western actors should promote and work with informal processes of justice. The article problematizes expert statements that posit that working with informal justice is somehow more 'Afghan-led' and less of an outside imposition than supporting the country's formal justice system. To the contrary, this article details how – discursively and institutionally – academic authority about what is locally appropriate in practice served to foreclose national debate and scrutiny about the organization and administration of justice. This amounted to a net erosion of accountability, reinforced by the subsequent militarization of the justice sector and governance more broadly. In conclusion, the article calls for greater attention to the broader fields of power in which claims of sensitivity to the local sentiments and reality in Afghanistan are made.

Introduction

Within international policy and practitioner circles devoted to peacebuilding, stabilization, and military interventions, there has been a growing orientation towards the local, the context-specific, and the informal as alternatives to attempts at 'Western' statebuilding (Albrecht et al. 2011; Boege et al. 2009). Working with and supporting non-state and ostensibly organic or traditional forms of governance are often presented as more appropriate and effective, as enabling less imposing forms of intervention, and even as more in line with 'critical theory' (Grissom 2010).

In this article, I explore the potential pitfalls of such strategies, and the democratic and empowering claims that surround them, through a detailed exploration of Western attempts to strengthen mechanisms of informal justice in Afghanistan.[1] I dissect the *governmental assemblage* (Li 2007) of institutional practices, political imageries, scholarly repertoires, and strategic considerations that made it plausible and possible to promote and to work with informal justice and, moreover, that gave such undertakings importance and urgency. I demonstrate that the interest in and ability to boost informal justice processes in Afghanistan rested on a temporary alignment between foreign military forces, non-governmental organizations, academic expertise, and neo-traditional local elites. Calls for recognition of and support for informal justice processes were premised upon assumptions about Afghanistan as defined by its non-stateness and localized governance, knowable (and manageable) through scholarly research and expert knowledge. In turn, NATO impatience over frustrated attempts to boost the formal justice system, in a situation where governance and justice were increasingly seen as integral to the war effort, made unlocking knowledge about Afghan-specific forms of governance a military imperative. Catering to these knowledge needs were a handful of research organizations that could provide, through the 'mapping' of local power relations and dynamics, the *intimate knowledge* allegedly required for outsiders to strengthen and refine informal justice mechanisms in a sensitive and informed manner.

Although, as the events recounted below will make clear, this assemblage unravelled in the end, I argue that it nonetheless revealed the contours of a specific and alternative set of governance relations. Yet, while certainly radically different from the universalistic ethos of earlier international visions for Afghanistan, the form of governance made visible in the agenda to strengthen informal justice was not necessarily more egalitarian. Rather, I suggest that it amounted to an erosion of accountability. Despite its claim to be more 'Afghan-led', the informal-justice agenda mainly resulted in exactly the opposite. At the discursive level, privileging academic expertise as able to devise solutions about what was locally appropriate served to foreclose the possibility of public debate in Afghanistan on what were essentially political questions tied up with competing visions of statehood. At the institutional level, the governance assemblage through which international 'engagement' with informal justice could take place was located not in national institutions but in a parallel and ad hoc constellation made up of nongovernmental organizations (NGOs) and researchers. Any semblance of accountability and national sovereignty was further undermined by growing military interest in the informal-justice agenda, which had the effect of moving the issue further out of public purview.

Defining informal justice

During the first decade of the twenty-first century, Afghanistan represented a rather extreme example of legal pluralism by design as well as default – a reflection of the turbulent history of 'statebuilding' in Afghanistan. The official legal framework was a patchwork of secular laws, codified laws derived from *sharia*, and uncodified Islamic jurisprudence. Moreover, this official legal framework coexisted and competed with localized, non-formal legal practices. 'The informal justice system' in Afghanistan is usually an umbrella term referring to all such practices of solving disputes or offences outside of the state courts (with the exception of those primarily carried out by religious figures in the name of *sharia*). More or less institutionalized, informal justice varies across regions and population groups. Often privileged or considered the ideal type is the image of the *jirga* (Barth 1959; Carter and Connor 1989, 7; Rzehak 2011). *Jirga* is a Pashto word for a purpose-specific gathering of entrusted men tasked to make a decision or resolve a dispute. Parties to a conflict typically each nominate one or several representatives, their background and numbers depending on the nature and seriousness of the dispute or violation and the relationship between the parties involved. Through discussion, the representatives will agree upon a settlement, to which the parties are expected to adhere. Failure to do so might result in social sanctions or even expulsion from the community. The focus is normally on restoration and compensation for the aggrieved party. Women seldom take part in the proceedings and can find themselves given away in marriage as compensation to the offended party, a practice called *baad*.

The representatives in a *jirga* are typically drawn from a small and relatively fixed 'roster' of senior men (Smith 2009) recognized for their skills in mediation and reputation for fairness and integrity, or general standing (or power) in the community. Although decisions are assumed by the parties to be in accordance with Islamic teachings (Barfield, Nojumi, and Thier 2006), the explicit framework of reference (into which violations and appropriate compensation are placed) is generally local customs and traditions, sometimes explicitly referred to as *Pashtunwali*.[2] Solving disputes through a *jirga* is regarded as a key tenet of *Pashtunwali* and can thus be understood as an exercise of affirming identity and community, whether positioned against adversaries, the state, or other localities, ethnicities, or tribes. Indeed, as Boesen (1983) points out, the Pashtun tribal system, as articulated in its idealized form, is 'based on the obligation of the aggrieved party to assert and re-establish his honour and social integrity by demonstrating his ability to take revenge or get compensation' (1983, 124).

It was these kinds of processes that increasingly caught the attention of various actors seeking to improve the Afghan justice system. This interest culminated in attempts to draft a national policy which would recognize informal justice mechanisms – often referred to as *jirgas* and *shuras*[3] – and integrate them into the formal system; and it is to this ill-fated initiative that the article now turns.

The 'national policy on relations between the formal justice system and dispute-resolution councils' (and its discontents)

In April 2009, a working group was established in the Afghan Ministry of Justice, tasked with the creation of a national policy that would bestow government recognition upon informal justice mechanisms and formulate a relationship between these and the formal court system. At this point, several years had passed where there had been substantial attempts to reform the formal justice system, following on from an emergent Western consensus that the justice sector had been neglected and constituted a weak link in the overall international attempt to restructure Afghanistan – partly due to the paltry efforts of the Italians who had been in charge of reforming the legal sector in the early years after the US-led invasion. A period of more extensive aid and a proliferation of 'rule of law' activities had followed, but quickly led to Western disillusionment as rapid results failed to materialize.

Suggestions about a hybrid legal system had been voiced on occasion, most prominently in the 2007 UNDP biennial Human Development Report for Afghanistan, which focused on justice sector reform. The report had called for 'a hybrid model of Afghan justice that articulates, in detail, a collaborative relationship between formal and informal institutions of justice' (UNDP 2007, 4). According to this model, traditional justice institutions would cooperate with and work alongside the state justice institutions (4). The report had proved to be unusually controversial for a publication of its kind. Its primary author, a UK-based academic and member of the Afghan diaspora, was reprimanded by government officials; the report itself was banned, and any citations from it declared illegal, in a decree issued by the Supreme Court (Suhrke 2011, 214). The Supreme Court had objected to what it regarded as a potential negation of the formal system's universal jurisdiction. The Court's officials were also accused of wanting to divert the considerable aid for the justice sector to themselves. Many Afghan human rights advocates also resisted attempts to boost the position of informal justice mechanisms. They viewed these practices to be open to abuse, as they followed no codified law and allowed human rights abuses against women and children; and their 'adjudicators' required no formal qualifications or vetting.

Nonetheless, partly due to the lobbying of international donors, the idea of a formalized relationship between formal and informal justice was repeatedly mentioned in various benchmark documents formulated as part of the donor-led reconstruction process.[4] In fact, by 2009, quite substantial attempts by various international agencies to 'engage' with informal justice processes were already underway. The United States Institute of Peace (USIP), a US research and policy institute, had been an early advocate of working with the informal system, starting in 2002. Following on from several commissioned research publications on the informal justice system in Afghanistan, and the coordination of a series of workshops and conferences from 2005 onwards, in 2008 USIP played an important role in securing the inclusion of a reference to the informal system in Afghanistan's (2008) National Justice Sector Strategy. According to USIP, this reference 'obligates the State to develop an official policy toward its relations with customary dispute resolution systems and to conduct activities that will strengthen these systems so that fair and effective access to justice for all Afghans is achieved'.[5] In early 2009, USIP set up what it termed *pilot projects*. These projects to 'test ways of designing or strengthening links between the state and informal systems to increase access to justice' (USIP 2010, 1) were implemented either by USIP itself or by partner NGOs.

In the southern province of Helmand, the UK government had also been working with informal justice processes for some time. In 2008, justice committees consisting of 'representative groups of senior tribal elders representing all the major tribes and sub-districts of a district'[6] were established, through UK initiatives, in two districts in Helmand. A year later, they were followed by additional committees in other districts, and the committees were incorporated into the Afghan Social Outreach Program (ASOP) to increase the visibility and presence of the Afghan government at the local level. Like the US strategy formulated later on, the involvement of the UK was rooted in military objectives. The UK government also funded a substantial research project on informal justice mechanisms across the country, which resulted in a series of publications by the Afghan Research and Evaluation Unit (AREU), a Kabul-based research institute (Gang 2011; Smith 2009; Smith and Lamey 2009).

Yet, the international actors involved preferred to anchor their activities in a national framework, or at the very least to secure the formal observance of a key tenet of established aid practice: *local ownership*. So it was that in spring 2009, with the Supreme Court still ambivalent, if not outright opposed, a working group tasked with drafting a national policy was formed by the Ministry of Justice. It consisted of representatives of the main international agencies involved in justice sector reform, as well as USIP, AREU, the Ministries of Justice and Women's Affairs, the Supreme Court, the Afghan Independent Human Rights Commission, and the Afghan Women's Network, an umbrella women's rights organization. This working group had been established largely due to the efforts of USIP and the UK government, which subsequently became prominent actors in steering the process. Based on the British experience in Helmand, the UK's Department for International Development (DFID) justice advisor was actively involved in the attempts to get the national policy adopted, while USIP provided the secretariat for the working group.

Most participants in the working group recounted the process as being long and cumbersome. From the start, many of the Afghan female representatives strongly opposed the very idea of a national policy which recognized informal justice mechanisms.

> The policy would give the *jirga*s and *shura*s a lot of power. The policy said that it would legalize their decisions, build their capacity and rights, allow them to decide on smaller criminal matters. All of this was dangerous for women's rights and human rights.[7]

The discussions crystallized around the question of whether the informal system was inherently harmful to women, a position maintained by many Afghan human rights activists, or whether it at times acted in women's favour, a contention put forward by Western researchers in particular. The debate was frequently heated, with Western participants suspecting the Afghan women activists of mere posturing, while they in turn accused their foreign adversaries of attempting to lock Afghanistan into a premodern condition. Eventually, the Afghan activists allowed the policy to go through. The grounds for this concession were somewhat different from the original intention of those who had first proposed the policy. Though they had envisaged a policy that would recognize the informal mechanisms and facilitate formalized cooperation between these mechanisms and state courts, the activists were now justifying the policy mainly with reference to the idea that it would enable increased state control over the informal system and limit its reach and excesses. The exhausted parties all appeared happy to accept this tactical divergence of interpretation for the time being.

The second point of contention was whether informal mechanisms should be given jurisdiction over criminal cases. Though there was agreement that murder and other 'serious crimes' should be the prerogative of state courts, USIP and DFID in particular wanted to permit the informal system to have jurisdiction over minor criminal cases. Others, including the Supreme Court, disagreed, arguing that this would be in contradiction with the Constitution and the (interim) criminal procedure code. Here, the international position prevailed.

What eventually emerged from the 10-month process was a very brief document, less than 4 pages (considerably shorter than the initial draft that was presented to the working group).[8] It stated that neither the formal nor the informal system on its own could meet justice needs in the country. It argued that the positive functions of the informal system should be strengthened, and at the same time, that practices and decisions that violated the human rights of women, men, or children (including *baad*) should be eliminated. The draft further stated that it was a matter of national policy to ensure that dispute-resolution councils were free from the influence of 'oppressive actors' and that no one should be compelled to appear before them. Furthermore, disputes resolved through informal justice processes 'not in contravention of Sharia, the Constitution, other Afghan laws and international human rights standards' would be recognized as valid decisions by the formal justice system, after registration with relevant government institutions. The policy also stated that serious criminal cases remained under the exclusive jurisdiction of the formal system, whereas petty criminal cases could be referred to the informal system, subject to the consent of the victim.

Following this agreement, the policy draft was prepared to be sent out for wider consultation. However, things took an unexpected turn when the new minister of justice, Habibullah Ghalib, declared his opposition to the very idea of the policy. According to members of the working group, the minister could not see the value of the policy, preferring instead to have a law. Moreover, he had earlier been involved in the drafting of a law on peace councils – a semi-official additional layer of mediation bodies – and wanted to relaunch a draft law along these lines. Alarmed at the prospect that the painfully crafted policy would be ditched, the US and UK embassies attempted to convince Minister Ghalib to change his mind. But this backfired, with the minister protesting that Afghan sovereignty was being violated and expressing his determination to replace the policy with a law. Thus, the process started all over again. A similar group of people started to convene, and many of the same controversies were reopened. To avoid repetition of the earlier, long-drawn-out process, after a few sessions (where barely a paragraph had been drafted) it was summarily decided that the *Taqnin* (the legislation-drafting department of the Ministry of Justice) would produce a first draft of the law and present it to the working group.

Shortly afterwards, in September 2010, a draft was presented to the working group by the *Taqnin*. However, it looked very different from what the international actors who had promoted the policy had intended. Compared to the policy agreed upon a year before, the proposed law was decidedly more to the taste of those who wanted to use the process as a way of regulating the informal justice system and limit its power, rather than a positive recognition of such processes. The draft contained none of the positive acknowledgments of such mechanisms. Instead, Article 1 declared the purpose of its enactment to be 'to regulate the affairs related to Shuras and Jirgas in the country'.[9] It stated that *jirga* members should have 'complete knowledge of Afghan laws' and be local residents, (Article 6) effectively disqualifying a large number, if not the majority, of current *jirga* participants. Moreover, the draft law declared that those members of *jirga*s and parties to disputes who did not observe its provisions should be prosecuted. (Article 24) To their horror, those who had started the process of developing the policy realized that they had ended up with a result that effectively criminalized the very system they had wanted to promote.

Although USIP and others expressed their concerns (see Wardak 2011), the working group never reconvened, and there was no sign of willingness from the *Taqnin*'s side to revise the draft law any further. But meanwhile, even as the Kabul-based sceptics succeeded, for the time being, in turning the process in the capital to their advantage, the international engagement with informal justice was expanding significantly. The international military had made informal justice integral to its campaign against Taliban insurgents, and in response, the biggest donor, the US, was allocating copious funds to informal justice. With increasing military interest in the justice sector, the question of whether to support informal justice was rapidly moving out of the purview of Kabul-based activists and officials, rendering formal sanction there irrelevant. However, before investigating in greater detail the constellations through which these experiments with informal justice took place, I want to explore the *rule of experts* revealed both in the contestations over the national policy and law and in the ad hoc activities 'on the ground'.

Contesting experts

Invoking research findings as an authoritative claim to truths about Afghanistan to which policy had to adhere became an important feature of contestations over the place of informal justice in Afghanistan. The 2007 UNDP report had stated that more than 80% of all disputes were solved by the informal system. The report's front page illustrated this claim in unambiguous terms. A painting showed a circle. The smaller upper part was filled by a judge presiding over a court, with the figure '20%' inserted; the larger part of the circle was filled by a gathering of mostly turban-clad men sitting around a table, presumably engaged in informal dispute resolution, with '80%' inserted. This claim developed into something of a 'factoid': information based on soft opinion and a very narrow evidence base, translated by constant repetition into an accepted fact (see Cramer and Goodhand 2011).[10] Frequently invoked as an argument for the recognition of or support for informal justice mechanisms, it became part of a broader body of academic and 'grey' literature asserting that the formal justice system was not just ineffective in most of the country, it was alien to Afghan culture. Most Afghans, it was argued, preferred the restorative justice of their customary ways, and often resented the retributive justice practised by the formal courts (Barfield and Nojumi 2010; Ledwidge 2009; Smith and Lamey 2009; Wardak 2004).

The employment of epistemic authority in discussions of the place of informal justice in Afghanistan displays traits of what Ludden (1993) calls an orientalist practice of knowledge production. At the heart of this practice lies the claim of the existence of enduring if not permanent features of Eastern people and reality – 'the real Afghanistan'. These features, being defined relationally and mostly in contradistinction to the West, constitute an objective 'truth' to be discovered by scientific inquiry and to serve as guidance and justification for policy and governmental intervention. Ludden's perspective alerts us to the importance of attending to the historical context and political effects of knowledge production. It reminds us that the interest in and validation of informal justice mechanisms in Afghanistan did not appear in a vacuum but within the parameters of a Western military operation that structured both empirical developments in Afghanistan and the kind of knowledge that was useful and could be accommodated.

Applying this analytical lens, it becomes clear that since the time of the first encounters of British India with Afghanistan, the production of scientific 'truths' about Afghanistan has been closely entwined with Western forays into the country. In turn, the particular Western routes of arrival and modes of entry into the country, termed 'the keyhole of the Khaibar Pass' by Mousavi (1998, 8), have generally privileged tribal, stateless, independent, and Pashtun imagery (see also Hopkins and Marsden 2011). As Hopkins (2008) points out, early descriptions of Afghanistan, defined by its tribes, by the early-nineteenth-century colonial scholar-agent Elphinstone, provided a template for subsequent Western scholarship on the region. Haroon (2007, 14) further suggests that the images and at times celebrations of autonomous and sovereign tribes which by the latter half of the nineteenth century had become conventional wisdom in British official circles must in turn be understood in relation to British strategic objectives in the 'frontier' region. She argues that the British Raj wanted to wrest the area away from the Afghan king by asserting that the people inhabiting the area known today as the Federally Administered Tribal Areas (FATA) were independent tribes with no history of living under a higher political authority. Later on such notions were resurrected, as Afghanistan took centre stage in the Cold War conflict and aid workers, diplomats, and intelligence agencies took to working with non-state actors in what were then called 'the liberated areas' (Carter and Connor 1989) and with what was often celebrated as the country's heroic tradition of resistance against central government institutions (Hopkins and Marsden 2011).

The intention here is not to suggest that such images were or are a mere invention, reducible to a Western plot. Instead, my objective is to highlight the constant interplay between expert knowledge and Western foreign and imperial policy in Afghanistan and how – due to the particular history of the latter – this interplay has resulted in a scholarly template that privileges political imageries centred on the tribal, the non-state, and the Pashtun. In turn, this underlines the importance of placing the truth claims of academics and experts in the historical context in which they are produced, in order to reveal their political underpinnings and effects. This exercise must also be applied to knowledge claims made and produced within the context of the most recent episode of large-scale Western involvement in Afghanistan, an undertaking attempted by this article.

As Ludden argues, as orientalist knowledge production becomes institutionalized and affirmed in government policies it quickly moves out of the hands of academics and then gradually takes the form of conventional wisdom, which 'has become so widely accepted as true, so saturated by excess plausibility ... that it determines the content of assumptions on which theory and inference can be built' (1993, 251). A publication from USIP (2010) illustrates how this dynamic was at play in discourses about informal justice, demonstrating that certain 'facts' about the informal justice system had become such conventional knowledge, at least within certain circles. The USIP report presents findings from its aforementioned pilot projects, which form the basis of recommendations. The document proceeds from a number of 'facts' now treated as official wisdom. Juxtaposing general Afghan 'unfamiliarity with and resistance to' state justice institutions with the 'widespread use and popularity' of informal justice, it states that 'many experts believe that as many as 80% of all disputes in the country are resolved in the informal system' (3). The two authors[11] conclude that 'informal mechanisms provide the best prospect of providing sound dispute resolution services to most Afghans today and in the future' (2).

Language drawing upon scholarly research as a source of authority and guidance for policy was also an observable strategy in the attempts to promote the recognition of the informal justice system in the ministry working group, although there such strategies were only partially successful. Some of the international participants pointed to research that demonstrated the widespread use of the informal justice mechanisms, their resonance with local people, and ambiguity (rather than a clear-cut negative effect) when it came to its impact on women. However, those who were against the policy (or law) contested this line of argumentation. They contended that although research might show widespread use of informal justice mechanisms, this was because the formal system was inaccessible and malfunctioning, not because of an inherent preference for *jirga*s. Thus, it was necessary to improve the formal system rather than to endorse informal justice mechanisms. They further claimed that *jirga*s were institutionally biased against women, for whom the best protection against family and community abuses was in the formal system. The opponents of the policy also objected to the researchers' representation of Afghanistan. One Afghan member of the working group complained that the arguments put forward by the academics in the group had conjured up images of Afghanistan as a timeless land where autonomous *qabila*s (sub-tribes) constituted the largest unit of political and social life, making the prospects of 'national solidarity' and therefore modern democracy seem implausible.[12]

Rendering informal justice governable and administrable – and profitable

Whilst academic claims that informal justice mechanisms constituted an unalterable part of Afghan reality had found limited acceptance in the working-group discussions in Kabul, expert knowledge was already integral to a series of ongoing efforts to make the informal field knowable and amenable to Western intervention. A closer look at the practices through which these efforts took place reveals a peculiar mode of knowledge production. As I will demonstrate, its dynamics turned the suggestion that the promotion of informal justice was Afghan-led completely on its head.

In general, the massive but increasingly troubled foreign military-and-aid operation generated a great demand for knowledge about Afghanistan, a demand reflected – and institutionalized – in a proliferation of research activities focusing on the country. Most blatantly in the service of military objectives – and therefore attracting considerable controversy – were the so-called 'human terrain teams': small groups of social scientists embedded with military forces (González 2010, 118). However, the human terrain teams were but one extreme component of a much broader knowledge–intervention nexus, which in important ways bore a resemblance to earlier orientalist projects of making knowledge about Afghanistan available for Western policy-making purposes. Yet there was also an important disconnection with colonial times. As we shall see, such knowledge production was no longer conducted solely by Western government officials but had become decentralized, marketized, and outsourced. Moreover, compared to colonial times, academic and expert knowledge was operating to a lesser degree with essentialized and enduring frames. Instead, there was more emphasis on context and on the fact that that local 'reality' varies across time and space. However, earlier templates of Afghanistan as defined by its non-state, tribal, and Pashtun character were still evident. Indeed, the lack of knowledge of these enduring features of Afghanistan amongst Western policymakers was often presented as a key deficiency in Western intervention and as an explanation for the difficulties it experienced. The role of experts in making this reality accessible (to Western interveners) was still considered crucial.

The recommendations in the USIP report referred to earlier are centred on the importance of context, political sensitivity, and research, thus highlighting the expert knowledge and skills required for the task at hand. The document emphasizes that organizations working with the informal system need to have 'intimate knowledge of the local political landscape' (13). A subsection called 'The Importance of Understanding and Adapting to Local Context' lists a number of questions those wishing to engage with informal justice must cover, such as major disputes in the area, the reputation and loyalties of the formal justice system and local government officials, ethnic and tribal dynamics, the role of local commanders, the influence of the insurgency, and economic relations (12) The report warns that ignorance of the local context, and failure to appreciate the 'inherently political nature of dispute resolution', might undermine efforts altogether. Attempts to engage might be rejected by the local community as illegitimate, or might fuel tension and indeed political destabilization, for instance if one group had been favoured over another.

An apparatus that could satisfy these 'intimate knowledge' needs was already in place. In response to the ever-expanding demand for local knowledge generated by the USIP's informal-justice project and a host of other international pursuits, a handful of Afghan NGOs (many with Western staff in key roles) and institutes had emerged, specializing in conducting research often referred to as 'mapping' exercises. Perhaps at one point the most successful and professionalized of these research NGOs was The Liaison Office (TLO, formerly the Tribal Liaison Office), which was founded as an Afghan NGO in 2003. In 2011, TLO had 150 staff, and 10 field offices, concentrated in the south and east of Afghanistan. The TLO website clearly speaks to NATO governments and donors as potential clients. Stating that 'one problem in Afghanistan is the lack of research and understanding to guide overall engagement and development initiatives', and that 'TLO's research and analysis section aims to fill this fundamental knowledge gap', the website lists amongst its research activities

> thorough research of the ground context in given areas in order to understand community structures, decision-making and conflict resolution mechanisms, stakeholders and their sources of power (actor mapping), conflict-generating factors between individuals and groups (conflict mapping), local capacities for peace, existing service provision, economic realities, and the impact of Afghan government and international development and stability initiatives. (TLO undated)

Furthermore, TLO announces that it 'specialises in'

> topic-specific research, including targeted conflict assessments (e.g., land and resource disputes, kuchi migration and settlement issues), studies of informal and formal justice systems, policy analysis and exploratory assessments of areas of strategic importance such as the Afghan districts bordering Pakistan (TLO undated).

The TLO was one of the implementers of the USIP pilot projects on informal justice and one of a handful of organizations[13] who had established themselves through a portfolio of various mapping and project activities. Some of the work undertaken by these organizations was in the form of stand-alone research projects, such as 'provincial assessments' – reports on the political landscape at the province level, or studies of why people joined or supported the insurgency. In addition, the insertion of research or 'mapping' as an integral part of various aid, reconstruction, and 'governance' projects, some of which were implemented by the research NGOs themselves, had also become commonplace. For instance, the Afghan Social Outreach Program, piloted by the British in Helmand (see above), included a 'mapping exercise' producing a short list of power holders in the area. The short list served as a first step in setting up local councils; the exercise was carried out by an Afghan NGO called Welfare Association for the Development of Afghanistan (WADAN).[14]

The way in which this knowledge production was structured generated or reinforced specific hierarchies. Local Afghans were, for the most, valued for their access to communities and their ability to gain rapport, to operate undetected in unstable areas, and to communicate in local languages, all of which made them essential to the overall enterprise. The material they gathered was merely raw data, subsequently to be validated, refined, and put into useful forms by trained experts, mostly foreign. At the same time, the constant emphasis on 'local reality' and an objective air of research gave the process an appearance of being Afghan-led, obfuscating the fact that the entire exercise was structured by larger fields of power.

Reinserting these mapping practices into their broader political context provides an important corrective to discourses claiming that informal justice was inherently preferable in Afghanistan or to Afghans. Most basically, the limited reach of the formal justice system in places like the southern areas of Helmand, Kandahar, and Loya Paktia could not be understood without reference to the ongoing armed struggle between coalition forces and insurgents in these areas, which made them insecure for government justice officials to operate in. The reported large-scale resort to informal justice mechanisms by local people could therefore have been at least partly due to the situation brought about by international military operations rather than an immutable cultural preference. More generally, the increased interest in the informal and the traditional had taken place in the context of the growing difficulties facing Western attempts to stabilize Afghanistan. The procurers of mapping services were, after all, members of the NATO coalition, and the direction of accountability in these activities went from the NGOs to Western capitals (via foreign embassies and military bases). Afghan government institutions, on the other hand, were rendered marginal. This tendency to circumvent national institutions became even more pronounced once the military expressed an interest in informal justice.

Enter the military: informal justice as counterinsurgency

The promotion of the informal justice system became entangled in new dynamics as it was entwined with the strategies and rationales of the international military. With the start of the Obama presidency in 2009, the US military increasingly articulated its activities in Afghanistan as 'population-centric' counterinsurgency (COIN). The COIN discourse explicitly drew upon the experience of the colonial wars of Britain and France, as well as the American war in Vietnam. It formulated a present-day COIN military strategy that focused less on eliminating the enemy and more on protecting the population. The population was understood as rational actors exercising a choice between supporting the insurgents or supporting the government. The key objective was to win their support, thereby denying the insurgents a friendly environment to operate from. Thus, argued the COIN subscribers, the US military had to adjust from a dependence on overwhelming military force to a focus on 'winning hearts and minds'. Winning hearts and minds was frequently understood to be possible through the provision of 'good governance'. This meant that the soldiers would have to deliver governance, or at the very least facilitate it. Their job, according to the 2006 counterinsurgency manual, was to be 80% politics and 20% soldiering. The manual's foreword stated:

> Soldiers and Marines are expected to be nation builders as well as warriors. They must be prepared to help re-establish institutions and local security forces and assist in rebuilding infrastructure and basic services. They must be able to facilitate establishing local governance and the rule of law. The list of such tasks is long; performing them involves extensive coordination and cooperation with many intergovernmental, host-nation, and international agencies (Petraeus and Amos 2006, p. iii).

The effect of the COIN's population-centric outlook was to frame ever-expanding fields (justice, administration, health, education) through the lens of military goals. Providing services and 'improving' Afghanistan was no longer merely a good in itself or a way of proving to Western liberal audiences that Afghanistan was being 'developed'. It became enlisted directly in the war effort as a way of winning over the population. Although a link between development aid and the prospect of defeating the insurgency had been made since the early days of the invasion[15] (Gilmore 2011), with the COIN doctrine, improving governance became an indispensable and routinized part of the war effort and something that the military had to take systematic control over. Questions of governance and service delivery were thus problematized as deficiencies that needed to be rectified (Li 2007, 7) – urgently, given the security implications.

A legitimate government was generally regarded to be a cornerstone of population-centric COIN. However, in the context of Afghanistan, this presented the international military with a problem. The Afghan government was an ambiguous partner in the eyes of many of its Western backers.[16] Massive international aid had not yielded the expected returns in terms of 'statebuilding', and the Karzai administration was regarded by many Western officials as increasingly quarrelsome, overly corrupt, and lacking in 'political will'. Given that the absence of good governance was now seen as a potential risk for the entire military venture, the military took to circumventing Kabul, delivering governance by working directly with province- and district-level officials (Lefevre 2009), and in part by working with 'informal' structures and authorities. The military policy thus largely became to expand 'governance', rather than the Karzai government, to parts of the country it had identified as key for winning the war. Centralized statebuilding had to give way to direct 'population control',[17] reminiscent of earlier colonial practices of indirect rule, but euphemized as 'localized governance'. To some, the partial abandonment of national frameworks constituted an inevitable trade-off that the COIN doctrine necessitated.

> For the purposes of COIN there is not a 'longer term' in which to work. The longer it takes, the better for Taliban war aims. They are keen to portray the government as ineffectual and chronically corrupt. They are of course right. COIN operators, working locally by necessity, are not going to be able to correct the faults of a disastrously compromised elite, and a largely unco-ordinated international effort that might take decades to bring positive effect. The solution lies, as with so much in the world of COIN, in local solutions. Local solutions, however, often collide with national aspirations. The awakenings movement in Iraq, which extracted much of the sting from the Sunni resistance cells, was hardly compatible with aspirations for state monopoly on force. Similarly, local justice initiatives may not strictly be compatible with traditional ideas of the judiciary holding the monopoly on final adjudicative authority. (Ledwidge 2009, 8)

As the quote above indicates, the justice sector in Afghanistan was one of the sectors that became entangled in these rationales. The provision of justice was regarded as a 'key service' by promulgators of COIN. It became commonplace to argue that in the justice sector the Afghan government and NATO found themselves in direct competition with the Taliban, as the latter often provided justice which although 'extreme and harsh' nonetheless had a 'comparative advantage'[18] by nature of its swift application. It followed that in this situation, to prevent a 'justice gap'[19] that could be readily exploited by the insurgency, there was *no choice* but to work with the informal justice system. This articulation suggested a convergence of COIN, knowledge of Afghanistan, and informal justice. However, this was a tenuous constellation. It only partly gained traction and it was certainly not seamless. Instead, there were unstable and temporal alignments, ad hoc experiments, and a certain amount of disquiet.

As already noted, the UK government had for some time carried out substantial experiments in supporting informal justice in Helmand province. In 2008, councils of elders, described as 'community justice support mechanisms', 'comprised of representative groups of senior tribal elders representing all the major tribes and sub-districts of a district', were established in two of the districts in Helmand.[20] These two initiatives were later formalized under the ASOP and extended to other districts in Helmand. The UK military prided itself in practising population-centric COIN before the rest of NATO forces, and the work with informal justice in Helmand was largely conceived and presented as a way of generating popular support for the Afghan government and international forces through the provision of justice as a service.[21] The more immediate practical imperatives of processing the large number of people detained by security forces were another important reason for the UK programmes. Based on the work in Helmand, the British DFID justice advisor also played a significant role in developing the national policy and generally advocated for an official recognition of the informal system.

The American government was more hesitant to make support of informal justice an official policy. However, it eventually took a clear position when it made support of informal justice one of the components of its overall rule of law strategy. As part of this, USAID allocated nearly half of its more than USD 30 million funds for the justice sector to the informal system (SIGAR 2011). The justification for doing so was heavily grounded in COIN, repeating the now conventionalized wisdom that the weakness of formal justice institutions was a security problem which required 'supporting the traditional justice sector in post conflict areas to provide immediate access to justice in support of stabilization efforts'.[22]

The USAID informal justice programme, implemented by the private contractor Checchi, was to take the form of a one-year pilot. It was to strengthen informal justice mechanisms, particularly in areas that had been 'cleared' by international military forces, by setting up networks of 'village elders', who would receive training and be invited to various events (USAID 2011). The project also attempted to resolve specific long-running disputes by convening various 'elders' across districts and facilitating cooperation between elders and government officials (USAID 2011). An assessment of the pilot some nine months later was overwhelmingly positive. It recommended that support of informal justice 'should continue as the mechanism can be rapidly revived through donor intervention to fulfil needs of a recently pacified community for justice while at the same time help prevent the Taliban from re-establishing themselves' (USAID 2011, 31).

In discourses that framed informal justice through a military or security lens, emphasis was placed on how the informal justice system delivered not only justice but also stability. It was suggested, both by various NGOs involved in 'informal justice' work and by the military, that the informal system played an important function in preventing conflicts from escalating and thereby being exploited by the insurgency. Hence, a growing convergence between justice, 'stabilization', and containment made it increasingly clear that the overarching objective was less about the provision of justice for the local population than it was about military victory for the NATO coalition.

The informal justice assemblage unravels

The original promoters of official recognition of the informal justice system were not wholly enthusiastic about an integration of informal justice with COIN. Early advocates of a greater role for informal justice, such as USIP and TLO, had been making overtures to the military and others about the importance of informal justice to COIN (USIP 2010). Yet, perhaps stunned by the speed at which their argument had become popularized, these advocates then appeared somewhat uneasy about the entry of other international actors into a field that they had carefully delineated and cultivated. Certainly, they were worried about the large sums of money being inserted into the informal system, and they expressed scepticism about the ability of military actors and larger government programs to apply the necessary finesse:

> As in the past, coalition and ISAF troops may feel assured that they are talking with the correct local Afghan leaders when in fact, they may be unwittingly drawn into one side of an on-going dispute. To avoid such pitfalls, it is critical that credible Afghan civil society partners be engaged after proper due diligence and investigation. (USIP 2009)

For its part, the US military showed some frustration with the fine-tuned approach to informal justice advocated by the original actors in the informal justice field such as USIP. Clearly not institutionally equipped to deal with the intricacies of context-specific community politics (something which was perhaps more within the skill-set of armies with imperial histories, such as the British army), the US military was often inclined more towards a research approach that could be presented in terms of baseline, statistics, and 'best tactics, techniques and procedures'. The latter was the phrasing used in an email invitation to a conference on informal justice at one of the ISAF bases in Kabul, where a number of 'experts' (including this author[23]) had been convened to discuss how the military could utilize informal justice to solve disputes. At the conference, the carefully argued presentation from USIP, which called for caution and analysis prior to 'engagement', clearly failed to gain much traction with the audience of senior military officers. Instead, it was the charts, statistics, and calls for large-scale training programmes of *jirga* elders, presented by the private contractor Checchi (who had been awarded a USD 28 million contract by USAID), which generated the most enthusiasm.[24]

But back in the *Taqnin* working group that was tasked with developing national legislation, the military endorsement of the informal system was presented as a *fait accompli* to sceptical Afghan participants. In an apparent outbreak of frustration over the slowness of the drafting process in the *Taqnin*, one of the internationals warned the Afghan members of the group that efforts to stop the informal system from gaining wider influence were futile. They should accept the need to have a law so that they could at least gain some influence over the process:

> You have to understand that the [foreign] military are engaging with the informal system. Italy, the US, everyone. The Afghan government might pretend that the informal system does not exist, but the military are all interacting with them. In Helmand, they are releasing prisoners. In Bamiyan, they might be doing something else. With this law you can at least ensure some harmony [of these engagements]. [Even] if the Afghan government pretend they do not exist, the military will still do this [work with informal justice mechanisms].[25]

In the end, this did little to convince the Kabul-based human rights activists of the need to have such a national law. Despite having secured a draft that was more in tune with their wishes to see informal justice mechanisms regulated rather than promoted, they preferred not to have any law or policy at all. In spring 2011, the law was taken off the cabinet's agenda through a promise extracted from the president after lobbying by Afghan human rights activists. The prospects of getting a national framework for the ad hoc experiments with informal justice seemed bleak.

Conclusions

By the end of 2010, the informal justice assemblage – a temporary and nascent mode of governance through a configuration of expert knowledge, NGOs, traditional elites, and military actors – was showing some cracks. Attempts to get local-level 'pilots' and ad hoc experiments sanctioned by national authorities had backfired. Those who earlier had courted the military with regard to the utility of informal justice for military purposes were expressing a certain ambivalence. At the same time, the doctrine of population-centric COIN, which had made engaging with the informal justice system a military necessity, was itself disintegrating. Reports from the south and east of Afghanistan suggested that assassination of insurgents (known as the 'kill or capture' strategy) rather than protection of the population was becoming the strategy of choice. In hindsight, population-centric COIN proved to be a temporary and partial experiment, directed in part to audiences in the West, rather than an all-compassing and dominant policy.

Regardless of whether this assemblage would gain further traction, survive in a modified form, or completely unravel, it had revealed forms of power at work whose political effects are significant. In sum, the effects of the informal justice assemblage were an erosion of accountability and disempowerment of local politics. In Kabul, expert knowledge steeped in orientalist frames was used in attempts to override political contestation about the currency of informal justice mechanisms. Western academic work which purported to provide 'Afghan-led solutions' was thus doing the exact opposite, foreclosing the possibility of national debate on what were essentially political questions about competing visions of social orders and who was authorized to dispense justice. Expert authority was also integrated into programme design and implementation, replacing universalistic notions of rights and uniform frameworks, and effectively moving adjudication out of the purview of the capital and the possibility of national scrutiny.

The expert knowledge at work in the informal-justice assemblage was mostly located within an external intervention, and as a result largely did not question its own terms. It took the form of a functionalist anthropology whose very premise, like earlier colonial ethnography, was to consolidate a social and political order defined by Western powers. Presented in this context, claims of its being Afghan-led were misleading. The negotiations (or tussles) over the informal-justice agenda demonstrate how justice and conflict resolution are also ultimately struggles over jurisdiction, authority, and sovereignty. While COIN discourse presented the military interest in informal justice as a matter of attracting popular support by providing justice, a closer reading also reveals a more immediate concern with establishing influence and presence in local areas in order to assert a measure of sovereignty. After the Taliban had been removed through military offensives, military actors spoke of a 'governance vacuum' that had to be filled. What was at stake here was a search for identifiable groups who could serve as local allies, and how to boost their authority.

In this, the military interest in informal justice did not differ from other historical processes in which rulers have set up or co-opted courts and justice bodies with the view to consolidating power. In the nineteenth century, Amir Abdul Rahman famously attempted, and to some extent succeeded, in using *sharia* courts to centralize power and undermine tribal autonomy (Kakar 1979). When in government, the Taliban themselves carried out highly publicized and more routine displays of power through the dispensation of justice based on their particular interpretations of Islamic law. As the insurgency gained force, they were also reputed to use the imposition of justice as a way of making their presence felt.

If a sovereign power was asserted or invoked in the informal-justice assemblage, it was not primarily vested in an Afghan central state. Rather, sovereignty was to be found in a hierarchically structured configuration of localized authority and intervening external powers. The COIN advocates and their allies were at pains to state that they were involved in restoring the organic and authentic institutions of Afghans. These 'authentic' and 'time-honoured' traditions, assuming timeless properties, were the primary rhetorical reference point of sovereignty and legitimacy – not the Afghan state. In actuality, however, authority over life and death was simultaneously located in other institutions and actors, namely external interveners. In this sense, the ultimate sovereign affirmed in the informal justice assemblage revealed itself as an imperial one.

As Stoler and Bond suggest, modern imperial forms of rule are characterized not by demarcated territories under explicit colonial authority but 'by wide thresholds of partial sovereignties and territorial claims that produce contradictory legal entitlements and ambiguous human rights' (2006, 95). The informal-justice assemblage was indicative of an intervention process in which the local population was increasingly rendered 'nationals but not citizens'; where local context and customs were accorded weight, but national institutions were not. In the evolving geopolitical order, Afghanistan appeared to be reverting back to its slot as a 'zone of exception', which in effect made its population, defined by its otherness, ineligible for modern citizenship or national sovereignty, instead to be governed through traditional authority – though assisted by local research organizations and a cadre of experts, and, in the last instance, validated by external powers.

In the end, however, the NATO coalition in Afghanistan could find no time for such a sophisticated form of governance. Faced with escalating insurgent pressure and growing impatience from their own political leadership, the military largely replaced COIN with a more brutal military strategy centred on targeted killings. Yet there are signs that the valorization of informal institutions of governance might at least have produced a useful legacy for Western powers seeking to extricate themselves from earlier pledges of building a democratic nation-state in Afghanistan in allowing them to claim that they were leaving behind a country in harmony with its own customs and culture. In reality, there is a distinct possibility that such claims will be little more than a veneer, thinly covering an actual landscape of propped-up militias, short-term deals with local power brokers, and continuing violence.

Notes

1. The material on which this article is based was collected during my Ph.D. fieldwork on gender violence in Afghanistan, mainly between 2009 and 2011, funded by the Research Council of Norway. My probing into the processes that I describe was not part of my initial research design but prompted by angry complaints of Afghan women's rights advocates over a proposed government policy that would bestow formal recognition on informal justice mechanisms. I eventually decided to explore the backdrop to the proposed policy in further detail: how the idea of such a framework had gained traction and what was becoming of the initiative. I carried out interviews with actors who had been involved in the process, and received permission to observe the meetings of the Ministry of Justice working group set up to develop the initiative.
2. Pasthunwali can be translated as 'Pasthun-ness' or 'the way of the Pasthuns'.
3. *Shura* means council or consultative process. Whilst *jirga* is a Pashtu word that refers more specifically to an ad hoc gathering to resolve a particular issue, *shura* is of Arabic origin and used in the languages of both Dari and Pashtu.
4. Such as in the Afghan National Development Framework (Islamic Republic of Afghanistan 2008a), the National Justice Sector Strategy (Islamic Republic of Afghanistan 2008b), and the communiqué of the 2010 Kabul donor conference (Islamic Republic of Aghanistan 2010).
5. http://www.usip.org/programs/projects/relations-between-state-and-non-state-justice-systems-afghanistan. USIP website, accessed 29th March 2011.
6. Support to the Informal Justice Sector in Helmand, April 2009. Internal DFID note. On file with the author.
7. Author's interview with an Afghan human rights official, Kabul, June 2010.
8. Draft National Policy on Relations Between the Formal Justice System and Dispute Resolution Councils, 10 November 2009. On file with author.
9. Law on Dispute Resolution Shuras and Jirgas. Draft 1. September 2010, Article 1. Unpublished document on file with author.
10. The 2007 Human Development Report (UNDP 2007) states that the percentages in its 20/80 circle are 'drawn from Asia Foundation (2006) and "Justice for All" (2005)'.
11. Described as a political anthropologist and traditional-justice specialist, and a lawyer and senior rule of law adviser, respectively.
12. Author's interview with member of the working group, Kabul, October 2009.
13. Other 'mappers' were the Cooperation of Peace and Afghan Unity (CPAU), WADAN, the Center for Afghan Policy Studies (CAPS), and the Peace Training and Research Organisation (PTRO). During parts of my Ph.D. fieldwork I was based at two of these institutions; CPAU and PTRO, although as a guest researcher I was not engaged to work on any of their projects.
14. Author's interview with DFID official, Kabul, July 2010.
15. Most notably through the establishment of Provincial Reconstruction Teams (PRTs).
16. This argument was also used by those who opposed COIN – who declared that with the present Afghan government COIN would never work.
17. This formulation is from a lecture by Antonio Giustozzi (2011).
18. Request for Task Order Proposal (RFTOP), Rule of Law Stabilization Program (RLS) Informal Component, United States Mission to Afghanistan. Attachment I: Statement of Work. US government tender document. On file with the author.
19. Request for Task Order Proposal (RFTOP), Rule of Law Stabilization Program (RLS) Informal Component.
20. Support to the Informal Justice Sector in Helmand, April 2009. Internal DFID Note. On file with the author.
21. http://www.helmandprt.com/delivering-justice.html Accessed 18th April 2011.
22. Request for Task Order Proposal (RFTOP), Rule of Law Stabilization Program (RLS) Informal Component.
23. During a trip to Kabul in May 2011, I visited the USIP's Kabul office for an update on their informal-justice work. I also asked if they had any suggestions about how to reach the relevant people within the US military who were working on this topic, as my attempts to set up a meeting had not led anywhere. Staff at the USIP generously invited me to join them at a panel at one of the NATO military bases a few days later, where various 'experts' would speak about the 'best tactics, techniques and procedures' through which the international military could best relate to traditional dispute mechanisms. Excited by the opportunity to do some participatory observation, I took part in this panel by making a few comments in response to the other presentations.

References

Albrecht, P., H. M. Kyed, D. Isser, and E. Harper, eds. 2011. *Perspectives on Involving Non-State and Customary Actors in Justice and Security Reform.* Rome: IDLO.

Barfield, T., and N. Nojumi. 2010. "Bringing More Effective Governance to Afghanistan: 10 Pathways to Stability." *Middle East Policy* 17: 40–52.

Barfield, T., N. Nojumi, and J. A. Thier. 2006. *The Clash of Two Goods: State and Non-State Dispute Resolution in Afghanistan.* Washington, DC: United States Institute of Peace (USIP).

Barth, F. 1959. *Political Leadership Amongst Swat Pathans.* London: Athlone Press.

Boege, V., A. Brown, K. Clements, and A. Nolan. 2009. "Building Peace and Political Community in Hybrid Political Orders." *International Peacekeeping* 16: 599–615.

Boesen, I. W. 1983. "Conflict of Solidarity in Pashtun Women's Lives." In *Women in Islamic Societies: Social Attitudes and Historical Perspectives*, edited by B. Utas, 104–127. London: Curzon Press.

Carter, L., and K. Connor. 1989. A Preliminary Investigation of Contemporary Afghan Councils. Report prepared for Agency Coordinating Body for Afghan Relief (Acbar) Peshawar, Pakistan.

Cramer, C., and J. Goodhand. 2011. "Hard Science or Waffly Crap? Evidence-Based Policy versus Policy-Based Evidence in the Field of Violent Conflict." In *The Political Economy of Development. The World Bank, Neo-Liberalism and Development Research*, edited by K. Bayliss, B. Fine and E. V. Waeyenberge, 215–238. London: Pluto Press.

Gang, R. 2011. "Community-Based Dispute Resolution Processes in Kabul City." In *Case Study Series.* Kabul Afghanistan Research and Evaluation Unit.

Gilmore, J. 2011. "A Kinder, Gentler Counter-terrorism: Counterinsurgency, Human Security and the War on Terror." *Security Dialogue* 42 (1): 21–37.

Giustozzi, A. 2011. "Kant, Hobbes or … Machiavelli? Facing the Grim Choices of State-Building in Afghanistan." Antony Hyman Memorial Lecture, SOAS, London, 15th March 2011.

González, R. J. 2010. *Militarizing Culture: Essays on the Warfare State.* Walnut Creek, CA: Left Coast Press.

Grissom, A. 2010. "Making it up as we go Along: Statebuilding, Critical Theory and Military Adaption in Afghanistan." *Conflict Security and Development* 10: 493–517.

Haroon, S. 2007. *Frontier of Faith: Islam in the Indo-Afghan Borderland.* New York: Columbia University Press.

Hopkins, B. D. 2008. *The Making of Modern Afghanistan.* New York: Palgrave Macmillan.

Hopkins, B. D., and M. Marsden. 2011. *Fragments of the Afghan Frontier.* London: Hurst & Company.

Islamic Republic of Afghanistan. 2008a. "Afghanistan: National Development Strategy 1387–1391 (2008–2013). A Strategy for Security, Governance, Economic Growth and Poverty Reduction." Kabul: Islamic Republic of Afghanistan.

Islamic Republic of Afghanistan. 2008b. "National Justice Sector Strategy." http://moj.gov.af/Content/files/National%20Justice%20Sector%20Strategy%20NJSS%20-%20English.PDF

Islamic Republic of Afghanistan. 2010. "Communiqué, Kabul International Conference on Afghanistan, Kabul 10th July 2010." http://unama.unmissions.org/Portals/UNAMA/Documents/Kabul%20Conference%20Communique.pdf

Kakar, H. M. 1979. *Government and Society in Afghanistan: The Reign of Amir 'Abd al-Rahman Khan.* Austin: University of Texas Press.

Ledwidge, F. 2009. "Justice and Counterinsurgency in Afghanistan: A Missing Link." *Rusi Journal* 154: 6–9.

Lefevre, M. 2009. "Local Defence in Afghanistan: A Review of Government-Backed Initiatives." Thematic Report. Kabul: Afghan Analyst Network.

Li, T. M. 2007. *The Will to Improve: Governmentality, Development, and the Practice of Politics.* Durham: Duke University Press.

Ludden, D. 1993. "Orientalist Empiricism: Transformations of Colonial Knowledge." In *Orientalism and the Postcolonial Predicament: Perspectives on South Asia*, edited by C. A. Breckenridge and P. van der Veer, 250–278. Philadelphia: University of Pennsylvania Press.

Mousavi, S. A. 1998. *The Hazaras of Afghanistan. A Historical, Cultural, Economic and Political History.* Richmond, Surrey: Curzon Press.

Petraeus, D., & J. F. Amos., 2006. 'Foreword' in *Field Manual 3–24/MCWP* (Marine Corps Warfighting Publication 3–33.5, Counterinsurgency). Washington, DC: Department of the Army.

Rzehak, L. 2011. "Doing Pashto. Pashtunwali as the Ideal of Honourable Behaviour and Tribal Life Among the Pashtuns." Thematic Report, Afghan Analyst Network.

Sigar. 2011. "Special Inspector General for Afghanistan Reconstruction (SIGAR) Quarterly Report to the United States Congress." July 30 2011.

Smith, D. J. 2009. "Community-Based Dispute Resolution Processes in Nangarhar Province." *Afghanistan Research and Evaluation Unit Case studies series.* Kabul Afghanistan Research and Evaluation Unit (AREU).

Smith, D. J., and J. Lamey. 2009. "A Holistic Justice System for Afghanistan." *Policy Note.* Kabul Afghan Research and Evaluation Unit (AREU).

Stoler, A. L., and D. Bond. 2006. "Refractions Off Empire: Untimely Comparisons in Harsh Times." *Radical History Review* 95: 93–107.

Suhrke, A. 2011. *When More is Less: The International Project in Afghanistan.* London/ New York: Hurst/ Columbia.

TLO. (Undated). "Research and Analysis, The Liasion Office." Accessed 27th March 2011. http://www.tlo-afghanistan.org/research-and-analysis.

UNDP. 2007. Afghanistan Development Report 2007: Bridging Modernity and Tradition: Rule of Law and the Search for Justice.

USAID. 2011. Afghanistan Rule of Law Stabilization Program (Informal Component) - Assessment – Final Report.

USIP. 2009. "Traditional Justice Workshop for General McChrystal." ISAF in Afghanistan, 27 Novermber 2009. http://www.usip. Accessed 18 April, 2010. org/in-the-field/usip-traditional-justice-workshop-general-mcchrystal-isaf-in-afghanistan.

USIP. 2010. "Informal Dispute Resolution in Afghanistan." *USIP Special report* United States Institute of Peace.

Wardak, A. 2004. "Building a Post-war Justice System in Afghanistan." *Crime Law and Social Change* 41: 319–341.

Wardak, A. 2011. "State and Non-state Justice Systems in Afghanistan: The Need for Synergy." *University of Pennsylvania Journal of International Law* 32: 1305–1324.

Index

Note: Page numbers in *italic* type refer to *tables*
    Page numbers followed by 'n' refer to notes